Classroom Management
for Middle-Grades Teachers

Classroom Management for Middle-Grades Teachers

C. M. Charles

San Diego State University

Marilyn G. Charles

Cajon Valley Schools, California

PEARSON

Boston ■ New York ■ San Francisco
Mexico City ■ Montreal ■ Toronto ■ London ■ Madrid ■ Munich ■ Paris
Hong Kong ■ Singapore ■ Tokyo ■ Cape Town ■ Sydney

Series Editor: *Arnis E. Burvikovs*
Series Editorial Assistant: *Christine Lyons*
Marketing Manager: *Tara Whorf*
Production Editor: *Michael Granger*
Editorial Production Service: *Chestnut Hill Enterprises, Inc.*
Composition Buyer: *Linda Cox*
Manufacturing Buyer: *Andrew Turso*
Cover Administrator: *Kristina Mose-Libon*
Electronic Composition: *Omegatype Typography, Inc.*

For related titles and support materials, visit our online catalog at www.ablongman.com.

Between the time Web site information is gathered and then published, it is not unusual for some sites to have closed. Also, the transcription of URLs can result in unintended typographical errors. The publisher would appreciate notification where these occur so that they may be corrected in subsequent editions.

Library of Congress Cataloging-in-Publication Data

Charles, C. M.
   Classroom management for middle grades teachers / C. M. Charles, Marilyn G. Charles.
      p. cm.
   Includes bibliographical references and index.
   ISBN 0-205-36128-5
      1. Classroom management—United States.   2. Middle school teaching—United States.   I. Charles, Marilyn G.   II. Title.

   LB 3013.C464 2004
   372.1102'4—dc21

                                                                          2003040429

Printed in the United States of America

10 9 8 7 6 5 4 3 2   08 07 06 04 03

CONTENTS

PREFACE

Purpose and Nature of This Book

This book is designed to help middle-grades teachers understand the nature and needs of early adolescent students, envision and plan a suitable educational program for them, and work with them efficiently and effectively. Its focus is on management—on handling skillfully the myriad conditions and concerns related to teaching and learning. Of central importance is helping students conduct themselves in ways that promote learning and personal growth. The importance of this endeavor, called behavior management, can hardly be overemphasized, as no other aspect of teaching so strongly affects the success and satisfaction of everyone concerned.

Management is usually thought of as something different and apart from teaching. *Teaching* suggests imparting knowledge, while *management* suggests handling details and arrangements. In actual practice, the two are inseparable, with management being one important aspect of teaching. To be effective, it must be based on a thorough knowledge of students and how to work with them. This book describes middle-level students at their unique stage of life and explains how to adjust programs and instruction accordingly. It emphasizes that effective teachers not only promote student growth in academic matters, but in character, self-discipline, and human relations as well.

Considerable attention is given to behavior management, but not the kind that forcibly keeps students in check. Forceful control too often makes students fearful, resentful, and unwilling to cooperate. Effective behavior management does not rely on force, but on respect, personal attention, and democratic decision making—factors that promote harmonious relations and the desire to learn. This kind of management, or discipline as it is often called, requires that teachers and students work together, on the same side.

Attention is also given to routine management matters, such as organizing the physical environment, arranging student seating and traffic patterns, handling materials of instruction, collecting and dealing with written work, and managing homework. How well teachers discharge these and similar tasks determines whether the class supports learning in a milieu of goodwill, or declines into boredom, lethargy, and conflict.

Other matters receive strong consideration as well. The importance of involving parents, family members, and community in middle-level education is explained, and suggestions are given for increasing parental involvement. Working with students of poverty and various cultural, linguistic, and ethnic groups is highlighted, with practical suggestions for increasing their opportunities. Advice is provided for helping students who require special accommodations or management. The effective use of computer technology is explored, and numerous Web sites useful to teachers are listed. Finally, legal, ethical, and professional considerations are examined. Explanations are given for what teachers are required to do, and not do, when teaching the young, and recommendations are made for contending more easily with the pressures of teaching.

For Whom This Book Is Intended

The book is intended for middle-level teachers, whether in training or already in charge of their own classrooms. It is recommended for middle-level administrators, too, because their decisions affect what transpires in the classroom. Although junior high and middle-level schools have been in existence for decades, teachers and administrators who serve in them have usually been trained as either secondary or elementary teachers. Yet, their students are notably different from either secondary or elementary students. They require programs and teaching tactics that meet their particular needs. Middle-grades teachers, therefore, need to know the nature of early adolescent students, how they behave, how they respond, what they are interested in, how they prefer to learn, and how they can best be taught.

Notable Features of the Book

Principles and Goals

The book begins with an historical overview of the purpose and nature of middle-level education, which will help readers understand the contexts within which today's middle-level teachers and students work. It then goes on to describe many important tasks in classroom management, as indicated in the chapter titles. When the principles advocated herein are realized, schooling, teaching, and learning will have reached specific goals:

1. The educational program is clearly adapted to the nature and needs of young adolescent students.
2. The classroom functions as a community of learners, with each member respectful toward all others and concerned about their welfare.
3. Parents, family members, and community cooperate with teachers and support the school program.
4. Democratic teaching prevails, with students closely involved in making decisions about matters that affect them.
5. Management aspects of teaching are discharged efficiently, allowing learning to proceed smoothly.
6. Teacher and students work together on the same side to improve learning and resolve class problems.
7. Conditions that usually foster misbehavior have been identified and removed or softened.
8. Positive behavior management is used to help students acquire self-control and behave responsibly.
9. Class character is strong, with students exhibiting self-direction, initiative, and responsibility.
10. The educational program fosters success for students with disabilities and those from various cultural, ethnic, linguistic, and economic groups.

11. Computer technology is extensively used for acquiring information and broadening educational opportunity.
12. Legal requirements are discharged dutifully, and ethical and professional demeanor is always evident in teachers and other school personnel.

Pedagogical Features

The following pedagogical features are included to make the book more useful:

1. *Chapter previews.* Each chapter begins with a preview that orients readers to chapter contents.
2. *Scenarios and examples.* Many scenarios and examples are used to add interest and impact.
3. *Field applications.* Chapters contain field applications and other in-text exercises that cause readers to reflect on information and relate it to class realities.
4. *End-of-chapter questions.* Questions at the ends of chapters can be used for reflection, assignments, or class discussions.
5. *End-of-chapter activities.* Activities at the ends of chapters are provided for reflection, self-improvement, cooperative work, discussions, and assignments.
6. *Writing style.* A reader-friendly writing style is used that is informal, yet scholarly.

Bibliography

Altogether the references at the end of each chapter compiled in the Bibliography contain approximately 300 citations of articles, books, and other materials that have important bearing on classroom management.

The Author Team

The authors are C. M. Charles and Marilyn G. Charles, father and daughter. C. M. Charles, of San Diego State University, is an educational psychologist specializing in innovative programs and classroom discipline and management. He has authored more than twenty books used nationally and internationally and has received many teaching awards. Marilyn G. Charles, of Cajon Valley Schools, California, has a solid reputation for excellence in teaching and service. She has twenty-five years experience in middle-level teaching and has served as mentor teacher in English and Spanish.

Organization of the Book

The book is organized into thirteen chapters. Where feasible, each chapter builds on or extends information presented in previous chapters. The book begins with the purpose and history of middle-level education and then moves to the nature and needs of middle-grades students, principles of working with early adolescent students, and many other topics important in middle-level education.

Acknowledgments

We want to express our thanks to Arnis Burvikovs and Christine Lyons at Allyn and Bacon and to Myrna Breskin, who were influential in getting this book into its final form. We would like to acknowledge the valuable comments and suggestions provided by the reviewers of this edition: Dr. Laura Van Zandt Allen, Trinity University; Dr. Jan Waggoner, Southern Illinois University; and Melanie W. Green, Appalacian State University.

1 The Purpose and History of Middle-Level Education

Chapter Preview

This chapter provides information about the nature and purposes of middle-level education and explains what sets it apart from education at other levels. A brief history of middle-level education is presented, together with the concerns that have brought it to its current state. New challenges facing middle-grades education are identified, as are trends that may lead to future development. The chapter presents a list of characteristics that many authorities consider indicative of quality middle-level schools and concludes with challenges and trends for the future.

Remembering Your Middle School Years

What do you remember about school during your middle-grades years, say grades six through eight? The school dress code? The grades you made? A favorite teacher? Your relationships with peers? Perhaps you were obsessed with a sport that was your passion and joy, or enraptured by an idolized actor or rock star. Maybe an environmental or humanitarian cause so captivated you that you felt you would do almost anything to support it. Maybe you remember trying to shut out your parents as much as you could, until you needed them, of course. Or perhaps you remember what so many students experience—the pervasive anxiety, the constant uncertainty, confusion, the need to look just right, to fit in.

Those concerns are almost always present in young adolescent students. They don't seem to change much over time, despite changes in the dynamics of schools, families, and adolescents. The structure of middle-level schools has certainly changed in recent years. The curriculum is evolving, and new styles of teaching and behavior management are coming to the fore. But the nature and needs of young adolescents remain surprisingly constant. The overriding question for educators is, how do we, today, meet those needs, and in the process provide a high-quality education for all students, regardless of ability or background?

Mrs. Amaro and Miss Amaro At School

The following vignettes present contrasting experiences of a girl, and later her own daughter, as they moved into the unnerving world of post-elementary schooling. These accounts

1

are separated by thirty-seven years. The first is of Estelle Riviere, who later became Estelle Amaro, the mother of Amy Amaro, whose account follows.

Estelle Riviere (later Mrs. Estelle Amaro)

First day of junior high, 1965. Estelle Riviere, butterflies in her stomach, has been standing for some time at the bedroom mirror. She had unrolled her hair from the curlers she slept in all night, brushed it into a flip, teased it at the crown, and given it a good coating of her mom's hair spray. Now she furtively applies a touch of lipstick and a bit of mascara, not specifically banned in her mother's no-makeup rule. She sings along with Herman's Hermits on the radio, puts on a new pleated white skirt, and rolls it at the waist to raise the hemline. Not too short, though, for fear the vice principal might, as was rumored, make her get on her knees to measure and then expel her or send her home if the skirt was more than two inches above the floor. She planned how, if called in, she would surreptitiously unroll the waistband. She didn't know who the vice principal was, or the principal either, but she was afraid of them. She put on her white anklets and the leather school shoes, and her outfit was complete. As she studied the effect in the full-length mirror, she suddenly felt like crying.

"Estelle!" It was her mother. "Mrs. Adams and Paula are here! Don't forget your lunch. Let me take a look at you. Do you have your notebook and purse?" Mom gave her a hug, told her she looked very nice, assured her she would have a good day, and reminded her to behave in class and do what the teachers told her. She added she would be there after school to pick Estelle up. She stood at the door waving as Estelle got into the back seat of the blue station wagon beside Paula.

Estelle was dreading the morning and wished she could have stayed home, or at least that her mother would have gone with her. But once in the car with Paula and Mrs. Adams, her mood improved. She was glad to see Paula was also wearing a white pleated skirt and carrying a blue binder and sack lunch.

When they arrived at Madison Junior High, Estelle was astonished at the number of students milling around. All six elementary schools fed to it, and Estelle had never before seen so many people her own age together in one place. In sixth grade, she had felt important and accomplished and knew everything about the school. Her last teacher, Mr. Butler, had let her do special projects and help in the class. He treated her as someone important. Here in Madison Junior High she suddenly felt little and alone in the crowd. She overheard some of the eighth-graders laughing and talking about the "peagreeners," and she knew they meant those like her, new to the school and green as peas.

She went into the office where several lines of students waited at a high counter, behind which the office staff stood, handing out schedules. She got in line behind Paula, only to find when she reached the front that she was in the wrong line. She hadn't noticed the lines were arranged alphabetically. She had to wait once more in the R through Z line. When the bell rang, Estelle still didn't have her schedule.

She found her way to the English class, late, where an unsmiling Mrs. Gallas pointed to a seat, gave her a book, and continued the lesson. At the end of the class, homework was assigned—twenty sentences to be diagrammed before tomorrow. She only knew a few people in that class, where seats were assigned and a no-talking rule was strictly enforced.

Estelle progressed through the rest of the day, to history, math, science, home economics, and physical education, each with a different teacher. All of her teachers seemed stern and businesslike. None seemed to take much notice of her. In most of the classes she got to sit by Paula, whose schedule was similar to hers.

She found physical education embarrassing and demeaning. She had to wear a royal blue one-piece sleeveless outfit with her name embroidered on the left pocket, and she had to get weighed in front of everyone else. After that the class did some folk dances and exercises in the gymnasium. The boys did their activities outside, so at least they didn't see the girls in their unbecoming outfits. Estelle was told that when you were on your period you had to say "R" to the teacher. (Estelle never understood why.) If you said "R," you only had to take half a shower. Estelle wished she could play speedball with the boys at lunch, as she had done in elementary school.

Estelle's schedule showed she would be in cooking the first semester and sewing the second semester, which she expected because the girls always had home economics while the boys all had woodshop. Most of her classes were organized in rows of desks, where students listened to the teacher and took notes. She learned that there would be great amounts of written work to turn in, and many tests to take. If you talked to someone during class you would get a scolding from the teacher. You were always to "do your own work." Estelle was good at following teachers' directions.

One of the strongest memories she had of that first day in junior high was how childish she looked in socks. Most of the older girls wore stockings. She decided to beg for a garter belt and some stockings and ask Mom if she could begin shaving her legs.

When her mother picked her and Paula up after school, both girls complained about the strict teachers and boring classes. They were excited, though,

about the cute boys. They decided junior high would be okay. Estelle wanted to get her homework done early so she could watch the Monkees on television that night.

By the end of Estelle's two years in junior high school, she had had twelve different teachers. She earned good grades from all of them by doing what was expected—listening, always doing the homework, and always studying for tests. Her teachers remained mysteries to her, as did the whys and wherefores of what she was learning. She was never assigned to work on a project with another student and never asked to defend an opinion or persuade another person to her way of thought. She never got to participate in after-school clubs or student activities—there were none. Years later she could only remember one of her teachers clearly, and that was because of his unfairness and negative attitude. But she did go on to high school, university, and graduate school. She was very successful academically, though many of her friends were not. She supposed their families didn't support education as much as hers did.

We now move forward thirty-seven years to the day when Estelle's youngest daughter, Amy, entered middle school.

Amy Amaro, Estelle's daughter

First day of middle school, 2002, and Amy Amaro had butterflies in her stomach. She watched in the mirror as her mom braided her long brown hair so it would be tidy and out of the way for school activities, and then Amy finished dressing while Britney Spears was on television dancing, singing, and looking perfect. Amy wore blue shorts, a white-and-blue T-shirt, and tennis shoes. Her backpack was by the front door, ready to go. The school had sent home a letter detailing what supplies she needed; she had them all. On Orientation Day, the Friday before the first day of school, she had met all of her new teachers and had gone on a tour of the campus. It was the second time she had been there. Her whole class had come over a few weeks earlier to see a concert and eat lunch with "the big kids in middle school." She knew where the restrooms and her classrooms were, she had met her

teachers, and she knew what her schedule was, but if she forgot, her advisory teacher, Mr. Brent, a very nice man, had a copy of it. His was the first class of the day, and he explained there would be seventh- and eighth-graders in attendance, too, and that they had all started out with him in sixth grade, just as Amy was about to. The older kids, remembering what the first days were like, were assigned to help the newcomers. There were seventh- and eighth-graders in her physical education classes, too, and in her electives. She learned she would have Mr. Brent for her advisory teacher all three years in middle school.

Before leaving for school, Amy reviewed her schedule for Estelle: "First, I have math and science for two periods with Mrs. Olivero. Then, physical education with Coach Herron. Coach said there will be boys in our class. For my elective wheel, I get technology arts first. Then lunch. Did you pack my lunch, Mom? They said the lines may be long the first day and we should bring our lunch so we have time to eat. Then, I have English and social studies with Mrs. Bigler. We can have clubs, too. I want Spanish and photography!"

Estelle smiled. "You sound all set."

"I'm just hoping I don't look stupid or that somebody makes fun of me. I'm worried if I can do the work the teachers expect. I hope they don't call on me in class."

When Mrs. O'Brien arrived with Tyneesha, Estelle gave Amy a hug and stood at the door and waved after her. Tyneesha had a new hairdo and wore a blue shorts outfit. Her backpack matched Amy's. Amy waved to Estelle and had a sudden feeling of loneliness. She wished she had another year in elementary school, where everything was comfortable and understandable.

Once at school, Amy and Tyneesha went to their advisory period to start the day. First thing, the school principal appeared on the class television monitor, giving a welcome to all students and relaying some school news. The assistant principals also said a few words, as did the counselors.

In advisory period, all the students formed into small groups and introduced themselves to each other and then rotated to meet other groups. Later, in science class, Mrs. Olivero showed some of the lab equipment and explained what it was for and how it was used safely. In math, Mrs. Olivero issued the textbooks, reviewed the topics they would be learning about, and explained expectations concerning classwork, homework, and periodic assessment. To pique interest, Mrs. Olivero demonstrated a few math memory "tricks" that the students found especially interesting. All of her classes mentioned school rules, the daily schedule, and incentives and rewards for good performance.

As for other students, Amy found some of them intimidating (some of the boys in eighth grade had noticeable mustaches) and some of the eighth-grade girls wore high heels and dresses. Amy felt little in comparison, but reminded herself that she was only in sixth grade.

Amy already knew she would be assigned to a "house" and taught by a team of teachers. She would have all of her classes, except for electives and physical education, with the same group of kids.

The Differences

You see from the first-day experiences of Estelle and Amy that both had similar feelings of insecurity, confusion, and fearfulness, offset by energy, curiosity, and desire to learn. But their school experiences were quite different. For Estelle, the experience was businesslike, conducted by no-nonsense teachers. It is not that her teachers were heartless—they were caring and well-intentioned, and were teaching in a manner which, at that time, was believed best for adolescent students.

In Amy's school, teachers and other adults seemed more understanding of and in tune with early adolescent students. They looked for ways to capitalize on students' impressive energy and enthusiasm, and therefore encouraged interaction and active learning. They tried to adjust the school experience to students' needs, and all in all projected a desire to provide well-rounded education for all students.

FIELD APPLICATION 1: Observe in a middle-level school to which you have access. Does the school seem to resemble more closely that of Estelle or Amy? In what specific ways?

The Purpose of Today's Middle-Level School

As depicted in the contrasting experiences of Estelle and Amy, today's middle-level school is notably different from yesterday's junior high school. It is designed to serve a different purpose. Junior high school was, as the name implied, a sort of lower-level high school. In 1965 it was almost identical to high schools of the day (which have now changed too), but was then seen by many as something of a holding tank for students who were not yet mature enough to do real academic work. Junior high was supposed to teach subject matter which, as in high schools, emphasized abstract ideas. Teachers taught through lecture–demonstration, and students were expected to show compliance, perseverance, and adultlike responsibility. Those expectations did not fit well with students who were not inclined to concentrate on academic subjects for long, or listen to lectures, or persevere on routine tasks, or behave as adults would like them to.

Educators recognize now that the old junior high focus and program were too narrow, the possibilities too limited, the activities too tedious, and the demands too stringent for the students they served. While students do need a firm grounding in academic pursuits, they need even more the security and guidance for developing confidence and character. Those qualities in turn form the foundation for good learning and personal relationships.

As viewed today, middle-level education serves not as a holding tank, but as an important phase in adolescent development that can be used for significant growth. This growth is accomplished in today's middle-level schools through small communities of student learners who have close contact with helpful teachers. Young people entering adolescence are beset with questions about who they are, what they value, how they want to live, why society functions as it does, and where they fit in. They have much to learn, and most of them want to learn.

How Middle-Level Schools Evolved

In the late 1800s, Americans were justifiably proud of their "common schools" that provided free basic education to most American children, grades one through eight. The rationale for the common school was that an educated populace was necessary to support America's participatory democracy. The common schools focused on reading, writing, speaking, arithmetic, patriotism, discipline, and morals of honesty, hard work, responsibility, courtesy, and respect for elders. Most young children attended school for at least part of the year, although few continued and completed high school. Of those who did, only a handful went on to university.

In the early 1900s, things began to change. As Diane Ravitch points out in her book, *Left Back: A Century of Failed School Reforms* (2000), this period saw America undergoing great economic and social change, moving rapidly from an agrarian to an industrial economy. Immigration was high and urbanization was occurring rapidly. Those new conditions called for school reforms that could help forge a nation from the diverse ethnic groups newly arrived and, at the same time, provide the young a means for improving their lives. Harvard president Charles W. Eliot led the call for higher standards for all students, in the belief that the intellectual capacity of immigrant and lower-class students was usually underestimated. He also believed that schools should give greater attention to different ways and rates of learning. William Torrey Harris, superintendent of schools in St. Louis, urged schools to provide the same quality education to working-class students as to children of the rich. In answering critics who complained about the cost of such education, he stressed that the best preparation for any participant in a democracy is the power to think (Ravitch, 2000). Harris was appointed United States Commissioner of Education by President Benjamin Harrison in 1889, a position he filled until 1906.

Earlier, Eliot and Harris, together with four university presidents, three high school principals, and a university professor, were brought together as "The Committee of Ten" to address the need for a nationwide system of education. Under the auspices of the National Education Association, this committee studied the nation's schools and made recommendations for improvement. Their report, issued in 1893, recommended three modifications that were considered radical at the time:

- High schools should provide an equal academic education for all students.
- Active learning methods should be emphasized over rote memorization.
- Instruction should be directed at individuals who learn in different ways and at different rates.

Critics were numerous. They decried the Committee of Ten's recommendations as ill-conceived, inefficient, and impractical. Middle-ground positions were suggested as alternatives, holding that most students should receive a practical curriculum to prepare for future occupations, while a few should be allowed to pursue academic studies that would lead to higher education.

Junior High Schools Appear

The Committee of Ten recommended that the school program for college-bound students should consist of six years of elementary school followed by six years of secondary school. Many school systems followed this plan, while others adopted a plan of eight years of elementary school followed by four years of high school. The Committee of Ten further recommended that all high school students should study mathematics, science, literature, history, foreign language, and the arts, no matter what their future occupation might be (Ravitch, 2000). These recommendations were hotly debated for a number of years. Influenced by those debates, the National Education Association (NEA) created a Commission on Economy of Time in Education, which in 1913 suggested the concept of a separate junior high school. They concluded that time was being wasted in the elementary schools and that necessary basic skills could be taught in six years. The Commission advocated a separate three-year school where the curriculum would be differentiated according to each student's future occupation. In 1915, the NEA backed this idea, and in 1918 the NEA's Commission on the Reorganization of Secondary Education (CRSE) came out in support of a separate junior high school. As schools adopted these proposals, public education became, in most states, six years of elementary school, three years of junior high school, and three years of high school. This was called the 6–3–3 plan, which endured for a half-century.

Although it is often believed that the junior high school developed because of dissatisfaction with the 8–4 plan, other forces played a major role. Colleges and universities were very influential in elementary and secondary education issues. They wanted better-prepared students, and pushed for a more rigorous curriculum, one which would begin earlier than ninth grade (Powell and Van Zandt Allen, 2001). A second force came from concern about an increasing dropout rate. It was hoped that the junior highs could help in this regard by easing the abrupt transition from elementary school to high school that afflicted students attending 8–4 plan schools (Anfara, 2001). Yet another concern centered on overcrowded schools, due to population growth after World War I. Communities could save on capital outlay by shifting grades 7–9 to a separate building (the old high school, perhaps) and just build one new school (George and Alexander, 1993). Most of these developments came from pragmatic responses to societal issues, rather than from consideration of the needs of young adolescent learners. Nevertheless, as Powell and Van Zandt Allen point out, the junior high school provided the opportunity to examine more closely this distinct age group and their educational needs.

The junior high became well established in subsequent years, but in truth the differences between junior and senior high schools were superficial, while the differences between students at the two levels were great. The universities wanted public schools to be more rigorous and academic. Their influence led to middle-level schools teaching through lectures, organizing teachers by department, providing elective programs that were specialized rather than exploratory, and grouping students by intellectual ability.

Only a few decades earlier, working-class children typically held jobs and worked long hours on farms and in factories and mills to contribute to the family well-being. Now a more nurturing view of the young had taken hold, with laws prohibiting child labor (except in farms and family businesses) and requiring attendance at school. This new view saw childhood as a time for wide experience and formal learning rather than work.

Educators were also becoming more aware of age-specific characteristics and began to realize the need for a junior high program different from that of either elementary or high school. Thomas Briggs (1920), an early authority in junior high school education, envisioned the junior high serving as a bridge between elementary and high school, with guidance and direction for students, integrated subject matter, and exploratory courses. Briggs's vision was not to materialize for many years to come. Even in the 1960s, junior high schools still had the structure and programs of high schools, but they were soon to change.

Early Efforts toward Middle-Level Education

In the second half of the twentieth century, a newer concept of middle-level education began to emerge, and by the end of the century it was in vogue. In 1963, William Alexander, often referred to as the "father of the middle school," described the sort of institution he and others envisioned as a "school in the middle," designed to meet the particular needs of early adolescent students. His plan called for moving ninth-grade students into high school. The earlier years of education would be divided into elementary school (kindergarten through grade four) and middle school (grades five through eight). Most schools, however, adopted a K–5, 6–8, and 9–12 configuration. The educational program in the new middle schools would include block scheduling, teachers trained especially to teach ten- to fourteen-year-olds, use of varied instructional techniques, and strong guidance services. Alexander was one of the authors of the first textbook for middle-level educators, called *The Emergent Middle School* (1968). He was instrumental in forming the Florida League of Middle Schools in 1972 and established the first program in middle-school teacher education at the University of Florida.

Although more attention was being paid to the nature and needs of middle-level students, other factors influenced the spread of the middle school. As George and Alexander (1993) point out, one such factor was the issue of school desegregation. School districts were under pressure to comply with mandates and found that, by reorganizing existing grade levels, this compliance could be achieved relatively easily. Also, population shifts in the Northeast and Midwest created the need to balance the enrollments at elementary and secondary schools in order to utilize existing facilities more efficiently. By moving sixth grade to junior high and ninth grade to high school (creating a middle school with grades 6–8) school districts were able to accomplish the balance needed.

In the 1970s, the Ford Foundation, decrying the lack of attention to students in the middle grades, commissioned a study to investigate research, attention, and advocacy pertinent to individuals in early adolescence. In addition, the Association for Supervision and Curriculum Development (ASCD) created a group to study the middle school and how it could meet the needs of the early adolescent learner. In 1975, it published its findings in *The Middle School We Need* (Gatewood, 1975), reporting that a notable gap existed between the theory and practice of middle-years education. The conclusions drawn from such efforts contributed to Joan Lipsitz's 1997 report, *Growing Up Forgotten: A Review of the Research and Programs concerning Early Adolescence.* This work helped focus educators' attention more concertedly on the needs of early adolescence.

Recent Efforts in Middle-Level Education

Activity related to student-centered schooling increased greatly in the latter part of the twentieth century and is still accelerating (Powell and Van Zandt Allen, 2001). By the end of the twentieth century, the junior high school, in its grades 7–9 configuration, had almost disappeared in the United States. While in 1971, 45 percent of middle-level schools included grades 7–9, the number today is less than 5 percent, while the 6–8 configuration has increased to over 60 percent. More importantly, middle-level programs have also changed significantly (National Middle School Association Research Summary, 2001). These changes originated in concerns previously mentioned and are being pushed forward by efforts such as those described in the following paragraphs.

A Nation At Risk.   In 1983, the National Commission on Excellence in Education published *A Nation at Risk,* which raised alarm about the condition of education in the United States. Achievement levels were declining and student dropout rates were increasing. This situation prompted a number of philanthropic foundations, educational researchers, university centers, and the U.S. Department of Education to seek ways to reverse these trends. The movement gained further momentum in 1995 when the International Association for the Evaluation of Educational Achievement sponsored the Third International Mathematics and Science Study (TIMSS). The results, released in 1996, revealed that eighth-graders in the

United States were not only falling well behind students from other industrialized nations, but that most of the lost ground occurred in the years between fourth and eighth grade.

National Middle School Association (1982, 1995).   Just before publication of *A Nation at Risk,* the National Middle School Association (NMSA) published a position paper specifying ten elements considered essential in good middle schools (NMSA, 1982, pp. 10–15). Those ten elements were:

- teachers committed to young adolescents;
- a curriculum based on student needs;
- a range of organizational arrangements;
- varied instructional strategies;
- a full exploratory program;
- comprehensive advising and counseling;
- continuous progress for students;
- evaluation procedures compatible with young adolescents;
- cooperative planning;
- a positive school climate.

Those ten elements have been incorporated in most of the newer efforts to improve middle school education. They were revised in 1995 and now describe the developmentally responsive middle school as characterized by:

- educators committed to young adolescents;
- a shared vision;
- high expectations for all;
- an adult advocate for every student;
- family and community partnerships;
- a positive school climate.

The NMSA also recommended that middle-level schools provide:

- a curriculum that is challenging, integrative, and exploratory;
- varied teaching and learning approaches;
- assessment and evaluation that promote learning;
- flexible organizational structures;
- programs and policies that foster health, wellness, and safety;
- comprehensive guidance and support services.

The Carnegie Report.   In 1989, the Carnegie Council on Adolescent Development published *Turning Points: Preparing Youth for the 21st Century,* in which it offered a set of recommendations for improving education for middle-grades students. Those recommendations included dividing large schools into smaller communities for learning, organizing instruction to ensure success for all students, preparing middle-grades teachers specifically to teach young adolescent students, engaging families in the education of the young, and connecting schools with communities.

In 2000, the Carnegie report was updated and entitled *Turning Points 2000* (see Jackson and Davis, 2000). In that report the original recommendations were updated as follows:

- Teach a curriculum grounded in rigorous, public academic standards for what students should know and be able to do, relevant to the concerns of adolescents and based on how students learn best.
- Use instructional methods designed to prepare all students to achieve higher standards and become lifelong learners.
- Staff middle-level schools with teachers who are expert at teaching young adolescents, and engage teachers in ongoing, targeted professional development opportunities.
- Organize relationships for learning to create a climate of intellectual development and a caring community of shared educational purpose.
- Govern democratically, through direct or representative participation by all school staff members, the adults who know the students best.
- Provide a safe and healthy school environment as part of improving academic performance and developing caring and ethical citizens.
- Involve parents and communities in supporting student learning and healthy development.

As a continuing part of the Turning Points effort, certain school districts have been selected and funded to put into practice the concepts advocated in the report.

Middle Grade School State Policy Initiative.   The Carnegie Corporation of New York now funds a program of grants to states to stimulate change in middle-grades education. Their goal is to effect reform by changing state-level policies to reflect the principles set forth in *Turning Points.* The states then establish professional development opportunities for teachers. By 1997, the Middle Grade School State Policy Initiative (MGSSPI) had supplied planning grants to twenty-seven states, with additional two-year grants to fifteen states. Since 1990, most states receiving grants have developed comprehensive policy statements for the middle grades, established certification requirements for middle-grades teachers, developed statewide frameworks for the middle-level curriculum, and added a middle-level focus to existing frameworks (Jackson, 1997).

Illinois Middle Grades Network.   In 1989, a U.S. Department of Education grant provided start-up funding for a program initiated and conducted by middle-grades practitioners in Illinois. Funding was later taken over by various foundations and has helped formalize the Illinois Middle Grades Network, an affiliation of schools and staffs that work collaboratively to implement reform and disseminate effective practices. The Network offers staff development and mentoring relationships to schools that desire to participate.

The effectiveness of the Illinois Middle Grades Network was assessed in 1997 by the Project on High-Performing Learning Communities (Felner et al., 1997). That assessment showed strong evidence that the well-implemented reforms were bringing about changes for the better, especially for students at risk of failure. Achievement improved notably in mathematics, language, and reading in schools where the Turning Points suggestions were "highly implemented." No corresponding improvements were evident in any of the "non-implemented" schools used for comparison. Further, students in highly implemented schools, according to self-reports, acquired greater self-esteem, experienced less fear of the future, and had less fear of victimization than did students in comparison schools. The researchers pointed out that even the highly implemented schools were works in progress, simply farther along the road to improvement than some of the other schools.

Middle Start Initiative.   The Middle Start Initiative, launched in 1994 by the W. K. Kellogg Foundation, was designed to help Michigan schools create more effective learning environments for early adolescent students, particularly those at risk of academic failure and those who are economically disadvantaged. Since its inception, Middle Start has expanded to five other states. Middle Start is a comprehensive initiative focusing on ten dimensions: curriculum, school climate, instruction, family involvement, student assessment, school–community partnerships, professional development, internal and external communications, school organization, and program evaluation (W. K. Kellogg Foundation, 2002). Middle Start utilizes self-study data and school performance data in planning and evaluating reform efforts.

Middle Grades Improvement Program.   The Middle Grades Improvement Program, begun in 1987 under sponsorship of the Eli Lilly Endowment, involved sixteen urban school districts in Indiana (Lipsitz, 1997). Those districts created their own improvement plans, with cooperative input from teachers, parents, and community agencies. Consultants were provided to the districts to assist in planning and implementing the improvements. The emphasis on data-based decisions helps focus plans for improvement.

National Forum to Accelerate Middle-Grades Reform.   The "National Forum" is a group of sixty educators, researchers, officers of national associations, and directors of foundations dedicated to improving education for young adolescents. In 1999, this forum launched a program called "Schools to Watch." These schools serve as exemplars of what is possible with time, dedication, and hard work. They share these three characteristics (Norton and Lewis, 2000):

- focus on academics;
- structure that addresses the developmental needs of young adolescents;
- social equity, manifested by every student's access to excellent teachers, resources, and supports.

Five common themes further characterize the "Schools to Watch":

- clearly articulated academic outcomes;
- changes in curriculum and teaching to help students achieve;
- built-in accountability;
- focus on areas for improvement;
- leaders with vision.

FIELD APPLICATION 2:   Arrange to speak with a middle-school teacher you know. Ask that person if she or he has heard of any of the recent initiatives described in the preceding paragraphs. If so, ask his or her opinion of them and if any are improving school practice.

Defining Characteristics of
Quality Middle-Level Schools

Programs and initiatives such as those described in previous paragraphs have been catalysts for reform and have prompted many agencies to join the middle school effort. The National Middle School Association and associated state organizations are helping improve middle school education by organizing conferences, arranging for visits to exemplary schools, and publicizing promising practices. State departments of education are issuing reports and directives related to middle school reform. Researchers are widening the scope of their investigations. Local school boards, superintendents, other school leaders, and teachers are taking up the challenge to provide the best education possible for their students, and are implementing many efforts to improve middle school education. From evidence so far available, the following provisions seem most likely to produce the desired outcomes (NMSA Research Summary, 2002).

   1. Teams of Teachers Working Together. Teacher teams seem to produce a positive effect all around. By working together with the same group of students, a team can more easily provide interesting programs, implement effective discipline, permit earlier and more effective academic interventions for students in need, and improve communication with students, parents, and others. They are also more likely to increase the students' sense of belonging and security, which seems to encourage their participation in class activities.

   Interdisciplinary teams provide benefits for both students and teachers. When students feel their teachers know them and care about their current achievement and future success, they are inclined to try harder and care more about their own success. When teachers know their students well, academically and emotionally, and have regular opportunities to discuss curriculum and instruction with the other team members, they are better able to take individual students' needs into account.

   Teams typically consist of two to four teachers, each responsible for a portion of the core curriculum, which frequently consists of mathematics, English, science, and social studies. By meeting regularly, teachers are able to discuss student achievement, involve guidance counselors to assist students, integrate curriculum, develop strategies for improving instruction, and communicate more effectively with parents (Erb & Stevenson, 1999a, pp. 47–48, cited in Jackson and Davis, 2000).

   Difficult challenges must be overcome in creating and maintaining a successful team. Teachers must be willing and able to compromise for the good of the team, and must support the decisions of the team. Teams must create procedures and discipline plans together, which can present problems when not all teachers are comfortable with the same management or discipline style. And, of course, team meetings take time, which must be made available if teams are to function effectively. Strong-willed teachers can make it hard for others to put forth ideas, while teachers who do not follow through with team plans undermine the success of the team. Team responsibilities must be shared, rather than falling to one person. Keeping the focus on the learning needs of the children helps team members work out their differences.

2. Advisory Program. The advisory program is a regularly scheduled time of interaction between an adult advisor and a small group of students. Its purpose is to provide a "comfort zone" for each student. Scheduling of the advisory period varies according to each school's design, but most practitioners conduct daily advisories, first thing in the morning, for no less than twenty minutes. At least one additional weekly meeting of longer duration is needed to help students work on school or community projects. For optimum benefit, individual meetings between the advisor and each advisee should be scheduled every month (Stevenson, 1998).

Jim Burns (1996, 2001) recommends team-based, "designated day" advisories, with flexible scheduling for various activities. For example, the advisory for Day One would be a brief (ten–fifteen minutes) meeting to communicate important weekly dates for the team—any scheduled quizzes, due dates for projects, special events, and general information relating to the interdisciplinary team. Day Two could be for individual and group goal-setting and monitoring of progress. Other days could be devoted to citizenship activities, service projects, communication skills, hobbies, and mini-courses on particular topics. Burns adds that, just as there is no one right way to teach, there is no one right way to operate an advisory group. The general conclusion is that advisories such as Burns describes do in fact lead to improved test scores, improved grades, fewer behavior-related referrals, and better attendance (Hopkins, 1999).

The ideal number of students in an advisory is twenty or less. The leader, a teacher or another staff member, makes a concerted effort to get to know each student well, sometimes beginning even before the school year starts by mailing each student a postcard during the summer, or inviting the advisees to a barbecue and "get-acquainted" activity. Although in some schools the advisories are grade-specific, in others the students stay with the same advisor during their years in the school. An advisory aims to create a feeling of "family" for the student by providing for adult–child and peer group interactions. Possibly the most valuable quality of a good advisory is that a caring adult guides and supports students through difficult times and in doing so positively affects their feelings, attitudes, and behavior at school.

FIELD APPLICATION 3: Arrange to speak with a teacher or administrator of a middle-level school. Inquire whether the school uses an advisory program as described here. If so, ask the person to describe the program and how well it seems to work.

3. High Levels of Student Activity in Learning. Adolescents are by nature full of energy, and, as John Lounsbury says (see Listserv, 2000), they learn best with their hands on and their mouths open. That is why middle school educators are encouraged to provide instruction that harnesses this energy and puts it to productive use. Students enjoy hands-on activities, collaborative projects, cooperative groups, problem solving, and other kinds of active learning. As we will see in later chapters, high activity adds interest and motivation that, in turn, lead to better learning, better attitudes, and more acceptable behavior.

4. Exploratory Courses and Programs. The concept of an exploratory curriculum has long been identified as a desirable element of middle-grades education. In theory, the entire middle-level curriculum should be challenging, integrative, and exploratory (NMSA, 1995). In practice, *exploratory* has come to mean an opportunity for students to select from optional courses that are appealing and that provide experiences and opportunities beyond the core curriculum. The exploratory curriculum complements the core curriculum, enabling students to see connections within learning. Topics in the exploratory curriculum often include career exploration, world languages, art, music, creative writing, technological arts, speech, and drama (Brazee, 2000).

5. Helpful Transition Programs. Early adolescents are often referred to as "in the middle" between childhood and adulthood, with all its ramifications. It is unfortunate they are said to be in the middle between this and that, which suggests they have left something good and are having to mark time while waiting for something else that is good. It would be more reasonable to say they are in the early adolescent stage of development. Nevertheless, we are at present stuck with the labels "middle" and "transition." Labels aside, we can focus on helping students function fully during early adolescence, while helping them move smoothly from one phase to another.

Elementary students entering middle-level schools experience strong feelings of excitement and fear, resulting in a mood that some authorities call "middle school malaise" (Mizelle, 1999). When they finish middle school and have to make the transition to high school, they will again experience malaise. Schools, teachers, and parents can help ease these transitions by providing information in advance about the new school, organizing social support for each student, and establishing good articulation between the faculties of schools involved (Mac Iver, 1990). The schools can do such things as invite incoming students to visit the campus, tour the site with an older student, meet with school personnel for information on programs and procedures, and meet with a panel of students for a question-and-answer session. Parental involvement throughout the process is very important as well.

Moving to a larger school can sometimes disrupt the social networks of students at a time when friends are very important. The transition team should provide opportunities for incoming students to get acquainted with current students and other newcomers. One way of accomplishing this is through "buddy" programs in which older students are paired with younger ones. Some teachers also use pen-pal programs of letter writing between current students and incoming students, and, on a larger scale, schools frequently use peer mentoring programs (Mizelle, 1999).

Vertical teaming, which refers to articulation and coordination of curriculum through the grades, can also help. With student comfort and achievement as the focus, educators can decide how best to address issues concerning which faculty members teach what, and when and how they teach it. When this is done, students can see how their formal learning is to proceed through the grades, no matter which type of school they attend.

6. Involvement of Parents, Families, and Community. We have noted how important it is for parents and family members to remain closely attentive to their child's progress through school. Their attention and involvement can be encouraged through a number of activities, such as:

- allowing parents and family members to help with homework or listen as a student explains a homework assignment;
- inviting them to attend school functions;
- inviting them to meet with teachers and administrators to discuss the educational program;
- participating in parent committees at the school;
- guiding students in making decisions and choices that may have long-lasting effects on their lives.

Many schools now have parent volunteer coordinators who work in parent centers that have been established on campus. The coordinator helps involve parents in many activities at school and helps keep them informed. Some coordinators compile information and articles into a monthly newsletter for parents.

Teachers, of course, must keep parents informed about their child's progress via formal progress reports and conferences as well as through informal notes and phone calls. Some schools have instituted Homework Hotlines where students and parents can call to get information on assignments for each teacher. Some even use a school Web site to communicate with parents. A growing trend is having student-led parent and teacher conferences, where the child shows and explains a portfolio of work-to-date to the parent. The process of preparing the portfolio, explaining it to the parent, and reflecting on the experience can be very positive (Cromwell, 1999). Chapter 4 is devoted to improving working relationships between schools and families.

7. Leaders with Vision. A middle-level school is not just a checklist of individual attributes. It is more like an orchestra, where the brass, strings, woodwinds, and percussion play individual roles that produce a joint outcome. Teachers, principals, students, staff, parents, and others all have key roles that, when not discharged well, damage the overall performance.

Good principals of middle schools are leaders who have clear visions of what the middle school should be and how it should perform. Those leaders know how to inspire teachers, staff, and students. While in this book we emphasize teachers as crucial in delivering education to students, the role of the school principal is paramount in keeping middle-level schools on track so they can provide the best education possible to students in attendance (Jackson and Davis, 2000).

Special Challenges in Middle-Level Education Today

Educators who have been involved in the middle school reforms have very positive feelings about them and believe the new efforts are yielding desirable results. Yet, many of those same educators feel the reforms have not gone far enough. They point to several additional challenges that need to be addressed.

Raising Student Achievement

A major challenge remains low levels of academic achievement. We noted that, in 1996, the Third International Mathematics and Science Study documented a decline in math achievement among middle and high school students. These were the same students who, in fourth grade, had scored above the international average on the tests. This puts middle school education and the American math and science curricula in the spotlight. According to William H. Schmidt, U.S. research coordinator for TIMSS, "The middle school is the crux of the whole problem and really the point where we begin to lose it" (quoted in Bradley and Manzo, 2000).

Policymakers were interested in following high-achieving fourth-graders as they progressed through middle school, so U.S. officials backed a follow-up study to see how they fared. The repeat of the Third International Mathematics and Science Study (TIMSS-R) took place in 1999, with the eagerly awaited results released in December 2000. American educators were hopeful that reform efforts in curriculum and instruction over the past decade would produce better results for U.S. students. However, the results were the same as found in the earlier test: after fourth grade, U.S. students fall behind their international peers for some reason (Schemo, 2000). A question we must face is why?

Educators believe they know some of the reasons, but have no conclusive answers. Some of the factors they point to are (see Tomlinson, 1995; Mills, 1998; Chaddock, 2000):

- We do not expect enough academically of early adolescent students.
- The percentage of students taught math by teachers who majored in mathematics is only 41 percent in the United States, compared with 71 percent for our international peers.
- The U.S. math curriculum tends to be very wide but not very deep, the opposite of other countries.
- Middle-grades teachers are not focusing sufficiently on preparing students for high school.
- Tracking students by ability level negatively affects the lower-tracked students' self-perceptions and motivation, which quickly results in racial and class inequities.
- Students are somehow escaping personal accountability for learning.

A different view is presented by David Berliner (2001), who analyzed the statistics from the TIMSS-R and concluded that it is not the schools that are failing in general, but that we are failing some of our students in particular. He says that, in a country as heterogeneous as America, average scores mislead, due to inequities in the quality of education. He suggests strongly that the solution is to adequately fund and equip schools that are failing students in our poorest neighborhoods.

Preparing Quality Middle School Teachers

Another challenge centers on the recruitment, training, and retention of high-quality teachers for the middle schools. The National Forum to Accelerate Middle Grades Reform

(2002) has issued a position paper on desirable teacher preparation, licensing, and recruitment, calling for the following:

- Mandatory requirements and middle-level licensure should be required for individuals desiring to teach in middle-level schools.
- Institutions that prepare middle-level teachers should have their programs scrutinized and accredited.
- Teacher education programs should include specialized programs for developing middle-level teachers and should assign to them faculty and staff with expertise in middle-level education.
- States should make middle-level teacher licensure specific to the middle grades (e.g., grades 5 through 8, or 6 through 9) and avoid significant overlap with licensure for the elementary or high school levels.
- Middle-grades licensure for content-area teachers (such as language arts, science, mathematics, and social studies) should be middle-grades subject-specific and middle-grades standards-based, including concentrated study in two or more academic areas. For other middle-grades teachers (e.g., special education, bilingual education), specialized training in middle-level education and early adolescence should be required.
- Colleges and universities should work in partnership with districts and schools to provide ongoing professional development and sustained support for both new and veteran middle-level teachers.

These suggestions are reflected in requirements for teacher education program accreditation established by the National Council for Accreditation of Teacher Education (NCATE). Those requirements are reviewed in Chapter 5.

Helping Beginning Teachers Experience Success

Once well-prepared teachers are hired, they need to receive close support from the school district and fellow teachers. The support process is not yet well established in most schools, with the result that an unduly high number of middle school (and other level) teachers leave the profession early in their careers (Terry, 2001). This situation can be remedied easily and should be made a priority by school administration and faculty. Mentor teachers can help new educators use the most successful practices and deal with the discouragement and frustration all teachers experience. School districts can provide quality professional development in content and pedagogy. In remarks made concerning professional development, Hayes Mizell (2001) stated that professional development should be tied to student outcomes. He suggested that effective staff development can be a lifeline for teachers needing support to meet the instructional challenges they face.

Teachers report that some of the best professional development comes from the process of working with "critical friends" (meaning other teachers) to analyze together assignments, student work, standards, and successes and failures. This process, with its frank conversations, can be instrumental in improving teaching practice (Jackson and Davis, 2000).

FIELD APPLICATION 4:   Arrange to speak with a first- or second-year teacher. Ask that person what specific problems he or she encountered and whether the school could have done anything to make things easier in the beginning.

Future Directions in Middle-Level Education

Middle-level education is being continually reformed, and several changes likely to continue in the near future are already evident.

Rethinking the Grade Levels Configuration

As we have seen, the junior high/middle school configurations have progressively changed over the years, from the 6–6, the model of 1900, to the 6–3–3 junior high model during the middle of the twentieth century, and on to the 5–3-4 middle school model prevalent today. Some school districts in Cincinnati, Cleveland, Milwaukee, and Philadelphia are rethinking the organizational plan and are once again opting for an 8–4 configuration, in the belief that this organization provides better benefits of continuity of curriculum, adult–student relationships, and smaller, safer schools (Harrington-Lueker, 2001). It remains to be seen whether this movement will become popular.

Looping

Looping refers to teaching teams and students staying together for more than one year—for example, moving on together from seventh to eighth grade. The potential advantages are that teams and students know one another better and there is less time lost at the beginning of the school year (Jackson and Davis, 2000). Potential disadvantages are that teachers may not be well qualified to teach their particular subjects and that students could benefit from associations with a larger variety of teachers.

Middle Grades Reform Models and Designs

Many different paths are currently being followed in middle school reform. Some of these paths are made available commercially or under grants from foundations, which allows school districts to contract with particular programs for help in designing and implementing reforms. To illustrate, two low-performing middle schools in Baltimore have contracted to use the Talent Development Middle School model, which emphasizes teaching coaches, professional development, and improved school climate (Niedowski, 2001). Another promising plan is the Turning Points reform model, which focuses on data-based inquiry and teacher collaboration to improve student learning (Jackson and Davis, 2000). Yet another is AVID (Advancement Via Individual Determination), actually a program rather than a reform movement that started with one teacher (Mary Catherine Swanson) in a single classroom in a single high school in San Diego in 1980 and is now used in more than 1000 schools in sixteen states. AVID's mission is to enable underrepresented students to succeed in rigorous curricula, thus improving their later success in higher education (see AVID, 2001).

Technology

The use of technology, particularly networked computers connected to the Internet, presents exciting possibilities for improving student achievement in a developmentally responsive, socially equitable way. Recognizing both the opportunities and the challenges associated with technology in the school program, the U.S. Department of Education established the Office of Educational Technology to set forth a strategic national plan (U.S. Department of Education, 2001). Their recommendations call for the following:

- All students and teachers should have access to information technology in the classroom, at school, in the community, and in homes.
- Teachers should use technology effectively to help students achieve high academic standards.
- All students should have technology and information literacy skills.
- Research and evaluation should drive improvements in applications.

Probably the most promising means of reaching these technology goals lies in teacher education, both preservice and in-service. Veteran teachers are accustomed to a model of teaching that gives little attention to technology, and many are still uncomfortable with computers. Beginning teachers, while usually comfortable with computers, do not know how to use them to teach effectively. These are concerns to be reckoned with, because, no matter how much technology is available to teachers, it is left to the individual teacher to plan and deliver instruction.

On the positive side, the interactive attributes of technology fit very well with the nature of middle-grades students, who have no trouble accessing the Internet and engaging in learning experiences that are interactive and motivational. Far from providing only factual information or entertainment, these experiences can serve to enhance higher-order thinking skills such as drawing inferences and making analogies (Quinn and Valentine, 2001). They can also integrate learning activities thematically across the curriculum, as is done in a series called "WebQuests," which are interactive expeditions that involve adventurers, scientists, other experts, and connected classrooms (see Dodge, 1997). Some examples are AmazonQuest, MayaQuest, and AfricaQuest.

President George W. Bush's education plan, entitled No Child Left Behind, maintained that schools should use technology as a tool to improve academic achievement. His plan proposed various grants to help educators use technology effectively, including the setting of performance goals to measure how technology improves student achievement. As results accrue, educators will be better able to make judgments about technology's effects on student learning.

QUESTIONS

1. Reflect on your own junior high or middle school experience. What stands out in your memory? Teachers, activities, special programs, academics, friends? Do those memories suggest anything to you concerning the kind of teacher you'd prefer to be?

2. What would you identify as the two most important influences that originally prompted the establishment of junior high schools?

3. Why did educators become dissatisfied with junior high schools, and why have they believed middle schools would serve students better?

4. Of the various grade-level configurations for the school years kindergarten through grade 12, which do you believe serve students best? Why?

5. Of the recent efforts in middle school education described in the chapter, which two do you think are most promising?

6. To what extent do you believe computer technology can improve school achievement? What evidence supports your beliefs?

ACTIVITIES

1. Suppose you are a member of a sixth-grade team that is planning activities to help new students make the transition more easily from elementary schools into your middle school. Describe five activities you think would be most helpful.

2. Analyze the descriptions of the "defining characteristics of quality middle-level schools" presented in the chapter. Which two of the seven do you think would be most valuable? Which two least valuable? Explain your reasons.

3. With a group of classmates, speculate on why American students' achievement in mathematics declines, in comparison to that of other countries, during the middle school years. Present your conclusions to the class.

4. Describe the teacher education program you believe would provide the best possible preparation for middle school teachers, within the present constraints of time and resources.

REFERENCES

Alexander, W., Williams, E., Compton, M., Hines, V., and Prescott, D. 1968. *The emergent middle school.* New York: Holt, Rinehart, Winston.

Anfara, V. (ed). 2001. *The handbook of research in middle level education.* Greenwich, CT: Information Age.

AVID, an educational reform program that works. 26 August 2001. *San Diego Union Tribune.* <http://www.middleweb.com/MGNEWS1/MGN0907.html.

Berliner, D. 2001. Our schools vs. theirs: Averages that hide the true extremes. 28 January, *Washington Post.* Outlook Section OP-ED.

Bradley, A., and Manzo, K. 2000. The weak link. *Education Week.* <http://www.edweek.org/ew/ew_printstory.cfm?slug=05msmain.h20>.

Brazee, E. 2000. Exploratory curriculum in the middle school. *ERIC Digests.* <http://www.ed.gov/databases/ERIC_Digests/ed447970.html>.

Briggs, T. 1920. *The junior high school.* Boston: Houghton Mifflin.

Burns, J. 1996. The five attributes of satisfying advisories. *Integrative Design.* <http://www.vla.com/idesign/attributes2.html>.

———. 2001. Frequent inquiries regarding advisory: Ten questions, with answers from Jim Burns. Integrative Design. <http://www.vla.com/idesign/advisory2.html>.

Carnegie Council on Adolescent Development. 1989. *Turning points: Preparing American youth for the 21st Century.* New York: Carnegie Corporation of New York.

Chaddock, G. 2000. US eighth graders beat global average in math. 6 December. *Christian Science Monitor.* <http://www.csmonitor.com/durable/2000/12/06/p1s2.htm>.

Cromwell, S. 26 April 1999. Student-led conferences: A growing trend. *Education World.* <http://www.education-world.com/a_admin/admin112.shtml>.

Dodge, B. 1997. Some thoughts about WebQuests. <http://edweb.sdsu.edu/courses/edtec596/about_webquests.html>

Felner, R., Jackson, A., Kasak, D., Mullhall, P., Brand, S., and Flowers, N. 1997. The impact of school reform for the middle years: Longitudinal study of a network engaged in Turning Points-based comprehensive school transformation. *Phi Delta Kappan, 78*(7), 528.

Gatewood, T. 1975. The middle school we need: A report from the ASCD working group on the emerging adolescent learner. Washington, DC: Association for Supervision and Curriculum Development.

George, P., and Alexander, W. 1993. *The exemplary middle school.* (2nd ed.). New York: Harcourt Brace.

Harrington-Lueker, D. 15 March 2001. Middle schools fail to make the grade. *Middle Web.* <http://www.middleweb.com/MGNEWS1/MGN0319.html>.

Hopkins, G. 1999. Advice about middle school advisories. *Education World.* http://www.education-world.com/a_curr/curr127.shtml>.

Jackson, A. 1997. Middle Grade School State Policy Initiative. *Phi Delta Kappa International.* <http://pdkintl.org/kappan/kfels973.htm>.

———, and Davis, G. 2000. *Turning points 2000: Educating adolescents in the 21st century.* New York: Teachers College Press.

Lipsitz, J. 1997. Middle Grades Improvement Program. *Phi Delta Kappa International.* <http://www.pdkintl.org/kappan/kfels973.htm>.

———, Jackson, A., and Austin, L. 21 March 1997. Speaking with one voice: A manifesto for middle-grades reform. *Phi Delta Kappa International.* <http://www.pdkintl.org/kappan/kman973.htm>.

———, Jackson, A., and Austin, L. 21 March 1997. What works in middle-grades reform. *Phi Delta Kappa International.* <http://www.pdkintl.org/klip973.htm>.

Listserv, Middle Web. 16 November 2000. A Listserv conversation with John Lounsbury. *Middle Web.* <http://www.middleweb.com/MWLISTCONT/lounsburychat.html>.

Lounsbury, J. 1996. Key characteristics of middle level schools. *ERIC Digests.* <http://www.ed.gov/databases/ERIC_Digests/ed401050.html>.

Mac Iver, D. 1990. Meeting the needs of young adolescents: Advisory groups, interdisciplinary teaching teams, and school transition programs. *Phi Delta Kappan, 71,* 458–464.

Mills, R. 1998. Grouping students for instruction in middle schools. *ERIC Digests.* <http://www.ed.gov/databases/ERIC_Digests/ed419631.html>.

Mizell, H. 2001. Professional development: The state it's in. *Middle Web.* <http://www.middleweb.com/HMstate.html>.

Mizelle, N. 1999. Helping middle school students make the transition into high school. *ERIC Digests.* <http://www.ed/gov/databases/ERIC_Digests/ed432411.html>.

National Commission on Excellence in Education. 1983. *A nation at risk: The imperative for educational reform.* Washington, DC: U.S. Government Printing Office.

National Forum to Accelerate Middle Grades Reform. 2002. National forum policy statement on teacher preparation, licensure, and recruitment. <www.mgforum.org>

National Middle School Association. 1982. This we believe. Columbus, OH: Author.

———. 1995. This we believe: Developmentally responsive middle level schools. Columbus, OH. Author.

———. 2001. Research Summary #3. <http://www.nmsa.org/research/ressum3.htm>.

Niedowski, E. 15 September 2001. Middle school reform is off to a bumpy start. *Baltimore Sun.* <http://www.sunspot.net/templates/misc/printstory.jsp?slug=bal%2Dte%2Emd%Eidde11 . . . >.

Norton, J., and Lewis, A. 27 June 2000. Middle grades reform. <http://www.pdkintl.org/kappan/klew0006.htm>.

Powell, R., and Van Zandt Allen, L. 2001. In Anfara, V. (Ed.). Middle school curriculum. *The handbook of research in middle level education.* Greenwich, CT: Information Age.

Quinn, D., and, Valentine, J. (2001). National Middle School Association research summary #19: What impact does the use of technology have on middle level education, specifically student achievement? National Middle School Association. <http://www.nmsa.org/services/ressum19.html>.

Ravitch, D. 2000. *Left back: A century of failed school reforms.* New York: Simon & Schuster.

Schemo, D. 6 December 2000. Worldwide survey finds U.S. students are not keeping up. *New York Times.* <http://www.nytimes.com/2000/12/06/national/06 EXAM.html>.

Stevenson, C. 1998. *Teaching ten to fourteen year olds.* (2nd ed.). New York: Addison Wesley Longman.

Terry, S. 6 August 2001. Rookie teachers aren't on their own. *Dallas Morning News.* <http://www.dallas news.com/education/433256_mentors-02irv..html>.

Tomlinson, C. 1995. Gifted learners and the middle school: Problem or promise? *ERIC Digests.* <http://www.ed.gov/databases/ERIC_Digests/ed3 86832.html>.

U.S. Department of Education, Office of Educational Technology. 2001. E-learning: Putting a world-class education at the fingertips of all children. <www.ed.gov/technology/elearning>.

W. K. Kellogg Foundation. 2002. Middle Start overview. <http://www.wkkf.org/Programming/Overview.as p?CID=40>.

2 The Nature and Needs of Middle-Grades Students

Chapter Preview

This chapter reviews characteristics of middle-grades students and identifies the needs that affect their behavior in school. Young adolescents, because of personality traits and maturity levels, require instruction and behavior management that are, at times, somewhat different from those used with students at other stages of development. Middle-grades students are unsettled by the numerous changes that are occurring rapidly in their bodies and minds. Their interests fluctuate rapidly, as do their emotions. In order to teach these students effectively, you need insight into their needs, changes, and characteristics. That insight allows you to organize instruction and class interactions to benefit your students best.

What You Need to Know about Students' Nature and Needs

Some years ago, Anne Harnett (1991) identified three special traits and three needs that set middle-grades students apart from students at other levels, and therefore require special attention. Harnett's three trait clusters were:

1. The principal element of early adolescent development is physical change, which varies greatly among individuals and is somewhat unpredictable.
2. A period of strong intellectual development occurs between ages 10–12, followed by increased ability to deal with abstractions.
3. The influence of families, teachers, and other adults becomes less important to these students and is supplanted in large part by the pervasive impact of peers.

Harnett's three needs clusters were:

1. The need for developing a personal set of values.
2. The need to accept and like oneself.
3. The need to understand adults and the adult world, and to develop meaningful relationships with adults.

Here we examine the traits and needs Harnett identifies, together with others suggested by various educators and psychologists, and explore their implications for education. These factors may not seem particularly important to you just now, but please give them careful attention. This knowledge will form the foundation on which your expertise is built and will help you teach more effectively and relate better with students. It will show what makes students' lives in school miserable or enjoyable, dreary or rewarding. It will explain the needs that motivate students and cause them to relate with others as they do. It will pinpoint what interests students and what does not. It will show you how to encourage acceptable behavior and work together on the same side with your students, thereby ending the distress of struggling against them. Finally, it will teach you how to relate to individual students on a personal level and make a lasting positive impact on their lives.

The Nature of Middle-Grades Students

People who visit a middle school for the first time are often astonished at the diversity so evident among the students. Most immediately obvious are the surprising differences in physical size and maturity. Some students are short, while others are tall. Some are large, some are small. Tall girls abound, many of them towering over the boys. Visitors not familiar with middle-grades students may be surprised to learn that these differences exist among students of approximately the same age.

> **FIELD APPLICATION 1:**   Observe students as they arrive or move about a middle-level school. Make notes about variations in physical size and appearance.

Group Nature and Individual Nature

We begin our examination of the nature of early adolescent students, ages approximately eleven through fourteen, by noting how they behave in groups. Then we will turn our attention to individual traits and behavior, which often run contrary to norms for the group.

Group Nature.   Group nature refers to middle-grades students' predominant ways of thinking, feeling, and acting. The better we understand these characteristics, the better we can teach them and anticipate how they will behave and react. The most noticeable characteristics of middle-grades students are that they are physically and intellectually diverse, emotionally somewhat volatile, impressionable, and changeable. These characteristics are, for the most part, determined genetically, although language and patterns of social interaction are learned.

Individual Nature.   Individual nature refers to a single person's ways of thinking, feeling, and acting. Individual nature is often different from group norms, or averages, although individual students at this level tend to defer to the group. While group nature tells us what we can expect of students, on average, it is the individual student we must teach. The variations among individuals are great, and although we know what to expect from the group, we are not very sure about what to expect from given individuals. At no other time in life are the variations so great—in physical size, muscular development, intellectual ability, emotional maturity, sexual maturity, outward personality, interest in learning, and so forth. These variations call for special consideration in the ways we treat and teach students, beyond what teachers at other levels must do.

A Time of Great Change

Many changes are occurring quickly among students at this phase of life. Some of the changes are noticeable to untrained observers, while others are obscure but nevertheless real. The interconnected physical and emotional changes begin to accelerate around age ten or eleven, reach a peak, and begin to subside somewhat at around age fourteen. Physical changes are the most obvious. Growth spurts and sexual changes are the rule of the day, occurring in some students a year or more before others. By age twelve, girls often suddenly grow taller than boys and develop outward sexual characteristics. Some begin their menses. Boys, although developing more slowly than girls, may suddenly grow in height and muscularity. The hormones associated with sexual maturity produce in both sexes a number of quickly occurring changes that perplex students, sometimes make them nervous and embarrassed, and leave them disconcerted. These changes often make it difficult for students to concentrate on school matters. It is helpful to discuss these changes frankly with students. Simple discussions in an advisory or class meeting format can explore changes taking place and help students see them as normal processes of maturation that everyone experiences.

Intellectual ability begins to soar for many students around age ten or eleven, and by age fourteen most are able to use abstract thought as adults do. Many, however, continue to think most of the time in the manner of younger children. The noted psychologist Jean Piaget (1950) discovered that before the approximate age of eleven students function intellectually at the "concrete operational level," using a thinking process that involves visualization of real objects and events rather than abstractions. By age fourteen or fifteen, however, the great majority has acquired the power to think abstractly. Their intellectual processes work as efficiently as do those of adults—in some cases more efficiently—although they do not yet possess adult wisdom. They can theorize. They can identify causes and effects, and purposes and places for everything. They can deal with abstract concepts and form intellectual relationships that bring understanding and pleasure.

Although this new reasoning capability exists, it does not develop properly without practice. For that reason, you might consider using instructional activities that involve increased amounts of problem solving and abstract reasoning. Students should be encouraged to analyze situations and form conclusions. They should think beyond the concrete aspects of the real world and the present, moving on to abstractions, logical applications, and propositional thinking (i.e., if so-and-so happens, then what happens as a result?). Frequent opportunities should be provided for analyzing, conjecturing, hypothesizing, theorizing, evaluating, making explanations, and doing creative thinking. Brain research by Diamond and Hopson (1998) suggests that these types of activities may improve brain development; hence, learning environments should be rich and stimulating.

This is not to suggest that thinking skills such as memorizing and categorizing should be set aside, nor that concrete thinking is no longer useful. Indeed, most adults, although easily able to do abstract thinking, still think mostly in terms of concrete objects and observed events. Adolescent students are similar, and they still profit from learning activities that feature tangible objects and realistic experiences.

A Need for Teacher Sensitivity

Changes occurring rapidly in the middle-grades years include many that can affect students to a significant degree, either positively or negatively, and require teacher sensitivity.

Students Are Uncertain, Even Fearful.   Can you imagine a more difficult time in life, psychologically speaking, than the years between eleven and fifteen? We all struggle through them, but in the process feel we get knocked about. We realize we are no longer little kids and are beginning to move toward adult life. We are filled with questions and concerns. What must we do with ourselves? What are we to become? How do we behave? How should we relate to others? How will we make a living? How will we manage when we have to be in charge of ourselves? Adolescents are equally troubled by adult expectations placed on them, such as learning in school, contributing to quality of family life, and showing initiative and responsibility. They have to deal with such concerns every day.

Do you remember the worries you experienced when moving from elementary school to junior or senior high? Many of us don't remember much about it now, while others retain indelible impressions. Donna Schumacher (1998) reminds us of the major concerns during that period of life, which we teachers sometimes overlook. She reports Gilbert Weldy's (1991, 1995) observations of students' fears about entering middle school—about getting to class on time, finding lockers, keeping up with materials, finding lunchrooms and restrooms, getting on the right bus to go home, getting through the crowded halls, remembering which class to go to next, changing classes, changing teachers, no recess, new standards of homework and grading, fear of a larger, impersonal school, social uncertainty and immaturity, and being mistreated by other students. These fears, corroborated by Anderman and Kimweli (1997), are addressed at school in transitional procedures and advisories, described in Chapter 1. While we may consider them to be of little importance today, they still afflict young adolescent students more than we imagine.

Emotions Are Volatile.   Most middle-grades students' emotions vacillate a good deal. As hormones surge and intellectual and physical changes occur, feelings become fragile and students may unexpectedly, and unreasonably (it seems to us), become angry, sad, upset, or withdrawn. Just as abruptly they may become joyful and giggly. Displays of compassion are seen frequently, as is callousness, and you often hear students complain that things are unfair and the world is not what it ought to be. This state of emotional flux persists through entry to high school. It annoys teachers, who may have forgotten that they themselves once experienced the same process. We may help students somewhat by acknowledging their feelings and discussing them nonjudgmentally when appropriate. We should refrain from telling students they are being silly or have nothing to worry about or are not acting grown-up.

Students Are Seeking—But What?   Students know life holds new opportunities for them, but find the opportunities unclear. They expect challenges and problems without much idea of what they are. They know they and their peers are changing, and they feel strong yearnings that are difficult to comprehend. They understand they are moving toward new roles in life, new relations with others, new meanings, new purposes. Change accompanied by uncertainty predisposes them to examine, at least abstractly, a variety of lifestyles, especially those of personalities in television, music, and film, whom they often try to emulate. By the way, you fascinate your students, too. They may try to hang around and chat with you, and if they do you may find the experience rather enlightening.

FIELD APPLICATION 2: Arrange to chat with a middle-grades student or two. Ask them how they like school, including what they like most and least about it. Ask if they are looking forward to becoming adults, and why or why not. Ask what sort of future they see for themselves.

Students Are Impressionable. Middle-grades students are easily influenced, though to many beleaguered teachers they don't seem so. They are paying very close attention to adult role models, including you. It may exasperate you that they become moonstruck by scrawny guitar players with wild hair and vile tongues, yet it is best for them (and you) that you remain accepting of this phase as a normal, even necessary, part of their personal development. You should also remain considerate of their feelings. Don't be surprised if some of your students idolize you as well. This presents a danger for you as well as a positive challenge. The danger lies in letting them get too close to you. You must remain friendly, considerate, helpful, and understanding, yet maintain a line of separation that you do not let them cross. At times you will need to find ways to remind them gently that you have great concern for them, but your concern is that of a teacher who cares about them, not as a close personal friend. The positive challenge lies in the opportunity you have to exert a positive influence on your students, in matters of learning, dealing with concerns, and building positive lives.

Self-Concept Is in Flux. The terms *self-concept* and *self-esteem* are often used interchangeably, but they have different meanings. *Self-concept* is shown in how you honestly describe yourself. *Self-esteem* refers to your feelings, good or bad, about yourself. Both self-concept and self-esteem fluctuate during the middle school years. Students may see themselves as competent one day and incompetent the next. They may be pleased with themselves at one moment and disgusted the next. Middle-grades students have the lowest self-esteem of any age group, probably because of life uncertainties and what is happening to them physically, emotionally, and socially. Many educators maintain that building strong self-esteem is a prime function of education. This belief has led them to try to teach students to feel they are very special, very competent, absolutely great, and the like.

Unfortunately, these teachings don't carry much weight unless there is something tangible to back them up. Kids can't feel wonderful about their accomplishments when they know, in their hearts, they've not accomplished anything. We do better to try to help students accomplish three things: (1) develop strong character, (2) become competent in learning, and (3) become skilled in personal relations. Students will know whether or not they are making progress in these matters. As they progress, self-concept becomes more positive, and self-esteem increases proportionately.

Keep in mind that students' self-concept and self-esteem are fragile, more so now than at any other time in life. It takes little to send them plummeting. On some days you get the impression that a given student considers herself the greatest invention of recent history, while on other days she sees herself as utterly incompetent and useless. In neither case do those self-perceptions reflect reality. At this stage in life, students profit from considering others' points of view and life realities. In Chapter 9 you will find many suggestions for helping students develop and maintain a productive sense of self.

Character Development Is Sensitive.   Human character is made up of a number of qualities, such as ethical behavior, consideration for others, honesty, personal dignity, and responsibility. These qualities and others are scrutinized in Chapter 9. Both individual character and class character are closely related to behavior and, hence, to class management and discipline. Middle-grades students are in the throes of learning about qualities that comprise character, exploring those qualities, clarifying their meanings, and deciding whether and to what extent they are important. During this time, their sense of honesty and conscience is growing rapidly. Whereas younger students consider it wrong to tell lies only when they get caught, young adolescent students have a more accurate understanding of honesty and its importance in personal relationships. They clearly know the difference between lying to embellish stories and lying to deceive others harmfully. A sense of conscience continues to develop along with this sense of honesty. Students know the difference between right and wrong and have begun to feel uneasy when they know they've done wrong, although the uneasiness remains affected by the fear of getting caught.

Predominant Psychological Pushes

Several additional psychological pushes are being felt by students at this age. Four of special importance are peer influence, the urge for personal identity, accepting and liking oneself, and determining what is correct, important, and worthwhile.

Peer Influence Dominates.   Rather abruptly, middle-grades students begin to feel uneasy about being in the presence of adults, seeming to be fully comfortable only with their peers. They are frequently embarrassed when seen in public with their families. This is hurtful to parents whose children are crucially important in their lives, but it is a natural part of progress toward personal independence.

It is surprising how quickly peer norms establish themselves and how strong they become. Suddenly, only certain styles of clothing, shoes, hair, speech, and attitude will suffice. Everything must be fully in keeping with the group norm; if not, the individual feels dreadfully ill at ease. It is hard for adults to understand this. Logically, you would think that students struggling for independent identity would depart from the group norm, rather than submerge themselves in it. The strong copycat syndrome troubles parents, as it does teachers, but teachers and families are well-advised to heed the following:

Your child and the children you teach will— WILL—try their best to live by peer codes of dress, personal appearance, and behavior. It is a natural phase, and there is little you can do to prevent it. If you try to make students behave otherwise, you will probably do more harm than good. You don't need to indicate that you approve of what they are doing, but neither should you indicate strong disapproval, even though you may find the whole scene distressing. To work effectively with students at any phase of life—but especially during early adolescence—you have to be tolerant, accepting, understanding, and helpful. You can destroy fragile relationships by denigrating adolescents or showing personal disapproval. At the same time, it is well to establish clear expectations for classroom behavior. You shouldn't send these expectations down from on high as commandments, but should discuss them thoroughly with students, explaining the reasons behind them. Students should give their input as well. Accede to their recommendations when possible, without compromising standards about which you feel strongly.

At the same time, students need to understand that a life focused mostly on peers doesn't provide much opportunity for valuable experiences that are otherwise available. The limiting effects of peer-centeredness should be discussed frequently with students, who themselves have no idea why they reject parental influence in favor of peer influence. Group discussions should be held about true independence, taking advantage of what others, especially adults, have to offer, and the positive as well as the limiting effects of devotion to peer norms of dress, appearance, ways of speaking, and worldview.

Students Are Struggling for Personal Identity.   Students' efforts to establish a personal identity, one separate from their parents, becomes very important at this time. Carlos increasingly wants to be known as Carlos Hernández, not Carlos the child of Mr. and Mrs. Hernández. As this phase unfolds, Carlos may become embarrassed when peers see him with his parents. His embarrassment hurts his parents' feelings. Though he is trying to disentangle his identity from theirs, however, Carlos still wants and needs their full support. Until he establishes a strong sense of identity, which usually emerges late in high school, he will at times alternately seem to love his parents, hate them, and feel ashamed of them. You can help students with the process of establishing identity by showing you consider them responsible and contributing members of the class, drawing attention to their accomplishments, and relating with them as social equals deserving of respect.

Students Need to Accept and Like Themselves.   For students, this is a time of questioning and finding fault. Since early childhood they have been evaluating and judging themselves against others, but now they do so more seriously. Am I normal? Am I weird? Am I different? Am I ugly? Am I incompetent? Am I stupid? Am I hopeless? Is there any way I can more be popular?

Answers to these questions don't come easily. Each student has to think them through. You can help by holding discussions about these concerns. Your purpose is not to answer the questions but to help students explore them and articulate their concerns. As they do so, they will see that others are experiencing the same or similar concerns. You might talk about things that bothered you during adolescence to show that everyone is plagued at times by the same questions. Encourage students to explore ways of dealing with the matters that concern them. Sometimes grandparents, uncles and aunts, and older brothers and sisters can help. It will come as a relief to students as they realize they are not weird, stupid, hopeless, or much different from anyone else.

Everyone Is Trying to Determine What Is Correct, Important, and Worthwhile.   Students are continually struggling to understand what, in life, is correct versus incorrect, important versus unimportant, and worthwhile versus worthless. They will eventually reach relatively stable conclusions, but meanwhile there are things you can do to help. Invite them to participate in thinking about or discussing their most cherished, and most disliked, people, objects, behavior, and activities. Ask them individually to think of ten objects, ten people, and ten activities they truly value or enjoy. Ask them to imagine moving to a foreign place where everything is unfamiliar. If they could take with them only three out of each category, which or who would they take? Why?

Predominant Changes in Social Behavior

As students move through the middle grades, there are several notable changes in the way they relate with each other and adults that occur during this time.

Interactions Are Becoming More Reasoned.   Prior to middle school, students went through a phase in which they were loud and argumentative. They enter middle grades in the same mode, but soon begin showing increased reliance on reason and persuasion. Their interest in competition is burgeoning. When they win they are exuberant; when they lose they are less than gracious but not so rancorous as before. They are beginning to respect others in the group and increasingly want to share each other's company. They tend to form groups, and their behavior reflects peer norms. This is a good time to work on developing a sense of fair play and consideration for others.

Rebelliousness Is Increasing.   As students strive for personal identity and independence, they simultaneously become increasingly rebellious. They probe at, and beyond, the limits of acceptable behavior, at home, in the community, and in school. Their willingness to defy your requests can cause serious difficulties unless you give some thought to dealing with such situations. You can rather easily prevent most conflicts between students and yourself, and should it occur there are helpful things you can do and say. We will explore such things in Chapters 7 and 8.

Views toward Rules and Authority Are Changing.   Primary grade students see little need for rules and enforcement, and many intermediate grade students violate rules whenever they can get away with it. Nevertheless, by the time they've moved into middle school, students recognize the need for rules and enforcement in maintaining comfortable social interactions. They want those rules to apply equally to everyone and to be enforced evenhandedly. They have stopped blindly accepting teacher authority. They often talk back, argue with teachers, and drag their heels before complying (if at all) with teacher requests.

Relationships with Teachers Are Changing.   Middle-grades students are beginning to lose, or have already lost, most of the childish awe they once felt for teachers. Awe is replaced with one of three sets of emotions, depending on the teacher: (1) disrespect combined with dislike for the teacher; (2) respect but little feeling of like or dislike for the teacher; and (3) respect for the teacher with occasional displays of admiration, affection, and hero worship. As we will see later, students respect you if they believe you accept and are trying to help them. They like you if you show personal interest in them, provide interesting activities, show them respect, and make yourself available. Those things cause students to respect and like you in return, and when that happens they will try hard to meet your expectations and please you. This point will be reemphasized from time to time in subsequent chapters. It is a major key to working effectively with young adolescent students.

The Needs of Middle-Grades Students

We now move from student nature to an exploration of the basic needs that motivate student behavior. We will identify those needs, note how they are manifested, and see how they are satisfied.

All of us, from adolescence onward, share a common set of fundamental needs. When any of our needs is left unsatisfied for long, we may become fixated on that particular need and expend undue energy attempting to satisfy it, or else we may try to compensate for it in unexpected ways. In either case, our behavior may become odd, erratic, troublesome, or annoying to others. Behavior that results from inability to meet needs is often socially troublesome and is disapproved. It can interfere significantly with teaching and learning.

Eight Psychological Needs

Eight psychological needs are especially important in human life and continually influence our daily behavior. Descriptions of these eight needs are presented in the following paragraphs. The list of needs has grown out of the pioneering work of Abraham Maslow, Rudolf Dreikurs, and William Glasser.

Maslow (1954) held that all humans are continually motivated by five basic needs, which he called Physiological, Safety, Belongingness and Love, Esteem, and Self-Actualization (meaning striving to develop ourselves fully). Maslow described the first four needs as "deficiency needs," which affect us adversely when not met, and the fifth as a "personal growth need."

Dreikurs (with Pearl Cassel, 1972) was one of the first to explain the connection between needs and misbehavior in the classroom. He believed that the prime need for all students was a sense of belonging, and that misbehavior occurred when students strove unsuccessfully to meet that need.

Glasser (1986, 1993, 1998) presented a somewhat different concept of human needs that he believes affect students in school and on which his contentions about quality teaching, learning, and education are based. Glasser identified five needs, which he called Survival, Belonging, Power, Fun, and Freedom.

C. M. Charles (2002) has proposed an expanded list of needs that seem more inclusive of factors that motivate student behavior in school and, therefore, help both students and teachers know more about what causes students to behave as they do. Knowledge of these needs gives teachers a better understanding of how to relate with students and provide them better instruction and learning environments. Charles's list of eight needs is as follows:

- *Sex*—We are driven to fulfill the sexual aspects of procreation, and want the emotional benefits associated with it. This need emerges strongly during the middle-grades years, although it cannot be satisfied in a socially approved manner for a number of years. Yet, you will see that it greatly affects adolescent students in a number of different ways. Schools and communities remain in a quandary concerning how, if at all, they can help adolescent students contend with this powerful need.

- *Security*—We continually desire to be safe, free from physical and psychological threat and danger.
- *Belonging*—We continually desire to be acknowledged as worthwhile persons, have strong connections with others, and be considered a valued partner or member of a group.
- *Hope*—We continually desire to believe our lives will continue well or get better, that a brighter future lies ahead for us.
- *Dignity*—We continually crave respect from others and want to think of ourselves as admirable people. (Please note that this desire for respect should be tacitly acknowledged in all our dealings with middle-grades students.)
- *Power*—We continually desire a degree of control in our lives, over people, conditions, and events that affect us.
- *Enjoyment*—We continually desire to have pleasure and find satisfaction in what we do and in those with whom we associate.
- *Competence*—We continually desire to be able to do things well and to feel that others recognize our competence.

The foregoing are called "needs" because they persist through our lives and because we do not function well or fully unless they are satisfied fairly regularly. They are different from interests and wants, both of which may be powerful but are relatively short-lived and do not much affect the quality of our lives. For example, we might have a strong interest in dancing, but our normal life functioning is not affected adversely when we are away from dancing for a while. And we might really, really, really want to go to the football game on Saturday night, but if we don't get to go our daily life won't be much damaged (although we might feel it definitely will be).

When their eight basic needs are being met satisfactorily, or else put on hold without creating excessive inner turmoil, students are able to participate in school in a relatively contented and productive manner. When any of the needs is not being met, students experience uneasiness, together with moderate to strong discontent. Discontentment motivates new behavior, which at times may be positive, as when Jonathan, feeling himself less accomplished than others in the class, redoubles his efforts to learn. More often, however, behavior resulting from discontentment is counterproductive, as when Julie, new to the school, feels so overwhelmed she withdraws into herself and declines to associate with others or take part in class activities.

How We Can Help Students Meet Their Needs

If you are to teach Julie well, you must determine why she behaves as she does and decide what you can do to help her. Perhaps by talking with her you can learn of her feelings of isolation or powerlessness, feelings that often arise when the need for security goes unmet. By talking with Julie and providing some of the security she requires, there is a good chance you can bring her back into a productive mode.

The process for helping students meet their needs is summarized as follows: (1) When a student's basic need is not being satisfied, the student then (2) begins to behave in unusual or self-defeating ways. When we notice those telltale behaviors, we (3) give the student appropriate help or attention, in a positive manner, that we believe will satisfy the underlying need, at least temporarily. This (4) restores the student to more normal functioning. But what exactly do we give the student that satisfies the need? The following paragraphs provide answers to that question.

Satisfying Students' Need for Security

Symptoms: Students whose need for security is not being met usually show one or more of the following behaviors: they seek closeness to or contact with you, kindness from adults and other students, and safety in all places and activities. Some of these behaviors, such as constantly seeking your attention or closeness, will annoy you. Others, such as avoiding places, activities, and other students they find threatening, may be less evident, yet you must be alert to them also. If such behaviors do not bring the results students want—or worse, if they bring disapproval or danger—students may withdraw further, feign incompetence, or simply stop trying.

Suggestions: Help students satisfy the need for security by providing an environment that is safe from threat and harm, not only physical harm but also psychological harm from bullying, teasing, taunting, and name-calling. Students also need protection from fear of failure, fear of teacher disapproval, and fear of speaking in front of the group.

What do you do? Show the affected student personal attention and kindness. Make it clear you do not expect students to be perfect, that you know they will make mistakes, that making mistakes is a valuable way of learning, and that you admire students who continue to try despite making mistakes. Discuss with the class the importance of all class members helping each other to feel comfortable. Stress acceptance without disapproval of others' appearance and mannerisms. Establish a formal class agreement about treating everyone as we, ourselves, want to be treated. Ask students to volunteer to help classmates, especially those new to the class. Encourage students to work as buddies with another, and to establish friendships with those who seem worried or under stress. If you accomplish these things while encouraging but not pressuring reticent students, they will soon begin to feel comfortable about being in the class and participating in class activities.

Satisfying Students' Need for Belonging

Symptoms: Students whose need for belonging is not being met may try continually to get your personal attention. They will also try to obtain attention and acknowledgment from peers and establish friendships and be included in groups. Attention seeking is very common in classes, as when Shawon shouts out and tries to get others to laugh. If those behaviors don't bring Shawon what he wants, he may hang about on the fringes of groups and try to curry favor there. He may bond with another student or two like himself and together they may adopt a "sour grapes" manner or bully or intimidate students less assertive than themselves.

Suggestions: Help all your students enjoy a sense of belonging in the class. Give them your personal attention every day, and encourage camaraderie. Exchange pleasant words with all your students regularly. Make provisions for students to participate meaningfully in groups. Give students responsibilities for seeing after the well-being of other students and the class environment. These provisions ensure helpful personal contact and a concomitant sense of importance, thus removing the motivation for attention-seeking behavior.

Linda Albert (1996) advises teachers to help students meet the need for belonging by enabling them to "connect" with others through positive relationships. As students make these connections, they become more cooperative and helpful with each other and more receptive to teachers. To facilitate these connections, Albert stresses what she calls "The Five A's": acceptance, attention, appreciation, affirmation, and affection.

Acceptance means understanding it is all right for each person to be as he or she is, regarding culture, abilities, disabilities, and personal style.

Attention means making oneself available to others by sharing time and energy with them.

Appreciation involves acknowledging the accomplishments of others by giving compliments, expressing gratitude, and describing how other individuals have helped the class.

Affirmation involves making positive statements about others that emphasize desirable traits, such as courage, cheerfulness, dedication, enthusiasm, friendliness, helpfulness, kindness, loyalty, originality, persistence, sensitivity, and thoughtfulness. Affirmations should be phrased as, "I have noticed your thoughtfulness" and "Your kindness is always evident."

Affection refers to displays of kindness and caring that people show each other. It is freely given, with nothing required in return.

Satisfying Students' Need for Hope

Symptoms: Students whose need for hope is not being met in school try hard to obtain evidence of progress. They may persistently ask you how they are doing. They may ask you how long a particular activity will last and when they will be able to do something more interesting. They want to experience success frequently. They want to know you believe a brighter future awaits them. In further attempting to meet this need, students often boast about their prowess, real or imagined, tell how good things were elsewhere or in the past, and continually ask others for approbation and verification of progress and competence. If students obtain no satisfaction from these efforts, after a time they become lethargic and yet more disenchanted with school. They may stop trying altogether and begin thinking of dropping out. Meanwhile, they gravitate to peers who share their feeling of hopelessness.

Suggestions: Help students satisfy their need for hope by encouraging them to learn meaningful information and skills in areas of personal interest. Draw attention to their successes. Help them document what they have learned. Discuss new learnings they might acquire in the future. Allow them to work cooperatively or investigate topics of strong personal interest. Try to help them have an enjoyable time in school. See if every day you can ensure they encounter something that makes school seem worthwhile and their progress satisfying.

Satisfying Students' Need for Dignity

Symptoms: Students whose need for dignity is not being satisfied persistently seek to achieve, feel successful, and receive recognition from others. They want to have their personal qualities and accomplishments acknowledged and often seek that acknowledgment from teachers and peers. They react poorly to being teased or called names. They may become overly sensitive and imagine or want to believe themselves superior to others. They may frequently put others down. If these behaviors don't satisfy their need for dignity, these students may become overly defensive, feel victimized, and react with hostility to perceived slights or disrespect.

Suggestions: You can help students satisfy their need for dignity by showing you respect them, interacting with them as social equals, and treating them as competent and valued members of the class, able to take on important tasks and conduct themselves responsibly. Talk with them personally. If necessary, conduct lessons that teach students how to react appropriately when threatened or provoked.

> **FIELD APPLICATION 3:**   Chat with a couple of middle-grades students. Ask how they feel they are treated by teachers at school. See if they feel respected, are brought into decision making, and are treated as social equals (meaning not talked down to or treated as a child). Ask if they would like to be treated differently than at present.

Satisfying Students' Need for Power

Symptoms: Students whose need for power is not being satisfied often behave in ways they hope will bring respect and admiration. They want to play significant roles when working with others and want to hold responsible positions in groups and the class. They will often try to ally themselves with you as well as with powerful students and attempt to exert influence in class decisions. If these behaviors fail to bring the gratification they seek, these students may try to control others who are less powerful. They sometimes become belligerent and vociferous and may engage you in power struggles in front of the class.

Suggestions: You can help students satisfy their need for power by bringing them into collaborative decision making and putting them in charge of tasks important to the class. Consider assigning duties such as distributing and collecting materials, checking roll, taking care of instructional media, handling electronic equipment, taking care of class plants or animals, keeping the room clean, greeting visitors, serving as ambassadors to other classes, and the like. Call on all students for input in class discussions and decisions, but make sure you don't allow any of them to dominate the class or your attention.

Satisfying Students' Need for Enjoyment

Symptoms: All students want to have a pleasurable time in school. It displeases them when they don't. They often blame lack of enjoyment on poor teaching or bad schooling. In fact, students complain about schools almost everywhere as being boring, no fun, and stupid. Students whose need for enjoyment is not being satisfied usually respond well to instructional activities that are fun, challenging, and intriguing. They like cooperative activities with other students and are drawn to charismatic teachers. They frequently seek interesting things to do—many of them nonproductive—that are not related to the lesson. They may also try to associate with other students who seem fun-loving, even if a bit disruptive. If these behaviors do not bring the satisfaction students seek, they talk, move about, and act out. They seek things to do other than the assigned activities.

Suggestions: Keep in mind that enjoyment is a very powerful need among middle-grades students. Help satisfy this need by providing instructional topics and activities that are especially engaging. When appropriate, allow students to work together, one of their favorite activities in school. Meanwhile, maintain a balanced sense of humor and share a good laugh with students from time to time. Let them tell an occasional joke or share an amusing anecdote. Call attention to the fun and enjoyment that can be found in most matters, including most subjects in the curriculum. Help them see that one of the most enjoyable things in school is exploring topics of special interest, learning them well, and sharing what they learn with others.

Satisfying Students' Need for Competence

Symptoms: Students whose need for competence is not being met seek tangible evidence of growth in skills and knowledge. They frequently ask how they can use what they are learning or how it applies to real life. They seek opportunities to excel. They want praise, congratulations, and laudatory comments from others. When these efforts are unsuccessful, students become frustrated. They exaggerate their achievements. They show off or boast excessively and say uncomplimentary things about teachers, school, and programs.

Suggestions: You can help students satisfy their need for competence by providing the opportunity and support they need to become excellent in academics, physical skills, special interests, and other matters they consider important. Find ways for them to demonstrate new capabilities to themselves, peers, families, and others and help them keep tangible records that document their growth.

> **FIELD APPLICATION 4:**   Chat with two or three middle-grades students. Ask whether they feel they are becoming more competent (skillful, knowledgeable) in school. Ask them what they can do now they couldn't do last year. Ask what they would like school to make them really good in.

Summary Reminders

We have noted a number of traits, concerns, and needs that all students contend with during the middle-grades years, and we have examined many things teachers can do to help. Based on these considerations, there are two points we should keep firmly in mind:

1. *All the changes we have noted are part of a natural, ongoing process.* The nature of any middle-grades student is not static. It is continually changing. The descriptions provided herein no doubt describe some of the realities for students with whom you work. That knowledge forms the basis of your professional expertise in helping middle-grades students succeed in school. Most of those characteristics and concerns are in transition for individual students, part of the process of moving from childhood through adolescence and on to adulthood.

As students complete the middle school years, some of their more remarkable traits soften while others come to the fore. The physical changes that begin with adolescence will be completed, for the most part. Sexual maturation will be largely accomplished and will no longer be so disconcerting to them. Uncertainties diminish about physical development, appearance, and personality, although of course they never disappear entirely. Peer norms, while still strong, do not dictate behavior so strongly as before. Personal identity has been established and relations with parents improve. Students are learning to interact more effectively with each other, and a new respect for teachers is developing. Intellectual development, especially the capability to engage in abstract thought, is almost complete. Students are now able to learn most of what they want to know about most matters. They still don't show much appreciation for the school curriculum, although some students enjoy parts of it very much. Most continue to resist authoritarian teachers who seem harsh and lacking in understanding.

Other life concerns begin to predominate as students move into high school. Matters such as dating and establishing close relationships with others gain momentum. Students begin to get a better idea of their personal capabilities and what they might want to do with their lives. They are becoming concerned about financial matters and how to make a living enjoyably. These matters do not concern you as a middle-grades teacher, of course. They simply illustrate the ongoing process of development across the school years and help highlight the issues that present the greatest challenges, and opportunities, as you help students along the way.

2. *Successful middle-grades teachers accept their students and adapt programs in accordance with students' traits and needs.* In the chapters that follow, we will explore how these adaptations are successfully accomplished.

The two principles articulated here, when put into practice, are the key to successful middle-level teaching. Learn about students' needs, traits, and differences. Consider them normal and natural. Look on them as keys to understanding and helping students. Do not consider them obstacles in your path. Adapt your program to students' traits as best you can. As you do so, you will find you begin to relate profitably with your students, help them significantly, and enjoy the process greatly.

QUESTIONS

1. A number of traits of middle-grades students were discussed as important in education. Which three do you consider to be the most important for teachers? Why do you consider them especially important?

2. Which of the behaviors listed in the section on "A Need for Teacher Sensitivity" do you feel affects students most significantly? Why do you think so?

3. What is your understanding of the difference between Piaget's "concrete operational" level of thinking and his "formal operational" level of thinking? Do the differences between the two really make much difference to teachers? Explain.

4. Of the eight human needs that were described, which did you have the most trouble satisfying during your early adolescence? (Please suppress for the moment your desire to mention sex.) Why do you believe the need you identify was so difficult to satisfy?

5. What is your understanding of the difference between needs and interests? Which do you consider the more powerful of the two in motivating student behavior?

6. Many people have contended that the school has a single responsibility, which is to teach students subject matter in the most effective, efficient way possible. Is there, then, any real justification for spending time considering middle-grades students' nature and needs? Explain your conclusions.

ACTIVITIES

1. Make a one-page justification for spending so much valuable time in your mathematics (or other) class giving attention to student traits and feelings.

2. With a fellow student, compose and role-play a situation in which one of you (the student) behaves in an unusual or inappropriate way. The other (the teacher) then tries to determine a particular need that is not being satisfied for the student. Use the descriptions given in the chapter for needs and associated behaviors when they are not being met.

3. In a group of fellow students, tell of an incident you experienced in school in which one of your personal traits was not accepted by the teacher, or one of your needs went unmet. Explain how you were affected. Allow your companions to give their views on how the teacher might have dealt with you more effectively.

4. Consider adaptations in lessons or personal relations that would help teachers work more effectively with students. In one page, describe three adaptations you put high on the list. Share them with fellow students and ask for their comments.

REFERENCES

Albert, L. 1996. *Cooperative discipline.* Circle Pines, MN: American Guidance Service.

Anderman, E., and Kimweli, D. 1977. Victimization and safety in schools serving early adolescents. *Journal of Early Adolescence, 17* (4), 408–438.

Charles, C. M. 2002. *Essential elements of effective discipline.* Boston: Allyn & Bacon.

Diamond, M., and Hopson, J. 1998. *Magic trees of the mind: How to nurture your child's intelligence, creativity and healthy emotions from birth through adolescence.* New York: Dutton.

Dreikurs, R., and Cassel, P. 1972. *Discipline without tears.* New York: Hawthorne.

Glasser, W. 1986. *Control theory in the classroom.* New York: Harper and Row.

———. 1993. *The quality school teacher.* New York: Harper Perennial.

———. 1998. *The quality school: Managing students without coercion.* New York: HarperCollins.

Harnett, A. 1991. Preparation of middle school teachers. *ERIC Digest 90–1.* Washington, DC: ERIC Clearinghouse on Teacher Education. ERIC Identifier: ED335 356.

Maslow, A. 1954. *Motivation and personality.* New York: Harper.

Mizelle, N., and Mullins, E. 1997. Transition into and out of middle school. In Judith L. Irvin (Ed.) *What research says to the middle level practitioner.* Columbus, OH: National Middle School Association.

Piaget, J. 1950. *The psychology of intelligence.* London: Routledge & Kegan Paul.

Schumacher, D. 1998. *The transition to middle school. ERIC Digest.* ERIC Identifier: 422 119.

Weldy, G. (Ed.). 1991. *Stronger school transitions improve student achievement: A final report on a three-year demonstration project "Strengthening Total Transitions for Students K–13."* Reston, VA: National Association of Secondary School Principals.

———. 1995. Critical transitions. *Schools in the Middle, 4* (3), 4–7.

3 Principles of Working with Middle-Grades Students

Chapter Preview

In the previous chapter, we noted the nature and needs of middle-grades students and the related implications for education. In this chapter we move ahead to consider student traits more closely as they relate to learning, positive human relations, a desirable attitude toward learning, and sense of satisfaction in the educational process. You will see that to be successful you must acquire a repertoire of knowledge, attitudes, and skills necessary for working with adolescent students, together with a steadfast adherence to certain principles of teaching.

Knowledge for Working with Middle-Grades Students

To work most effectively with middle-grades students, you need to know not only their characteristics and the needs and interests that affect their behavior, but also what they enjoy, prefer, and dislike in schools and teachers. A number of assertions are made in the following paragraphs concerning what students like and dislike in school. The lists, which are not necessarily hierarchical, have been formulated by the authors of this book from students' needs and feelings as explained by Maslow (1954), Biddulph (1997), Mee (1997), Glasser (1998), and Wong and Wong (1998). The authors have drawn certain conclusions, as well, from their many years of experience with adolescent learners.

Brief Review of Nature, Needs, and Interests of Middle-Grades Students

In Chapter 2 we explored the nature, needs, and interests of learners in the middle grades. We saw that rapid physical and other developmental changes are occurring for those students, accompanied by fluctuating emotions. These changes and uncertainties make it difficult for students to focus on learning as we would like. Yet, these students are very energetic and impressionable, making them especially amenable to many experiences that can significantly improve their lives. These students can and will expend great effort delving into topics they find enjoyable and meaningful, but may not give much effort to activities they don't enjoy. Unfortunately, some of the subjects we try to teach in middle grades fall into the latter category. It is therefore necessary that we find ways to brighten and make more attractive all subjects we teach.

What Middle-Grades Students Strongly Dislike in Schools and Teachers

It will be useful for you to take into account what students find unappealing or off-putting about school and teachers. That knowledge will enable you to avoid or correct those conditions and more easily draw students into willing participation in worthwhile learning. The following is a review of what students very much dislike and will avoid when possible. While teachers often attach value judgments to student behavior, please remember that students are as they are, whether that appeals to us personally or not. Our task is to use what we know about our students as a basis for making education more effective for them. As we do this, teaching becomes more satisfying for us, too.

Dislikes Related to Needs
- Insecurity, feeling unsafe, feeling worried
- Sense of hopelessness, no conviction that school is worthwhile
- Threat to personal dignity, fear of belittlement, of being inconsequential
- Lack of acceptance, feeling unacknowledged, an outsider, unwanted
- Powerless, having no control of or input into events that affect one personally
- Boredom, no activities that are pleasurable or rewarding
- Incompetence, incapable of doing what others can do and what is expected

Dislikes Related to Class Activities
- Sitting still for long periods
- Keeping quiet for long periods
- Working by oneself
- Memorizing facts for tests
- Completing lengthy writing assignments
- Doing repetitive busy work
- Completing long reading assignments
- Engaging in individual competition where there is little or no chance of winning
- Having little or no choice in activities, assignments, or assessment

What Middle-Grades Students Like in Schools and Teachers

If you can avoid things students dislike, while building your program around the things they do like, you can be sure your students will enjoy both you and the class. When that happens, you will find teaching satisfying and rewarding. Among the things students find most appealing in school are the following:

Likes Related to Needs
- Security, the feeling of safety without worry
- Sense of hope, the feeling that school is worthwhile and success is possible

- Personal dignity, feeling respected and worthwhile
- Belonging, feeling a part of things, being valued, having a place in the class
- Sense of power, with some control of and input into events in the class
- Enjoyment of activities that are pleasurable or rewarding
- Competence, capable of doing what others can do and what is expected

Likes Related to Class Life and Activities
- Teachers who are friendly, enjoyable, and interesting
- Attentive support and help from the teacher
- Camaraderie, enjoyable associations with classmates
- A curriculum featuring topics that are naturally intriguing and worthwhile
- Interesting instructional activities that are enjoyable and productive
- Opportunity for and likelihood of success and accomplishment
- Having attention drawn tactfully to personal accomplishments

In Students' Own Words

Cynthia Mee (1997) interviewed large numbers of middle-grades students and asked them questions about a number of topics. Here are some of their comments that bear on educational practice.

Advice for my teachers: Lighten up, be more caring, give less homework, teach so we can have fun, stop yelling, stop being mean, have a sense of humor

What makes me happy: Being treated nice, getting good grades, hanging out with friends, not having homework

The worst thing about my age: For fifth- and sixth-graders, being caught between a kid and a grown-up, being youngest in school, getting beat up, getting ignored

For seventh- and eighth-graders, too much homework, stress, lack of trust, not being taken seriously

What makes me feel bad: Being disliked, teased, yelled at, getting poor grades, being alone, not being accepted, having no money

What makes me feel good: Good grades, compliments, doing things with friends, getting presents, sleeping, canceled tests, brothers and sisters not around, listening to music, feeling loved (for 7th and 8th graders, music is important)

My idea of a good teacher: Makes learning fun, is nice, cares about students, humorous, understanding, doesn't yell, doesn't have favorites, doesn't give a lot of homework

What I dislike about school: Homework, tension, students who act bad, sitting in a desk, boring lectures, hard chairs, reports, tests, everything, too many classes (all grade levels, and boys in particular, mentioned disliking discipline procedures)

FIELD APPLICATION 1:   Talk with a few middle-grades students. Ask them to tell you the three things they like most, and least, about school. Take notes and analyze them later to see if their likes and dislikes are similar to those mentioned in the foregoing paragraphs.

Attitudes for Working with Middle-Grades Students

The personal attitudes you project concerning students, learning, and teaching strongly affect the climate and activities in your classes. The following are some of the attitudes known to serve teachers well. To the best of your ability, develop and display these attitudes sincerely.

- Maintaining a respectful attitude toward your students at all times.
- Understanding and accepting students for who they are, including race and ethnicity, language, customs, ability, strengths, and shortcomings.
- Considering students to be your social equals and treating and talking with them as such, not as inferior beings.
- Believing in your students, in their innate value, potential, ability to do the right thing, and capability of succeeding and contributing.
- Truly desiring to be consistently helpful, all the time in all matters, including recognizing when your efforts are being well-received and when they are not.
- Being steadfast in your determination to help students learn, develop self-discipline, and get along with each other. Being persistent, yet capable of rolling with the punches when you are treated unpleasantly.
- Remaining flexible, maintaining a sense of humor, and keeping a sense of proportion by recognizing that most issues are minor and can be resolved cooperatively.

FIELD APPLICATION 2:   Observe a fellow teacher and ask him or her to do the same for you. Determine which of the attitudes listed above are evident in the observed behavior. Be specific. Think about your personal style of teaching and honestly appraise it in light of the listed attitudes.

Skills for Working with Middle-Grades Students

The remainder of this chapter is devoted to skills that help you work more effectively with students. These skills include comprehending students' perspectives on reality, establishing a basis of respect for all, enhancing personal relations, communicating effectively, enhancing the curriculum, enhancing instruction, and providing helpful feedback.

Establishing a Basis of Respect for All

If you cannot sincerely respect your students and make that respect evident, you will have a difficult and distressing career. What students want from teachers more than anything else is consideration and respect. They react poorly (as does everyone) to being talked down to, treated inconsiderately, demeaned, disapproved, slighted, or publicly criticized. Not only must you treat your students in a respectful manner, you must do all you can to help them see the value of treating their classmates in a similar way. One of the best things you can do for your students, and yourself, is work in collaboration with the class to instill a class climate of consideration and respect. This topic should be discussed frequently by the class. Encourage the class formally to establish respect for all as a basic working agreement.

Comprehending Students' Perspectives of Reality

Stephen R. Covey (1989), writing about human relations, explains the importance, even the necessity, of seeing situations from other persons' points of view. We know that students often see things differently from us, but we naturally tend to work from the basis of our personal perspectives. When our perceptions are different from those of students, we are likely to encounter problems.

Covey says the way to understand others' views (in this case, the views of students) is to ascertain what they are saying from *within their perception of reality*. Covey explains that we can access students' views by using "empathetic understanding." When students say something that seems incongruous, nonsensical, or untrue, take their remarks seriously, but ask questions such as:

> Can you help me understand . . .
>> what that means to you?
>> why that bothers you?
>> why you like that so much?
>> what we could do with that information?
>> how you feel I should respond?

Once you believe you understand what students are really saying, respond along these lines: "I think I understand what you mean and how you feel. I may be wrong, but I have a somewhat different view that I would like to explain to you, in the hope that we might find a way to resolve the concerns both of us have."

> Here is how I see the situation . . .
> This is what has been bothering me . . .
> Can you understand what I mean by . . .
> Do you see any ways we might find a solution that will satisfy both of us?

This process reflects Covey's basic principle of communication, which is:

> First seek to understand the other, and only after that seek to be understood.

FIELD APPLICATION 3:   Work together with a fellow teacher or student teacher. Role-play a scenario in which a student might be reacting poorly to a lesson or teacher treatment. When it is your turn to play the teacher, practice using the suggestions Covey presents for grasping the student's perception of reality. Later, when you have an opportunity, use the skills in talking with a disgruntled student.

Enhancing Personal Relations

Personal relations have to do with how we treat each other. When we say "good" personal relations, we mean dealing with each other in ways everyone finds proper, beneficial, or satisfying. In the classroom, we are concerned not only with how we interact with students, but also with how students treat each other.

There are certain things we can say and do that help us get along with our students and work with them contentedly. We want to attract their attention and convey the impression that we are nice people with whom to associate. We want to gain their trust. We want them to cooperate with us, learn a great deal in school, enjoy the process, and have good feelings about school, teachers, and education. To the extent we accomplish those things, we achieve the educational outcomes we hope for. Some of the skills that you and members of your class should find helpful follow.

Make a Good First Impression
- Smile at the other person and say hello.
- Introduce yourself: "My name is . . . What's yours?" Allow the other person to introduce him- or herself. Make sure you get the name right. Repeat it and if necessary ask the individual how to spell it. Associate the name with something you know well so you won't forget it. Use it at once.
- Ask the other person something specific to the situation: "Alicia, how do you feel about speaking in front of the class like this?"
- Use a happy smile that is genuine, not condescending or derogatory.
- Open up communication further. Make comments such as, "That's interesting. Tell me more about it." "Why do you suppose you feel that way?" "Wonder if other people have that same feeling?" As the other person responds, listen carefully in order to grasp what he or she is saying and what it seems to mean to them. From time to time ask if you are understanding correctly.

Confer Dignity on Others.   Conferring dignity is one of the most powerful techniques for exerting positive influence on others. We confer dignity when we show respect for others, when we considerately help them feel valued. We do this by remembering and using their names and mentioning something positive about them. We do it by treating them courteously as equal human beings, asking their opinions, listening, and acknowledging their contributions. When we do these things, others begin to seek us out, ask our advice, and cooperate with us. In the process we receive a great bonus: others confer dignity on us. Many people never seem to understand that they cannot gain stature by gossiping and running others down. That tactic actually produces the opposite effect and makes others mistrustful of you. Point out to your students that the best way to build a solid reputation is to be ethical, treat everyone with respect, and mention others' admirable qualities.

Build Trust with Others.   The best educational experiences for teachers and students alike occur within high levels of mutual trust—that is, when students trust you and you trust them. Some students come to you very trusting and remain that way unless you do something to damage their trust. Others are wary, and forging bonds with them may take a while. The strategy for building trust is always to interact with students on the principles of kindness, consideration, helpfulness, fairness, and honesty. In class meetings, discuss those five principles and ask how teachers and students can show them in class.

Rely on Students for Guidance.   You can count on students to help establish a climate in the class that brings satisfaction to everyone. Students understand and will support provisions made for personal needs, helpfulness, respect, consideration, problems, conflicts, and working together. They know the difference between proper and improper behavior, can see that misbehavior has a number of causes, and are capable of understanding how those causes can be dealt with. They clearly know when learning is enjoyable and when it is not, and can tell you why. They know when they feel treated well and when they feel slighted or demeaned. They know school suits them better when instructional activities are fun and students and teacher treat each other well. They know the value of self-discipline, self-direction, and personal responsibility, although at times they may act as though they never heard of those concepts. Ask students about them. Listen to what they say. Not only does this provide guidance, but it helps develop the sense of "we" that characterizes the best classes.

As a rule of thumb, consider at every turn how you can involve students in planning class matters. Ask them to help resolve problems, take responsibility, and give productive feedback on curriculum, lessons, and teaching. Involving them in this way allows you to move away from teaching that "does things to" students and replace it with teaching in which students work together with you.

Treat Students as Good Salespeople Treat Customers.   We want to get along well with our students, for their sake and ours, and we want them to get along with each other. Toward that end, we can learn a valuable lesson from skilled salespeople. They extend a friendly welcome to customers, smile, try to put them at ease, and ask how they can be of help. They treat customers that way in part because their livelihood depends on it. Even when no sale is made, the customer retains an inviting impression that might bring him or her back later. Word gets around. The same is true for teachers and students. We educators are not in the sales business, at least not directly. We don't have to ask our potential customers (students) how we might assist them, but it helps if we do. Take a moment to think about how you would treat students if your income depended half on how much they learn and half on how much they like the way you treat them.

Troublesome Errors in Interpersonal Relations

We have seen some tactics for relating better with students. Now let's identify errors we might make that damage those relationships.

Slighting Students.   We slight students by giving them scant attention, dismissing their concerns with silly or callous remarks, disregarding contributions they make, or failing to give them credit they deserve. If you do these things, you undo all you have hoped to accomplish. It is better to give students undeserved recognition and credit than fail to show them consideration and appreciation.

Putting Students Down.   Put-downs—insensitive or disparaging comments made to students—are often of a personal nature. We must avoid calling students inept or lazy or stupid, or imply such meanings. We must not speak sarcastically to them and then laugh as if we didn't mean it. The intent of such messages is all too clear.

Discounting Out of Hand.   Imagine Adrian's reaction when he tells you he will have his work done by tomorrow but you reply, "How many times have I heard that from you?" It would be much better if you said, "Thank you, Adrian. I believe I can count on you. Will you give it to me first thing in the morning?"

Communicating Effectively

To a surprising degree, how you communicate with students determines your effectiveness as a teacher. Relationships are built in large part on good communication and are easily destroyed by poor communication. You may think words are just words, messages just messages, directions just directions. But the proper word at the proper time can foster excitement, while an improper word can cast a pall.

Mr. Abramson

Antowine and Jerrold are talking in the back of the room during math. Everyone is supposed to be working quietly. Mr. Abramson, helping a student at the front, straightens up and looks at them sternly. He says sharply, "Antowine! Jerrold! No talking back there! I don't want to tell you again!" He holds his stare until they have slumped back over their work. How do you think Mr. Abramson's comments make Antowine and Jerrold feel? Do you suppose he has increased their eagerness to cooperate with him?

Mr. Berensen

Sheree and Monala are talking in the back of the room during English. Everyone is supposed to be working quietly. Mr. Berensen, circulating among students at work, eases alongside them and asks quietly, "Do you girls need some help?" They get back to work without saying anything. Mr. Berensen adds, "If you have difficulty, let me know." How do you think Mr. Berensen's words make Sheree and Monala feel? Would they remain inclined to cooperate with him?

Congruent Communication.   Many years ago, Haim Ginott (1971) provided sound advice on using communication to build students' dignity. His advice had to do with "congruent communication," which is especially helpful when students make mistakes or behave improperly. When Mai carelessly lets paint drip on the floor, how should Mrs. Soames react? Should she berate Mai? Should she remind her that it is the third time she has done it? Should she look exasperated and tell her to get paper towels and clean it up?

Ginott said teacher responses should always address the situation and never the character of the student. Accordingly, when Mai drips paint, Mrs. Soames should say pleasantly, "That needs to be cleaned up. Do you know where the towels are?" In saying that, she addresses the situation. She doesn't imply that Mai is clumsy or careless, thoughtless or hopeless. Her facial expression is benign. Her voice carries no tone of exasperation. She doesn't roll her eyes or turn her palms up to heaven. Mai cleans up the spots while the class goes on about its business.

Reason-Specific Communication. Most communication between teachers and students occurs as ongoing give-and-take, such as instructional input, questions about assignments, and discussions about lessons and other issues. This communication is not done with a particular purpose in mind other than to exchange information. However, at times we can use communication to accomplish specific purposes such as giving students personal attention, reviewing their feelings about learning, discussing their concerns about class matters, and informing families about class activities and progress. Let's see briefly how each can be done and what it accomplishes.

Giving Personal Attention. We noted earlier that each student wants to be noticed and validated by the teacher. Some teachers give personal attention as students enter the room, by smiling, saying hello, and greeting as many as possible by name. Some, while circulating during periods of work, stop by each student and quietly ask a question or make a positive comment. Students very much appreciate personal attention of this sort.

Listening. Thomas Gordon, acclaimed author of *Parent Effectiveness Training* (1970), *Teacher Effectiveness Training* (1974), and *Discipline that Works* (1989), has made major contributions to promoting effective listening in the classroom. Gordon devised a set of listening skills he called passive listening, acknowledgment, door openers, and active listening. These skills help teachers listen to students more effectively and can be taught to students to help them better listen to each other, as well.

Suppose you are listening to Julian, who is trying to explain why yet again he has failed to complete his homework. When Julian first begins to speak, you use *passive listening*. You say nothing, but show receptiveness through eye contact, taking a seat by Julian, and remaining alert.

As Julian talks, you use *acknowledgment responses* such as nodding and saying "uh-huh" and "I see."

If Julian has difficulty saying what's on his mind, you may help with *door openers* such as, "Could you tell me more?" or "It sounds like you have something to say about that."

As Julian expresses himself further, you use *active listening*, which shows understanding of his message by reflecting it back. Without making judgments, you say something like, "You are not able to get your homework done because your mother makes you work after school and then mind your little brother while she works at night. Is that right?"

Comprehending. Stephen R. Covey, whose "empathetic understanding" was described earlier, maintains that listening is not merely taking in the words of other people, but "getting inside their head" to grasp their deeper hopes, fears, realities, and difficulties. You might remember he says that when working with others we should try to understand them well before trying to make ourselves understood. Covey says most of us don't know how to listen empathetically and thus may not properly understand the other person. Covey cautions us:

> Empathetic listening takes time, but it doesn't take anywhere near as much time as it takes to back up and correct misunderstandings when you're already miles down the road, to redo, to live with unexpressed and unsolved problems. . . . People want to be understood. And

whatever investment of time it takes to do that will bring much greater returns of time as you work from an accurate understanding of (their) problems and issues . . . (1989, p. 253).

Responding Helpfully.   When it was time for the mathematics lesson, John said to Ms. Stapleton, "I don't feel good. Can I go to the nurse's station?" Later in the lesson Maree tells Ms. Stapleton the work is too hard for her. The next day Miguel says he didn't do his homework because the assignment was stupid.

What are these students telling Ms. Stapleton? Are the messages literally true, or do they imply something their words don't indicate? When you think you might be receiving a hidden message, listen to tone of voice and observe body mannerisms. They may tell you a great deal about the student's needs or feelings. Consider again what the students said to Ms. Stapleton:

1. Early in the math lesson, John holds his brow, says to Ms. Stapleton, "I don't feel good. Can I go to the nurse's station?"

Analysis: John may actually be ill or he may be trying to get out of the lesson. Here you'd best let him go to the nurse's station where he can rest or receive medical attention if needed. If this pattern repeats, find a quiet opportunity to talk with him and at that time ask, "John, I am wondering if there is something about the class that is making you feel upset. If there is, I'd like to know. I want the class to be good for everyone and that includes you. I'd really appreciate your help."

2. Ms. Stapleton, circulating among working students, sees Maree has made no progress. She asks why and Maree says, "This stuff is too hard."

Analysis: The work may actually be too hard for Maree, as she says, or her mind may be entirely elsewhere. If you believe she is troubled by a personal problem, say, "I'm sorry, Maree. I truly want you to enjoy this work. What could I do to help?" These words may not resolve Maree's difficulty, but they will give her attention and comfort she desires.

3. When Ms. Stapleton collects homework, she finds Olmo hasn't done his. She says in front of the class, "Olmo, you had the assignment just like everybody else. I don't want any excuses. You haven't tried." Olmo replies, "You know why? That stuff is stupid. Nobody goes around bisecting lines with a compass. That's the dumbest thing I ever heard of."

Analysis: Ms. Stapleton has learned enough about Olmo to foresee his reaction, but in any case she should not have reprimanded him in front of the class. Her best course of action now is to get out of the situation with the least possible damage to Olmo's dignity and her own. She should say, "Olmo, I can see you don't feel good about this work. I may have made a mistake about it. I want these assignments to be valuable for you. Let's think about it overnight and discuss it tomorrow. Will you help me in this matter, Olmo?" Olmo may be the only student reacting negatively, but what you have said lets him off the hook and gives you a reprieve as well.

4. When Ms. Stapleton tells students to get out their math books, she hears a chorus of groans from the students.

Analysis: The groans deliver a sincere message about boredom. When students are bored in school, it is not their fault. It is useless to reprimand them for their behavior or lecture them about the importance of mathematics. Ms. Stapleton must take the blame for a lackluster lesson and do something about it. She might say, "Class, I can see you don't enjoy this activity. I think mathematics is very important and I hope you think so, too. Maybe we can find a better way to learn these important skills. Would you think about it overnight? I will too, and perhaps we can find some new ideas tomorrow. For right now, let me tell you how a great man of the past, Archimedes, used mathematics to make a machine that could lift enemy ships out of the water and sink them. He used levers. Can you guess how?"

Avoiding Arguments with Students.   Many teachers, when responding to student excuses and complaints, slip out of a helpful mode into a confrontational one. They don't want to accept thoughtless complaints and, truthfully speaking, they don't like students telling them they are wrong. Their natural inclination is to dispute such contentions by arguing with the student. You are well advised to resist that temptation. Arguing with students is a no-win proposition, for two reasons: First, you can never actually win the argument (meaning persuading students you are right and they are wrong), and second, in trying to win the argument through authority or force you damage trust you have tried to establish.

What should you do when you have disagreements with students? Consider their point of view and try to understand it. You might be in the wrong. If you are, admit it and go on from there. If you feel you are correct, seek a middle ground that satisfies both of you. Here is how you might proceed:

- Listen carefully to the student. Keep calm. Hear her out. Don't deny or contradict what she says.
- Drop your defenses. If you are offended, resist the impulse to strike back. Try for understanding.
- Don't tell the student she is wrong. Doing so attacks her intelligence, perception, and reason, all related to her personal dignity.
- When the student has had her say, tell her you have considered carefully what she said. Say, "I am often wrong, but . . . " Then briefly state your position. Tell her you'd like to find a solution to the disagreement that satisfies her concerns as well as yours. If that can't be done immediately, set the issue aside temporarily and discuss it further when feelings have subsided.

This is not to say you never try to change students' opinions. One of your main duties is to help them see different points of view and allow them to change their behavior when they gain new perspectives. But you don't accomplish this by arguing. You accomplish it through example, stories, lessons, and discussions. And, of course, you can give your own opinion as well.

Encouraging.   When students are worried or have made a mistake, your objective is to help and encourage them. You don't want to make them feel worse or push them away. Yet, when trying to be helpful we often do the opposite of what we intend. Thomas Gordon (1989) has described twelve common types of teacher responses that discourage students and stifle communication. He calls them "roadblocks to communication." Imagine that student Dale is supposed to be writing a composition in class, but he learned just last night that his parents intend to separate. He didn't sleep much and now can't concentrate on the assignment. Dale could use some comfort and encouragement, but Mr. Askew does not detect Dale's need. He thinks Dale is procrastinating, which he sometimes does. Mr. Askew asks Dale what the problem is. Dale shrugs and says "Nothing." Then he adds that he doesn't understand how to do the assignment. The following are examples of comments Mr. Askew might then make that would discourage Dale and make him unwilling to talk further.

> *Giving Orders.* "Dale, you get busy. I think you know how to do that composition. No more wasting time. Get your name and date on your paper and get to work."
>
> *Warning.* "Dale, I'm telling you for the last time to get to work. If you don't, you'll be taking that home with you tonight along with a note to your parents."
>
> *Preaching.* "Dale, you know you are expected to complete all your work. We are not doing this for the fun of it. It's for your own good, don't you see that? If you don't try to learn this, you're never going to write well at all. You will never look like an educated person."
>
> *Advising.* "Dale, let me give you a piece of advice. When I was younger I was much like you, never doing what I was capable of. A good teacher got me out of that. He told me to set some personal goals for myself and work toward them, step-by-step. I think you'd benefit from that. I'd like you to come up with a plan and try it."
>
> *Criticizing.* "Dale, I can't believe you are fooling around again. Didn't we just talk about this last week? You have ability but you are not using it. I'm really disappointed in you."
>
> *Questioning.* "What's wrong, Dale? You have been sitting here ten minutes and still have nothing on that paper. Can't you even try? Do you think something bad is going to happen if you write a few lines? What's the matter with you anyhow?"

While Mr. Askew's responses to Dale may be common, they hinder rather than help. What could Mr. Askew do that would be better? Consider the following responses, which provide encouragement instead of finding fault.

- "Dale, can you get this assignment completed by the end of the period?"
- "Writing is not easy, is it? Many people have a difficult time at first. Let's see if we can begin with a title."
- "Sometimes we feel like working and sometimes we don't. We might be tired or our minds might be elsewhere. Do you ever have feelings like that?"
- "Dale, I can tell you are having difficulty getting started. Is there something about the assignment that bothers you? I'd like to correct it, if there is."
- "Dale, I feel something is not right for you. I don't want to pry. If you feel like talking, I'll listen now or I'll be here in the room right after school."

Even with "better" responses from Mr. Askew, Dale might choose to keep his troubles to himself. But that is better than Mr. Askew and Dale struggling against each other.

To encourage students, we should acknowledge the validity of their feelings. We accomplish nothing positive by denying them, which degrades students' dignity and makes things worse. We should always keep foremost in mind what Ginott (1971) called the teachers' hidden asset, which he says is always to ask ourselves,

How can I be most helpful to my students right now?

Reviewing Feelings about Learning.   Teachers routinely have students review their progress but usually focus on what students have learned rather than on their feelings about the activities. Students' reactions to instruction can teach you more than you might imagine. Consider setting aside a few minutes at the end of each day, or perhaps in the advisory period, for students to discuss what they are enjoying most in their school activities and what they are not enjoying. Drop your defenses and let students speak frankly. Ultimately, you will be grateful for what they teach you.

Discussing Class Business and Concerns.   Most authorities on class management advocate the use of classroom meetings, introduced many years ago by William Glasser (1969) and now widely used in education. Glasser contended that classes function best when students are brought into making decisions about class functions and problem resolution. He described class meetings as follows: The class is seated in a tight circle that allows good eye contact. The operating principle of class meetings is that problems are identified and solutions sought, but blame is never assigned to anyone. Everyone has a say. The teacher serves as leader to get the discussion under way, then acts as a group member. Concerns can be raised by students or the teacher. The group seeks general consensus or a solution acceptable to all. The teacher makes sure that each student is heard and no one is ridiculed, stifled, or blamed.

To introduce class meetings as a component of the ongoing program, Jane Nelsen, Lynn Lott, and H. Stephen Glenn (2000) suggest asking students if they would like to be more involved in the decisions that affect them at school. Alfie Kohn (1996) suggests posing questions such as the following:

- What makes school awful sometimes?
- Can you remember an experience during a previous year when you hated school, when you felt bad about yourself, or about everyone else, and you couldn't wait for school to be over?
- What exactly was going on when you were feeling that way? How was the class set up?"

When students show willingness to try class meetings, agree on times when they should be scheduled. Frequent meetings are useful while students are learning the process. After that, a half-hour meeting per week is usually enough.

Thirteen Operating Principles That Lead to High-Quality Classrooms

The following thirteen operating principles have been composed by the authors from information drawn from a large body of literature and from their own experiences and those of other teachers. They believe that by applying the principles you can work more effectively and enjoyably with students.

1. *Approach Your Students in an Exemplary and Charismatic Manner.* Conduct yourself ethically in all dealings with class members and school personnel by being honest, trustworthy, helpful, and considerate. Also, use your charisma to advantage. Charisma refers to the intangible attraction that people are able to exert on others. It is a trait students very much prize in teachers. They like teachers who are interesting, energetic, and intriguing. They delight in teachers' special talents, experiences, and knowledge. Teachers sometimes feel they don't have an abundance of personal charisma, but all of us have some degree and can increase and make good use of it. The question is, how? Suggestions for increasing charisma are presented toward the end of Chapter 5, should you wish to look at them now.

FIELD APPLICATION 4: Identify a teacher you know who seems very popular with students. Try to determine whether, and to what extent, that popularity is related to teacher charisma. If you think charisma is playing a significant role, see if you can determine, specifically, what in the teacher is attractive to students.

2. *Develop a Set of Class Agreements Concerning How the Class Is to Function.* Your classes operate much more smoothly if you and your students agree on a set of clear understandings about how the class is to function and students are to conduct themselves. Such understandings can be formalized in two different ways.

In the first, you make a set of rules about how students are to conduct themselves and explain those rules to the students. For enforcing the rules, you explain pleasant things that will occur when students follow the rules, and unpleasant things that will occur when students break the rules. You make sure students understand the rules and consequences clearly. Tens of thousands of teachers use this approach, and you may wish to use it, too. However, for what we hope to accomplish in today's classrooms, a second approach serves better.

In the second approach, you work with your students to develop a set of agreements concerning how the class will operate and how students and teacher will behave. By involving students in formulating the agreements, you increase the likelihood they will abide by them. A suggested procedure for reaching the agreements involves a series of introductory sessions.

The Purposes of the Introductory Sessions

The introductory sessions should achieve the following:

- initiate a collaborative relationship with your students;
- engage students in dialog concerning how the class might best serve everyone's needs; and
- reach class agreements about matters of curriculum, instruction, class character, behavior, interpersonal relations, and quality learning. As the discussions proceed, you may wish to consider additional topics.

The Sessions

A series of introductory sessions is described here in some detail. You will see that instead of telling students what to do, you ask questions that cause students to think about class behavior and procedures. Out of the ensuing discussions come conclusions about what will serve the class well and what will not. The conclusions are worded succinctly and are thereafter called class agreements. This process can be done in a series of seven sessions, each requiring approximately twenty minutes, or in some cases a bit more. In these discussions students should be seated in a tight circle. If your classroom, lab, shop, or gymnasium does not allow this possibility, make the best arrangement you can for students to have eye contact with each other.

Session #1. *Presenting Yourself to Students, and Students to You*

This session presumes you and the class are new to each other. If you decide to introduce this procedure after you have already been working with a class and know the students, skip this first session.

As students come into the class area, smile at them, make eye contact, and greet them verbally. Allow them to settle into chairs or at tables you have arranged in a circle, or assign them to their seats. (If you use a seating chart, give all students copies. That will help them learn each other's names quickly.) Tell them you are pleased to see them, eager to know them better, are looking forward to working with them, and would like to discuss their ideas for making the class as useful and enjoyable as possible. From the class list, call each student by name. Make eye contact, smile, and, if necessary, ask if you have pronounced the name correctly. Do your best to learn all names quickly—this is very important to students. Do the introductions expeditiously; don't draw the process out.

In no more than two minutes, tell students just a bit about yourself. Let your personality show while you maintain your decorum. Very briefly mention such things as family, pets, hobbies, interests, and why you became a teacher. Keep this short. In future days and weeks you can add more details about yourself, such as places you have traveled, special skills you possess, and unusual experiences you've had.

After introducing yourself, tell the students you'd like to learn something about them. From your class roster call on individual students, or ask them to work in pairs and introduce each other. Suggest they mention something especially memorable about themselves, such as unusual hobbies or experiences. Move quickly and try to get around to all students, even if it makes this first meeting run long. Make notes to help you memorize names. As the session ends, thank the students and tell them that at the next session you want to learn what they like and dislike about school.

Session #2. *Drawing Students Out on How They'd Like the Class to Function*

Have with you a chart and marker for taking notes. Tell the students you are interested in organizing the class (or improving its organization) to help them learn important information and have an enjoyable time doing so. Begin by asking:

1. What are some of the things you like best about school?
   (They typically say they like sports, being with friends, and doing art, music, and extracurricular activities. A few may mention learning, good teachers, computers, laboratories, and library.)
   Down the left side of your chart, make a list of what they say.
2. Ask what they like, specifically, about each of the things you've listed. Write their comments on the right side of your chart.

3. Ask if they think it would be possible for this class to emphasize some of the things they've mentioned, especially those on the right side of the chart.

Thank the students for their contributions. Tell them you want the class to include topics and activities they enjoy, insofar as possible. Tell them you will follow up on their suggestions at the next discussion.

Session #3.   Feedback on Previous Suggestions, and Drawing Students Out on What They Prefer in Teachers

Begin the session by reiterating what students previously said they like best in school. Ask if you have understood their comments correctly. Reassure them you will give their suggestions serious consideration. Turn to a fresh page on the chart and:

1. Ask if they have had a teacher they really enjoyed and respected. Ask them not to mention names, but indicate what that teacher did that made such a good impression. (They will probably say the teacher was nice, neat, interesting, helpful, fair, and had a sense of humor. They may mention activities they liked or the teacher's special talents.) Write what students say down the left side of your chart.
2. Review students' comments. Where needed, ask for elaboration, such as, What does a "nice" (or "neat") teacher do? What does a helpful teacher do? What does "we really had fun" mean? Make notes on the right side of the chart.
3. Tell students you want to be the kind of teacher they enjoy, insofar as you are able. Tell them you will give feedback on their suggestions at the next discussion and see how you can incorporate them into your style of teaching. Thank them for their thoughtfulness.

Session #4.   Feedback on Preferred Teacher Traits, and Drawing Students Out Concerning Behavior in the Class

Review students' comments about teachers from the previous session. Ask if they have corrections or additions. Reassure them you will try to be the sort of teacher they enjoy, insofar as you are able.

Now draw students out concerning how they like their classmates to behave in school.

1. Ask students to think of a classmate who has behaved in ways they admired or appreciated. Without naming names, let them tell what the classmate was like. List the behaviors down the left side of your chart.
2. When several behaviors are listed, go back and ask why those behaviors are appreciated. List the comments on the right side of the chart.
3. Ask students how they like fellow members of classes to treat them. Make notes on the left side and go back and again ask why.
4. Expand the question to the kinds of behavior they most appreciate from other students when the teacher is presenting a lesson or they are working together on assignments. Ask why. Just before the end of the session, ask students if they agree on the behaviors and reasons you have listed on your chart. Ask if they think it would be possible to have those kinds of behavior in this classroom.

Thank them for their input. Tell them you will keep the notes for further consideration.

Session #5.   Feedback on Desirable Behavior, and Exploration of Undesirable Behavior

Quickly review students' contributions about behavior they appreciate in others, in various situations. Verify that you have summarized their ideas correctly.

Now ask about the kind of behavior they *dislike* in their classmates. On the left of your chart, make a list of the disliked behaviors. Ask students why they dislike them. Jot the reasons on the right side of the page.

When several behaviors have been listed, ask students why those behaviors occur. Then ask how they might be prevented from occurring. Your students may have some trouble with this, so ask if there are things teachers and students can do that will cause students to *want* to behave properly, not things that make them afraid to misbehave. Take notes. If they get stuck, ask directly about removing causes of misbehavior, providing enjoyable activities, and living by the Golden Rule.

After they have shared some ideas, say something like the following: "Suppose, despite everything we do, someone in the class misbehaves, does something that we as a class do not approve of. What should we do then?" Students typically suggest punishment of some sort. If they do, then ask, "Could we help those persons understand their behavior is harmful to the class or to themselves? Does punishing help them, or does it just make them feel bad and resentful?" Tell students you don't want to use punishment or be unpleasant or fight against them in any way. "That doesn't do us any good. What I'd prefer is to correct whatever is causing the person to misbehave. That is how I would like to go about it. Put yourself in that student's place. Would you prefer being punished or having conditions changed so you simply wouldn't feel like misbehaving any more?"

Thank the students for taking the matter seriously. Tell them that in the next session you will explore how their suggestions might be put into practice.

Session #6.   Preparing Class Agreements

Before the session, prepare a fresh chart that summarizes the following:

> What students said they like best about school.
> What students said they like best in teachers.
> Behavior students said they like in classmates.
> Behavior students said they dislike in classmates.
> How class members who misbehave might be helped to behave better.

Show students the chart and say, "Here are the ideas you have had about what makes school enjoyable and worthwhile. I'd like to see if you would be willing to add a sixth item that says all of us, you and I, will make a strong effort to do high-quality work. Would you agree to that?" (Explain what you mean by *high-quality* and discuss the point as necessary.)

Say: "Now I'm wondering how we might make these things happen in our class. You have said you like school to be interesting and fun, and in that regard you have mentioned studying interesting topics, working together with friends, and having more group activity and less working by yourself. If you want to agree to that, let's make a statement about it and together we will do our best to make everything we do as enjoyable as possible." The class might come up with the following statement:

"We agree to do our best to make school interesting and enjoyable."

Follow with the remaining topics, and make a class agreement about each of them. You may need an extra session for this. When this activity is completed, prepare a chart that shows the agreements and display it in class. Give it a prominent title, such as "Our Class Agreements."

Suppose your class has settled on the following agreements (given for illustration only):

1. We will do our best to make the class interesting and enjoyable.
2. Our personal behavior will always be ethical, considerate, and responsible.
3. We will keep the classroom orderly and comfortable.
4. We will do high-quality work we can be proud of.
5. If anyone breaks an agreement, we will do what we can to help the person want to behave properly.

Session #7. Procedures for Intervening Helpfully When Misbehavior Occurs
Display a chart of the agreements in the class. Say: "Here are the agreements we have reached that will guide our behavior in the class. Look at them again. Are there any you would want to change? delete? add?

All right, then. Let's suppose somebody breaks one of the agreements. We have said that, if that happens, we will help the individual want to conduct him- or herself properly once again. I'd like to suggest it will be my duty to intervene—that is, to step in and take action—when agreements are broken. You can assist by being considerate toward the person we are trying to help. When I intervene, here is what I'll attempt to accomplish:

- stop the misbehavior;
- deal with what is causing the misbehavior, if I can determine what it is;
- help the person return to proper behavior;
- reduce the likelihood that the situation will occur again; and
- leave the person's feelings and dignity intact.

If the misbehavior is relatively serious, I may want to discuss it with the entire class. Sometimes this is desirable, sometimes not. I'll use my judgment about that. If misbehavior is very serious, I may need to call the office for immediate assistance.

Now, what do you think I should do or say when someone is misbehaving and I need to intervene?" Jot the class's suggestions on a chart. After some discussion, the class might arrive at suggestions such as the following. If they are agreeable to you, write them out. Make sure the class understands that you may use any of them, in any order. Explain that you will point to or otherwise indicate the agreement being violated and do or say the following:

For Minor Misbehavior
- Nothing more than make eye contact with the student
- "Perhaps I can remind you of this agreement?"
- "I am not comfortable with what is happening here. Could I ask for your consideration and help?"

For Lethargy or Lack of Interest

- "I can tell you are not very interested in this (topic or activity). What can I do to make the experience better for you?" (Suggestions are considered at this time.)
- "Class, this doesn't seem to be working as we had hoped. What do you think the problem is? Can we resolve it, or should we change to a different activity?" (Suggestions are considered at this time.)
- "Class, I don't feel (*something such as the quality of our work recently*) has been up to the expectations we hold for ourselves. Perhaps we might discuss this matter in a class meeting." (Class meeting is used later, involving problem solving.)

For Recurring Difficulties

- "We are having problems keeping this agreement. Why is that, and how can we resolve the matter?" (Suggestions are considered at this point. Problem solving used.)

For Resistant Problems or Conflicts

- "Could you meet with me later? We need to work together to straighten this out." (Public discussion or private conference follows. Problem solving used for resolution.)

For Hurtful Events or Serious Conflicts

- "Let's meet together and see if we can help each other work this out." (Conference ensues. Plans are made for resolution and follow-up.)
- "When you have cooled down, let's talk together to see if we can settle this problem." (Private conference follows. Conflict resolution is used.)

For Gross Defiance or Dangerous Behavior

- "You must go immediately to (*separate parts of the room; suspension room; principal's office*). I really hope we can talk about this later and get it settled."
- Call office for immediate assistance, if necessary.

Once class agreements have been formalized and put in place, review them periodically. Ask students if the agreements are clear, if they are serving well, and if they need to be modified in any way.

3. *Work to Foster Respect and Build a Sense of Community in the Class.* We have considered respect, its value in the class, and how it is encouraged. Many authorities include respect in a "sense of community" in the classroom, where each person becomes concerned about all other members of the class and where everyone works together for mutual benefit.

To build this sense of community, give your class frequent opportunities to collaborate. Class meetings can be devoted to talking about how the next unit in history might be approached, or what came across best and worst in the recent English compositions. Academic study pursued in cooperative groups enables students to make connections while learning from each other. And units in language arts and literature can be organized to promote reflection on helpfulness, fairness, and compassion. Excellent opportunities for collaboration are also available in class activities such as producing a class newsletter or magazine, staging a dramatic or musical performance, or doing community service activities as a class.

William Purkey (2002) suggests that a community of learners can be advanced through using an "invitational curriculum" that makes all aspects of teaching and learning as attractive as possible. To read a brief presentation of Purkey's ideas, refer to his paper presented on the Internet at *www.invitationaleducation.net*

4. *Emphasize Trust as a Basic Class Value.* To trust others means you feel you can count on them to support you and stand by you, all the time, in all situations, and never harm you. Trust of this sort between teacher and students is essential if learning is to occur well, meaning not only academic achievement, but also desirable attitudes, personal relations skills, and personal responsibility and self-control.

Students will not work closely with us if they do not trust us. Establishing and maintaining trust is our job, not theirs. To make this happen we must display ethical qualities, consistently, over time. This procedure is best understood in terms of the Golden Rule—that is, simply treating students as we ourselves like to be treated. Ethical qualities required for trust include kindness, consideration, faith in students' potential, helpfulness, fairness, honesty, and patience. The nature of these qualities and the role they play in establishing trust are explained in Chapter 9.

5. *Strive to Build Collaboration and a Sense of Class Ownership.* Collaboration refers to working in close partnership with your students where, together, you plan and make decisions that affect the class. Collaboration brings a number of desirable qualities to the class. It puts you and your students on the same side, where you can work together to ensure effective teaching, learning, and class behavior. It gives students a much-needed sense of positive power and makes them inclined to support decisions they help make. It establishes their stake in maintaining the well-being of the class and does away with the somewhat antagonistic posture frequently seen between teacher and students. Finally, collaboration makes possible some of the most important aspects of effective teaching, such as meeting needs, providing mutual support, developing self-direction and self-control, establishing trust and consideration for others, and building a class sense of community.

The more closely you collaborate with students, the more purposeful and responsible they become. Without collaboration, you are likely to find yourself frequently at odds with them, with neither of you fully able to meet your needs or enjoy the class. With collaboration, however, you are able to pull together, thus increasing mutual sensitivity and concern. We do need to be clear about one thing: collaboration does not suggest you and your students always have an equal say in matters that affect the class, nor does it imply that you turn ultimate control over to your students. As class leader, you have the final say, and at times may have to veto students' suggestions. In those cases you are obliged to explain clearly your reasons for doing so.

6. *Always Maintain a Helpful Attitude toward Your Students.* Helpfulness is a fundamental quality of effective teaching. Students respond to it positively, and to us as well when we use it. It is fair to say that in most settings helpfulness is our most effective teaching tactic. It attunes our minds and those of our students to success in school and encourages us to work together to achieve it.

Helpfulness is seldom forceful in nature, except when we are protecting students from danger. In the helpful mode, we do not try to make students do anything. Instead, we attempt to intrigue them, entice them, and use inspiration, encouragement, support, and close collaboration. When we do those things—and many others that will be explained later—students soon begin to behave appropriately because they see the social value in doing so. Before long, it seems to them the natural thing to do.

Most teachers would love to teach this way, but are afraid of losing control of the class. For the time being, open your mind to the possibility that the opposite will occur— that a gentle, helpful approach, properly used, will eliminate most misbehavior, make students more cooperative, and lead to stronger learning and more positive attitudes.

7. *Teach in Accordance with Student Needs and Proclivities.* In Chapter 2 we reviewed students' needs and natures, and in this chapter we have reviewed many of their perspectives on schooling. Take those needs and perspectives seriously into account and make your program consonant with them.

8. *Make Frequent Use of Cooperative Learning That Includes Group Goals and Individual Accountability.* This principle provides a number of conditions prized by present-day educators. Student motivation will be high. Cooperation skills will be developed within the group. A sense of group enterprise and camaraderie will grow. Individual accountability ensures that every student remains actively involved and contributing. The nature of the activities allows the use of multiple intelligences (Howard Gardner [2000] presents evidence that humans have many separate kinds of intelligence, each playing important roles in personal success). Students also learn through varied means, with personal preferences such as reading, listening, discussing, working with their hands, and so forth. Cooperative learning models can allow students more frequently to use the learning style they prefer.

9. *Assiduously Avoid What Students Dislike in School and Capitalize on What They Like.* Early in this chapter you saw lists of many things students like and dislike in school. The point was made that in order to keep motivation high and learning strong, we should avoid what students dislike, when possible, and emphasize topics and activities they enjoy. Please think deeply about this rather simple-sounding suggestion.

10. *Draw Attention to Student Accomplishments.* The need to feel competent strongly motivates student behavior and helps determine their attitude toward school. To gain and maintain a sense of competence, students need tangible evidence that they are contributing to the class or growing in areas they consider important, such as academic learning and certain skills. Students use two sources of information to judge whether and to what extent they are achieving. The first source is their own knowledge of what they can do now that they couldn't do before. The second is feedback from others acknowledging their progress and prowess.

While almost all students want approbation from teachers, most do not like to see particular students singled out for praise repeatedly. All students want to feel competent and want their turn in the limelight. Find ways to recognize every student's talents, accomplishments, contributions, progress, and laudable personal qualities.

11. *Establish and Maintain Positive Relationships with Students' Families.* Teachers acquire reputations in interesting ways. Generally speaking, they are seen as good teachers if families like them, have average reputations if families don't know anything about them, and have undesirable reputations if families dislike them. Parents form their impressions from what their children tell them and from how well teachers keep them informed about their child's progress. Most parents think you're neat if you treat their child well, but get very upset with you if children say you are mistreating them. Because your sense of well-being is so dependent on how families see you, it is eminently worthwhile to keep them informed about your program and their child. You can do this occasionally by telephone, but a concise class newsletter works better, and in many communities an Internet Web page better still. Many suggestions for building sound relationships with families are presented in Chapter 4.

12. *Strengthen Class Character.* Class character refers to the overall personality and behavior of the class, especially as concerns ethical behavior, steadfastness, and assumption of responsibility. Character, comprised of a number of traits, resides in individual students. As character is strengthened in individual students, it becomes stronger for the class as well. Chapter 9 examines class character and explains how you can improve it overall.

13. *Practice and Teach Conflict Resolution.* Conflicts are strong clashes of will that occur between students or between student and teacher. They usually engender heated emotions, with considerable threat to the dignity of the persons involved. Conflicts typically lead quickly to misbehavior as both sides put forth threats and throw up shields against loss of dignity. Conflicts can usually be worked out satisfactorily for all disputants, but people seldom know how to resolve them unless trained to do so.

Good conflict resolution, the type you should use and teach to your students, strives to find solutions that allow both sides to feel they have gotten more or less what they wanted. The procedure by which this is done is commonly called *win/win conflict resolution.* This procedure for resolving conflict occurs as follows:

1. Disputants identify and clearly explain their primary concerns.
2. Each side listens carefully and tries genuinely to see the situation from the other's point of view.
3. Through discussion, the disputants identify possible solutions that might be acceptable to both. They explore these solutions until they find one acceptable to both.
4. The solution is implemented, allowing good relations to remain intact.

QUESTIONS

1. Early in the chapter it was advised that you adopt six "attitudes" concerning your work with students. Which of the six would you find most difficult to maintain? Do you believe you can realistically project any of those attitudes that might not be natural to your personality?

2. What is your understanding of Covey's process of "empathetic understanding"? Do you feel it is a valuable skill? Is it one you can use?

3. What does the concept of "conferring dignity" mean to you? How would you explain the concept to one of your friends?

4. What do you understand "congruent communication" to mean? How would you explain the concept to one of your friends?

5. The concept of "class as a community" has received considerable attention. Do you feel teachers of classes such as mathematics need to be concerned with class community? Explain.

6. Thirteen principles of working with students were presented toward the end of the chapter. Which two of those principles do you consider most important, and which two least important? Why?

ACTIVITIES

1. Suppose one of your students criticizes an assignment you have made, but you think the assignment is reasonable and helpful. Mindful of the futility of arguing with students, write out what you would say that might satisfy both you and the student.

2. Select one of the thirteen operating principles for high-quality classrooms and outline what you would do to teach in full accord with that principle.

3. With three or four colleagues, review Cynthia Mee's findings about students' likes and dislikes in school. Determine how well her findings correspond with your personal experiences as a student and teacher.

4. Analyze the seven sessions described for establishing class agreements. Make changes in them that you think would make them more useful, and explain your reasons.

REFERENCES

Biddulph, S. 1997. *Raising boys.* Sydney, Australia: Finch.

Covey, S. 1989. *The seven habits of highly effective people.* New York: Simon & Schuster.

Gardner, H. 2000. *Intelligence reframed: Multiple intelligences.* New York: Basic Books.

Ginott, H. 1971. *Teacher and child.* New York: Macmillan.

Glasser, W. 1969. *Schools without failure.* New York: Harper & Row.

———. 1998. *The quality school: Managing students without coercion.* New York: HarperCollins.

Gordon, T. 1970. *Parent effectiveness training: A tested new way to raise responsible children.* New York: New American Library.

———. 1974. *T. E. T.: Teacher Effectiveness Training.* New York: David McKay.

———. 1989. *Discipline that works: Promoting self-discipline in children.* New York: Random House.

Kohn, A. 1996. *Beyond discipline: From compliance to community.* Alexandria, VA: Association for Supervision and Curriculum Development.

Maslow, A. 1954. *Motivation and personality.* New York: Harper.

Mee, C. 1997. *2,000 Voices: Young adolescents' perceptions and curriculum implications.* Columbus, OH: National Middle School Association.

Nelsen, J., Lott, L., and Glenn, H. 2000. *Positive discipline in the classroom.* Rocklin, CA: Prima.

Purkey, W. 2002. Invitational education. <www.invitational education.net>.

Wong, H., and Wong, R. 1998. *The first days of school.* Singapore: Harry K. Wong Publications.

4

Establishing Sound Relations with Parents, Families, and Community

Chapter Preview

This chapter reviews the long-standing tradition of parental, family, and community involvement in educating the young. It explains why such involvement is important, identifies a number of approaches for encouraging involvement, and suggests strategies you and your school can use for increasing parent, family, and community interest, involvement, and support.

Tradition of Parent, Family, and Community Involvement in Education

As we saw in Chapter 1, the public school system in the United States was originally established through the cooperative involvement of parents, educators, and community, with each giving strong input into how America's youth should be educated. From the beginning, local school boards, elected by and representing the citizenry, provided advice and consent in all educational matters. Communities, through representative boards of education, assumed primary responsibility for the schools, although they carefully considered input from professional educators and other sources. Standards of behavior were agreed on and teachers were given the authority to enforce those standards.

As society changed in response to industrialization, urbanization, and the influx of poor and illiterate immigrants, the structure of public education changed. Small autonomous school districts gradually merged into larger ones, guided by centralized administrations that, in turn, implemented mandates from state governments. For a time, public involvement in and support for education waned. Today, it has resurged strongly and now plays a key role in providing better education for citizens and immigrants.

The present desire to involve parents and the broader community in matters of education is made evident in a plethora of statements from the U.S. Department of Education, the National Education Association, the National Middle School Association (NMSA), teacher associations of the various states, parent–teacher associations in all the states, the National Association of Secondary School Principals (NASSP), and documents such as *Turning Points 2000*. The Carnegie Council on Adolescent Development (1989) included close parent participation among its eight recommendations for exemplary middle schools. In a letter to California Teachers Association members dated September 2001, President Wayne

Johnson announced the joint endeavor between the CTA and California PTA to increase public awareness and family involvement in public education. He concluded, "It's only when families and teachers work together as partners that children get the best opportunity to succeed." This conviction was echoed in the *NASSP Bulletin* where Van Voorhis (2001) wrote: "The value of parent involvement in schools has received increasing attention as an effective school reform strategy. There is growing evidence that parent involvement at the school can positively influence students' success in school regardless of the family's income or education . . ." In *NEA Today Online,* Michelle Green (2000), states: ". . . everybody acknowledges the critical link between parental involvement in school and student success." *Turning Points 2000* (Jackson and Davis, 2000) contains a summary of the findings from 66 studies on parental involvement and student performance. Anne Henderson and Nancy Berla (1994) state: "The evidence is now beyond dispute. When schools work together with families to support learning, children tend to succeed not just in school, but throughout life."

Implications for Teachers and Schools

A large percentage of educators now in service were trained at a time when little attention was paid to the issue of parental involvement in education. Truth be known, many educators believed families should attend to raising their children and let teachers teach them, without either interfering much in the other's business. Parental involvement was typically limited to chaperoning at field trips, dances, and other special events. Educators considered themselves to be solely in charge of curriculum and instruction, and did not look forward to parents calling them or visiting the school or class. Such "intrusions" were often viewed as troublesome, needed only when there was a problem with a student. Most teachers felt more comfortable when they had little or no contact with students' family members.

Elora Taylor's Transformation

In 1990, Ms. Elora Taylor had been teaching English for twenty years. At that time she was in a traditionally structured junior high school that offered a departmentalized curriculum for seventh and eighth grades. Classes were grouped by ability. Ms. Taylor was proud to say she taught English to seventh-grade gifted students, that she was a specialist in Shakespeare, and that her course of study was rigorous.

Despite her acknowledged expertise, Ms. Taylor was wary of parents. She treated them with respect, but they made her anxious and suspicious, so much that she went on the defensive whenever they approached her, even before she knew what they wanted. Many of her students' parents were professional people, strong and successful advocates for their particular children. They often had an intimidating manner and usually got what they wanted from teachers.

Most of Ms. Taylor's students were identified as gifted as early as third grade. They knew each other before coming to junior high because they had participated in districtwide contests in math, essay writing, and academic decathlons. But in Ms. Taylor's class there suddenly appeared a young man, Martín Morales, born in Mexico and recently arrived in the United States. Martín was a quiet, shy, purposeful boy who wore starched white shirts and pressed trousers and carried his belongings in a navy blue backpack. The problem he presented for Ms. Taylor was that he could barely speak English.

Ms. Taylor rushed immediately to the counselors, wanting to know why they had placed him in the gifted class. He was in way over his head, out of his league, she said. How was he going to live up to her standards? Being there, she said, was not fair to

Martín or the other students. The counselors only told her that Martín's mother had insisted on it, adamantly. Ms. Taylor fumed about the situation but resigned herself. What could she do? In the next reporting period she "gave" Martín a grade of C.

Two days later, Martín's mother appeared at Ms. Taylor's classroom door just as school ended. With her were two little girls in ruffly dresses, with a long-stemmed red rose they shyly handed to Ms. Taylor. Mrs. Morales tried in poor English to speak about Martín and his grade. Ms. Taylor couldn't understand her well, so decided to reply in her rudimentary Spanish, hoping she wouldn't give offense. Mrs. Morales was very appreciative and called her Maestra. She wanted to know what she could do at home to help Martín improve his performance at school. Ms. Taylor wanted to say that the best thing for Martín would be to move into an easier class, one less demanding. But seeing the determination in Mrs. Morales's eyes, she simply said that she would give him special attention and get other students to help him as might be necessary.

That year, 1990, Ms. Taylor organized a Renaissance Faire to showcase her students' projects, essays, and mastery of scenes from *Macbeth* and *Romeo and Juliet.* For those scenes, students were required to memorize lines and, in costume, enact the roles for parents and others in attendance.

Mrs. Morales had come by several more times to visit Ms. Taylor, wanting to know about Martín's progress, his class behavior and effort, and what cos-tume he would need for the performance. As the days passed, Ms. Taylor began to see Martín in a different light. He was always well mannered, and the effort he was making in difficult circumstances was increasingly apparent. Ms. Taylor recognized the support he was getting from home, too. Martín's mother didn't want her son to be "basic"; she wanted him to be all he could. Although she didn't have much money, she got him a witch's robe and hat. At the faire, she was proud and delighted to see Martín recite his lines in *Macbeth.*

In the weeks that followed, an interesting transformation occurred in Ms. Taylor. She thought more about desire and effort and overcoming obstacles, and not so much about making students fit her high standards. Thanks to Mrs. Morales, she began to realize that all parents, including those who seemed haughty and demanding, only wanted the best for their children. She even began to think of ways to increase parent involvement, rather than avoid it. The transformation was gradual, of course, but it took hold strongly. Now, more than a decade later, Ms. Taylor finds herself very attentive to the nature, needs, and desires of each of her students. She still expects much from them, but focuses more on them as deserving students than on making them live up to rigid standards. She enjoys them and likes to have contact with their parents. Not infrequently she still sees Martín, in her mind, walking down the corridor carrying his navy blue backpack.

Why Parental Involvement Is Important

Why do we want family members involved in our business of teaching their children, even when at times it is inconvenient and nerve-racking? The answer is, their involvement provides us better support from home, the students behave better in class and learn more, and everybody ends up better satisfied, at least most of the time. Richard Riles, former U.S. Secretary of Education, states:

> Thirty years of research shows that when family and community members are directly involved in education, children achieve better grades and higher test scores, have much higher reading comprehension, graduate at higher rates, are more likely to enroll in higher education, and are better behaved (quoted by John Lounsbury in "Understanding and Appreciating the Wonder Years," an on-line article on the National Middle School Association Web site, October, 2001).

This contention is not surprising. As we saw in Chapter 2, students at this age have a burgeoning need for independence and identity separate from their family. Yet, at the same time they retain a very strong need for familial security and support. They naturally vacillate between these two strong forces, but this transitional phase occurs more satisfactorily when school and family work together, both understanding what is happening in students' lives and both working to provide student self-fulfillment within a climate of support.

In a study on improving relations among schools, parents, and community, researchers Rutherford and Billig (1995) selected nine middle schools to answer two major questions: (1) How can schools and districts best involve families and the community as partners in education reform?; (2) How do family, school, and community interact most effectively? Based on their findings, Rutherford and Billig made the following suggestions:

1. *Take proactive steps to improve the contributions that can be made by family, school, and community.* Families can include middle graders in some aspects of family decision-making. Schools can provide programs specifically designed to meet the needs of students and their parents. Communities can reach out to provide internships in the workforce as well as service opportunities. In all these efforts, it is important that positive achievements of early adolescents be publicized.

2. *Turn challenges into opportunities.* As students make the transition from elementary school to middle school, they undergo physical and emotional changes that sometimes lead to breakdowns in communication between parent and child and between parent and school. To help family members stay involved in their children's education, schools can provide information on the nature and requirements of middle school and how family members can help their children achieve academic success.

3. *Productive relationships among family, school, and community are crucial in these joint efforts.* The school must take the lead in establishing relationships and providing opportunities for them to thrive.

4. *Decision making should be shared by teachers, students, and parents.* Students' and parents' roles in school, at home, and in the community undergo change when students enter middle school. Both should be allowed to share a certain amount of responsibility with the teacher in making decisions that affect them. Students and family members should be represented on site councils, PTA boards, and other advisory committees, while student-led parent–teacher conferences allow the student to take responsibility for communicating with parents about goals and achievements at school.

5. *Sustaining involvement requires strong leadership.* Good leaders should be identified in the school and in the community. They should have the energy and vision to make parental involvement a school priority and help faculty and staff implement participatory programs.

6. *Support for teachers is essential.* Teachers are the direct educational link between child, family, community, and school, and as such it is imperative that they receive training in how to involve families and communities in middle-level education. Teachers need to know what is expected of them and receive support in their efforts to design good programs.

7. *Provide better connection of families to the school program.* Family members are often left wondering about how to deal with multiple teachers, more challenging course-work, and their child's growing desire for independence and autonomy. Schools should consider provisions that occasionally allow students and family members or guardians to attend class together in the evenings.

Joyce Epstein (discussed in Dianda and McLaren, 1996) suggests six approaches that help teachers and schools encourage parent participation.

1. *Provide information concerning parent roles.* Schools should assist families in pro-viding home environments that better support children as learners. Information for doing so can be made available through workshops, videotapes, reading material on parenting and child rearing, and on-campus learning opportunities in computer technology, English as a Second Language, preparation for graduate-equivalency diplomas (GED), and other sub-jects of interest. When family members become learners, they more eagerly support the school program for their children.

2. *Communicate about programs and progress.* Schools can communicate regularly with family members about the programs provided for students, and about the group and individual progress of students in those programs. Effective communication can be done through notes, telephone calls, E-mail, newsletters, information meetings, Homework Hot-lines, and school and class Web sites. At times it will be necessary to provide translators for meetings and translations of written materials. (Note: Be aware that extensive communica-tion can consume huge amounts of time. Choose carefully your modes of communication and streamline them for efficiency.)

3. *Encourage and obtain parent volunteers.* Schools can recruit parent volunteers and train them to help in a number of school activities. One effective way of attracting parents is to include a card requesting volunteers in with the required enrollment materi-als sent home with each student on the first day of school. This card can feature a variety of ways family members can be involved, from providing baked goods for special events to chaperoning field trips to working in classrooms or grading papers at home. The school's volunteer coordinator can create a database of parent volunteers to share with the faculty.

4. *Improve conditions for learning at home.* The school can assist families with infor-mation on homework and ideas for working more effectively with students at home.

5. *Bring family members into decision making.* Family members can be actively recruited to serve on school committees, thus giving them a voice in school matters and a feeling of commitment to the school.

6. *Collaborate in community concerns and events.* Schools can identify and compile lists of community resources that can help strengthen the educational program. Examples include working closely with city recreation departments to create after-school and leisure time programs for students, using AmeriCorps tutors to provide one-on-one assistance to children, connecting students and families with community services as the need arises, and building close relationships with local business and commercial entities.

FIELD APPLICATION 1:   In a middle-level school—one where you teach or in which you have an interest—inquire about the level of parent involvement. Determine if there is a school policy on parental involvement, or if the matter is left up to individual teachers. If a program is in effect, ask how it is implemented.

Steps toward Parent Involvement

How do we translate into actual practice ideas such as those offered by Rutherford, Billig, and Epstein? Let us first examine some principles of involvement and then more detailed suggestions for implementing them.

Principles of Involvement

We should be mindful of the following principles as we think more fully about how best to involve family members in school programs. The principles apply in general. Begin on the assumption that they are accurate for all family members with whom you deal. Family members not inclined to be helpful will let you know. Even in those cases, you accomplish something positive by inviting their participation in their child's education. The principles are:

- *Parents have genuine concern about their child's education.* Most parents are deeply concerned about their child's education, and they especially want to know about their child's achievement, behavior at school, relations with other students, and attitude toward learning.
- *Family members are willing to help.* Many family members are willing to help provide quality learning experiences for their child, both at school and at home. However, they seldom know specifically how to do so.
- *Clear communication between teachers and family members is essential.* Teachers and administrators need to establish manageable communication links between school and family members, so that family members are kept informed about three things: school matters affecting their child, experiences and progress of their child, and areas in which their help would be valued.
- *Parent involvement in decisions affecting school and students should be cultivated.* This is advisable for two reasons. First, family members offer perspectives on educating the young that are closely tied to community values and aspirations. Second, if we want to cultivate good parental involvement, we need to give them status greater than that of mere helper.
- *Parental roles at school must be clarified.* It is necessary to identify, and make explicit, ways in which family members can help in the school program.
- *Family members need to be taught how to help.* Many parents want to offer to help teachers but don't know how to do so. Teachers must think through their programs to identify areas where help is needed.

■ *Family members need to receive acknowledgment for their contributions at school.* Such acknowledgment can be provided in various ways, among which are expressions of personal gratitude from teachers, letters and personal words from administrators, mention in the school newsletter, and recognition at school assemblies and awards nights.

Presenting Yourself and Communicating

Middle-level teachers who seem to be most successful—and at the same time enjoy solid reputations within the community—are those who go out of their way to communicate with family members and enlist their help and support. In this endeavor, there are several points to keep in mind.

What Parents Want. Virtually all parents think of their child as their most precious possession, their best reflection of themselves, their best extension into the future. They expect you to hold Jonathan or Jennifer central in your thoughts; never mind that there may be thirty to thirty-five other students in the class and perhaps 150 or more throughout the school day whose family members expect the same. They want you to care about their child as a person and provide understanding, encouragement, and support. And they want you to inform them about your educational program, their child's success and progress therein, and anything else related to their child's life at school. Wise teachers recognize these realities and capitalize on them.

How to Present Yourself to Parents. Be friendly but professional in your contacts with parents. They see you as professional and knowledgeable. They don't want you to be wishy-washy, silly, or disorganized, nor do they want you to treat them as long-lost best pals. Of course, they don't want you to be gruff and intimidating either. Be considerate, remain approachable, and show family members you value their collaboration.

How to Communicate with Parents. Be sure to communicate clearly. This is no time to show off your impressive vocabulary or command of complex sentence structure. Don't try to impress family members with the numerous acronyms (GATE, ELP, IEP, IGE, GED, AFDC, SDAIE, ADD, ad infinitum) that so easily trip off your tongue. Use short, direct sentences with words everyone understands.

Venues for Communication

While at times you may engage in chitchat and exchanges of pleasantries with family members, the most effective communication occurs within more formal structures. There are a number of ways you can accomplish this.

Unscheduled Contacts. You never know when a parent will contact you at school or by telephone and want to talk, usually about some problem that involves his or her child. When that happens, relax, stay calm, and make sure you understand what the parent is talking about. If there is a misunderstanding, straighten it out tactfully. If you have made a mistake, admit it and reassure the parent you will correct it. If the parent is upset, be accepting and try to see the situation from the parent's viewpoint. Thank the parent for bringing the matter to your attention. Calmly explain your understanding of the situation or your views on it. Don't argue with the parent. Ask if the two of you can work together for the child's benefit. Ask if they have suggestions for doing so. Be a good listener. Reassure the parent you always want to do the best you can for their child.

Formal Conferences. At times you will need to meet formally with family members concerning their child. Usually these conferences concern one or more of three matters: continued misbehavior, special needs, or poor academic performance. Prepare yourself accordingly. The following suggestions should be helpful in making the conferences productive and relatively nonthreatening.

Before the Conference
1. Prepare a folder with the child's name attractively written on it.
2. In the folder include (depending on the purpose of the conference)
   - a summary of work covered to date
   - a profile of the child's performance in that work
   - samples, good and bad, of the child's work
   - tests that back up your evaluations
3. Make notes to remind you of incidents that corroborate your assessment of the student's behavior.

When the Parent Arrives
1. Greet the parent in a cordial, relaxed manner. Sit side by side with the parent at a table rather than across a desk. This conveys a message of cooperation.
2. Begin by chatting about the child as a worthwhile person with whom you are pleased to be working. Mention good traits. This reassures the parent.
3. Guide the parent through the student's folder, commenting on records and work samples it contains, or
4. Encourage the parent to explain his or her concern. Listen carefully. Be accepting. Do not argue or criticize. That only causes resentment. Parents cannot be objective about their own child.
5. Now describe the problem as you see it. Be factual. Comment only on what you have observed. Don't express negative judgments about the child's character. Also explain what you feel the causes of the problem might be and how you think they can be addressed.
6. Ask if the parent has suggestions about how the two of you can work together for the child's benefit. Make suggestions of your own. See if you can agree on a plan of approach.
7. If appropriate, work with the parent to add a home action plan that will benefit the child.
8. End the conference by reassuring the parent that you will follow up and keep him or her informed. Remember that parents can be your strongest allies. Let them know you feel that way and show you want the best for the child.

Back to School Night. Early in the year your school will probably host an open house, at which time students' parents visit the school and classrooms. Parents need to know a number of things about their child in school but often never ask the appropriate questions. Many feel they shouldn't meddle; many feel insecure about approaching the teacher and don't want to feel embarrassed. Many would like to help but don't know how. Some, because of language difficulties, do not feel able to help. If you take time to inform reticent parents about what they need to know, you will earn their esteem and support. Toward that end, briefly explain the following:

- The *educational program* provided in your class, a summary of your curriculum, requirements, grading procedures, and special activities. Emphasize how these things serve the child's interests. This doesn't have to be communicated all at once; you can spread it out over time.
- The *expectations* you hold for their child, including class work, behavior, homework, makeup work, and the like, explaining that they are designed to help the child be more successful in school.
- How you will *help students meet* class expectations; that is, how your discipline system works.
- *What family members can do to help* further the progress of the child.
- *Information* about special activities and events.

After your presentation, family members may wish to ask questions and speak with you individually about their child. The following are some of the questions they are likely to ask. Answer them as though their child were always at the center of your thoughts.

- How's my child doing in school?
- How does my child get along with others?
- Does my child cause problems?
- What is my child best at?
- What does my child need to improve on?
- Is there anything I can do to help at home?
- What after-school opportunities are there for my child?

If any of your responses show the child in a less than favorable light, don't be surprised if parents reply with comments such as:

- He never was that way before (even though he probably was, and to which you say, "I hope we can work together on this, for his benefit").
- She was very popular in her other school (which may or may not be true, but to which you say, "She will be popular here, too, if together we can encourage her to be more friendly to others. Let's see if we can work together on this").
- He is just like his father, who never completed anything he started (to which you say, "Here are some things we might try. Will you help at home?").
- Her mother is the same way, just loves to talk (to which you say, "I really like your daughter. She's a neat girl. It's just that the excess talking sometimes disturbs the class and keeps her from getting her work done. I think I know how to help her. Can I count on your support?").

Newsletters. Many teachers send home one-page newsletters every month, or more frequently if possible. The newsletters typically include items such as important dates, field trips, special activities, holidays, and class accomplishments. Some teachers also include suggestions for helping students with homework and a learning activity in which the family can participate together. It is better to keep newsletters short and to the point. They never should degenerate into breezy notes that single out a few students for attention. Many teachers post their newsletters on special class Web sites. The students themselves are capable of producing the newsletter, with your guidance, and they can learn much from doing so. Good newsletters increase parent interest, involvement, and support. They are well worth the effort.

Written Notes. Personal notes are helpful for sending parents brief messages such as reminders about upcoming events. They can also call attention to the student's accomplishments, good behavior, and displays of responsibility. Students should deliver these notes and be allowed to read them—otherwise the notes may never reach home. Notes should be translated, as needed, into the primary language of the parents.

E-mail. Depending on your community, many or most families may have computers at home with E-mail capability they use every day. With their permission, you might wish to exchange information with them via this medium. It is an easy way for you to get information to parents, and easy for them to respond. However, as mentioned earlier, you may need to take some precautions here to keep yourself from being inundated with E-mail from parents. If that happens, learn to reply with necessary information in a friendly way, but keep the messages short and to the point.

Web Sites and Class Home Pages. Increasing numbers of teachers are creating home and class Web pages for their classes, and are using them to maintain contact with students' families. Typically, these pages contain announcements, homework assignments, and other news and information of interest to all parents. Setting up a Web page is not difficult. If you don't know how to do it, a media person at your school or fellow teacher will show you, or you can learn through any number of manuals on the topic. Your school district may have its own server dedicated to this purpose, and most servers for electronic mail include provisions for establishing a Web site in their service package. You can find these by using keywords such as "free space" or "free Web hosting." Sites available to you usually have enough space for you to use multiple pages if you wish.

The home page need not be elaborate in appearance. Parents want information, not frills. They especially want to know about homework, for which you can use a separate page to post assignments each day or at the beginning of the week, with updates as changes are needed. They also like to know about class activities. As indicated earlier, you may wish to post a class newsletter on the site also, on a page separate from homework. On yet another page, post examples of outstanding student work and photographs that show class events.

Remember, however, that before you display any student's name on the Internet, picture, work, or other items that identify the student personally, obtain parents' signed permission for doing so. Your district will probably have permission forms for you to use. If not, you can make your own. Consult with your site principal to make sure you have covered all contingencies.

Telephone Calls. Family members rarely receive phone calls from the teacher except when their child is in trouble. It is good public relations to surprise the parents occasionally with brief, friendly messages such as:

> "Mrs. Appleton, this is Miss Cabrera, Alex's teacher. I just wanted you to know that Alex did excellent work in math this week. I am proud of him, and you can be, too. Tell him I said so. Thank you for your support, and I'll call you again before long."

With that you say good-bye and hang up, thereby avoiding a lengthy chat with what will certainly be an appreciative Mrs. Appleton.

If the message has to be about an unpleasant matter, it should be delivered in a way that requests help:

> "Mrs. Engles, this is Mr. James, Jeff's teacher. I am calling to let you know there's a problem at school I need your help with. It is not serious, but it does need attention. Jeff has received four citations for misbehavior in the past two weeks. I am concerned about him. I know you don't want him misbehaving in an unruly manner or breaking school rules. I have spoken with him about this matter and I'd like to ask you to do the same. We don't want to punish Jeff. All we want to do is get him to follow the rules, for his own benefit as well as that of others. May I count on your support in helping Jeff?"

Performances and Displays. Like many teachers, you may wish to put on student performances and displays of student work for parents, relatives, and friends. Such events include musical productions, plays, choral verse readings, readers' theatre, science fairs, art exhibitions, and athletic events. Family members usually turn out in numbers for such occasions. You can use this time not only to show what you and your students have done, but also to indicate the special activities that contribute to the children's well-rounded education. These events, incidentally, contribute strongly to teachers' good reputations.

Student-led Conferences. Parent–teacher conferences at report card time are a matter of course in elementary school settings, but are less common in middle schools, due to time constraints in setting up conferences for large numbers of students. However, depending on your teaching position, you may have the opportunity to participate in such conferences. Middle-grades students benefit from the opportunity to reflect on their own learning and demonstrate understanding and new skills. Some middle-grades teachers structure conferences with family members so that the student takes the major responsibility for selecting work for a portfolio and discussing the selections in light of strengths, weaknesses, and goal-setting. Students are asked to explain their work and its quality to the parent, along with how they feel they have benefited from the experience.

> **FIELD APPLICATION 2:** Interview a teacher you know personally who teaches in a middle-grades school. Ask how he or she communicates best with parents, what teachers at the school think about involving parents, and any concerns teachers in the school might have about communicating with parents.

Concerning Increasing Parental Involvement

There are a number of things we can do to obtain help and support from family members.

Making Family Members Feel Welcome at School.   Family members are not likely to come to school (except when irate) unless we make them feel welcome and wanted. Teachers, administrators, and a friendly and helpful office staff can initiate a welcoming tone by greeting family members with a smile and a pleasant tone of voice. They should answer family members' questions, deal with their concerns in a manner that is helpful and professional, and otherwise show by word and deed that family participation is valued. Ultimately, most family involvement comes at the specific request of classroom teachers. It is very helpful, however, for schools to provide parent centers, where volunteers can work on projects, meet other parents, and borrow books and other resources. Many family members also appreciate printed information concerning parenting and relationships with teenage children. In addition to parent centers, many middle schools have a parent coordinator who serves as liaison between family and school. The coordinator answers questions, helps resolve problems, and helps match parent volunteers to staff members who have requested help.

Involving Parents in Decision Making. Parent leadership opportunities exist for volunteers interested in serving on school committees such as School Site Council, Bilingual Advisory Committee, or District Advisory Committee for Title I (a federal program providing funds to schools with high percentages of low-income families). In many schools, there are elections for these leadership positions. All parents are invited to attend general meetings. Parent leaders active in these ways are often invited to sit on interview committees for principals or other administrators when those positions are open.

Clarifying Parent Roles at School. Not every parent has the time or interest to be involved in a leadership role. The parent coordinator will help match up family members with their interests, whether it be sponsoring and coordinating special events or chaperoning field trips and other school events. Some family members are eager to help teachers on an ongoing basis with grading papers or filing or creating special materials in the Parent Center, while others are more comfortable helping occasionally behind the scenes, by baking treats or phoning parents about upcoming meetings. There are also parents who will only come to school to see their own child, whether to see a performance, witness an award presentation, or have lunch. "Meet and Eat" is a luncheon event some schools provide once a month, when family members come to school and have lunch with their child, an activity that is very popular with both family members and students. Another popular event is "Tagalong Day," when family members attend school with their child and go through the daily schedule with them, thus gaining a new appreciation for students, teachers, and programs. Some parents like to share information about their professions or jobs with groups of students on Career Day, while others may use their connections in the community to arrange tours of businesses or obtain donated materials or services for school projects.

Helping Parents Know How to Help in School. Many parents want to be involved at school but don't know how. Parent volunteer orientation meetings can make family members aware of opportunities and the important roles they can play at school. Some schools hold such meetings at community centers, church halls, and even at family members' homes, to lessen the discomfort some family members feel in going to the school campus. Some schools have access to a calling system that can send out a phone message to all students' homes, and this can be used to advantage in letting family members know of upcoming opportunities.

The Helping Role. Family members who wish to be involved in working with students in the classroom on an ongoing basis need to receive training in how to speak and relate with students and how to carry out functions they are assigned. Although family members may appear at times to be inept in working with students, we should always assume they care about other children as well as their own, want them to do well in school, and will respond positively to our suggestions. We often find that family members who want to help in the classroom are quite keen about becoming more deeply involved in their child's education. Those individuals often prove to be strong supporters of teachers and schools.

Coordinate Community Service Activities.   You can use the community to teach students about responsibility, helping others, and experiencing success outside of school. One of the most difficult aspects of this valuable outreach is time: time to coordinate the activities in the community, time to engage the community in providing resources and support for the students and the school. Family members can take a leadership role in organizing these activities.

Help Students at School.   Family members are usually quite concerned about their child's performance on achievement tests and are happy to know they can help their child raise his or her scores. Green (2000) reports that one school formed a Dad and Grand-dad's Club, where male volunteers read to students, mentor their academic work, and perform other valuable services such as coordinating fundraising for the school, hosting teacher appreciation activities, and beautifying the school grounds. In these ways, men not only provide direct help to students, but show they care about school, students, and education in general.

Some family members become valued assistants in providing quality learning in the classroom. Often they are well educated and may have even wanted at one time to be teachers. It is common for such family members to help with clerical work in the class, in taking attendance, distributing and collecting materials, recording grades, helping produce class bulletins, seeing that information reaches other family members, and so on. Given some instruction and guidance, many can fill teacher-aide roles such as monitoring students at work, working with individual students who are experiencing difficulties, and overseeing and providing guidance in group work. In all cases, the classroom teacher assumes ultimate responsibility for what the parent assistant does.

Help Students at Home.   Most students benefit when parents help them with school assignments. Unfortunately, students most in need of help often have parents who, for a variety of reasons, are afraid or unable to come to school. Teachers often interpret this reticence as lack of interest and so hesitate to involve these parents in home-based learning (Ascher, 1988). However, teachers can help family members work effectively with their children and so should not hesitate to communicate with parents or guardians. Given encouragement and guidance, these parents can do much to help their children.

Some of the specific duties parents can perform are providing suitable places for homework, monitoring homework, interacting with the child, reviewing and checking assignments, helping students develop specific skills, and providing appropriate rewards when students complete projects and other assignments. Family members should be advised that their child may resist having assignments monitored and checked at home. Should this happen, it is possible to structure homework so that family members and children occasionally work together on assignments. Teachers who make this provision are urged to make the assignments especially interesting, so as to encourage interaction between students and family members (Van Voorhis, 2001).

Book Talk.   Nancy Morris and Isabel Kaplan (1994) describe a middle school "book talk" program in which family members interact with their children. Students and their family members agree to select and read books from a list of fifteen titles. Groups for each book are limited to ten participants who are allowed three weeks to read the book before discussions began. Discussions in the groups are coordinated by facilitators who have read the book. With the group seated in a circle, the facilitator initiates the conversation with some general questions. Participants then converse freely. Family members and students report positive feelings about the experience.

Reading Club.   Kathy Folsom (1994) describes a program in which family members join a reading club. They agree to read with their children daily and turn in reading logs. Every month, children are allowed to choose a free book as their reward for participating in the club.

Interactive Homework.   Epstein, Salinas, and Jackson (1995) developed an interactive homework program called TIPS (Teachers Involve Parents in Schoolwork). The program includes specific assignments for different subjects, with each assignment containing clear objectives, instructions for completing the assignment, and suggestions for involving parents. The assignments are made weekly or bimonthly, so the students have time to ensure parents' participation. The assignments are integrated with the curriculum and are graded. Students are responsible for completing the assignments, and family members are asked to provide feedback to the teacher.

Providing School Adjunct Programs.   The hours from 3:00–8:00 P.M. are hazardous for children, especially for those without adult supervision. Many children go home with no adult present and no organized activities available. Unsupervised, they sometimes find activities that endanger themselves or the community and that affect their behavior and achievement in school. This uneasy time can be replaced with well-designed after-school programs in which students engage in a variety of positive activities that provide exercise as well as interactions with adult role models. Some after-school programs are held at schools, run by school personnel or community groups. Others occur at recreation centers attended by parents and siblings. These centers can use the school's standards of behavior, thus demonstrating solidarity with the school.

In addition, businesses often "adopt" schools and provide financial support, sponsor special events, and donate materials. Many allow their personnel to become involved in tutoring, mentoring, explaining, and demonstrating. In San Diego, California, for example, a partnership was established between Rubio's Baja Grill restaurant chain and Monarch School, which serves homeless and at-risk students in the downtown area (Millican, 2001). Ralph Rubio, cofounder of the chain, read about the school and believed he could help its students by creating a student-run restaurant where they could work as well as attend school. In this manner they would learn work skills that would help break the cycle of poverty they were accustomed to. Students helped develop the concept of the restaurant, including the design, logo, and menu. Vendors participated by donating materials and equipment. Students, many of whom work in the restaurant (named Cabo Café and Grill) learn the business from restaurant executives.

The Leadership Role.   Family members can also help schools by assuming leadership roles in various noninstructional activities at the school. The state of Kentucky, for example, features a training program called the Commonwealth Institute for Parent Leadership. Even if your state does not have such a program, there are many things your school can do to develop parent leadership, such as the following (suggested by Henderson and Raimondo, 2001):

- Include family members in the school's staff training for meeting standards for all students.
- Include specific techniques for collaboration between school and family members in all aspects of staff development.
- Help family members maintain a focus on student achievement in all activities. When displaying student work, display standards and scoring rubrics associated with that work.
- Explore district, state, and federal programs to see what possibilities there are for funding a parent training program.

FIELD APPLICATION 3:   Talk with a parent you know who has a child attending a middle school. Ask how, and to what extent, the school and individual teachers communicate with the parent. Ask if the parent is ever invited to the school or to participate in school activities.

Establishing a Learning Community That Involves Parents.   The term *learning community* refers to a group of people concerned about learning who are connected to each other by a common set of beliefs, feelings, and relationships (Belenardo, 2001). Learning communities usually improve when family members are included in them. Family members can be taught computer skills that help them participate in their child's learning. Those who have not graduated from high school can use free on-site instruction that helps them earn a graduate equivalency diploma (GED). By participating in such learning activities, family members show they value education. Michelle Green (2000) describes a school that uses a yearly survey in which family members indicate their interest and preferences for becoming involved in various school-related activities. The school uses the results in monthly parent-enrichment seminars, presented during the day and in the evening as well. Sessions are recorded on video for family members unable to attend the seminars.

Once programs are in place for welcoming family members to the school, teachers can get them into the classroom and onto decision-making committees. Then if family members are encouraged to participate at home, a community of learners begins to grow. If all goes well, these efforts can result in the following (Belenardo, 2001):

- *The school program will reflect the shared beliefs and expectations of parents, teachers, and administrators.* Ideally, this will include high academic standards, a schoolwide behavior management program, and productive instructional practices.

■ *Individuals will show a willingness to go above and beyond what is expected.* The efforts of each individual contribute to a successful school, thus providing a sense of satisfaction for all involved.

■ *Everyone will experience a sense of being a part of something valuable.* Activities link parents, students, staff, and administrators to the school's traditions. All members are accepted and have a strong sense of belonging. Individuals are recognized for their performance and contributions.

■ *Members become connected through care and mutual respect.* Teachers and family members reach out to help students succeed. Cooperative interdependence is evident in interdisciplinary teams, a sense of collegiality on campus, and teachers and family members working together to improve programs.

■ *Members have regular contact with one another.* Family members are participating in school activities and interacting with other family members as well as teachers, students, and administrators.

■ *Leadership is strong and proactive.* Leadership is focused on what is best for students. It seeks ways to bring out the best in everyone involved.

Despite considerable effort by teachers, staff, administrators, students, and parents, there may still be a number of parents who are reluctant to participate in school activities. We will never be able to get all of them involved, but here are some things we can do to provide additional encouragement (from Gutloff, 1997):

■ *Reach out to meet family members in their homes.* Sometimes circumstances such as financial hardship or lack of appropriate child care can make it difficult for family members to participate. In such instances, home visits can be arranged and conducted by a parent coordinator or volunteer who personally informs family members of school events and invites them to attend. For this approach to be successful, a nonjudgmental, nonauthoritarian, partnership attitude must be displayed. The major theme must center on benefits to students, and the presentation should specify opportunities for family members to participate.

■ *Accommodate different languages.* Lack of proficiency in English can create a barrier between family members and the school. Providing translators for meetings and written translations of school information and reports is most helpful. It is important to have bilingual personnel on-site to make phone calls and meet with family members. Keep in mind that a seeming lack of enthusiasm may be a parent's way of showing deferential respect for the educator.

■ *Provide genuine help to parents and their children.* Inform parents about resources that help encourage success in school. Help parents understand that new habits, such as limited TV viewing, can help students do better in school. Most parents want to know more about homework expectations. Time-tested practices that influence children in developing study habits can be very useful. If parents request information, a helpful resource is Anne Henderson's small book entitled *Parents Are Powerful,* published by the Center for Law and Education (1996). This booklet informs parents about their rights, how to deal with problems at school, what a middle school student should be learning, how parents can get involved, and other useful topics. In an introductory letter to parents, Henderson writes:

> You are the most important people in your children's lives. No one will have a bigger impact on whether they do well—in school and through life. And no one cares about them more than you do (p. 1).

At the conclusion of this letter she reminds parents, "Not only is it your right to be involved, it's the right thing to do" (p. 5).

All in all, there are two keys to maintaining effective relationships with family members, communication and acknowledgment. You have to make sure you *communicate* the following clearly to family members:

- They are welcome at school.
- You want their help.
- Their involvement will benefit their child and other students.
- They can be given any training they might need.

Then as family members become involved, you have to *acknowledge* their contributions and show they are appreciated by telling them so personally, sending them thank-you notes, mentioning their accomplishments in newsletters, and recognizing them at special events.

When Things Don't Go Well

As we have seen, it is best for everyone when parent and teacher show concern and involvement in the student's growth and development as a person and learner. As Stevenson (1998) puts it, the "power of concurrence" that exists when home and school work together in concert can have enormous influence on students. That is not to say that you will always see eye-to-eye with parents. At times you won't like what they do or say, and they may be critical of you, which makes you feel professionally (and personally) under attack. It hurts to feel there are those who think you are mistaken, don't value your contributions, or simply don't like you, and there may be times when, no matter how well-intentioned you are, you make a mistake in dealing with a parent or child, as happened to Gary Glanville.

Gary Glanville

Gary Glanville was at home on a late Sunday afternoon when he received a call from his principal, Mary Beth Barnes. It was very unusual for her to phone him at home, especially as she would see him at school the next morning. He felt a twinge of apprehension.

She got right to the point. The father of Susan, one of Gary's students, had, uninvited, read his daughter's journal (a class activity) and was particularly upset by an entry that expressed her feelings about her parents' pending divorce. Gary had responded to the entry with a comment on his own divorce and had suggested if Susan needed to talk about the matter, he would be available to listen. Principal Barnes said the father had gone "ballistic" about Gary's invasion of family privacy and had called her, the superintendent, and various members of the community to complain. She asked the father to meet with her and Gary at school the next morning to try to resolve the problem. She said she supported Gary as a teacher and would back him fully, which he appreciated no end.

Gary spent the night feeling sick, confused, angry, humiliated, misunderstood, horrified, and scared. He had worked hard to be an honest, caring, ethical professional, and now it seemed one person's reactions might ruin his professional credibility, all because he had tried to respond considerately to a young girl's feelings about her family crisis. Now he was depicted as a meddler, prying into and infringing on private family matters.

In the meeting the next morning, Gary apologized to the father, admitting that he could have used better judgment in his response to Susan's journal entry. The father began to give him another lecture about teachers staying out of family matters. Principal Barnes intervened by calmly saying that Mr. Glanville was known for doing his best on behalf of students and for being concerned with aspects of their lives that affected them at school. She added that he was respected by colleagues and members of the community and had a strong following among parents.

The father was still upset when the meeting ended, but nothing more came of the incident. To Gary's surprise, Susan was allowed to remain in his class. Gary wondered about that, but let the matter lie as if nothing had happened, although he never had a sense of closure. Gary asked his students not to write about personal family matters in their journals. From the experience he learned two lessons that served him well in subsequent years:

First, while pleasing family members must not be teachers' first consideration when making professional decisions, realistically, to be successful, a teacher must understand family members' feelings and anticipate their reactions.

Second, in any conflict one must remember that the parties operate in different contexts and that their perceptions of the same event can differ markedly.

Two years later, the father's second daughter was placed in Gary's class. Principal Barnes only told him that the father had made the request personally. Gary never had spoken with Susan about the incident, but he surmised Susan had supported him.

FIELD APPLICATION 4:   Talk with a middle school teacher and ask if he or she has ever had difficulties relating with parents, or if any colleagues have. Ask, without identifying individuals, what the problem was, how it was handled, how the teacher and parent felt about it afterward, and what lessons were learned from the experience.

QUESTIONS

1. Suppose you were asked to explain why it is beneficial to all concerned for family members to be involved more closely in their child's education. What would you say?

2. Suppose you want family members to work with you to make homework assignments more meaningful or satisfying. What sorts of things might you want the family members to do?

3. What are five activities or duties in your class that a parent or family member could easily do, thereby freeing you for more direct contact with students?

4. Whose primary responsibility do you think it is—the school's or individual teacher's—to encourage and establish linkages between classrooms and community businesses and agencies? Why?

5. Do you feel it would be helpful to produce a class newsletter to keep family members informed about your class and its activities? If so, what would you want to include in it? How frequently would you send new issues? What means would you use to make sure the family members saw the newsletter?

6. Regarding Rubio's school restaurant mentioned in the chapter, what do you see as benefits for the school and its students? What do you see as benefits for the Rubio company? What problems might you anticipate with such an arrangement?

ACTIVITIES

1. With a partner, role-play parent–teacher conferences on the following situations:
   a. An angry mother wants to know why her son has received a grade of D from you. He has assured his mother that he has made A's and B's on all his assignments.
   b. A father wants to meet with you because his daughter complains that you are picking on her and embarrassing her in front of the class.
   c. A doting mother of a high-achieving son wants to keep talking with you well beyond the time allotted for the conference.

2. Suppose you and a colleague are placed in charge of a center at your school to provide wholesome after-school activities for students. Work together to decide what you would provide at the center. Indicate what help you might need with human and material resources.

3. You have two mothers who say they can willingly and reliably come to your class(es) three days a week to help for one or two hours each day. You are receptive to the idea. Outline what you would prefer that the mothers do. Indicate how you would train or otherwise prepare them for their tasks.

4. A well-educated retired couple, with a granddaughter in your class, volunteers to coordinate a parent–student educational activity once a month, in the evening at their home. Outline what you would like to see them provide or do. Indicate how you would encourage students and family members of your class to participate. Indicate how you would evaluate the results of the plan.

REFERENCES

Ascher, C. 1988. Improving the school–home connection for low-income urban parents. *ERIC Digest.* <www.ed.gov/databases/ERIC_Digests/ed293973.html>.

Belenardo, S. 2001. Practices and conditions that lead to a sense of community in middle schools. *NASSP Bulletin 85* (627), 29–30. <www.nassp.org/news/bltn_prac_cond1001.html>.

Carnegie Council on Adolescent Development. 1989. *Turning points: Preparing American youth for the 21st Century.* New York: Carnegie Corporation of New York.

Dianda, M., and McLaren, A. July 1996. A pocket guide to building partnerships for student learning. NEA. <www.nea.org/partners/pocket.html>.

Epstein, J., Salinas, C., and Jackson, V. 1995. *Manual for teachers and prototype activities: Teachers involve parents in schoolwork (TIPS) language arts, science/health, and math interactive homework in the middle grades* (Rev. ed.) Baltimore: Center on School, Family, and Community Partnerships, Johns Hopkins University.

Folsom, K. 1994. Developing and implementing a plan involving parents to improve the reading interests of middle school students. Nova Southeastern University: Ed.D. practicum.

Green, M. 2000, September. Getting help from home. *NEA Today Online.* <www.nea.org/neatoday/0009/cover.html>.

Gutloff, K. 1997, October. Make it happen: How to involve hard-to-reach families. *NEA Today.* <www.nea.org/neatoday/9710/cover.html>.

Henderson, A. 1996. *Parents are powerful.* Washington, DC: Center for Law and Education. <www.cleweb.org/>.

Henderson, A., and Berla, N. (Eds.). 1994. *A new generation of evidence: The family is critical to student achievement.* Washington, DC: Center for Law and Education.

Henderson, A., and Raimondo, B. 2001, September. Unlocking parent potential. *Principal Leadership 2* (1). <www.principals.org/news/pl_prnt_ptntl.html>.

Jackson, A., and Davis, G. 2000. *Turning Points 2000: Educating adolescents in the 21st century.* New York: Teachers College Press.

Johnson, W. 2001, September. CTA President's message to members. Mailing to CTA Members. Sacramento: California Teachers Association.

Lounsbury, J. 2000. Understanding and appreciating the wonder years. Month of the young adolescent. <www.nmsa.org/moya/moyajhl.htm>.

Millican, A. Cafe gives at-risk kids a real lift in life. *San Diego Union-Tribune,* 29 October 2001, Local news B1, B3.

Morris, N., and Kaplan, I. 1994. Middle school parents are good partners for reading. *Journal of Reading 38* (2), 130–31.

Rutherford, B., and Billig, S. 1995. Parent, family, and community involvement in the middle grades. *ERIC Digest.* <www.ed.gov/databases/ERIC_Digests/ed 387273.html>.

Stevenson, C. 1998. *Teaching ten to fourteen year olds* (2nd ed.). New York: Longman.

Van Voorhis, F. 2001. Interactive science homework: An experiment in home and school connections. *NASSP Bulletin.* <www.nassp.org/news/bltn_sci_ hmwrk1001.html>.

5 Professional Preparation and Instructional Practice

Chapter Preview

This chapter presents recommendations concerning how teachers should be prepared for classroom teaching and how they can best present instruction. The preparation aspect reviews recommended training programs and necessary perceptions for teaching. The instruction aspect deals with how to organize and conduct lessons for maximum student benefit.

Desirable Preparation for Teaching

This portion of the chapter concerns how teachers can best be prepared for teaching in the middle grades. It touches on: (1) professional education, (2) understanding the interplay among instruction, management, and discipline, and (3) attending to the prevalent traits of middle-grades students.

National Forum to Accelerate Middle-Grades Reform: Policy Statement

The following sections describe the preparation you should be receiving before beginning your career as a middle-level teacher. The recommendations presented here were set forth by the National Forum to Accelerate Middle-Grades Reform in their 2002 policy statement on teacher education, licensure, and recruitment. The recommendations (abridged here) are:

- Mandatory requirements and middle-level licensure should be required for individuals desiring to teach in middle-level schools.
- Institutions that prepare middle-level teachers should have their programs scrutinized and accredited.
- Teacher education programs should include specialized programs for developing middle-level teachers and should assign to them faculty and staff with expertise in middle-level education.

- States should make middle-level teacher licensure specific to the middle grades (grades 5 through 8 or 6 through 9) and not overlap significantly with licensure for the elementary or high school levels.
- Middle-grades licensure for content-area teachers (such as language arts, science, mathematics, and social studies) should be middle-grades subject-specific and middle-grades standards-based, including concentrated study in two or more academic areas. For other middle-grades teachers (e.g., special education, bilingual education), specialized training in middle-level education and early adolescence should be required.
- Colleges and universities should work in partnership with districts and schools to provide ongoing professional development and sustained support for both new and veteran middle-level teachers.

The National Forum goals suggests that teachers receive special preparation in order to further the following goals:

1. **Academic excellence.** Middle-grades teachers must have a deep understanding of the subjects they teach and how to help young adolescents learn the concepts and skills in the curriculum.
2. **Developmental responsiveness.** Middle-grades teachers must have a solid understanding of early adolescence, as well as the skills and dispositions to work with young adolescents' unique developmental challenges. They should be able to motivate young adolescents to engage actively in their own learning.
3. **Equity and cultural diversity.** Middle-grades teachers must have a wide repertoire of skills and appropriate attitudes to enhance learning and development for an ethnically diverse school population.

These recommendations are not yet implemented everywhere. In 2002 the majority of states did not require that middle-level teachers hold a special credential; most teachers were still preparing for either elementary or secondary teaching. When they move into middle-level teaching, they must make a number of adjustments, often with little assistance. While only 20 percent or fewer of today's middle-level teachers have received formal training for middle-level teaching (NMSA National Forum Policy Statement, 2002), the picture is changing. Many states have implemented more appropriate licensing regulations, and 86 percent of all states make available a specific middle-level credential, although only 42 percent actually require it for middle-level teaching (NMSA National Forum Policy Statement, 2002).

NCATE Accreditation of University Programs

The recommendations set forth by the National Forum have been incorporated into the programs provided by most universities that prepare middle-level teachers. Accreditation requirements help ensure that the requirements are given serious attention. Most universities periodically request, and undergo, external accreditation of their various schools and departments. This accreditation is done by specialized agencies for the purpose of ensuring program quality and institutional reputation. One of the preeminent accreditation agencies for education is the National Council for Accreditation of Teacher Education, known as NCATE. This agency sets forth program requirements that must be met before it will put its stamp of approval on a given program. The process of accreditation is rigorous and demanding, with very high standards. The following paragraphs review what NCATE requires before it will accredit a university program for preparing middle-level teachers.

I. ***The program must be identifiable.*** In order for a program to be considered identifiable, it must contain the following:
   A. a written conceptual framework that makes explicit the underlying professional commitments, dispositions, and values on which the program is based; a statement of philosophy and goals; an associated rationale for coursework and field experiences; and a description of program evaluation;
   B. a clear specification of the knowledge, pedagogy, and field experiences that are designed especially for teaching at the middle level.

II. ***The program must emphasize the nature of early adolescence and the needs of young adolescent students.*** This emphasis must be shown through specification of the
   A. physical, social, emotional, intellectual, and moral characteristics of the developmental period of early adolescence within social and cultural contexts;
   B. changes in family settings, social contexts, threats to health and safety, and risk behaviors in contemporary society that affect healthy development of young adolescents.

III. ***The program must enable beginning teachers to apply their knowledge of the nature of early adolescence and the needs of young adolescents.*** The ability to make these applications is shown by the following:
   A. teachers can plan developmentally and culturally responsive instruction;
   B. teachers can design appropriate school programs for middle-level students and function within them.

IV. ***The program must prepare professionals who understand the rationale for, the role of teachers in, and the function of:***
   A. interdisciplinary teams
   B. teacher-based guidance programs
   C. flexible grouping and scheduling arrangements
   D. activity programs
   E. working with colleagues within the framework of the entire school community
   F. working with families, resource persons, and community groups.

V. ***The program must prepare professionals who can design and employ teaching and learning approaches appropriate for young adolescents that:***
   A. honor individual differences among learners by utilizing multiple approaches to thinking and learning;
   B. incorporate learners' ideas, interests, and questions into the exploration of the curriculum and pursuit of knowledge;
   C. emphasize the interdisciplinary nature of knowledge while drawing on the resources inherent in separate subjects;

    D. teach the basic concepts and skills of inquiry and communication as integral to all learning;

    E. cultivate skills in recognizing and solving problems;

    F. utilize multiple grouping strategies that emphasize interdependence, cooperation, and individual responsibilities;

    G. employ accountability measures that balance evaluation of academic learning with assessment of individual growth and development;

    H. include multiple strategies for evaluation and assessment.

VI. *The program must prepare professionals who can collaborate effectively with:*

    A. colleagues, to improve schools and advance knowledge and practice in their fields;

    B. families, resource persons, and community groups to achieve common goals for young adolescents.

VII. *The program must include:*

    A. preparation in two teaching fields that are broad, multidisciplinary, and encompass the major areas within those fields;

    B. at least one course designed specifically for teaching pedagogy appropriate for young adolescents.

VIII. *The program must provide field experiences in grades 5–8 that involve:*

    A. early and continuing involvement in a variety of middle-level settings;

    B. observation, participation, and teaching experiences ranging from individual to large group settings;

    C. full-time student teaching of at least ten weeks, supervised by a qualified teacher and a university or college supervisor.

> **FIELD APPLICATION 1:** Analyze the program of teacher education that is preparing you to work with middle-grades students. How well does it meet the recommendations put forth by the National Forum and NCATE?

Understanding the Interplay of Instruction, Management, and Discipline

In order to be an effective teacher at any level you must have a clear understanding of the meanings of and relationships among teaching, instruction, behavior management, and management of the classroom environment.

Teaching encompasses the totality of what you do at school to help students learn. Key components of teaching include instruction, behavior management, and management of class routines.

Instruction is the act of conducting lessons, the main procedure by which information and skills are taught. In this chapter you will see a number of suggestions concerning planning and presenting instruction.

Behavior management is a part of teaching that helps students conduct themselves in ways that best permit efficient, enjoyable learning. Effective behavior management energizes students. It encourages and helps them develop self-control and responsibility, while enhancing the ability to relate well with others. As we will see in Chapters 7 and 8, good behavior management attracts, entices, persuades, and guides students, without force or coercion.

Management of the classroom environment has to do with organizing efficient learning environments and procedures that enable the program to function smoothly and productively. It involves planning in advance, foreseeing opportunities and potential problems, attending to the myriad details of classroom teaching, dealing with materials and incidentals, assessing the program, and other matters, which we explore in Chapter 6. It enables you to stay on top of things and keep the class running smoothly.

As you can see, instruction, behavior management, and management of environment and procedures are not separate from teaching, but rather integral parts of it. As a whole, they help you conduct good lessons efficiently and facilitate maintaining good relations, communication, attending to special needs, helping students as necessary, assessing student progress and program effectiveness, resolving problems and conflicts, and enlisting the support of family members.

Understanding the Traits of Middle-Grades Students

In order to become an excellent middle-level teacher, it is essential that you understand young adolescent students, especially their needs, behaviors normal for their age, what they like and dislike, and how they are likely to act in various situations. In Chapter 2 you saw descriptions of the characteristics and needs of middle-grades students, and in Chapter 3 you examined basic principles of educating middle-grades students. Teachers who cannot adapt instruction to students' traits are never very successful. They have difficulty comprehending why students behave as they do, why they so often resist, and why they seem so unappreciative of effort expended on their behalf. Student interests, though transient, also play powerful roles in attention and motivation.

It is very important that you be sensitive to the genuine traits of adolescent students and not be deceived by first impressions. Robert Tauber (1997) reminds us that most teachers form early impressions of their students that are often incorrect. These expectations are seldom warranted, yet they affect how we relate to students, such as how frequently we smile, nod, make eye contact, lean closer to certain students, and offer praise. They also affect our willingness to devote time to certain students. It is known that those first impressions are related to students' body build, gender, race, ethnicity, name, attractiveness, dialect, and socioeconomic level (Collins and Plahn, 1988; Kenealy, Frude, and Shaw, 1988; Brylinsky and Moore, 1984). Unwarranted first impressions can easily lead to unreasonable expectations. Therefore, put first impressions aside. Give all students the benefit of the doubt and approach all of them respectfully and helpfully. The trust you show in them will usually be returned to you.

Meanwhile, be aware that students are equally prone to forming unfounded first impressions of you. Give some thought to how you can make a positive initial impression that will get the class off to a good start, such as being friendly and helpful, maintaining a pleasant demeanor, and showing personal interest in all your students (Hunsberger and Cavanagh, 1988).

Considerations in Planning Instruction

At this point we begin an exploration of instruction and how it is done best in middle grades. This will help you better understand what accomplished teachers include in their instructional efforts, as well as how they plan instruction and present lessons.

What Do We Try to Teach?

Think of the curriculum as your program for learners. There is an official curriculum and a functioning curriculum. The official curriculum is a written statement of goals, topics, and procedures. It is clarified through curriculum guides, textbooks, and other materials. Most teachers follow the official curriculum fairly closely, but virtually all depart from it to some extent. The functioning curriculum, on the other hand, consists of the topics, activities, and materials you actually use. Your functioning curriculum will probably be based on the official curriculum, but will be enhanced by some of your own ideas and preferences. The changes you make to the official curriculum are condoned and welcomed, so long as they remain consistent with the general purpose of your class.

Your functioning curriculum—and your ideas and preferences will change from year to year—should embody what you believe best contributes to the knowledge, skills, attitudes, values, and personal relationships you want your students to acquire. How do you work toward that end? Steve Biddulph, in his acclaimed book, *Raising Boys* (1997), has this to say about school:

> The learning environment of today's schools seems designed to educate senior citizens, not young people at their most energetic. Everyone is supposed to be quiet, nice, and compliant. Excitement doesn't seem to belong in this kind of learning (though many wonderful teachers do manage to bring some fun and energy into their classes, and many children catch this spirit and run with it). The passivity required by school contradicts everything we know about kids, especially adolescents. Adolescence is the age of passion. Boys and girls crave an engaged and intense learning experience, with men and women who challenge them and get to know them personally—and from this specific knowledge of their needs, work with them to shape and extend their intellect, spirit, and skills. If kids aren't waking up in the morning saying, "Wow! School today!" then something is not right (p. 130).

Biddulph may be going a bit far in saying something is drastically wrong with education when kids don't jump out of bed and exclaim, "Wow! School today!" That's not much in keeping with teenage nature; nevertheless, his contentions have a basis in truth. He correctly points out that adolescents have a surplus of passion and talent that enables them to become actively engaged in topics they consider important. It is up to you to help them access and interact with such topics.

How Do We Organize Instruction?

Many people think a teacher organizes instruction as follows: decides which pages students are to read in the textbook, has students read those pages, holds a discussion about the information, conducts an activity or two, assigns seatwork and/or homework, and sooner or later gives a test on the material. While some teachers do in fact organize instruction in this way, there are a number of alternatives that produce better results. Generally speaking, you should make sure your functioning curriculum abounds with topics that students find meaningful, significant, interesting, challenging, and worthwhile. Let students participate in deciding on those topics. Further, you see your primary role not as dispenser of information, but as helping students interact with interesting topics in such a manner that they learn eagerly and well.

A number of specific approaches to teaching are consistent with those guidelines. Each approach or method serves a particular purpose and is suited to certain topics. Presently we will call attention to some of those methods of teaching. Let's note first that instruction is usually intended to produce certain specific outcomes or else cause students to engage in certain valuable experiences. The first is referred to as outcomes-based instruction, and the second as experience-based instruction.

Outcomes-Based Instruction.   This approach identifies specific knowledge or skills we want students to acquire. The outcomes are stated in advance and class activities are organized to ensure that students attain those outcomes. This approach is planned through a "backward design" in which teachers first specify the desired outcomes and then organize instruction to help students reach those outcomes. This approach is useful for teaching factual information and skills, such as mathematical facts and processes, skills in drawing and writing persuasively, and correct use of language. Miss Nguyen frequently uses this approach when teaching English vocabulary, grammar, and public speaking.

Experience-Based Instruction.   The method identifies, or helps students seek out, experiences believed to enrich their lives, open up new vistas, and encourage the pursuit of new topics. Experiences refer to students' interacting, actively or passively, with certain situations and events. Familiar examples of such experiences include listening to music, watching films, reading stories and books, going on field trips, and taking responsibility for the class environment. Experiences are justified on the basis of the relatively intangible benefits they bring to students, even when no specific knowledge or skill is acquired as a result. You may sometimes identify experiences for students to engage in, while at other times you help students pursue on their own experiences they find interesting. Miss Nguyen uses this approach when she encourages her students to explore different genres of literature, and Mr. Stallings when he asks students to carefully explore a lawn, garden, park, or waterway and take note of the life forms, sounds, and activities therein.

Good outcome-based and experience-based approaches both feature interesting activities for students. Many good lessons emphasize both outcomes and high-quality experiences. That is, they provide rich, interesting experiences that lead to desirable knowledge and skills. Familiar examples of such activities include reading, listening, imitating, discussing, writing, investigating, role-playing, analyzing, and producing creative products. The attractiveness and instructional quality of activities and experiences are of prime importance because they must attract and hold student attention, encourage them to cooperate and participate, enable them to acquire and develop knowledge and skills, cause them to want to learn more, and leave them favorably disposed toward learning.

How Do We Attempt to Instruct?

The stereotypical instructor, in many people's eyes, stands in front of the class, lectures, makes notes and drawings on the chalkboard, questions students, and scolds those who are not paying attention. In actual practice, teachers nowadays use a surprising variety of teaching styles, or specific approaches, to help students learn. Writers such as Cruickshank, Bainer, and Metcalf (1999) and Joyce, Weil, and Calhoun (2000) have identified and analyzed more than thirty different styles of teaching, each useful for certain topics and situations. Included among the various methods are the familiar lecture method, read-review-recite method, discussion method, project method, inquiry method, interactive method, and experiential method.

More on Outcomes-Based Instruction.   Outcomes-based instruction is exemplified in "direct teaching" or "clinical teaching." This type of instruction (also referred to by William Glasser [1998a and b] as "boss teaching") is well-known and has been widely used. Teachers set the objectives, do the planning, organize activities, arrange groups, give explanations, direct and correct student work, keep records, and evaluate results. In other words, they organize and control almost everything, although they frequently discuss these matters with students to help learning and check on understanding. This method became very popular in the late 1970s and early 1980s, due mainly to the influence of Madeline Hunter (1967/1995) who called the method "clinical teaching." Hunter's method always followed the same sequence and was thus easy to teach and easy to use. After clinical teaching came into vogue, educators realized it helped teachers organize well and keep students on-task, but did not serve for many other things they wanted to accomplish. To illustrate how a teacher, using direct teaching, might initiate a unit of instruction, consider how Mr. Márquez introduces his unit on South American geography.

Class, today we are going to begin our study of the geography of South America. You will be expected to do the following things:

- Learn the names of the South American countries.
- Locate those countries on a blank map.
- Describe the types of terrain typical of each country.
- Name two products associated with each country.

- Describe the population of each country in terms of ethnic origin and economic well-being.
- Name and locate the three most important rivers in each country.

We will learn this information from our textbooks and encyclopedias. You will have two tests, one at . . . (and so on)

More on Experience-Based Instruction.   A second major type of instruction is referred to as experience-based teaching. We noted its usefulness in providing quality experiences and opening up new interests for students. This approach is exemplified in "lead teaching," popularized by William Glasser (1993, 1998a and b), which emphasizes student creativity, problem solving, self-direction, and responsibility, all done under teacher leadership but not close teacher direction. (Please note that *lead* refers to leading students, not the metal used to weigh things down.)

Glasser feels that boss teaching, in which the teacher is in charge of everything, is too often uninspiring and tends to promote misbehavior and low morale. He urged teachers to replace direct teaching with what he called lead teaching, in which students assume important responsibilities for their own learning, such as helping select appealing topics and activities and trying to do high-quality work (see Glasser, 1998a, 1998b). Lead teaching puts students and teachers into a working partnership in which each makes decisions and assumes responsibilities. Glasser claims students rarely resist education when allowed to learn in ways they enjoy, such as through discussion, group work, physical activity, collaboration, and creative projects. Similar approaches to teaching have been popularized by William Purkey (Purkey and Stanley, 1991; Purkey and Strahan, 2002), in what he calls "invitational teaching and discipline," and Alfie Kohn (1996, 1999), in what he calls "classroom learning communities."

Earlier we saw how Mr. Márquez introduced his unit on South American geography using direct instruction. For comparison, let's see how Mr. García introduces his unit, using a lead teaching manner.

Class, have any of you ever lived in South America? You did, Samuel? Which country? Peru? Fantastic! What an interesting country! I used to live in Brazil. I traveled in the Amazon quite a bit and spent some time with jungle Indians. Supposedly they were headhunters at one time. But not now. At least so they say. Tomorrow I'll show you a bow and arrow from that tribe I brought back. Samuel, did you ever eat monkey when you were in Peru? I think Peru and Brazil are very alike in some ways but very different in others. What was Peru like compared to here, Samuel? Did you get up into the Andes? They have fabulous ruins all over Peru, I hear, and those fantastic *Chariots of the Gods* lines and drawings on the landscape. Do you have any photographs or slides you could bring for us to see? What a resource you could be for us! You could teach us a lot!

Class, Samuel lived in Peru and traveled in the Andes. If we could get him to teach us about that country, what do you think you would most like to learn? (The class discusses this option and identifies topics.)

We have the opportunity in our class to learn a great deal about South America, its mountains and grasslands, its dense rain forests and huge rivers, and its interesting people and strange animals. Did you know there are groups of English, Welsh, Italians, and Germans living in many parts of South America, especially in Argentina? Did you know there are still thought to be tribes of Indians in the jungles that have no contact with the outside world? Did you know that almost half of all the river water in the world is in the Amazon basin, and that in some places the Amazon River is so wide that from the middle you can't see the shore on either side?

Speaking of the Amazon, I swam in a lake there that contained piranhas, and look, I still have my legs and arms. Surprised about that? If you wanted to learn more about living in the Amazon jungle, what would you be interested in knowing? (Discussion ensues.)

How about people of the high Andes? Those Incas, for example, who in some mysterious way cut and placed enormous boulders, big as houses, into gigantic, perfectly fitting walls? Samuel knows about them. The Incas were civilized and powerful, with an empire that stretched for three thousand miles. Yet they were conquered by a few Spaniards on horseback. How in the world could that have happened? If you could learn more about those amazing people, what would you like to know? (Discussion continues in this manner. Students identify topics about which they would be willing to make an effort to learn.) Now let me see what you think of this idea: I have written down the topics you said you were interested in, and I can help you with resources and materials. I have lots of my own, including slides, South American music, and many artifacts I have collected. I know two other people who lived in Argentina and Colombia that we could invite to talk with us. We can concentrate on what you have said you would like to learn about. But if we decide to do so, I want to see if we can make this deal: We explore what interests you; I help you all I can; and you, for your part, agree to do the best work you are capable of. We would need to discuss that to get some ideas of what you might do that would show the quality of your learning. In addition, I hope I can persuade each of you to evaluate yourselves regularly as to how well you believe you are doing. Understand, this would not be me evaluating you, it would be you evaluating yourself, not for a grade but for you to decide what you are doing very well and what you think you might be able to do better. What do you think of that idea? Want to give it a try?

Interactive Instruction. Fredric Jones (2001) has introduced a modified direct instruction approach in which students respond frequently. He calls it "say-see-do teaching." Its advantage is that it provides continual interaction between teacher and student. Jones contrasts interactive teaching with traditional direct teaching, as follows. He sees direct teaching as occurring in the following paradigm:

(Teacher) input, input, input, input, input—(Student) output

This approach, Jones claims, contains built-in factors that contribute to student misbehavior. The large amount of teacher input overloads students' minds and causes them to disengage from the lesson. Students sit passively for too long. The urge to do something builds up. The teacher does not adequately "work the crowd," that is, interact with individual students, particularly in the back of the classroom.

Jones's say-see-do teaching calls on students to participate much more actively. The teaching process involves repeated cycles of three phases: the "say" phase is teacher input, the "see" phase is teacher demonstration, and the "do" phase is student activity using what the teacher has explained and shown. Jones depicts it as follows:

Teacher input—student output—teacher input—
student output—teacher input—student output

Because interactive teaching keeps students actively involved, they remain more alert and cover more ground. Because they are called on to process the information immediately, they understand it better and remember it longer. Moreover, students thus involved have substantially less opportunity or desire to misbehave. You see an example of interactive teaching in Mrs. Lewis's Spanish lesson on using adjectives.

Mrs. Lewis is teaching students how adjectives are used in Spanish differently from English. The following are fragments from her lesson:

Say Phase—verbal explanation: Mrs. Lewis explains: "In Spanish, adjectives are placed differently than in English. There are exceptions we will learn about later, but in general adjectives in Spanish are placed *after* the noun they modify rather than before the noun, as is done in English. For example,

suppose we are walking with a friend and see a lake in the distance. In English we might say, 'That is a pretty lake.' We say the adjective first (*pretty*), followed by the noun it modifies (*lake*).

"In Spanish, the order of noun and adjective are reversed. To say 'a pretty lake' in Spanish, we say 'una laguna bonita.' Here the noun (*laguna*) comes first, and then it is described by the adjective (*bonita*)."

See Phase—visual representation: "Let me show you on the board." (Mrs. Lewis writes on the board "a pretty lake" and underneath it "una laguna bonita.")

Do Phase—student activity. "Class, think for a moment about which are the noun and adjective in these two phrases." She calls on two students, Charley and Denise: "Charley, in these two phrases, which word is the noun and which is the adjective? (Charley answers correctly.) Thank you. Denise, what is different about the sentence structure between the English phrase and the Spanish phrase? (Denise answers correctly.) Thank you."

Say Phase again: "Open your workbooks to page 32. Thank you. There you see some written examples of what we have been talking about, using different nouns and adjectives. Take a look at them and mark which you think is the adjective and which is the noun in each sentence. Let's do the first one together."

See Phase again: Students examine the first sentence in the workbook and, following Mrs. Lewis's directions, mark the noun and adjective. Mrs. Lewis calls on two students to see if they have marked the sentences correctly.

Do Phase again: Mrs. Lewis asks students to mark the nouns and adjectives in the remaining sentences. This takes about five minutes. Mrs. Lewis circulates among the students to see how they are doing. She asks them helpful questions and provides encouragement.

Say Phase again: Mrs. Lewis now introduces an exception to the general rule, having to do with the adjectives *mucho* ('much') and *muchos* ('many'), showing they are placed before the nouns they modify, as in *mucho dinero* ('much money') and *muchos árboles* ('many trees').

See Phase again: Mrs. Lewis once again writes two phrases on the board and shows students how the noun and adjective are placed.

Do Phase again: Mrs. Lewis asks students to turn to a new page in their workbooks and mark the noun and adjective in ten sentences. She circulates among the students while they complete this activity.

Say Phase again: Mrs. Lewis tells the class she would like them to work in their cooperative groups and practice together saying certain phrases correctly. She opens a chart on which are written ten phrases in English. Students already know the Spanish words for the English in the phrases.

See Phase again: Mrs. Lewis asks Linda to help her demonstrate what she wants the class to do. Linda and Mrs. Lewis demonstrate.

Do Phase again: Mrs. Lewis asks students to work in groups taking turns saying the phrases correctly in Spanish. The other members of the group listen to see if the phrases are said correctly.

(The lesson may culminate with a group discussion concerning what was learned, with students providing new phrases on their own.)

Cooperative Learning.   Cooperative learning is a method of instruction that has surged in popularity in recent years. It involves two or more students working together to complete specific tasks. Ideally it incorporates group goals with individual responsibility. It can be used to advantage in conjunction with both direct instruction and lead teaching. It encourages cooperation and positive give-and-take, and calls on every student to contribute. It has the capability of bringing about the following (Slavin, 1991):

- Distribution of leadership: All students have turns at being group leaders.
- Positive interdependence: Activities can be set up to make student groups dependent on each other.
- Social skills acquisition: To work effectively in a group, students must learn to listen, share, take turns, and show responsibility.
- Group autonomy: Students are, up to a point, left to resolve their own problems rather than be rescued by the teacher. By doing so, they become more autonomous and self-sufficient.

An example of cooperative learning is seen in Ms. Winston's sixth-grade class where students are learning about whales.

Ms. Winston has organized the class into six cooperative learning groups, each of which has five members. She has asked each group to learn as much as they can about one particular kind of whale, including the gray whale, beluga whale, killer whale, blue whale, right whale, and humpback whale. She has collected resources for students to consult. When the first group session is completed, the groups are re-formed so that each new group contains a student now considered to be expert on one of the types of whales. Each new expert teaches the other four students about that particular whale: its appearance, where it lives, what it eats, whether it is endangered, and so forth. Students take notes and make drawings, knowing that one of them will later move on to another group and serve as the expert teacher there. This process continues until all students have served as teacher for a group. Ultimately, every member of the class will have prepared a booklet that contains drawings and facts of each type of whale.

In such cooperative activities, students assume various roles in the group and work with little teacher intervention. The teacher monitors the process and provides assistance when necessary. Cooperative learning can be organized to make students dependent on each other, as in the example on whales. Because students do their work with little teacher involvement, they learn how to make decisions for themselves and show resourcefulness and responsibility.

Your Instructional Decisions. You will probably, at times, want to use direct teaching, interactive teaching, lead teaching, cooperative learning, and any number of other instructional approaches, depending on the topics being explored. All these approaches work well, provided you match them to what you hope to achieve. In all cases, remember that students appreciate activity, variety, novelty, challenge, mystery, team competition, setting new standards, and using computers. They like to hear and learn language that has rhythm, rhyme, and metaphor. They like to tell and listen to stories. They like to role-play, perform skits, and give performances. They like rhythmic activities with repetition, music, chanting, clapping, and dancing. If you build some of these things into your lessons, students will seldom complain of being bored.

> **FIELD APPLICATION 2:** Observe instructional procedures in a middle-grade class. Is the teacher using what you would call outcomes-based instruction, experience-based instruction, or a combination of the two? How can you tell? To what extent do you feel the approach is consistent with what the teacher hopes to achieve?

Teachers' Personal Qualities That Attract Students

Regardless of the style of instruction you are using at any given time, remember to take advantage of your personal qualities that affect students positively. Those qualities include:

- charisma—attractive appearance, enthusiastic, stimulating, helpful;
- understanding and accepting students for who they are, including race and ethnicity, language, customs, ability, strengths, and shortcomings;
- considering students to be your social equals and treating and talking with them as such, not as inferior beings;

- believing in students, in their potential, ability to do the right thing, and capability to succeed and contribute;
- being consistently helpful, all the time in all matters;
- remaining steadfastly determined to help students learn, develop self-discipline, and get along with each other;
- showing flexibility, maintaining a sense of humor, keeping a sense of proportion, and showing that most interpersonal concerns can be resolved amenably.

Procedures in Conducting Lessons

We now move from how to organize instruction to how it is delivered, or conducted. We will consider how to begin lessons, attend to motivation, provide input, supervise practice, lend support, and assess the results.

Initiating the Lesson

Lessons are typically begun in one of three ways: (1) reviewing progress on an ongoing topic and indicating what will be done next, (2) making connections between old and new learning, or (3) intriguing the students and inviting them to participate in something new. Teachers open new lessons by saying things such as:

(When reviewing progress and previewing what comes next): "Good morning, class. Take your landscape drawings from your folders and place them on the table in front of you. Thank you. Yesterday we completed the backgrounds and added shading to bring out light and shadows on the clouds and mountains. Today we are going to add foreground features, including a few trees, a fence, and a road. All right, watch me."

(When making connections between old and new learning): "Bonjour, classe! Comment allez-vous aujourd'hui? Class, for some time we have been working on conjugating French verbs in the present tense, to tell what someone is doing or what is happening at the present time. You have done very well on that. Today we enter into something new, which is to learn how verbs are used in the past tense, to tell what someone did or what happened in the past."

(When intriguing students and inviting them to participate): "Good morning. Nice to see you looking happy and eager to learn. (Shows a picture of a beluga whale). Anybody know what kind of whale this is? Yes, it is a beluga whale. You can see Mother Nature has made it white, given it a big brain, and put a pleasant look on its face. A question for you: I know most of you are interested in whales. Do you know how many different varieties of whales there are? Any guesses? Do you know the names of the different varieties, what they look like, where they live, and what they eat? If you learn those things, you will know more about whales than 99.9 percent of all the people on earth. An awesome thought, isn't it? If you wanted to learn about whales, how might you go about it? Any ideas?"

Attending to Motivation

Motivation refers to the impulse or desire to do, engage in, or avoid something, and it also refers to what teachers do to entice students into the lesson; hence, lesson plans often include a section entitled "motivation." Motivation is said to be of two types that come from different sources. *Intrinsic* motivation resides within us and stems from our human needs and interests. *Extrinsic* motivation is applied from outside the person, either through unpleasant coercion or pleasant intrigue, challenge, or enthusiasm. It may be more realistic to say there is only one type of motivation, but that it can be activated in various ways. In past years, teachers often activated motivation through fear of failure or reprisal. Now the more enlightened activate it through appealing activities and interesting possibilities.

Middle-grades students are interested in thousands of different things, but are not normally intrinsically motivated to learn parts of speech, algebraic processes, or the connections between cultural groups and their respective religions, even though we teachers might believe such knowledge and skills are enormously important in students' lives. When our teacher sense of what is important does not correspond with what students consider important, what do we do?

Some present-day authorities say that if students can't see the importance of what we want them to learn, we should consider dropping that topic and moving to something they *are* interested in. That's a lovely idea that would resolve many difficulties with motivation, learning, and behavior, but it only works when students already know what they like and it shuts off new experiences that are important and perhaps exciting.

A second possibility is to try to make bland or unfamiliar topics more appealing. Because we have abandoned threat and fear, we must find something that will bring intrinsic motivation into play. Some teachers are very good at this. Charisma helps, but the following are even more effective:

■ *Use novelty, challenge, mystery, puzzlement, and excitement* to energize students. Miss Nguyen in the English lesson says, "There may or may not be a double entendre somewhere on each of these pages. If you think you find one, raise your thumb so I can see it. If you can explain what it means, wiggle your thumb."

■ *Use color, sound, movement, and student activity* to attract and hold attention. Ms. Lewis uses songs, rhymes, and skits to help her students practice French vocabulary, pronunciation, and conversation.

■ *Assign individual and group projects,* as a means of adding sense of purpose to what is being learned and encouraging student self-control and responsibility. Ms. Eggleston and Mr. Peete have students keep portfolios of their best writing and artwork, which they later share with others and use in telling parents and family members what they are learning in school.

■ *State clear, reasonable expectations and requirements* to avoid confusion and enlist student cooperation. Mr. Timkins writes assignments on charts, explains them to students, checks for understanding, and leaves the chart on display while students do their work.

■ *Provide continual support, help, feedback, and encouragement* to assist students over rough spots and keep them on track. As often as she can, Miss Moore teaches her domestic science lessons in a say-see-do interactive manner. She explains one step at a time, models the step, and then immediately asks students to do what she has explained. Later, she circulates among students, quietly making helpful suggestions and encouraging comments.

■ *Listen to student concerns and remain flexible enough to change when doing so is warranted.* Mr. Proybal holds brief class discussions at the end of each week in which he asks students to comment on the lessons they liked best, those they liked least, and those they found most difficult. He listens carefully and uses student suggestions to improve his lessons.

■ *Provide numerous opportunities for students to display their accomplishments* to the class and larger audiences. Mrs. Cooper schedules displays of students' science projects and invites family members and community members. Mr. Wilder's students frequently stage skits and other performances for assemblies and the school's closed-circuit television.

■ *Emphasize student accountability* concerning behavior, work habits, and production of quality work. Mr. Adamo's students keep records and samples of their work and periodically discuss with him their ideas for further improvement. Similarly, Mr. Simpson has students keep ongoing charts for privately rating themselves each day on their behavior, effort, and progress. He discusses their records with them privately.

■ *Give students responsibility.* Mr. Li asks students to make decisions about how they wish to learn and conduct themselves. He asks that they make sure they do not put themselves in harm's way or disturb others, but otherwise allows them considerable latitude. He only asks that they explain and justify their decisions when asked to do so. When they fail to conduct themselves or learn in a responsible manner, Mr. Li asks them to reflect on why the outcomes were not as intended and make a new plan that will work better.

■ *Work to build class spirit.* Class spirit, a sense of meaningful endeavor and pleasure, seems to promote active student involvement, better behavior, higher-quality work, and higher levels of energy. Among the factors that appear to energize class spirit is a strong sense of class purpose. Mrs. Iwai involves her art students in producing murals that depict core values stressed in their school, while Mr. Johannsen and Mr. Ammens hold monthly competitions between their classes in activities such as vocabulary, knowledge of books and authors of juvenile fiction, and creative illustrations for book jackets.

FIELD APPLICATION 3: Talk with some middle-grades students. Ask what their favorite subjects and lessons are, and why. Ask if they have ideas about how teachers could make lessons more interesting.

Providing Informational Input

Lessons call on students to do one of two things: (1) involve themselves with new information, skills, or experiences, or (2) review, practice, or apply skills and knowledge previously learned. The most common source of new information is you, the teacher. Teachers are good at providing new information, teaching new skills, and showing students how to interact with the new information.

The second most-used source of new information is the textbook. Despite recurring predictions that textbooks would become obsolete because of the plethora of information available from other sources, they have remained teachers' and students' most trusted adjunct. Most classes use them. While textbooks are criticized as being too bland, too superficial, and too concerned with political correctness, they are nevertheless well organized and easily used.

Increasingly, teachers are relying on multiple sources of information that greatly enliven their programs. Examples include:

- the Internet (As you will see in Chapter 12, the Internet now makes available informational resources in enormous abundance from an incredible variety of sources.);
- reference materials, of great variety, applicability, and levels of sophistication (One need only look in a university library—or even a school library—to be almost overwhelmed by their quantity and quality. They are available free on the Internet, too.);
- physical apparatuses, such as those routinely used in science laboratories, shops, physical education programs, and most ordinary classrooms (maps, globes, overhead projectors, computers, and so forth);
- audio and video players, with tapes and discs available on a wide variety of topics;
- agency and business liaison people, such as community representatives for police, fire protection, and local businesses;
- people of renown, such as authors of juvenile books, musicians, and artists, many of whom make themselves available to schools;
- people with special skills, such as model-makers, storytellers, antique car fanciers, and the like;
- representatives of various ethnic groups who can share aspects of their cultures and traditions.

Making the Information Usable

Information that is provided, or sought out, may need to be processed to make it more understandable and useful. Both teachers and students have responsibilities in this regard.

Teachers select the information or refer students to sources where it can be obtained. They also make sure students understand the information. When teachers deliver or interpret the information, they often manipulate it to make it more easily understandable, usually by explaining, demonstrating, modeling, or elaborating.

Students' responsibilities with new information are: (1) to make sense of the information and absorb it, or acquire the skill; (2) remember the information or skill; and (3) use the information or skill appropriately. Students usually accomplish these things by listening, observing, emulating, reciting, putting information into their own words, demonstrating what they have observed, applying the information, evaluating the information, or doing creative work.

Strengthening Learning

Teachers can do several things to help students strengthen learning—make it more accurate, easily remembered, and easily used. We do well to remember that anything worth teaching is worth remembering, and if it is not worth remembering, it is not worth teaching in the first place. Students are said to forget approximately 90 percent of what they learn in school. How is that for efficiency? We seem to remember best the skills we use frequently and the knowledge that interests or affects us directly. Those are the kinds of learning we should emphasize, remembering that different students find different things meaningful and useful. Here are some of the things you can do to help students strengthen learning:

- Keep students actively involved. Do what you can to help them remain attentive and respond frequently.
- Apply what you have learned about students' needs and interests.
- Stress that you want them to acquire information and skills they consider useful.
- Show students various ways to organize information, through outlines, clusters of related concepts, sequences, and associating it with who, what, where, when, and why.
- Ask students to make immediate and frequent application of what they are learning. Help them with meaningful practice.
- Assign special responsibilities related to learning. For given topics you are teaching, put Carmen in charge of keeping track of facts and reiterating and explaining them. Put Arthur in charge of explaining and reiterating relationships—what caused what, and what is related to what. Put Suong in charge of applications—what is used for what, and how it is used, and so forth.
- Teach students how to use memory aids, such as sequencing and associating. Consider obtaining a book that explains such devices and teach students to apply the techniques to material being learned. Examples of such books are Harry Lorayne and Jerry Lucas's *The Memory Book* (1996) and Cynthia Green's *Total Memory Workouts: 8 Easy Steps to Maximum Memory Fitness* (2001). Students find the techniques explained in such books useful and fascinating.
- Use frequent review and frequent application. Don't treat old learnings as if they are relics to be stored in the basement. If they were important enough to teach in the first place, revisit them regularly.

Providing Helpful Support

The concept of helpfulness in teaching was given prominence many years ago by psychologist Haim Ginott (1971), whose ideas were presented in Chapter 3. He found helpfulness to be so effective he called it "the teacher's hidden asset." Nothing else, he said, influences students in such a positive way. You might remember that he urged teachers to ask themselves continually, "What can I do right now that will be most helpful to my students?"

Students almost always react positively when they believe you are trying to help them, although their idea of helpfulness may not correspond to your own. Being helpful does not mean lowering standards or doing students' work for them, nor does it involve trying to "make" students see, understand, work, or behave in certain ways. Rather, it involves meeting students' needs, lending support, asking questions that open new possibilities, and giving helpful hints. It involves providing a quality work environment and kind, respectful treatment. It involves showing you want to make the class comfortable and interesting. In all class matters, and especially in times of turmoil, continually ask yourself, "Is what I am doing right now helpful to my students?" Don't be reluctant to tell students of your desire to help them succeed.

Because the helpful efforts mentioned so far all focus on students, you might get the impression that teachers should function only as helpers, while leaving the important decisions to students. Of course this is not the case. Good learning and good behavior depend on your leadership. It is your duty to raise issues that need to be considered and to establish directions, set the tone, and make it easier for students to fulfill their obligations. These are things good leaders do, whether of nations, corporations, or classrooms.

Maintaining a Positive Atmosphere

Students' main objection to school is that it is boring. They say there is not enough excitement, variation, and challenge to keep them interested. We may want to blame students for not recognizing the marvelous opportunity they have for acquiring a good education and call them hedonistic ingrates who could use structure in their lives. But students these days do speak their minds honestly and act in accordance with their feelings and attitudes. That is why so much emphasis is now placed on making lessons meaningful and entertaining. We can't force students to learn. We can only entice them.

Students will involve themselves in classes that are interesting and will learn from them. It is your responsibility to make that occur, and you have seen how to do so. In addition, you will get good results from the following tactics:

- Use your charisma. (Charisma is discussed further at the end of this chapter.)
- Inject humor when appropriate. Allow students to laugh some of the time (but not all of the time). Let them see the humor in human foibles and note the unexpected and humorously bizarre behavior humans are capable of. Let them enjoy jokes and plays on words, but don't let them have fun at the expense of others. Students say they especially enjoy teachers who have a sense of humor. Just be careful that you don't cross the line that separates humor from buffoonery, or positive humor from hurtful humor.
- Make frequent changes in pace and activity. Students get tired of the same thing, day after day. Talk with them about this. Find out what they prefer. Sometimes a simple change can improve their attitude.
- Maintain and project a sense of hope for the future. Be optimistic. Stay upbeat. Consider how things can get better. Help students know they can learn and improve themselves by doing so. Help them understand that nobody is destined to fail and that everybody can become truly excellent in something.

Constantly Assessing Lesson Effectiveness

During lessons, do your best to monitor how everything goes. When problems appear, deal with them before they get out of hand. Here are some things to watch for and suggestions for attending to them:

Restlessness. Several class members are fidgeting. They are trying to stick with the task, but are pulling at their hair, tapping their pencils, shuffling materials, and glancing at the clock or out the window. This is a sign that the lesson has lost its appeal. Perhaps it has gone on too long. Ask students if they are tired. Ask if they can stick with the activity for five more minutes, or need a break.

Inattention. You see one or more students not paying attention while you give directions or make explanations. Consider whether your input is taking too long. See if you can get quickly to the point. Ask the class if they understand.

Failure to Participate. One or more students are not following along in the lesson. They are not taking part in discussions, are not listening, are on the wrong page, are looking out the window, or not working as assigned. Move alongside them. Ask if they are having trouble. Ask how you can help.

Withdrawal. One or more students have clearly withdrawn from the lesson. They may have pushed their materials aside, closed their books, laid their heads down on the desk, or are just sitting there with arms folded. This may be more serious than simple inattention. It often occurs when students feel personally insulted, find the work overwhelmingly difficult or frustrating, or have lost hope they can succeed. When you have the opportunity, discuss the situation with them. Find out, without prying into personal matters, what is troubling them. Show your willingness to help.

Failure to Follow Directions. One or more students raise their hands, not knowing what to do. Or they sit there, looking at their materials but doing nothing. Or they work at the assignment but do the wrong things. When you see such things, ask the students if they understand what they are supposed to be doing. The problem can probably be traced to inattention or inability to remember what to do. Monitor this closely. Give students enough help to get back on track, or ask a fellow student to help them.

Failure to Complete Assignments. You notice that one or more of your students fails to complete assigned work. This may be an isolated incident or ongoing behavior. Avoid this by keeping students moving along purposefully during class work. Talk with them if something seems to be interfering with their progress. Do what you can to help them overcome their difficulty.

Muttering When New Assignments Are Made. When you hear less-than-joyful mutterings from the class, ask sincerely what is concerning them. Try to find out if students are bored with the topic, find it meaningless, or don't like the drudgery. When you determine the source of the discontent, discuss how the matter can be improved.

Lightly misbehaving. Students are talking, laughing, making unwarranted noise, or mildly annoying others. At this point, stop the lesson and ask what is wrong and if the lesson needs to be changed somehow. If you think students are simply being inconsiderate, ask what might be causing them to bend class agreements about considering others or doing the best work they can.

Evaluating Student Progress and Keeping Records

One of your major duties in teaching is to evaluate student progress, assign grades, and keep records. These matters require more attention than space allows in this chapter. You will find them listed in Chapter 6, where suggestions are made for assessing work, using portfolios and performances, and assigning grades.

Reflecting on Your Teaching

Just as you want to encourage your students to reflect on their learning and look for ways to refine and improve their performance, so will you profit from doing the same for yourself (Stevenson, 1998; Jones, 2001). Consider making daily entries in a logbook as a history of what is occurring in your class. Note important incidents, ideas, and insights. Some students are certain to behave in ways that exasperate and confound you. In the log indicate your reactions and what you might want to do in the future. Also note anything in the class that might be affecting students adversely, such as noise, discomfort, inconsiderate students, difficulty with the subject, or the ways you relate to students. Ask yourself why some students do well in class and others do not, what obstacles they might be facing, and what you might do to help. Thinking and writing about these matters may bring you new insights and possible solutions.

As you begin reflecting systematically on your class and teaching practices, consider establishing a professional portfolio for yourself in which you place evidence of your successes and efforts at improvement. You will attend in-service sessions, you will receive letters of praise from parents and administrators, you will be involved in "extra" professional responsibilities, and you will create lessons in which you take particular pride. Soon your portfolio begins to indicate where you have been professionally, where you want to go, and what you are doing to get there. Here are some suggestions for what you might want to include (write the dates on all materials included):

- notes from in-service and staff development meetings, with reflections on what you learned there;
- letters and notes from family members of your students;
- personal communications from the administration;
- abstracts of favorite lessons you have developed and presented, with comments on their success;
- teaching and community awards and honors;
- any other materials you consider informative about your experiences as an educator.

A Final Note about Charisma

Charisma is your personal attractiveness that draws students to you and makes them want to cooperate with you. It is conveyed through deep knowledge, special skills, facial expressions, friendliness, enthusiasm, bodily carriage, sense of humor, wit, compassion, sensitivity to others, and manner of speaking. Think of those mannerisms for a moment. You might wish to appraise yourself with regard to the following:

Smiles. Students are attracted to teachers who smile and appear sure of themselves. Look your students in the face and give them genuine smiles. An old Chinese proverb claims, "A man without a smiling face must not open a shop." This applies to teachers as much as shopkeepers.

Friendliness. You show this quality when you quickly learn and use students' names and chat with them individually. You may not be able to speak with each student every day, but at least give them an individual greeting, with eye contact and a smile that shows you are pleased they are in the class.

Deep Knowledge. Students enjoy teachers who have breadth of knowledge and deep understanding. They very much enjoy knowing about marvelous or mysterious things and they want to understand natural phenomena. They like discussions in which you analyze past events and speculate knowingly about the future.

Special Skills. Students enjoy teachers who share special skills, such as drawing, playing a musical instrument, mimicking public figures' voices, doing magic, and so on. Share some of your special abilities with students now and then.

Enthusiasm. Students gravitate to teachers who are enthusiastic, but shy away from those who are not. Genuine enthusiasm enlivens everyone. Not all teachers are naturally enthusiastic. If this is the case for you, practice behaving in an enthusiastic manner until you can project it convincingly.

Sensitivity and Compassion. Students appreciate sensitive teachers who pick up on their feelings of depression, disappointment, or hurt. When you do so, don't pretend nothing is wrong, or tell students to buck up, or plow ahead no matter what. Students don't expect you to solve their problems, but they want your sympathy and acceptance. When you see students who seem especially troubled, ask them privately if something is bothering them and if they'd like to talk about it. If they want to talk, arrange a time and place. If they decline, don't pry. Tell them in a warm way that you are available to listen if they feel like talking.

Insights into Your Personal Life. Students want to know about your personal life. Let them in on it, but only in small doses—an interesting snippet here and there. Let them know if you have a spouse, significant other, children, or pets. They like to see photos of them and know what you do on outings. They are eager to know about your hobbies and favorite foods and movies and television programs. You might also share some of your unusual experiences. All of us have done things others find fascinating. We have held unusual jobs, traveled domestically and abroad, or worked in places such as national parks, inner cities, or farms. If you have memorabilia, share some of it with your students occasionally. All these things help students see you as a real person.

> **FIELD APPLICATION 4:** Observe a teacher of your choice. Assess the teacher's charisma in terms of the qualities described above. How do you see yourself in comparison? Are there things you might want to explore to increase your charisma with students?

QUESTIONS

1. How would you explain the interrelationship among teaching, instruction, behavior management, and management of environment and procedures?

2. How would you explain the differences between direct instruction and lead teaching?

3. Do you consider Jones's Say-See-Do teaching more a direct teaching method or a lead teaching method? Why?

4. To what extent do you believe teachers can motivate students to make more sustained effort? Explain your conclusion.

5. Do you agree with the contention that if something is not worth remembering it is not worth teaching in the first place? What exceptions or gray areas do you see?

6. Overall, do you have more personal affinity for lead teaching or direct teaching? Explain.

ACTIVITIES

1. Early in the chapter you read a section on desirable professional preparation for teaching in middle grades. With that in mind, assess how well you think you are prepared, or are being prepared, to teach. Use the criteria of a philosophy of middle-level education, traits of early adolescents, cultural and linguistic considerations, practical teaching skills, command of the subjects you are to teach, and ability to increase student motivation.

2. For a lesson you feel competent to teach, indicate what you hope the lesson would achieve. Describe activities and experiences that would lead to your goals. Would you be using a lead-teaching approach or a direct-teaching approach?

3. Describe how you might help students remember and apply what they have learned. Be as specific as possible.

4. Working with a group of colleagues, discuss how you might develop professional portfolios, what you would want to include in them, and how you world organize them.

REFERENCES

Biddulph, S. 1997. *Raising boys.* Sydney, Australia: Finch.

Bruner, J. 1960. *The process of education.* New York: Vintage.

Brylinsky, J., and Moore, J. 1984. The identification of body build stereotypes in young children. *Journal of Research in Personality, 28,* 170–181.

Collins, J., and Plahn, M. 1988. Recognition, accuracy, stereotypic preference, aversion, and subjective judgment of body appearance in adolescents and young adults. *Journal of Youth and Adolescence, 17* (4), 317–334.

Cruickshank, D., Bainer, D., and Metcalf, K. 1999. *The act of teaching* (2nd ed.). Boston: McGraw-Hill.

Ginott, H. 1971. *Teacher and child.* New York: Macmillan.

Glasser, W. 1993. *The quality school teacher.* New York: Harper.

———. 1998a. *The quality school: Managing students without coercion.* New York: HarperCollins.

———. 1998b. *The quality school teacher.* New York: HarperCollins.

Green, C. 2001. *Total memory workouts: 8 easy steps to maximum memory fitness.* New York: Bantam.

Hunsberger, B., and Cavanagh, B. 1988. Physical attractiveness and children's expectations of potential teachers. *Psychology in the Schools, 25* (1), 70–74.

Hunter, M. 1967. *Teach more—faster!* Originally published: El Segundo, CA: TIP. Published in 1995, Thousand Oaks, CA: Corwin.

Jackson, A., and Davis, G. 2000. *Turning points 2000: Educating adolescents in the 21st century.* New York: Teachers College Press.

Jones, F. 2001. *Fred Jones's tools for teaching.* Santa Cruz, CA: Fredric H. Jones & Associates.

Jones, J. 2001. How to make a practice of reflection. *TeachNet.* <www.teachersnetwork.org/docs/ntol/howto/develop/c13310,.htm>.

———. 2001. How to prepare a professional portfolio. *Teachnet.* <www.teachersnetwork.org/docs/ntol/howto/develop/c13309.htm>.

Joyce, B., Weil, M., and Calhoun, E. 2000. *Models of teaching* (6th ed.). Boston: Allyn & Bacon.

Kenealy, P., Frude, N., and Shaw, W. 1988. Influence of children's physical attractiveness on teacher expectations. *Journal of Social Psychology, 128* (3), 373–383.

Kohn, A. 1996. *Beyond discipline: From compliance to community.* Alexandria, VA: Association for Supervision and Curriculum Development.

———. 1999. *The schools our children deserve: Moving beyond traditional classrooms and "tougher standards."* Boston: Houghton Mifflin.

Lorayne, H., and Lucas, J. 1996. *The memory book.* New York: Ballantine.

National Forum to Accelerate Middle-Grades Reform. 2002. National forum policy statement on teacher preparation, licensure, and recruitment. <www.mgforum.org/teacher/refs.htm>.

Purkey, W., and Stanley, P. 1991. *Invitational teaching, learning, and living.* Washington, DC: NEA Professional Library.

Purkey, W., and Strahan, D. 2002. *Inviting positive classroom discipline.* Westerville, OH: National Middle School Association.

Slavin, R. 1991. Synthesis of research on cooperative learning. *Educational Leadership, 48,* 71–82.

Stevenson, C. 1998. *Teaching ten to fourteen year olds* (2nd ed.). New York: Addison Wesley Longman.

Tauber, R. 1997. *Self-fulfilling prophecy: A practical guide to its use in education.* Westport, CT: Praeger.

Managing Arrangements, Routines, and Incidentals of Teaching

Chapter Preview

This chapter considers the management of classroom environment, routines, and incidental matters. Although these things are seldom emphasized in teacher education, you will find it very difficult to teach if you can't handle them effectively. You probably know teachers who are so good at their jobs they make teaching look effortless. Their secret lies, in part, in their excellence in managing routines and incidentals. They are good at them because they anticipate, plan for, and give attention to conditions and situations that become problems when left to chance. This chapter explains how to manage these seemingly inconsequential, but very important, aspects of teaching.

The Importance of Classroom Management in Teaching

Teaching, in its totality, is rather like a theatrical production. The teacher, with varying degrees of input from students, is the playwright, producer, director, manager, often the lead actor, and always the person in charge. Students fill roles as audience, actors, and critics. They also write (in their minds at least) reviews of the show, and their reactions determine whether you become acclaimed in your work or are considered merely another performer going through the motions.

Your classroom is the set. Within that space you create furniture groupings that allow actors to receive attention and move about easily. As art director, you select props to create the ambience you desire—relaxed, purposeful, and interesting. As prop master you manage the many tools student actors use. As manager, you do the accounts—attendance, work receivable and payable, and bottom-line reports. As playwright, you make adjustments to the script so the audience understands the plot and actors know how to play their parts.

You are responsible for all the people and objects in the setting. Not the least of your concerns is arrangements, routines, and incidentals. It is surprising how nice teaching can be when you don't continually have to answer questions such as, Where do I turn this in? Can I go to the bathroom? Can I sharpen my pencil? I was absent yesterday . . . did I miss anything? What are we doing today? What's my grade? Where are the colored pencils? Good management takes care of these things and allows you to provide a positive atmosphere, with little conflict, where energy is concentrated on purposeful activity. At the same time, you remove much of the continual struggle that wears so many out, and you have more time and energy to work with your students.

Organizing the Physical Environment

The physical environment involves seating, traffic patterns, display areas, and storage. The room contains four areas teachers can manipulate—floor space, wall space, countertop space, and storage space. Many teachers use the ceiling as a fifth area, but please leave the ceiling unadorned and unused. Attaching materials to it may increase fire hazard, set off motion alarms, and be in violation of local fire codes.

Teachers have different preferences for how they set up their classrooms. Some enjoy creating visually stimulating classrooms with a wide variety of materials, charts, pictures, decorations, and slogans. Others prefer to keep the classroom lean and efficient. For them, heavily decorated classrooms are too cluttered and distracting. There is no right way in this matter. Effective teaching and learning can occur within both these settings.

Involving Students

You and your students have an equal stake in keeping the classroom clean, orderly, usable, and pleasant. You can involve students extensively in maintaining the classroom environment. Include them in the process as decision makers and give them active roles. There are several ways students can be actively involved.

Taking Active Roles.   All in all, classes function better when students are assigned significant responsibilities. Students with such responsibilities are often called class aides, assistants, or monitors. They help with a variety of classroom chores, such as caring for plants, distributing and collecting materials, creating folders of work for absent students, collecting student work, returning student work after grading, serving as messengers, greeting visitors, answering the intercom, sharpening pencils, straightening art materials, and so forth. Using student assistants increases students' sense of ownership in the class and, at the same time, frees time for you to work more closely with students.

Decision Making.   In class meetings, devote time to discussing students' preferences for what the physical environment ought to be. Examine matters such as neatness, cleanliness, order, aesthetics, availability of materials and equipment, and handling and care of materials and equipment. Encourage students to give input on how order and activity can be balanced.

Providing Feedback.   Wise teachers continually assess student reactions to all aspects of the instructional program. They make a point of asking students to reflect on and evaluate what is occurring in the class, specifically what students feel is going well and not so well. They respond to student feedback in a positive manner, implementing suggestions they consider helpful and professionally proper. In this way, they give students a degree of ownership of the class while simultaneously improving the program.

Seating Arrangements

One of the first things a teacher has to decide is how to position students for various group and individual activities. This calls for careful consideration of seating arrangements, activity areas, teacher's station, and traffic patterns. Because today's classrooms accommodate students of physical and linguistic diversity, it is important to consider space in relation to students' special needs.

In the not-so-distant past, student desks were anchored to wooden runners where they remained unmoved. These days, teachers arrange seating at their discretion to meet needs indicated by subject matter, activities, and collaborative work. Popular seating arrangements now include rows, circles, horseshoes, chevrons, and modular tables. Fredric Jones (2001) advocates creating an "interior loop," or walkway, within student positions, to present the fewest barriers between the teacher and individual students in the classroom. This allows the teacher easily and efficiently to "work the crowd," as Jones says, which refers to maintaining ongoing interactions with the class and individual students.

Teacher's Station

The teacher's station, usually a desk, should be placed in a position that oversees the entire class, ideally to the side or the back of the room. Some teachers like to display personal photos and give their station visual appeal. Many feel they add status by displaying teaching certificates, advanced degrees, and special awards. Whatever you place there, keep your station neat, which may require some effort if you are not a tidy person by nature. A messy teacher's desk sets a bad example for students and can cause parents and professionals to question your personal self-discipline. Make it a habit to clean and straighten your desk every day before you leave.

Traffic Patterns

Traffic patterns refer to routes established for students to move about the room. Locations of doors, display boards, white boards, storage areas, and, in some cases, sinks and drinking fountains, affect these patterns. Try to organize movement to eliminate congestion, waiting, and unnecessary contact, which waste time and frequently lead to disruptive behavior. Contrary to popular belief, well-managed classrooms are not necessarily quiet and still, but can show a great deal of student movement—obtaining and returning materials, turning in assignments, sharpening pencils, entering and exiting the classroom, reorganizing for group work, doing demonstrations and performances, approaching the teacher, and so on.

Display Areas

A number of areas in the classroom can be used to advantage for displaying such things as models, maps, student work, and art prints.

Chalkboards and White Boards.   Chalkboards or white boards will take up much of your wall space. They are routinely used to post daily information, assignments, weekly row or table points, explanations, and demonstrations. Students love going up to the board to work (such as doing math procedures), draw (such as cartooning and making backdrops for skits), and play games (such as Pictionary®, spelling games, and other instructional games).

Bulletin Boards.   Bulletin boards or corkboards are present in nearly every classroom. While often used only for posting decorations, they have useful instructional purposes as well. Consider using them to display daily bulletins, class birthdays, assignment lists for students returning from an absence, postings to help students become responsible for keeping up with class and school events, and a calendar of school events.

Decorative bulletin boards can also serve instructional ends. For example, prints of well-known art can be posted and, while attractive in their own right, can be used as a means of teaching students about art, artists, and the times and cultures in which they lived. Most students enjoy having their work displayed on corkboards, too. They are proud of the recognition and enjoy looking at what others have done. If you post student work, make sure you include something from every student at some point in the semester or year.

Windows.   Don't forget to consider windows as display areas. Allow some of the displays to face outward. Your students and their friends will congregate outside your room before and after school to see the artwork and photographs you post.

Walls and Corners.   Large maps can take up a whole bulletin board, and if your subject is geography or social studies, you may want to leave them there all year. Large rollup maps can be installed just above the white board to be used when necessary and out of the way at other times. Charts of classroom procedures and rules deserve a prominent place, particularly while students are learning new routines. Some teachers like to post inspirational slogans and mottoes, and many schools urge teachers to display posters about traits being emphasized in character education.

Countertops.   Countertops provide ideal placement for student file folders and/or portfolio folders. Use hanging files in covered boxes or crates for neatness. Use wire baskets or plastic letter trays for storing printed materials and collecting student work. Many teachers use countertops to display models, plants, and aquariums.

Storage

Keeping things orderly in their appropriate places suggests you know exactly what you are doing. This is very important to your sense of well-being, because modern classrooms contain a surprising number and variety of supplies, instructional materials, reference books, textbooks and workbooks, maps, globes, charts, science apparatus, recorders, projectors, and the like. Most of these things must be kept out of the way except when being used in specific lessons, but should always be easily obtained when needed. This means you need to decide how and where you will store such materials, how you (or class assistants) can find them when they are needed, and how your students can readily access them. Most teachers store instructional materials in file cabinets, on shelves, and in closets and cupboards.

File Cabinet.   The school should furnish you a file cabinet. If you don't have one, speak with the secretary or the custodian. If none is available, speak with your principal about ordering one. You will be creating and accumulating material and documents and you must have a neat, accessible place for them. Once you have a file cabinet, you need some hanging folders and manila folders. You might want to put a wire basket on top of the filing cabinet for papers to be filed. Go through the basket and file materials at least once a week.

Shelves.   Shelves are the most common storage areas for textbooks, workbooks, reference books, novels, models, videos, CDs, and the like. They are also used for bins that contain various worksheets, objects, games, paper, and other supplies. You may be assigned a classroom that has no shelves. If so, you can easily make them from finished boards and concrete blocks, available at building supply stores. You can also use countertops for storing books and equipment. Small tables work in a pinch. Ask your principal or colleagues. Somebody will find what you need.

Cupboards and Closets.   Classroom cupboards and closets can be used to store supplies of paper, pencils, glue, paints, scissors, crayons, rulers, and pens. Be sure to organize the materials carefully and place them in labeled compartments. (You will want to teach students how to obtain and replace the materials properly.) Collections of materials for special projects and units can be kept in file boxes and stored in cupboards. Make sure they, too, are well organized and clearly labeled. Large posters and charts can be kept in cardboard file boxes or in cupboards.

TVs, VCRs, DVDs, and microprojectors are standard equipment in many classrooms. You may need to bring in your own CD player for music. You will require a secure place to store CDs and instructional videos. These items can be kept in closets or special storage facilities provided by the school. You will need to keep these compartments locked.

In addition, you will require items for cleaning, such as a broom, rags, and cleaning solutions, which will be provided by the school in accordance with health and safety standards. A small vacuum cleaner is very useful, but you will probably have to provide it yourself.

> **FIELD APPLICATION 1:**   Arrange to observe a classroom. Note and diagram the physical environment as concerns seating arrangement, traffic patterns, display areas, and storage facilities. Do you see improvements you could make?

Needs Associated with Roaming

Sometimes teachers new to a school do not get assigned a classroom of their own. This situation is referred to as "roaming" because you have to move from classroom to classroom to teach your classes. It is challenging, but certainly possible. You will most likely use colleagues' rooms while they are having planning period, so establish good relations with those individuals. In each room, you should have a desk or teacher station to use. You will also need a bit of bulletin board space. You may have to share materials, or else tote everything with you each day, for which you may need a rolling cart, a briefcase on wheels, and a great deal of patience. On the positive side, you can learn a great deal from the experience because you see other teachers' ways of organizing classrooms.

Laying Out the Semester or Year

The Calendar

Before beginning the year or grading period, lay out a calendar of events that affect your class. Your school will probably provide you a lesson planning book that shows a year's calendar, with notations of national holidays and certain non-holidays that affect the normal program, such as (if you are teaching in the United States) Valentine's Day and Halloween. If you are teaching elsewhere, similar days should be noted. As you lay out the year or semester, take into account all the holidays, vacation times, teacher in-service days, and days when students will not be present. Your school district calendar, separate from the plan book, will indicate teaching days, in-service days, parent–teacher conference days, and dates when report cards are due. Your school site's calendar will indicate back-to-school and open-house nights, if you have them, and perhaps dates for school assemblies and special events. While these matters interfere with normal teaching, they also excite and motivate students and provide themes that you can use to good advantage.

Once you have marked the calendar, you will have a more accurate view of the sequence of events and the blocks of time available for teaching. Now you can make additional notations that offer an even more complete picture of what the months will bring. Assuming a traditional September-to-June schedule, as in the Northern Hemisphere, you will find it helpful to anticipate the following (these illustrations are for schools in the United States).

Late August, Early September.   School begins the week before or after Labor Day, and everyone is excited. These first days tend to be a time of fairly good student behavior. Students may be unsure of the new setting, and usually hope they have nice teachers who treat them well. This is a good time for high-interest teaching units; they help get you off to a good start with your students. It is now that you should establish and carefully teach routines and expectations. Rosh Hashanah and Yom Kippur are often celebrated this month, or in October in certain years. Check with your principal regarding the school's policy of drawing attention to religious holidays and discussing their meaning.

October.   If your school has a parents' back-to-school night, it will probably occur in October, although it might be in September. At that time you will be expected to describe your program to those who attend, talk with family members personally, show them samples of their child's work, and answer their questions. Rosh Hashanah and Yom Kippur may be celebrated this month. Halloween occurs at the end of the month and students in most schools will be excited and distracted. Many teachers provide stories and writing and art activities on the Halloween theme. Again, check with your principal about school policy.

November.   Three events of interest occur this month. Election Day, the first Tuesday of the month, might be of major interest. Veterans Day, November 11, is a school holiday, but may be moved to provide a three-day weekend. Thanksgiving, late in the month, is a time of excitement. Two days of school will be missed (in some districts, three days or even the entire week).

December.   The last one-third of the month will be given to vacation, leaving the early two-thirds, for most students, a time of excited anticipation over Hanukkah, Kwanzaa, and Christmas. Check school policy regarding mention of or attention to these celebrations. Regardless of policy, students will be thinking about gifts, travel, feasts, family events, and the like.

January.   Teachers and students return from holiday excitements to normal school routine with varying degrees of interest, but at this time everyone is amenable to getting back to work. Martin Luther King Day, January 15, is normally set to provide a long weekend at mid-month, and the days that precede it offer an appropriate time for emphasizing African American history, music, art, and literature, although these topics are usually considered in February, when many schools emphasize Black History. Chinese and Vietnamese new year is celebrated sometimes in this month and sometimes in February. The professional football playoffs leading to the Super Bowl are underway, and many students will be interested in them.

February.   This month seems to pass quickly because it is short and contains long weekends and dates of interest. Professional football's Super Bowl is played at the beginning of the month. Presidents' birthdays (Lincoln, February 12, and Washington, February 20) are observed with one or two long weekends—check your school calendar. Valentine's Day, February 14, is a time of great excitement in most middle schools.

March.   After the fast pace of February, March seems to slow down. Student enthusiasm may wane. However, with fewer outside distractions students can concentrate better on schoolwork, so this is a good time to complete longer units of study. Saint Patrick's Day receives secular attention on March 17.

April.   Most schools take a week or two weeks spring vacation early in this month, and many students travel or receive visitors. The month brings commemorations of Passover and Easter. Check with your principal to determine school policy regarding them. Most schools devote considerable time to preparing students for standardized tests that are usually administered in May.

May.   Achievement and other standardized testing is usually done this month. Schools typically offer concerts and drama productions for the public. Your school may invite family members to visit the school, which allows teachers and students to demonstrate some of their accomplishments. Mother's Day occurs this month. Memorial Day falls on May 30, but usually is observed on Friday or Monday to make a long weekend.

June.   The end of the school year is approaching, making the final weeks a time of activity and distraction. Teachers are concerned about report cards. Many awards ceremonies are conducted near the end of the school year. Students' minds are on summer, and a few are concerned about promotion or moving to another school.

In districts with year-round school calendars, Independence Day, July 4th, will affect planning for the first week of July. Some years the Olympic Games and the national primary elections will be of interest.

The attention given here to the yearly calendar does not imply that it is the driving force behind curriculum organization, but only that outside forces may impede or enhance normal instruction. Keep the notations at hand as you use your curriculum guide and textbooks to plot out instruction for your students. Pencil your plans on a separate chart because, before finalizing them, you probably will make a number of changes. A point to remember: to the extent possible, begin instructional units on Mondays (or the Tuesday following a long weekend) and have them end just before holidays, long weekends, or vacation times, as it is difficult to recapture student enthusiasm after such breaks. You may need to shorten or even bypass some of the units included in your curriculum guide in order to fit everything in your schedule.

Plans for First Day and First Week

It might seem that once you have laid out your schedule and organized the classroom environment, students will automatically be ready and eager to learn with little supervision. That is not the case, however. From the beginning of class, you must help students learn work routines and class procedures. By doing so you reduce confusion, increase instructional time, and maintain your composure. Students appreciate the security of knowing what to do and expect. Successful teachers know that the first few minutes of a class set the tone for the rest of the period. To begin your class effectively, try the following suggestions.

Greet the Students at the Door.   Stand at your classroom door between passing periods. Position yourself so you can see both your classroom and the hall. Watch student behavior in the hallways and be ready to greet students individually as they enter your room. Harry Wong and Rosemary Wong (1998), among others, recommends shaking hands with students as they arrive. Some teachers do this with great success, while others prefer to offer a smile and verbal greeting.

Use a Prepared Seating Chart and Assign Students Their Seating.   This eliminates a great deal of confusion for everyone. The seating chart will also help you learn students' names quickly. It reminds students that it is your prerogative, not the students', to decide who sits where. Many teachers laminate a blank chart and use small stick-on notes to place the students initially. Copies can be distributed to students to help them learn each other's names quickly. Changes can be made later as necessary.

Have an Assignment for Students to Begin as Soon as They Enter.   In many schools, students begin by writing the day's assignments and activities in their planners. They copy it from the white board, the overhead, or class television monitor. Help students learn habitually to fill in their planners. This does away with the annoying question that is otherwise asked repeatedly, "What are we doing today?" Provide an opening drill or study sheet or other quiet, individual assignment, and train students to begin it immediately after filling in the planner. If you use a prepared handout as the opening activity (often referred to as "bell ringer"), hand it to students as you greet them at the door. Some teachers use silent reading or journal writing as their opening activity. As students work, you can circulate, check on planners, and take roll.

> **FIELD APPLICATION 2:**   At a middle-level school, request information about yearly calendars and lesson plan books. Ask to see copies, if possible. Talk with a teacher about how she or he uses them, if you can.

Planning Lessons

Lesson plans contain the ideas, strategies, and techniques by which you instruct students. Find out what your administrator expects in the way of formal lesson plans. Your district or school may have a specific format for you to follow. If possible, ask to see examples. Devise lessons and units of instruction that are in keeping with the school curriculum guide. Estimate how much time you will need to:

- motivate and focus students and access prior knowledge;
- provide or access needed materials and resources;
- provide for presenting new information;
- provide for cooperative learning or seatwork;
- assess learning.

Write your plans in pencil, for you will often need to change them as you work. Consider formatting your lesson plans on the computer, which will save time and provide a clear, easily accessible record of what you and your students have accomplished. In addition to your daily lesson plans, prepare some activities and directions for emergency substitute teachers, should you need them. These plans can be one-day enrichment lessons or special self-contained units. They provide great peace of mind if you have to miss school. Also make two or three lesson plans involving high-interest activities and keep them on hand to use when, for whatever reason, your lesson plan for the day must be abandoned.

Handling Routine Matters

Checking Attendance

Keeping track of attendance is an hourly chore you must deal with quickly. Your grade book is the legal record of attendance and it is important that you keep records accurately. Use a seating chart, as suggested. Teacher Jim Hamilton has devised an attractive way of making them. Using a QuickCam and PageMaker® software, he snaps a digital photo of each student, adds their name, and puts the photos in place on the seating chart, which he can then print out. This chart is especially helpful to guest teachers.

Distributing and Collecting Materials

Good materials management is essential to smooth-running classes. Schools provide textbooks, workbooks, and worksheets, while students supply materials such as a three-ring binder, notebook paper, dividers, pencil pouch with pens and pencils, and a scientific calculator. Some students also carry with them colored pencils, scissors, a glue stick, and decorative pens. Many students will not have such materials unless the school provides them. Check to see if your school furnishes construction paper, markers, glue, and the like from a central supply location, or if the school gives you a budget for ordering supplies you need.

Materials kept in the classroom must be stored out of the way yet be easily obtained, distributed, and replaced. As materials are needed, students can receive them from supply monitors or get them from the shelves. Use class monitors to collect and return materials at the end of work periods.

School textbook and workbook policies also vary. Students are typically issued textbooks and workbooks for the class with the understanding they are responsible for reasonable care, must have the books in class as needed, must return them at the end of the semester or year, and must pay for any that are lost or severely damaged. Make sure you inform students and their families clearly as to which days the textbooks will be required in class. If you don't, the books are likely to be in lockers or at home when students need them. Some schools prefer to issue a class set of the texts and workbooks to each teacher who is then responsible for them. Teachers indicate how students are to use the books. The books can be stored on shelves or in cupboards. Class assistants distribute them when needed. Design a checkout procedure for students who wish to take the books home or use them for extra study.

Teach students how to use and care for instructional materials and give them reminders from time to time. Emphasize conservation and encourage recycling and reuse of construction paper and drawing paper.

Be sure to end activities in time for necessary cleanup. Otherwise, students will want to rush out the door when the bell rings, without cleaning up their area. Teach students to pick up stray paper, straighten their desks, and be seated before you dismiss them. Do not allow yourself to feel pressured by their exasperation in being made to wait until the room is clean. It won't take long for them to become efficient at getting the room tidy.

Procedures for Hall Passes

Passes are used when students must leave the room to go to the restroom, drinking fountain, health office, counseling office, or front office. Students will try to abuse their use, especially for visits to the restroom and health office. Draw students' attention to the class and/or school rule that requires students to use the restroom during passing periods, lunch, or PE. Most students will comply, although some will see what they can get away with. In an attempt to be fair to all students, some teachers issue three restroom passes to each student at the beginning of the grading period. Students use them at their own discretion, including going to the drinking fountain. Students sign out on a clipboard kept near the door for this purpose, indicating name, date, time, and destination. Students mark the time when they return, sign the pass, and clip it to the board. This procedure eliminates questions about how many passes each student has used. It also provides helpful information to the assistant principal in case of vandalism in the restrooms. Passes that students have remaining at the end of the grading period can be redeemed for bonus points or a modest treat, or entered into a raffle for a bigger prize.

Most students never request to go to the health office. A few must go there daily at given times to receive medication. Others have inhalers stored there in case of an asthma attack. Occasionally someone gets injured in PE. You may notice that some students ask to go to the health office right before time for a quiz or oral report. Others may decide, just as independent work begins, that they just can't wait any longer for a bag of ice for their sore finger. Tell these students that their presence in class is important and ask if they can stick it out. If they say no, write the pass and send them. The health office will take care of providing the ice and sending the student back to class, documenting their visit in a log. The health worker will call the parent and arrange for transportation home if the matter is serious. Don't waste the class's time by trying to determine if the student is "really" sick.

Procedures for Call Slips, Intercom Calls, and Other Interruptions

Sooner or later you will be in the midst of giving instructions or demonstrating a skill when the intercom buzzes, or a student office aide enters with a call slip, or an announcement is made over the intercom. A parent may have called and needs a message delivered to their child. A school health concern may have arisen, such as head lice and the need to check for them. Students may be called out to receive special services, counseling, or consultation with administrators. These and numerous other interruptions are disruptive and annoying. Remember, though, that the interruption is for a reason, and the person behind it is doing a necessary job.

Train a student assistant to sit near the intercom and answer with your name and room number and say, "Student speaking." If the information is not confidential, the student can pass on the information to the appropriate person without interrupting the lesson. If the information is an "all-call" over the loudspeaker, the message is for the entire student body and staff. The class should be trained to stop talking immediately so the message can be heard. As for call slips, the office monitor will most likely bring the slip to you so you can give it to the appropriate student. Office personnel do their best to keep interruptions to a minimum.

Dealing with Paper Communications

Set aside a time for going through your professional mail each day, both paper mail and electronic mail. If E-mail contains information you want to keep, print it out. Do your best to touch each piece of paper once only. Have files or a three-ring binder ready to receive information from the district, school board, or professional organizations. Keep files on all parent contacts, student disciplinary actions, and behavior contracts.

> **FIELD APPLICATION 3:** Observe in a classroom to determine how attendance is checked, how materials are distributed and collected, how hall passes are used and kept track of, and how student assistants (if any) are used.

Managing Instruction

As noted earlier, it is beyond the scope of this book to go into detail about the large variety of effective teaching methods, the purposes for which they are designed, and how they are used. If you are interested, consult Joyce, Weil, and Calhoun's *Models of Teaching* (2000). However, we will review a few management aspects of instruction that you might find useful, such as getting students' attention, giving instructions, helping with work habits, providing assistance during work time, and teaching students how to request help.

Getting Students' Attention

You should never try to instruct the class when you do not have everyone's attention. Normally, all you have to do is say something like, "Attention, everyone. Would you look at me, please." Because class activities are sometimes noisy, you may want to devise a signal that tells students they are to stop what they are doing immediately and give their attention to you. Some teachers flick the lights on and off. Others use a verbal cue, such as "Focus!" The important thing is the students know the signal and have rehearsed enough so they can comply without thinking. Be patient and consistent. Remember the students have several teachers who may use different signals.

Giving Instructions for Assigned Work

When giving work assignments, inform the students precisely what they are to do and when and how they are to do it. Every teacher complains about students' saying, "I don't know what to do," only seconds after receiving directions. The problem can be avoided by giving directions and, at the same time, jotting reminder notes on the board.

> Ladies and gentlemen, attention up here, please. Everyone. Thank you. Listen carefully to your assignment. At your desks I want you to do problems 2, 4, 6, 8, and 10 on page 32. [Jot "p. 32" on the board.] You may work quietly with your partner, and you'll have twenty minutes to complete your work. [Jot "quiet," "partner," and "20 min." on the board.] When you finish, put your papers in the in-basket. [Jot "in-basket."] Then you may pick up tonight's homework assignment and get a head start on it. [Jot "hw".] Once again, page 32, items 2, 4, 6, 8, 10. Work quietly with your partner. Put finished work in the in-basket, then begin homework. I'll circulate to help if you need me. OK, let's get to work.

This procedure suffices for most short assignments. When assigning a long-term project, print out an assignment sheet detailing the various components of the project and specific directions for completion. Provide examples if possible, as well as the due dates for each component, with one final due date for the whole project. A posted chart showing this information and reminders in your daily agenda will keep everyone on track.

Helping with Students' Work Habits

If you organize your class so it attends to student needs as described in Chapters 2 and 3, and if you establish a discipline system as described later in Chapter 7, your students will be on a good footing and should be able to work productively and enjoyably. It would be naïve, however, to suggest that students, even with those provisions, will never be inattentive, noisy, or inclined to procrastinate or goof off. Here are a few suggestions you may find helpful.

Dealing with Inattention

Students become inattentive to your lessons for the following reasons:

- They find the topic or activity boring.
- They get stuck and don't know what to do.
- They have become overly satiated—that is, they have had all of it they can stand for the time being.
- Their minds are focused somewhere else.

To limit inattention, make sure topics and activities are interesting. If you are unsure about new activities, be ready to fall back on those you know students enjoy, such as group work, role playing, or doing dramatizations. Make sure students know why the topic is valuable and what they are supposed to do. If lessons go on too long, break them into smaller parts and insert rest periods or other activities. For lessons that tend to drag, use Say-See-Do teaching, which maintains high levels of teacher–student interaction. If these efforts fail, ask students if something is bothering them. If they have concerns, decide whether they should be discussed at this time.

Dealing with Noise

Middle school students can be loud, especially when engaged in discussions or debates or when telling a story to a group of classmates. If you have assigned collaborative creative work, the noise level may become disconcerting. Even if you tolerate noise well, don't assume neighboring classes and teachers appreciate it. When noise reaches a certain level, signal for immediate attention, explain that the noise level is too high for comfort, and ask the students to make a conscious effort to speak more quietly. If it gets too noisy again, you might change the activity to "E-mail," a time when pairs of students conduct their discussions by writing messages to each other.

Dealing with Procrastination

Many students habitually procrastinate and can't seem to get things done on time. Even the best disciplined among us have difficulty maintaining focus when working at unexciting tasks or those that are too complicated or too long. To avoid procrastination among your students:

- Keep instructional tasks as interesting and as short as possible while covering what is intended.
- Break long tasks into a series of shorter steps, and place a deadline on the completion of each step.
- Emphasize a time limit and occasionally call out the amount of time remaining. Or, use a timer to display time on the overhead. Students can monitor the time and their progress.
- Use incentives. "As soon as everyone has finished, we can play Jeopardy®" (or some other preferred activity).

Dealing with Note-Passing

All teachers, when scanning students' eyes during an enthralling lesson, occasionally notice a student who is enraptured by a note received. When that happens, don't take it personally. Calmly ask the student to put the note in a box you keep handy and tell the student he or she can have it back later. You can subsequently discuss the matter with the student, if you wish, but for the present do as little as possible to disrupt your lesson. Never read the note aloud to the class. That shows lack of respect for students' feelings. However, do advise the class in advance that, if you intercept a note, for the interest of student safety you may read it privately and discuss the contents with school counselors.

Providing Assistance during Work Time

As students work individually at assigned activities, they invariably encounter difficulties that require your assistance. We have a few suggestions for helping students avoid or overcome those difficulties.

Directions and Reminders.   Give directions clearly and briefly. Post visual reminders if they are needed and allow students who have forgotten part of the assignment to ask other students for help.

Teacher Movement.   To provide assistance efficiently, you must be able to reach each student quickly. You have taken this into account when arranging class seating. Some teachers prefer to move in a predetermined pattern among the desks to be near students, comment on their work, and give help in a regular rotation. Others prefer to station themselves centrally to observe all students at work and move quickly toward those who show signs of difficulty. Your visibility and proximity help students remain on-task.

Providing Help Efficiently

Students who require assistance should receive it quickly, in no more than a few seconds' time. Fredric Jones (2001) reports that teachers typically spend an average of about four minutes per student when giving individual help. He says teachers question the student and then wait for a reply, which may be erroneous, fumbling, or non-forthcoming. Instead of questioning students, Jones would have teachers do the following, in twenty seconds or less:

- At first contact, quickly find anything the student has done correctly and mention it favorably, such as, "Good job up to here."
- Give a straightforward prompt that will get the student working again, such as, "Watch the decimal" or "That word means . . . "
- Leave immediately, being sure to pay brief attention to the work of nearby students who have not requested help.

Jones maintains that this technique of rapid movement has two positive effects: it allows you to help more students during work time, and it breaks down the dependency syndrome in which students raise their hands helplessly and wait. Jones says, "Be positive, be brief, and be gone."

Harry and Rosemary Wong (1998) mention how distracting it is for students to raise hands to get your attention. They advise teaching students to hold up fingers to signal in accordance with a predetermined system. For example, the index finger indicates the student wishes to speak, two fingers requests permission to leave seat, and three fingers means the teacher's help is needed. Other suggestions involve placement of a textbook or an index card to indicate that help is requested.

Students can rely on fellow students for help as well. Many teachers emphasize mutual assistance, especially in cooperative learning. The teacher may tell students, "Ask three, then me." When students have to wait for help, they know to move ahead to the next exercise if they can. If unable to do that, they take out a book and read silently until help is available.

> **FIELD APPLICATION 4:**   Obtain permission to observe how a teacher introduces a lesson, gets students' attention, gives directions, provides new information, and helps students at work.

Dealing with Emergencies

Your school has established procedures to follow in the event of fire, earthquake, tornadoes, and bomb threats or gunfire on campus. These procedures will have been carefully planned and you are expected to know and follow them exactly. You are responsible for your students in these situations. Together you should practice the required routines until every student knows exactly what to do. You must take these drills seriously and convey the seriousness to students as a matter of life and death. Set high standards for student compliance and accept nothing less.

Making Visits Outside the Classroom

Your class will probably routinely attend school assemblies, visit the library, go to the computer lab, and go outside for lessons. Decide how students are to move from place to place and train them accordingly. Do you want them in lines? Do you want quiet in the hallways? Where are they to be seated? How should they enter when they arrive? Students will meet your expectations if you make them very clear. Review the expectations to make sure students understand. Should students not comply with the standards you have set, have them turn around and start over again. This will help them understand you mean what you say.

Receiving Visitors to the Class

Visitors come to your class from time to time, including administrators, family members, and other teachers. Teach your class to expect these visitors and to acknowledge them and make them comfortable. You might wish to assign a student assistant the task of greeting visitors and showing them to a chair kept available for this purpose. Visitors who are there to evaluate you or the class may want to keep a low profile and not disturb the dynamic. If you want to introduce the visitor to the class, do so. At least inform the class who the person is and why he or she is there. This satisfies students' curiosity so they can return to the lesson.

Preparing for Guest (Substitute) Teachers

All teachers occasionally miss class for one reason or another, and at such times a guest teacher has to fill in. Adolescent students are prone to baiting substitute teachers and making work difficult for them. To make things go well, write up plans a day or two in advance, ready in case of emergency illness. Appoint two students per class to help the substitute locate needed materials, answer questions about routines, and provide other help. Make sure all students know guest teachers are to be treated with consideration and helped, not hindered. Have an up-to-date seating chart available with attendance sheets. Also provide a copy of behavior agreements. Include your teaching schedule and the names of neighboring teachers. Ask the guest teacher to leave you a note about what was accomplished, who helped, and who hindered.

Dealing with Completed Work

One of a teacher's most time-consuming tasks is dealing with completed work. Teachers routinely take home stacks of papers to be checked, graded, recorded, and returned. The following suggestions will help you more easily manage this burdensome task.

Receiving Completed Work

Harry and Rosemary Wong (1998) suggest teaching students to pass completed work to the side, across the rows, rather than up the rows to the front. Instead of passing the papers from hand to hand, students should place the stack of papers on the next student's desk, and so forth. If your students are seated at tables, ask them to place their papers at a designated spot on the table. Then a student assistant can pick up all of the papers and place them in a basket. At the end of the day or period you can move papers from the basket to a folder for correction and recording.

Checking Completed Work

Even though you have asked students to turn in their work, it is not necessary to check everything in detail. Much independent work is for practice only and necessary feedback can be given as you circulate and monitor students while they work in class. Advise your students that the homework or class work will be discussed the next day, at which time they can make corrections, a valuable part of the learning process. Prompt feedback is important, for it usually pinpoints erroneous concepts and allows students to make adjustments. Of course you should check student work when judgment or very accurate correction is required and when the work is done for a grade. And make sure you correct any work you want students to take home with them. Parents are almost certain to notice errors you might not have marked.

As for tests and quizzes, it is better that you grade all of them yourself. True, it is daunting to face 150+ exams, so consider varying the formats for easier checking. For some tests, students can put their answers on Scantron forms that can be machine-checked. This gives students practice in taking standardized tests.

Returning Completed Work

When work you have checked is ready to return to students, clearly explain:

- what you want students to do with the work;
- where the work should be kept if it is to be retained;
- whether students should record their scores or grades in the grade log;
- whether students should redo the work to improve quality;
- how long students have to complete any modifications.

Unless you communicate your requirements clearly, most students will glance at their score or grade and then throw the work away. Unless you want students to improve their papers during class, return them at the end of a period, rather than during work time. Otherwise, students will surely drop what they are doing to look at the scores and then express elation, resignation, or distress.

Managing Homework

The value of homework continues to be debated, with effective teachers holding different views. However, graded homework assignments seem to provide substantial academic benefits for students, perhaps because they make more effort when they know their work will be graded. Homework can also help students learn time management and develop responsibility for their own learning. The following suggestions might help make homework a more valuable educational experience.

- Keep the homework burden relatively light.
- Make it something especially interesting and worthwhile. Don't assign busy work or tasks that are boring and tedious.
- Speak with students about its value to them.
- Involve parents or family members to a limited extent such as requesting they discuss homework and class activities with their child. You may encourage parents to work along with students on some of the assignments.
- Grade the homework or assess it otherwise, and later conduct class activities that build on the independent work.

Absent Students and Makeup Work

Unless you establish a procedure to help absent students make up assignments they have missed, they will ask at inopportune times, "Did I miss anything yesterday?" You then feel obliged to stop what you are doing (such as starting the day's lesson) and get the materials and explain them, or put them off until later, hoping you don't forget. If possible, post homework assignments on your school's Homework Hotline or Web site and keep it up-to-date. Also make sure each student in your class has one or more "study buddies" they can contact about the day's assignments. These partnerships should be set up at the beginning of the semester or year, complete with telephone numbers. Place needed papers in an "Absent Student" folder. When students return, they can obtain the papers. Ask students to copy the planner from another student for the days they missed.

Students should know where and when to access the folder containing the papers you have set aside for them. You must have a policy on how much time is allowed to complete the work they missed. Keep in mind the student has makeup work in other classes in addition to yours. A general rule of thumb is to allow two days' makeup time for each day missed.

Dismissing the Class

When the period draws to an end, allow time for cleanup. Have students remain seated until dismissed. Use the last few minutes to review what was learned that day, anticipate tomorrow's lesson, provide last-minute reminders, and compliment students for their cooperation. Stand at the door as students leave so you can wish them a good day or pass along a private word of praise. Be very clear about what you expect. Otherwise, students will start "packing up" several minutes before the period ends and try to line up at the door. Teach students it is you, not the bell, who dismisses class.

Assessment and Evaluation

One of your major duties is to keep track of each student's progress toward class goals. This is done for four reasons: (1) to identify areas of strength and weakness in student learning;

(2) to maintain records of student performance in school, which are useful when students seek employment or wish to pursue higher education; (3) to be able to report to parents how well their child has been doing in school; and (4) to help in establishing levels of performance for the school, state, and nation.

For the most part, the responsibility for assessment, evaluation, and reporting falls to individual teachers. Teachers seldom receive much training in assessment and evaluation, yet are expected to make those determinations accurately, objectively, and fairly, and, further, to assign grades commensurate with student performance. These tasks are burdensome and troubling for most teachers. Here are some suggestions you might find helpful.

Goals and Standards

Make sure you have a clear understanding of what your students are supposed to be accomplishing. Normal expectations are found in curriculum guides, teachers' manuals that accompany textbooks, standards set by school districts and individual schools, and standards set forth nationally. The goals and standards to be assessed will normally be of three types:

- content, which focuses on *knowledge*—that is, the information that should be learned;
- skills, which focus on students' abilities to perform certain *mental procedures* (e.g., think critically, solve problems, follow mathematical algorithms) and *physical procedures* (e.g., use a keyboard, play a musical instrument, make technical drawings);
- values and character traits, such as effort, self-control, responsibility, ability to get along with others, and so forth.

Terminology

Teachers both assess and evaluate students in the three foregoing categories. In *assessment* you find out the extent to which students have progressed toward the established goals. This is normally done in two ways, by observing students and having them take tests. In *evaluation* you make judgments about how well students are doing, either in terms of established expectations or by comparing their performance against that of students elsewhere. When evaluation is done in terms of expectations, it is called "criterion referenced." When done in terms of comparisons against others, it is called "norm referenced."

For many years norm-referenced evaluation predominated in U. S. education, and it still holds for standardized tests, such as achievement tests used in virtually all schools. Recently, increased emphasis has been placed on criterion-referenced evaluation. Here, one does not compare students against each other, but instead judges the progress students have made toward class or grade expectations. Increasingly, students are being brought into the evaluation process, where they, too, assess their efforts and make judgments about progress and quality. A popular strategy is to teach students to evaluate their mastery of stated objectives by asking them to select and perfect samples of their work for inclusion in personal portfolios.

Newer Alternative Procedures in Assessment

All teachers struggle to determine, accurately and fairly, how well their students are learning. In the past, this process often included little more than graded assignments and occasional tests. The grades on those efforts were about all the feedback students got on their performance. Newer efforts, however, entail *ongoing assessment,* in which student efforts and progress are continually monitored. The process is in keeping with the meaning of the word *assessment,* which comes from a Latin root meaning to "sit beside as a second judge." *Assessment* in its best sense involves the teacher working alongside the students, offering feedback and guidance. The teacher gives instructions to the students, then coaches them as they complete their work, providing continual feedback about what is working, what is not, and what needs to be done differently. This process is not one-sided: students and teacher both have input and both consider what the other has to say. The resultant repeating cycle of performance and feedback is very helpful to student understanding and skill development.

But what kind of feedback do you give in this approach? First, students must know what they are expected to do and learn. The feedback you give them as they work is mostly informal: responses to their questions, comments to students as they work, and suggestions that help them keep on track or clarify or change focus as needed. By working in this way, your students' results are a reflection of your own efforts as well as theirs. This is not a contest of wills, in which you try to make students learn. It is a cooperative effort to help them learn, and you can accept some of the accolades (or blame) for their accomplishments. As this process continues, students acquire skills of working cooperatively with each other and being able to conduct assessment in cooperation with their peers.

Procedures and Devices in Alternative Assessment

Students are informally assessed by teachers all the time, not only with regard to achievement but also to effort, relationships with others, and class behavior. Some of those informal assessments are ultimately given a grade or mark on the report card. In the past, these judgments were made without reliance on formalized devices and procedures. Now, alternative assessment procedures help teachers more reliably understand what is happening with each student. The following are some of the devices and procedures educators presently use to advantage.

Concept maps—diagrams that show the essential concepts of the unit of instruction and their relationships, giving a picture of what students are supposed to learn and are learning.

Learning logs and *book response journals*—places for students to express personal reactions and to ask questions about ideas encountered in the material being learned, for reflection and learning to express themselves better.

Cooperative learning activities—activities structured so that the group works together toward a common goal, with each individual being accountable in the process.

Discussions—class discussions that encourage students to express opinions, listen and respond to others, acknowledge feelings, and make suggestions.

Response groups—small groups of students who have read the same book or studied the same events or ideas and subsequently share their observations, reactions, and conclusions.

Demonstrations—observable formats such as performances, drawings, paintings, photography, music, dramatic presentation, or oral presentations such as speeches, debates, and analyses in which students express their understanding of ideas.

Comparison organizers—devices often used in literature study to allow students to show their understanding of similarities and differences in character, mood, theme, setting, and plot. Similar organizers using appropriate criteria are used in other subjects as well.

Portfolios—collections of individual students' work completed over time. Students collect, select, and reflect on each piece they choose for inclusion in the portfolio. This helps greatly with ongoing assessment and offers an opportunity for students to look back, see what they have accomplished, and consider how their efforts can be improved further.

Elizabeth Hebert (1998) and her colleagues studied student portfolio use over a ten-year period and concluded that:

- students need help understanding the purpose of portfolios so they can make their selections accordingly;
- students assign more importance than at first expected to selecting and organizing work for inclusion in the portfolio;
- rigid standards concerning what should be included are not helpful because there is no correct list of items to include;
- parents or guardians need detailed information about portfolios and how they are used (see McTighe's comments in the next paragraph);
- frequent opportunities are needed to celebrate progress evident in the portfolios;
- portfolios and standardized testing, combined, provide much greater insight into students' progress than does either alone.

Jay McTighe (1996/1997) has reported the benefits she sees, as a principal, in her school's use of portfolios:

- much improved documentation of student progress;
- basis provided for faculty to acknowledge instructional successes and refine instructional strategies;
- increased parental attention to, and support for, the school program because students explain portfolios to their families;
- greater sense of student ownership of their learning.

In the past, students have felt that assessment is something done to them, not a process in which they are involved. Portfolios and other newer assessment procedures allow them to participate in meaningful analyses, receive helpful feedback from others, refine their work accordingly, and get still more feedback before their work has reached completion.

Designing and Using Rubrics

A rubric is an assessment guide that teachers and students can use jointly. It lists the criteria for evaluating a piece of work and provides examples of quality, ranging from excellent to poor. Rubrics are used to clarify the teacher's expectations when an assignment is given, and they make it easier to show students how to meet expectations and take responsibility for doing quality work. Rubrics are most effective if students are involved in their design. Proceed as follows:

- introduce the concept of rubrics, explain what they mean, and show some examples;
- show students samples of previous students' work (anonymous, of course) that reflect various levels of quality, as described in the rubric;
- guide the class in discussing the factors that differentiate between levels of quality;
- describe the characteristics of high-quality work and emphasize that high quality is the level students are striving for;
- help the students put into their own words the various levels of quality and show them how to use objective language rather than vague terms such as *neat* or *creative;*
- write out the student expressions and explain they are criteria that will be used to judge quality (explain what the word *criteria* means);
- limit the number of performance criteria so they can all be observed in one product or performance;
- agree on the completed rubric and post it in the class before students begin work;
- refer to the list of criteria when discussing progress with students and encourage them to use the list when working together or evaluating their work.

Grading

Ultimately you have to assign a mark or "grade" to individual students, based on their performance. For decades grading has been, and remains, a major source of frustration and stress for teachers and students alike. There are so many decisions to make in grading. How good is good? What levels of performance should be labeled with the grading letters or marks? Is late work acceptable, and is it judged with the same criteria as work done on time? Will you ask students to redo work that isn't up to standard? Can students retake tests they have failed? What if a student gets A's on every test but turns in no homework?

Questions like these have prompted teachers to develop assessment rubrics, for use in making judgments about the quality of students' work. While rubrics are helpful and provide a broad basis for making judgments, they can't be used in place of grades. Although various marking systems have been used in the past, anything other than letter grades seems to confuse parents and guardians, most of whom are familiar with the traditional grades. Moreover, school districts remain bound to grades because that is what universities want, and that demand is passed down to high schools and, in turn, to middle schools.

So what principles should you follow in grading? The following is probably your best course: to assign grades as accurately and objectively as possible, provide ample opportunities for students to demonstrate their learning and keep many samples to back up your judgment. Help students see a clear connection between their efforts and the grades they receive. For fairness in grading, formulate a very clear grading policy and communicate it well. Robert Marzano (2000) suggests using a rubric with scores assigned to each quality descriptor, with the recommendation that teachers use scores with half-point increments, making the judgment more accurate. Keep many scores and marks for each student in your records.

Students will not see grades in the same light you do. Barbara Davis (1993) points out that many students consider grades to be signs of approval or disapproval and take them very personally. You may have heard students say, when receiving less than an optimal grade, "Mr. Smathers doesn't like me." Or, if the grade is very good, they may say, "Thanks a lot, Miss Romero, for giving me the A." When Miss Romero replies that the student earned the grade, the student smiles knowingly, often not really believing it.

Discuss these matters with your students and try to help them understand that the function of grades is to communicate each student's level of learning *at a particular time.* Some authorities advise you to base grades solely on academic performance, without considering a student's behavior, effort, participation, attendance, punctuality, or attitude. Others think it important to consider effort and participation. You can make this judgment. In any case, don't let grades come as a surprise to students. Keep students fully and clearly informed about how well they are doing.

QUESTIONS

1. In this book we have considered, among other things, curriculum, instruction, behavior management, and management of procedures and incidentals. How would you describe the relationships among those four aspects of teaching?

2. What are your preferences concerning how "rich" to make the classroom environment, so an advantageous balance is struck among stimulation, usefulness, and clutter? Do you think this is mostly a personal preference, or is there an objective logic behind a preferred balance?

3. How would you arrange seating to be amenable with the activities you would emphasize?

4. How much importance would you assign to matters such as checking attendance, distributing and collecting materials, and monitoring hall passes? Explain.

5. Checking completed student work, including homework, can be an enormously time-consuming task. Do you think you would check all such work? If not, how would you give feedback to students?

6. What would you do to make sure you are following school expectations concerning grading and reporting?

ACTIVITIES

1. Diagram how you would set up the physical environment of your classroom, showing seating patterns, teacher station, storage areas, display areas, and so forth.

2. Describe what you would include in a folder you would keep available for guest (substitute) teachers. Would you want them to report to you about the class? How?

3. Describe how you would prefer to evaluate student work and keep records of student performance. Explain your preferences concerning homework, including how much, what kind, parental involvement, checking, and giving feedback to students.

REFERENCES

Davis, B. 1993. Grading practices. *Tools for teaching.* <http://uga.berkeley.edu/sled/bgd/grading.html>.

Hebert, E. 1998. Lessons learned about student portfolios. *Kappan Online Article.* <www.pdkintl.org/kappan/kheb9804.htm>.

Jones, F. 2001. *Fred Jones's tools for teaching.* Santa Cruz, CA: Fredric H. Jones & Associates.

Joyce, B., Weil, M., and Calhoun, E. 2000. *Models of teaching* (6th ed.). Boston: Allyn & Bacon.

Marzano, R. 2000. Transforming classroom grading. <www.ascd.org/readingroom/books/marzano00 book.html>.

McTighe, J. 1996/1997. What happens between assessments? *Educational Leadership 54* (4). <http://www.ascd.org/readingroom/edlead/9612/mctighe.html>.

Wong. H. 2001. (selection of tips for teachers). <www.glavac.com/harrywong.htm>.

Wong, H., and Wong, R. 1998. *The first days of school.* Singapore: Harry K. Wong.

7 Promoting Desirable Behavior in Your Classroom

Chapter Preview

This chapter presents information to help you encourage and maintain desirable behavior in your classes. It defines undesirable behavior and points out its detrimental effects on teaching and learning. Conditions that promote misbehavior are identified, as are the places and people who may be at fault. Suggestions are given for eliminating or softening the undesirable conditions and replacing them with effective alternatives that enable students to work harmoniously with you and each other.

Extent and Effects of Student Misbehavior

Undesirable student behavior—also known as misbehavior or poor discipline—is badly interfering with teaching and learning. Increasing numbers of students are disrespectful to teachers and others, disdainful of teacher requests, and inclined to incite trouble in the class. Many are lethargic and make little effort, seeming not to care whether they learn. They find little pleasure in school except for association with friends. Distressing numbers of these students, although physically present, have, for all practical purposes, dropped out of the educational process.

This situation perplexes and frustrates teachers, who believe all students can learn, especially within an environment of camaraderie, enjoyment, and goodwill. They truly want their students to profit from the educational opportunity they are afforded. But, despite their efforts, not many teachers enjoy the level of success they hope for, and they realize that, because of some students' misbehavior, even their best-behaved students are not learning as much as they could or should.

The increase in misbehavior and the slowdown in learning have been with us since the 1960s. We have tried to counter both by setting higher standards, shaping students up, keeping them on-task, and monitoring them very closely. Experience is at last teaching us, however, that we cannot force students to learn or behave as we want them to, no matter how high we set standards or how much we scold, reprimand, coerce, force, bribe, punish, or demand. Those tactics simply don't work with today's students, and, in fact, never made students actually want to learn or behave well. We now realize those outdated tactics produce student resentment, resistance, and desire to escape from demands of the classroom.

Student misbehavior presents the greatest obstacle to your success in teaching. It has the potential even to destroy your career. But it can be managed positively, so that students enjoy school and you enjoy teaching. Please take very seriously the suggestions made in this chapter. Nothing else you learn about teaching will serve you better.

The Meanings of Undesirable Behavior, Desirable Behavior, Discipline, and Behavior Management

Undesirable Behavior

Undesirable behavior has no clear definition, although we will soon assign it one. Essentially it is the same as misbehavior, which most people think of as kids' doing what they know they shouldn't. Some people feel that cheating, lying, showing disrespect for adults, and intimidating others are always misbehavior, regardless of the circumstances in which they occur. Confusion about the term has caused psychologist Thomas Gordon (1989) to conclude that *misbehavior* is a label teachers and parents apply to any behavior they disapprove of, regardless of what it is or where it occurs.

Here we will define the term a bit more precisely. Let's agree first that undesirable behavior in the classroom is any behavior that intentionally damages learning or personal relationships. With that in mind, let's define *undesirable behavior* and *misbehavior*—as applied to the classroom: undesirable classroom behavior (or misbehavior) is any behavior that, through intent or thoughtlessness,

1. interferes with teaching or learning,
2. threatens or intimidates others, or
3. oversteps society's standards of moral, ethical, or legal behavior.

There are thirteen types of undesirable behavior regularly seen in classes everywhere.

1. *Inattention*—daydreaming, doodling, looking out the window, thinking about things irrelevant to the lesson
2. *Apathy*—a general disinclination to participate, sulking, not caring, not wanting to try or do well
3. *Needless talk*—chatting during instructional time about things unrelated to the lesson
4. *Moving about the room*—getting up and moving about without permission, congregating in parts of the room
5. *Annoying others*—provoking, teasing, picking at, calling names
6. *Disruption*—shouting out during instruction, talking and laughing inappropriately, causing "accidents"
7. *Lying*—deliberate falsification to avoid accepting responsibility or admitting wrongdoing or to get others in trouble

8. *Stealing*—taking things that belong to others
9. *Cheating*—making false representations or wrongly taking advantage of others for personal benefit
10. *Sexual harassment*—making others uncomfortable through touching, sex-related language, or sexual innuendo
11. *Aggression and fighting*—showing hostility toward others, threatening them, shoving, pinching, wrestling, hitting
12. *Malicious mischief*—doing damage intentionally to school property or the belongings of others
13. *Defiance of authority*—talking back to the teacher, hostilely refusing to do as the teacher requests.

We normally think of misbehavior as pertaining only to students, but teachers sometimes misbehave in the classroom too, as we shall see.

Desirable Behavior

Fundamentally, desirable classroom behavior is that which shows consideration and respect for others. We like to add other attributes as well, such as cooperation and helpfulness. This definition departs somewhat from the traditional meaning of *good behavior,* which connotes obedience, acquiescence, keeping quiet, doing as directed, and remaining somewhat subservient. Oftentimes, behavior that is quiet and subservient does not promote initiative, taking risks, or assuming responsibility. Most of us who taught years ago deemed behavior good or bad in terms of "how people were supposed to behave." We had the feeling we should stifle bad behavior, not only because it interfered with teaching and learning, but because it simply was not how human beings were supposed to behave.

Many teachers still hold that view, but when we reflect on why students should be respectful, why they should be considerate, why they should do their work, and why they shouldn't bother others, we begin to gain a more pragmatic concept of behavior as a means of promoting learning. Behavior that increases educational opportunity can rightly be called "desirable." When we help our students behave considerately, our classes function better and everyone profits. We know many ways to encourage that kind of behavior, as you will see in this chapter and the next.

Discipline

Most people think of discipline as either (1) overall behavior in the classroom (i.e., Mr. Jones has good discipline in his class) or (2) what teachers do to make students behave, such as scoldings, threats, admonition, punishment, or other attempts to "make" students do as they are told. While these two concepts will probably stay with us for some time to come, neither indicates what we try to achieve in today's classes. The former concept of discipline, per se, is falling by the wayside. We are abandoning the notion that forceful techniques can be used to "correct" students who do not live up to expected standards of behavior.

Behavior Management

Behavior management refers to what we do to help students conduct themselves desirably, as concerns relations with classmates and teachers. We do not use behavior management to force students to behave in any particular way, because we know that force is ineffective, actually counterproductive. Neither do we try to condition students unknowingly to behave in particular ways. We are aboveboard in all matters of classroom behavior. We explain what is needed for the best and most enjoyable learning and draw students into working cooperatively with us to bring about a classroom that fosters goodwill and promotes learning. Instead of unpleasant force, we use positive enticement. We provide intriguing activities and a pleasant environment in which to learn. We involve students in making decisions, including class agreements about work and behavior. We provide encouragement and support. We try to eliminate conditions that might encourage misbehavior, and we try to be good models for our students. When students have difficulties, we help them work things through.

What Effective Behavior Management Accomplishes

Behavior management is supportive and encouraging, never abrasive, demanding, or coercive. It is a way of drawing students into considerate cooperation with the teacher and other students. By taking this respectful, helpful approach, we can usually accomplish the conditions described in the following paragraphs.

1. Maintaining an Effective Environment for Learning
The prime purpose of education is to help the young acquire attitudes, values, skills, and information that improve the quality of their lives and society as a whole. Such learning occurs best in environments that are reasonably well ordered, free from threat, relatively free from disruptions, and encouraging of exploration and interaction.

2. Promoting Good Personal Relations
Our personal sense of accomplishment and satisfaction is dependent in large measure on how we are treated by others. The treatment we receive from others depends in part on how we treat them. Most of us want to be accorded respect, accepted as worthwhile, and treated with consideration. We are more likely to get what we want when we accord those same things to others. We want to enjoy friendships and to be able to work with others harmoniously, so we must do our part there, too. When we have disagreements, we want to resolve them equitably while maintaining positive feelings. We cannot expect to enjoy any of those things unless we treat others with respect. Effective behavior management emphasizes the golden rule. At times it also requires us to teach students how to speak effectively with others, cooperate, and show respect and consideration.

3. Helping Students Develop Self-Control
Personal self-control enables students to learn better. It helps them maintain a sense of purpose and direction and avoid incidents that take them on tangents or lead to damaging con-

frontations. One of the major purposes of behavior management is to help students develop inner discipline, the ability to control and direct themselves in various situations.

4. Heightening Students' Sense of Purpose

Humans desire to find meaning in life. Meaning refers to understanding, of course, but also includes sense of purpose. Each of us, knowingly or unknowingly, tries to clarify what is important to us, how our lives are made better by those things, how we can best pursue them, and how we can avoid damaging others or the environment in that pursuit. Effective behavior management helps students develop a clearer sense of purpose concerning what they wish to experience, what they want to learn, and how they want their lives to progress.

5. Fostering a Sense of Responsibility

Our society emphasizes individual freedom of choice, as concerns expression, activity, and relationships. However, in a democratic society all freedoms must be linked to responsibility, meaning the rights of others must be taken into account and not transgressed. Responsibility entails showing consideration, behaving ethically, and accepting the legitimate consequences of one's behavior, whether positive or negative. Effective behavior management heightens student initiative and choice, but is always anchored in responsibility.

Strategies Used in Behavior Management

We have seen that behavior management is intended to promote safe and encouraging classrooms, good personal relations, self-control, sense of purpose, and sense of responsibility. These qualities, in combination, provide a fertile environment for learning. We have seen, too, that effective behavior management is enticing rather than coercive. Please give up once and for all any feeling that you can, with good results, make students do anything they don't want to do. When you use force, students resist. When you make demands, they subvert them. When you speak derogatorily, they lose respect for you. When you treat them inconsiderately, they lose trust in you. When you lecture them, they tune you out. It is true that, when you have very highly motivated learners (or very fearful ones), you can deal with them abrasively and get good results. But most students in school today are not highly motivated to do as you want, some are not very afraid of you, and a few are quite willing to defy you in front of others.

Instead of trying to rely on forceful tactics, adopt an approach in which you try to energize students, draw them to you, and make them want to cooperate with you. Be friendly. Speak directly to each student as often as possible. Make yourself accessible to them. Try to understand and accept them. Try to meet their needs. Use personal charisma to enliven your classes. Teach topics students find interesting, and, when that is not possible, employ instructional activities students are known to like.

When you do these things, you build trust with students. You show you are on their side, trying to help, rather than opposing their wishes. But, at the same time, you never say, "Hey, kids, anything goes in here. Do whatever you like." You remain purposeful and resolute. You believe in good learning and quality teaching, and you make that belief clear. If you treat students well, they begin to feel at ease with you. They take an interest in your life (don't encourage them too far in this direction). They see you as a human being with needs similar to their own. They begin to like you, respect you, and trust you. They begin wanting to please you. They lose interest in disrupting class and making your life difficult. They tell friends and family members you are a good teacher. They work with you and remember you years later with fondness and appreciation. That is what makes teaching so rewarding. All this becomes possible when you truly help students and treat them with consideration.

Preventing Misbehavior

Continually having to deal with misbehavior has driven many teachers to distraction. No one flourishes in such conditions. Through relatively little effort, however, you can prevent most undesirable behavior from ever occurring in the first place. Prevention is the key, and it can be accomplished through the following: (1) attending to students' needs, (2) addressing and removing catalysts of misbehavior, (3) emphasizing student dignity, (4) enhancing personal relations, (5) developing student character, and (6) establishing trust. If you put these six strategies in place, and if you and your students give them ongoing attention, you will have an enjoyable and satisfying class in which students learn and prosper. Let's examine these preventive techniques more closely.

Attending to Student Needs

Chapter 2 presented a discussion of eight basic needs that motivate student (and teacher) behavior. Psychologists began giving serious attention to needs some time ago. As early as 1943, Abraham Maslow (see Maslow, 1954) described his famous "hierarchy of needs," which he believed provided the key to understanding human motivation and personality. The relationship between needs and motivation in school was later explained well by psychiatrist Rudolf Dreikurs (see Dreikurs and Cassel, 1972), who taught that all students have a primary goal (need) for belonging. When that primary goal is not satisfied, students turn to the "mistaken goals" of seeking attention, seeking power, seeking revenge, and withdrawal, all of which can constitute misbehavior in the classroom. William Glasser, also a psychiatrist and a major authority in school discipline, set forth a somewhat different explanation of needs that underlie student behavior (see Glasser, 1998). He listed survival, belonging, power, fun, and freedom as predominant needs that motivate students in today's schools and stressed the importance of satisfying those needs. More recently, educational psychologist C. M. Charles (2002) set forth an expanded list of student needs that motivate behavior in middle schools: sex, security, belonging, hope, dignity, power, enjoyment, and competence.

Although human needs are essentially the same for everyone, they vary in intensity according to age and individual personality. Also, different people try to satisfy them in somewhat different ways. In school, those attempts frequently result in undesirable behavior. If you help students meet or otherwise deal with their needs in a positive manner, you will simultaneously help them behave better in the classroom. (Of course you need to meet your needs, too, without misbehaving while doing so.) Let's take a moment to review some of the needs and what you can do to help (the following material is condensed from the more lengthy exploration presented in Chapter 2).

The Need for Security.   Provide an environment that is safe from threat and harm, not only to physical harm but also psychological harm from bullying, teasing, taunting, name-calling, fear of failure, fear of teacher disapproval, and fear of speaking in front of the group. Show students personal attention and kindness. Discuss the importance of all class members helping each other feel comfortable. Stress acceptance without disapproval of others' appearance and mannerisms.

The Need for Belonging.   Give students your personal attention everyday and encourage camaraderie. Exchange pleasant words with all students regularly. Make provisions for them to participate meaningfully in groups. Give them responsibilities for seeing after the well-being of other students and the class environment.

The Need for Hope.   Encourage students to learn meaningful information and skills in areas of personal interest. Draw attention to their successes. Help them document what they have learned. Discuss new learnings they might acquire in the future. Allow them to work cooperatively or investigate topics of strong personal interest. Try everyday to make sure they encounter something that makes school seem worthwhile and their progress satisfying.

The Need for Dignity.   Always show respect for your students and insist that they treat each other the same way. Interact with them as social equals and competent and valued members of the class, able to take on important tasks responsibly. Talk with them personally. If necessary, conduct lessons that teach students how to react appropriately when threatened or provoked.

The Need for Power.   Bring students into collaborative decision making and put them in charge of tasks important to the class. Consider assigning duties such as distributing and collecting materials, checking roll, taking care of instructional media, handling electronic equipment, taking care of class plants or animals, keeping the room clean, greeting visitors, serving as ambassadors to other classes, and the like. Call on all students for input in class discussions and decisions, but make sure you don't allow any of them to dominate the class or your attention.

The Need for Enjoyment.   Provide instructional topics and activities that are especially engaging. When appropriate, allow students to work together. Maintain a balanced sense of humor and share a good laugh and a joke from time to time. Call attention to the fun and enjoyment that can be found in most matters, including most subjects in the curriculum. Help them see that one of the most enjoyable things in school is exploring topics of special interest, learning them well, and sharing knowledge with others.

The Need for Competence.   Provide opportunity, encouragement, and support for students to become excellent in academics, physical skills, special interests, and other matters they consider important. Find ways for them to demonstrate new capabilities to themselves, peers, families, and others and help them keep tangible records that document their growth.

> **FIELD APPLICATION 1:**   You will find it interesting and enlightening to ask students what they think misbehavior is. Ask questions that orient their thinking in accordance with the definition of undesirable behavior presented earlier. Discuss the thirteen types with the students and see if they agree that they constitute misbehavior. Ask them if they believe they could work with teachers, as a team, to prevent those misbehaviors from occurring.

Catalysts of Misbehavior

By "catalyst of misbehavior," we mean a condition or set of conditions that frequently instigate misbehavior, though they do not always do so. Such behavior may seem to occur out of the blue, but it can almost always be traced back to one or more causative conditions. We can identify a number of such catalysts, at least twenty-two of which teachers can soften or deactivate, thereby substantially reducing student misbehavior. Of course we cannot control certain societal factors that promote misbehavior, such as abominable living conditions and a milieu of violence and lawlessness. The best we can do for students in those situations is to help them enjoy alternative experiences in school that exemplify a better way of life. Of the twenty-two catalysts listed here, some originate in individuals, some in groups, some in instructional environments, and some in school personnel. (Note: The catalysts are listed numerically in the following paragraphs, not to indicate a ranking of any sort, but to help identify them for class discussions.)

Dealing with Catalysts That Originate in Individual Students.   Nine causes of misbehavior originate in individual students: *unmet needs, thwarted desires, expediency, urge to transgress, temptation, inappropriate habits, poor behavior choices, avoidance, and egocentric personality.* Two of these causes—unmet needs and thwarted desires—are easily corrected, but must be kept in balance through continual attention. Two others—inappropriate habits and poor behavior choices—are learned behaviors that can be eliminated through relearning. The remaining causes that originate in individuals are inborn traits that never leave us, although their influence can be controlled. Here are explanations of the nine causes that originate in individual students and suggestions for dealing with them.

1. Unmet Needs
Students continually try to meet their inborn needs. We have identified eight such needs that strongly affect student behavior: sex, security, belonging, hope, dignity, power, enjoyment, and competence. When any of these needs is not being satisfied, students become unsettled and more prone to misbehave.

Suggestions Concerning Unmet Needs. By being sensitive to students and their behavior and by talking with them, you can identify needs that are not being met and can help students satisfy them in acceptable ways.

2. Thwarted Desires

When students fail to get something they want badly, their behavior may temporarily become unacceptable. They may complain, be destructive, sulk, pout, act out, or criticize others.

Suggestions Concerning Thwarted Desires. When students misbehave out of keen disappointment, tell them you can see they are not feeling well and ask them if there is anything you can do to help. Show you are sympathetic, but don't dwell on the problem. Get them interested in something else, if you can. Their distress will soon run its course.

3. Expediency

Students always look for ways to make their lives easier and more enjoyable. They take shortcuts, conveniently forget what they are supposed to do, look for ways to get out of work, and intentionally break rules. While expedient behavior does not often appear in classes that are interesting and lively, it appears frequently in those that are dull and boring.

Suggestions Concerning Expediency. Hold discussions with your students about expediency and its troublesome effects. Ask them why they sometimes take the easy way, such as reading book summaries or reviews rather than the assigned book, rushing through a writing assignment, or copying others' ideas. If they are comfortable enough to answer honestly, they will probably say it is because they don't like the work, don't see the point in it, or don't want to spend time on it. Ask them what *would* encourage them to give their best effort. Listen to what they say and make use of their suggestions if you can.

4. Urge to Transgress

All of us feel the urge to transgress rules and regulations, and we often do so, even when we know there is a chance we will get caught or even harm ourselves or others. Students succumb to this urge frequently, especially when class activities are not appealing. They intentionally cheat, take shortcuts, tell lies, break class rules, and annoy others.

Suggestions Concerning the Urge to Transgress. Discuss this urge, its effects, and how it can be controlled sensibly. Explain that it is a natural phenomenon that affects all of us, one that when acted on occasionally brings satisfaction but more frequently brings unpleasant consequences. Discuss the reasons for rules, including how they equalize opportunity and help us live together harmoniously. Point out that when rules are broken, someone often suffers as a result. Discuss the meaning of ethics, ethical conduct, and personal character (topics treated in Chapter 9). Have students tell what they have seen people do that revealed high ethical character. Ask why ethical people are generally admired. Never allow students to see you transgress rules, expectations, or ethical codes of conduct.

5. Temptation

Students regularly encounter objects, situations, behaviors, and people they find powerfully attractive. Examples include music and lyrics, desirable objects, ways of speaking, styles of clothing, ways of conducting oneself, and cheating on tests and assignments. Although many of these things become mild or severe misbehavior, students nevertheless find them so attractive they will occasionally do, adopt, mimic, acquire, or associate with them, even though they are forbidden.

Suggestions Concerning Temptation. Conduct frank discussions with your students in which you analyze temptation together and help them understand why certain objects, styles, and opportunities are so seductive. Help students foresee the undesirable consequences of following disapproved styles and manners. Help them clarify the lines that separate the approved from the disapproved and reinforce their resolve to resist factors that are likely to harm them.

6. Inappropriate Habits

Inappropriate habits are ingrained ways of behaving that violate established standards and expectations. Jason uses profanity. Maria is discourteous, inconsiderate of others, and calls them names. Larry always looks for the easy way, even when it makes him misbehave. Josh is aggressive and combative. Some of these habits are learned in school, but most are acquired in the home or community.

Suggestions Concerning Inappropriate Habits. Bring inappropriate habits to students' attention without pointing a finger at anyone. Discuss their harmful effects and, if necessary, teach your students acceptable alternatives. Habits you might want to consider include poor manners, name-calling, teasing, verbal put-downs, cheating, lying, and disregard for others. Ask your students how they might rid themselves of these undesirable habits. Help them see that, if they do so, they can present themselves in a better light, be accepted better in school, and make the class more satisfying for everyone. You can use nonthreatening skits and dialogs to help students practice desirable behavior.

7. Poor Behavior Choices

When students attempt to meet their needs, their behaviors are sometimes acceptable, sometimes not. The difference may not be clear to students, who seldom put any real thought into how they can meet their needs appropriately. Alicia, in trying for attention, annoys others so much they avoid her. Alan, trying to meet his need for power, refuses to do what the teacher requests, thereby distressing the teacher and setting a bad example for others. Alicia and Alan are trying to meet legitimate needs, but do not realize their behavior choices are doing more harm than good.

Suggestions Concerning Poor Behavior Choices. To help students such as Alicia and Alan, ask the class questions such as:

- What are some of the things you have seen students do to (e.g., get attention, be acknowledged, get better grades than they deserve, get out of work, become members of groups)?
- Does their behavior usually get them what they want?
- What do you think those students could have done that would have brought better results?
- As time passes, will those students' efforts still be effective, or will they produce undesirable results?

8. Avoidance

No one likes to face failure, intimidation, ridicule, or other unpleasant situations and treatment. One way to escape those things is to avoid situations where they might occur. At times, avoidance is the best way to deal with a particular issue, but in school we can't always avoid situations we find unpleasant. Consider Norona, who refuses to participate in a group assignment. Her refusal seems to show disdain for the teacher, but her real reason for refusing is that she is intimidated by the prowess of her peers and doesn't want them to know she is inept. Her avoidance is hampering her personal growth and worrying the teacher.

Suggestions Concerning Avoidance. To help students such as Norona behave advantageously in circumstances they dislike, show them how to face unpleasant situations and work through them. Rather than singling out Norona, try asking the following in a group discussion:

- Are there things you try to avoid in school, such as people, events, or activities you find frightening or embarrassing?
- Which of those things could best be dealt with through avoidance (e.g., a clique that is maligning other students)? Which cannot be dealt with through avoidance (e.g., giving an oral report in front of the class)?

Select three or four that fall into different categories, such as things that are feared, disliked, embarrassing, demeaning, or provocative.

- What are the advantages and disadvantages of avoidance in each of these situations?
- If you must confront the situation, how might you do so successfully? For example, if Jayson is terrified of standing in front of the class and making a report, ask "Is it ever possible to make a strength out of what appears to be a weakness? How might that be done?" (Possibilities: using the extra motivation to advantage; perhaps admitting publicly that one is not very capable but is eager to learn from others.)
- Can students learn from situations that make them uncomfortable? (Yes, often very desirable learning.)
- What is the worst thing that can happen in class if we make a mistake? Can mistakes help us learn?
- What could a person do to reduce fear of mistakes or unpleasant situations? (Perhaps practice in pairs, then small groups, then large groups.)

Set up two or three scenarios involving avoidance and have students practice what to say and do in those situations.

9. Egocentric Personality

Students with egocentric personalities focus primarily on themselves, consider themselves superior to others, and believe they do no wrong. Most classes contain one or more such students.

Suggestions Concerning Egocentric Personality. To help these students behave more appropriately, ask questions such as the following in class discussions:

- Are the needs and interests of all students important, or do only certain students deserve attention?
- Is one person often entirely right and everyone else entirely wrong?
- Is everyone entitled to an equal opportunity in the class?
- How should you and I react to a person who always wants to dominate, be first, be right, and quarrel with those who don't agree? (Make sure the proffered suggestions are positive in nature, not negative.)
- Do you think it would be a good idea to make a class agreement for ourselves about equal opportunity, sharing, cooperating, and conducting oneself in a manner that does not antagonize others? (This might all be incorporated in an agreement such as, "We will always treat others as we would like to be treated.")

FIELD APPLICATION 2:   Observe a class in session and see if you note instances of temptation, avoidance, expediency, and egocentric behavior. What specifically were the students doing? What do you hypothesize to be the causes of their behavior? Was the teacher aware? How did he or she respond?

Dealing with Catalysts That Originate in Class Peers and Groups.   Two significant causes of misbehavior originate in class peers and groups—*provocation* and *group behavior*—both of which are highly contagious.

10. Provocation

A great portion of school misbehavior results from students' being provoked by annoyance, insult, or boredom. Heather is trying to study, but Art's incessant chatter frustrates her to the bursting point. Marty calls Jerry a name and Jerry responds hotly. Randall is trying to pay attention but finally disengages from the lesson because he neither understands the content nor sees any point to it.

Suggestions Concerning Provocation. Provocation often produces strong emotions that reduce self-control and increase combativeness. Discuss this phenomenon with your class. Ask:

- Can you name some things people say or do that upset you so much you want to retaliate? How do you feel when this happens?
- If you retaliate, is it likely to improve the situation or make it worse? What might you do that would resolve the incident peacefully?
- Is provoking others consistent with the class character we are trying to build?

Such discussions, supplemented with purposeful practice, help students learn to maintain self-control and act and speak more calmly when upset.

11. Group Behavior

Students often succumb to peer pressure or get caught up in group emotion and, as a result, may misbehave in ways they would not consider if by themselves. It is difficult for students to disregard peer pressure, easy to get swept up in group energy and emotion, and easy to justify one's misbehavior as "only what others were doing." Because Kerry and Lee want to look cool to their peers, Kerry defaces school property, and Lee bullies weaker members of the class, even though those acts are not what Kerry and Lee would do if by themselves.

Suggestions Concerning Group Behavior. Discuss this phenomenon with your class in ways such as the following:

■ Tell the class about some event in which a friend of yours, let's say Sarah, behaved badly just because others were doing so. Indicate that Sarah is now very embarrassed about her behavior and wishes no one knew about it.

■ Ask your students if they know any stories like Sarah's they can share, without mentioning names the class might recognize. If they share stories, guide the class in analyzing one or two of them. If they don't contribute a story, have a fictional one ready for their consideration. After hearing or recounting the story, ask questions such as:

1. Is the behavior something the person will be proud of later?
2. Why do you suppose the person behaved that way? (perhaps fun, comradeship, testing limits, being seen as clever or "cool")
3. What do you think the long-term results will be for the person? (perhaps an unpleasant story to remember, regret, guilt, getting caught, being found out, worry, disappointing one's family, possible punishment, living with knowing you did the wrong thing)
4. How do you think the possible benefits compare with the probable harmful effects?
5. Once you do something you are ashamed of, is there any way to make amends?
6. How can you stay away from, or keep out of, group activities that are unlawful, unethical, or against the rules?

Dealing with Catalysts That Originate in Instructional Environments.   Four causes of misbehavior originate in instructional environments: *physical discomfort, tedium, meaninglessness, and lack of motivation.* You can easily correct them.

12. Physical Discomfort

Students become restless or frustrated when made uncomfortable by inappropriate temperature, poor lighting, or unsuitable seating or workspaces. *Suggestions:* Attend to comfort factors in advance and ask students about them. Make corrections as necessary.

13. Tedium

Students begin to fidget after a time when an instructional activity requires continued close attention, especially if the topic is not very interesting. *Suggestions:* Break the work into shorter segments or add something that increases the interest level.

14. Meaninglessness

Students grow restless when required to work at topics they do not comprehend or for which they see no purpose. *Suggestions:* Make sure the topic is meaningful to students, that they understand it and see its relevance and importance in their lives.

15. Lack of Motivation

Students have little interest in what they are expected to learn and therefore make little effort to learn it. *Suggestions:* Select topics and activities in which students have natural interest. When that is not possible, introduce into those topics some elements students are known to enjoy, such as novelty, mystery, movement, competition, group work, and role-playing.

Dealing with Catalysts That Originate in School Personnel.   Seven causes of misbehavior originate in school personnel. They include *poor modeling, lack of personal attention, disregard for students' feelings, uninteresting lessons, ineffective guidance and feedback, poor communication,* and *coercion, threat, and punishment.* These catalysts are associated mostly with teachers, but also at times with administrators, clerical staff, health personnel, cafeteria personnel, custodial personnel, and family members working in the school. We can easily eliminate the causes for which we are personally responsible, but when the causes originate in other school personnel, we must proceed tactfully. At times you might be able to talk personally with an individual who is, say, using inappropriate language or trampling students' feelings. Often, the best way to address a concern is to mention it to the principal, who can take direct action or include it as an agenda item for the next faculty meeting.

16. Presenting Poor Models of Behavior

At times all of us are inconsistent, irresponsible, and short on self-control, and we sometimes treat students with discourtesy or disregard. We can't expect to be perfect, but we must realize that when we treat students poorly—which is to say, in ways we would not want to be treated—we damage relationships we have been trying to build. Imagine the effects on Mrs. Alexis's class when, after urging all students to speak respectfully to each other, she hotly says to Misti, "Sit down right now and shut your mouth!"

Suggestions About Modeled Behavior. Always be the best model you can for your students, who watch you very closely and often pattern their behavior after yours (especially when you misbehave). If you do anything inappropriate, you can soon expect to see your students do the same.

17. Showing Little Interest in or Appreciation for Students

We sometimes fail to show interest in students or appreciation for them as individuals, despite knowing they want our attention and want us to be interested in their lives. If we disregard them repeatedly, students may become wary of us or may disruptively seek the attention they desire.

Suggestions About Interest in Students. Give each student as much personal attention as possible. Go out of your way to greet them, exchange a friendly word, show you are aware of their difficulties, try to help them feel at ease, and acknowledge their progress.

18. Disregarding Students' Feelings

Some teachers teach in an autocratic manner with little regard for students' feelings. They order students about, point out their inadequacies, and speak to them sarcastically. This hurts students' feelings, made worse when they think they are being treated unjustly. Students often respond by sulking, refusing to cooperate, talking back angrily, or plotting revenge.

Suggestions About Students' Feelings. Be alert to students' feelings, whether they are of happiness and optimism or distress, sadness, frustration, fear, boredom, or pessimism. Acknowledge their feelings considerately. Talk with students about them when it seems appropriate to do so. Show your concern and willingness to listen.

19. Presenting Uninteresting Lessons

Students rally to us when we make our classes interesting, but they keep their distance when classes are dull. At times all teachers feel like telling students, "Here is the lesson and you know the expectations, so show some responsibility and complete the assignment as you know you should." This feeling is understandable, but rarely does it accomplish anything positive. Nevertheless, some teachers, especially those suffering from overload, sometimes resort to this approach.

Suggestions Concerning Interest. Do all you can to make your lessons enjoyable. Boredom makes school stultifying for you and your students alike. It is not difficult to provide engaging topics and appealing activities. Students want you to be enthusiastic, to have sparkle, and behave attractively. You want the same from them. Work on that and everybody will behave themselves better.

20. Ineffective Guidance and Feedback

Without proper guidance and feedback, students do not understand what you expect them to do or how they should do it. Neither do they have a good understanding, once they have completed their work, of what they have done well or poorly, how they could do it better, or how much progress they have made. Under these circumstances, it is difficult for them to take their work seriously.

Suggestions About Guidance and Feedback. Make sure students understand clearly what they are supposed to do and how they should do it. Check to make sure they understand before they begin working. During their work, and again after they have finished, provide feedback concerning what they have done well or poorly and how they can improve. Ask them to give their opinions about it as well.

21. Communicating Ineffectively

Some teachers do not understand how to communicate with students on a personal level. Students want you to exchange pleasantries with them. They want to know your views on things, and want to tell you theirs. They also want to know what is expected of them academically and how they are to conduct themselves. Students need personal communication from you; it is one of the main ways they receive personal validation.

Suggestions Concerning Communication. Go out of your way to speak regularly with students in a friendly way. Avoid comments that hurt feelings or dampen enthusiasm. Say things that increase optimism and bolster confidence. Build students up when you can, but do so honestly. No need to fake it. You can find genuinely positive things to say to, and about, each of your students.

22. Coercion, Threat, and Punishment
Students don't like to be forced to do anything. They don't like to be threatened. They don't like to be punished. They react negatively to such tactics and drag their heels and sometimes refuse to participate. If you treat them abrasively, they keep a watchful eye on you, fearful of being scolded, embarrassed, or demeaned, and they will almost certainly develop negative attitudes toward you and school and will long for the day they can escape your clutches.

Suggestions Concerning Coercion. Give up coercion, threat, and punishment (meaning intimidation, belittlement, and humiliation). Replace them with considerate helpfulness, personal attention, and good communication. You can win student cooperation through kind treatment and personal enthusiasm. These days, students simply cannot be bullied into learning.

> **FIELD APPLICATION 3:**   Spend a day at school and inconspicuously observe what school personnel say and do. Do you see incidences of behavior by adult personnel that you consider inappropriate in school? Relate a specific example or two, explain the possible undesirable effects, and suggest what might be done to improve the situation.

Attending to Your Own Misbehavior

At this point let's take a moment to consider teacher misbehavior. Teachers are unusually dedicated, conscientious, and hardworking. They care a great deal about their students. Yet we know that some, because of unfamiliarity with effective techniques or because of habit, frustration, or personal problems, occasionally do things that provoke conflict, inhibit student progress, and leave the class dispirited. Because teachers know this is undesirable and know how to avoid it, it is fair to call their actions misbehavior. If we are intent on improving behavior, we must address not only student misbehavior but our own as well. Here are some of the factors associated with teacher misbehavior, a trap you will wish to avoid.

Habit
Teachers sometimes become set in their ways of teaching and interacting with students. They may have learned their teaching style from their own teachers and over the years have remained comfortable with it.

Suggestions. Watch closely to see how students react to you. Do they seem friendly? Afraid? Attracted to you? Eager to cooperate? Eager to please? If they are reticent, fearful, hard to motivate, uncooperative, or unfriendly, analyze your teaching carefully and try to determine which of your behaviors might be causing trouble. Hold a discussion with students about teaching and ask them to tell about favorite teachers from the past. Pay attention to what they say and try adopting some of the characteristics or practices they like.

Unfamiliarity with Better Techniques

Some teachers have not had occasion to learn about newer, more effective ways of teaching and relating with today's students, ways that better promote desired learning, behavior, and attitudes.

Suggestions. Ask students what some of their favorite class activities are. Ask other teachers about techniques they use in working with students. Consult books, professional journals, and especially Internet pages that describe up-to-date practices. Attend workshops on humane discipline, human relations, and character building.

Frustration

Some teachers are beaten down from continually having to deal with student misbehavior or inconsiderate parents. This leaves them stressed and makes it difficult for them to work with students in a kind, helpful manner.

Suggestions. If you feel frustrated, you are probably trying, unsuccessfully, to force students to comply with your expectations. You cannot teach happily in this way. Your frustration will disappear when your students become cooperative, willing to learn, and considerate toward each other and you. You can make that happen by removing the causes of misbehavior and enticing students through personal attention, an interesting curriculum, and an attractive style of teaching.

Provocation

Students sometimes do and say things intentionally to get under your skin, hoping to see you become upset and befuddled and, perhaps, lose self-control.

Suggestions. Never provoke your students in ways that cause them to retaliate, and do not allow yourself to be provoked by them. When they try to provoke you, disregard their comments and actions and proceed as if nothing has happened. If you feel you must respond, only say, "I really regret you feel that way" or "What might I do that will make things better for you?" If they suggest you do something demeaning or dangerous, tell them, "I don't believe debasing or harming myself will make things better for you, but if you have a positive suggestion, please write it out for me and I'll consider it and see if we can work together. For now, I'd very much appreciate your cooperation."

Failure to Plan Proactively

Many teachers do not think ahead sufficiently to foresee potential problems. They get caught by surprise and have difficulty saying or doing the right things.

Suggestions. Think carefully about problems that might arise in class or reactions students might have to topics, lessons, your requests, or unexpected events. Try to learn from mistakes you make in confrontational situations and practice better ways of responding should similar situations arise again. By anticipating potential difficulties, you can change your plans to keep the problems from arising and you can prepare yourself to deal with whatever might eventuate. Verse yourself on what to do when people are injured or become suddenly ill, grow defiant, or get into fights. Decide what you will do and say if an unauthorized visitor comes into the room, if a parent berates you, if the class moans when you make an assignment, and so forth. Determine how you can respond decisively to such eventualities, yet maintain positive relationships.

Emphasizing Student Dignity

Dignity refers to self-respect, to a self-image of correctness, competence, and responsibility. The more respect we have for ourselves, the less likely we are to cause trouble for others. Focusing on student dignity is a valuable tactic in reducing misbehavior.

As you saw in Chapter 3, there are many things you can do to confer dignity on students. You can show you value them as people and class members. You can remember and use their names and mention something notable about them. You can show them full respect (even when they sorely try your patience) by treating them courteously as equal human beings, asking their opinion, listening to them, and acknowledging their contributions. If you do these things, students will seek you out, ask your advice, and cooperate with you.

Enhancing Personal Relations

Personal relations have to do with how we treat each other in a variety of situations. With help, most students can improve relations with teachers, other adults, and fellow students. The procedures for doing so are easily learned.

Efforts Beneficial to Students and Teachers.   The following efforts help students and teachers improve relations with each other:

Making a Good Impression
People react to us in terms of the impressions we make on them, such as whether we appear intimidating or kind, receptive or closed-minded, considerate or inconsiderate. We make a good impression when we smile genuinely, introduce ourselves if necessary, and memorize and use the other person's name. If we can then say something cordial or interesting, we become even more attractive.

Opening Up Communication
Some of us can easily chat with strangers at the drop of a hat, while others find doing so awkward and difficult. Those in the latter category find it helpful to get other people started talking about themselves and their experiences. Respond with comments such as "That's interesting. Tell me more about it." "What do you think we'd have to do if we tried something like that? Would it be possible?" "I've never worked on anything like that. How could we make it happen?" As they respond, listen carefully in order to grasp not only what they say but also what it means to them. Take mental notes. From time to time ask if you are understanding them correctly. Meanwhile, be sure you do not make statements or act in ways that turn the other person off, such as dominating the conversation, adopting a superior attitude, disregarding what the other person says, telling them how they are wrong, looking elsewhere while they talk, or failing to respond.

Predisposing the Other Person to Cooperate

At times we find ourselves in a working relationship with people who, for one reason or another, don't want to do their part. Their reluctance might be due to fear, lack of time, or simple disinterest. If you understand the reason for their reluctance, you can usually resolve it. For example, Tony is assigned to work with a new student named Dennis. The two of them are to prepare an oral report on the moons of Saturn. Dennis seems to like Tony and is interested in the topic but says he has to work after school and doesn't have time to practice any speeches. He says he will write his part out and Tony can read it to the class. Tony suspects that Dennis is worried about speaking in front of the class. He says, "Dennis, I'm wondering if we could try this: for our presentation, let's pretend one of us is an astronomer who knows a lot about the moons of Saturn and the other one is a science reporter for the newspaper. We can write up a list of questions for the reporter to ask, and the astronomer can answer them. Would you be willing to try that? Which role, reporter or astronomer, would you want to play?"

Building Trust

Trust is the feeling of being able to count on another person to accept us, show concern for our well-being, and never harm us. Trust grows within a milieu of ethical principles such as kindness, consideration, helpfulness, fairness, and honesty. In class meetings discuss those principles with students and, as a group, explore what they entail. Help students reflect on how those principles are displayed in personal behavior. Ask students if they feel the class can live by them most all the time.

Using Positive Body Language

A powerful medium teachers have for conveying messages to students is body language, also called nonverbal communication. Body language consists of physical mannerisms we display when interacting, such as facial expression, eye contact, gestures, posture, and proximity. Sometimes our body language supports what we are saying, while at other times it does not. When what we are saying with words seems different from what we are saying with our bodies, the message sent by our bodies is the stronger. Imagine that you are introduced to someone who says, "Delighted to meet you," but gives you an unenthusiastic handshake and looks away from you with a bored expression. Do you believe he or she is really delighted? How about if the individual smiles, gives you a warm handshake, and invites you to sit down? It's a different story then, isn't it?

The old saying about actions speaking louder than words holds true in all human interactions. Stephen R. Covey (1989) claims that, on the average, only 10 percent of our communication is conveyed by words, 30 percent by the sounds we make when speaking (e.g., inflection, emphasis), and 60 percent by our body language. We are more likely to understand what a person is really feeling or saying by interpreting speech sounds and body language than by relying verbatim on spoken words.

Students easily understand the importance of eye contact, facial expression, and body positioning when communicating with others. Most Western societies emphasize eye contact, although not all do. Many Eastern societies tend to avoid it. If you encounter cultural differences, make appropriate adjustments. Most people consider a smile or a pleasant expression welcoming and receptive. Nodding while looking at the other indicates agreement or understanding. When you stand near another person and face them, you are indicating receptiveness. When you maintain distance or turn to the side, you appear to shield yourself from the other person. That may not be what you intend. We can help students learn to match body language to their intentions.

Sending Clear Verbal Messages

Be aware of words used and how they sound. Words are very powerful. Not only do they help convey what we intend, they have the power to instill hope or mislead and hurt. We saw Covey's contention that 30 percent of the meaning we garner from what others say comes from the sounds they make when speaking, rather than from the literal meaning of their words. These sounds, such as intonation, inflection, and emphasis, modify the meanings of words. Compare the word *yes* when spoken flatly with *yes* spoken with a rising inflection. The first can be taken literally, but the second can convey various unclear meanings such as, "What do you want?" or "What are you up to now?"

Reacting Positively to Others

Suppose someone is sharing information with us. We want to remain on good terms with the individual so we can continue working together productively. How should we react? We know we should pay attention to what the person says, but how should we respond? Should we be entirely honest, even if what the other person says sounds crazy? The answer is yes. We should be honest, but tactful if there is danger of offending the other person. If our reaction is positive, fine. We can nod and show agreement. If uncertain, we can ask for more information, such as "Tell me more about that," or "You know, that idea is new to me. Could you explain it a bit further?" If we disagree with what he or she says, we should give our opinion gently. The best way to do this is to say, "I may be wrong, but . . . " and then give our view. "I may be wrong . . . " is one of the best ways to disagree with others. It doesn't put them on the defensive so much, and they are usually willing to hear your opinion.

When we agree with what others say, and when we find them interesting, we turn toward them, look at them, nod, and remain alert. When we disagree, we tend to look away, purse our lips, and appear inattentive. These messages come across clearly. If we hope to collaborate with people with whom we disagree, we must not alienate them. If we maintain good relations, we have a chance of working productively or even persuading them to our point of view. To make that possible, we can look at them, nod, and remain attentive. In that way we show interest in their views.

Following Through on Agreements

Students should know that we have to follow through on agreements if we hope to maintain positive relationships. Suppose Marcia is working with Tim to plan a flyer announcing the upcoming science fair. Tim would like to list the titles of the science exhibits and the names of the people involved in each. Marcia feels the flyer will attract more attention if done in a futuristic theme with high-quality illustrations. The two agree to produce prototype flyers that meet their specifications, so they can show them to others for feedback. If Marcia and Tim want to continue on good terms, both will need to follow through on their agreement.

What, Specifically, We Should Make Sure *Not* To Do

Just as there are specific things we try to do when interacting with others, so are there things we must make sure not to do. We have noted that we often harm relationships if we slight others, put them down, or discount their contributions out-of-hand. There may indeed be times when you feel others have not done their part or followed through, or are simply lazy and stubborn. You may think they are taking advantage of you and you might do well to tell them so. But if you do, focus only on the work done or not done. Don't make remarks about their character that are personally hurtful. If you do, they probably won't work with you anymore.

When Are Personal Relations Skills Best Learned and Practiced?

Personal relations skills are best introduced and practiced in class meetings. They can be further explored and enacted in discussions, demonstrations, and role-playing. We can provide students a safe venue while they learn what to say, how to say it, how to use body language, and how to maintain positive feelings during disagreements. Then, of course, the skills are to be applied in everyday interactions. Ask students to discuss how well they believe they are doing individually and collectively. Tactics concerning what to do when personal relations go sour can also be discussed, and strategies for correcting mistakes can be explored.

This concludes our examination of desirable and undesirable behavior and how we can identify and eliminate causes. In Chapter 8, we will see how to deal with undesirable behavior when it does occur.

> **FIELD APPLICATION 4:** Obtain permission to interview a teacher of your choice. Ask what he or she does, if anything, to establish and maintain good personal relations among students and between teacher and students. Ask what advice he or she would offer beginning teachers who want to establish positive personal relations in their class.

QUESTIONS

1. How many of the catalysts of misbehavior that originate in students are related to needs and failure to meet them? Which are they?

2. Would you say the following statement is true or false: "Most discipline problems in class are caused by provocation." Explain.

3. Do you buy the argument that teachers misbehave in class and that their misbehavior can be detrimental to students? Explain.

4. Of the personal relations efforts that were described, which do you consider yourself strong in? Which are weaknesses?

5. Examine the nine catalysts of misbehavior that originate in individual students. While those causes are known to promote misbehavior, do they have positive qualities as well? If so, what are they?

6. Of the nine causes of misbehavior that originate in individual students, which do you think you can reduce easily, and which do you think will present difficulties? Why?

ACTIVITIES

1. Summarize the steps you would take to prevent the occurrence of misbehavior in your classes. Which of the suggestions made in the chapter seem most helpful, and which least helpful?

2. Describe factors that might cause you to misbehave when working with students. Devise a practice regimen to help teachers avoid the sorts of teacher misbehavior described in the chapter.

3. Work with a fellow student to practice making appropriate responses when you are provoked by students and/or confronted by an angry parent. Share your efforts or role-play them for others.

4. Analyze the personal relations efforts listed as useful to students and teachers. Write out a plan for strengthening yourself, especially in weaker areas.

REFERENCES

Albert, L. 1996. *Cooperative discipline.* Circle Pines, MN: American Guidance Service.

Canter, L., and Canter, M. 2001. *Assertive discipline: Positive behavior management for today's classroom.* Los Angeles, CA: Canter & Associates.

Charles, C. 2002. *Essential elements of effective discipline.* Boston: Allyn & Bacon.

Covey, S. 1989. *The seven habits of highly effective people.* New York: Simon and Schuster.

Curwin, R., and Mendler, A. 2001. *Discipline with dignity.* Upper Saddle River, NJ: Merrill.

Dreikurs, R., and Cassel, P. 1972. *Discipline without tears.* New York: Hawthorne. Reissued 1995, Penguin-NAL.

Glasser, W. 1998. *The quality school: Managing students without coercion.* New York: HarperCollins.

Gordon, T. 1989. *Discipline that works: Promoting self-discipline in children.* New York: Random House.

Maslow, A. 1954. *Motivation and personality.* New York: Harper.

Nelsen, J., Lott, L., and Glenn, H. 2000. *Positive discipline in the classroom.* Rocklin, CA: Prima.

8 Managing Misbehavior in a Positive Manner

Chapter Preview

This chapter continues an exploration of effective behavior management. In Chapter 7 we examined a number of strategies for preventing undesirable behavior. In this chapter we explore ways of dealing effectively with misbehavior that does occur, as it will to some degree in all classrooms. The strategies described herein are categorized into two groups, in accordance with the severity of the misbehavior. Strategies in the first group are for benign misbehavior such as inattention and unwarranted talking. The tactics suggested can be considered "supportive" because they help students stay on-task when the first signs of misbehavior appear. Strategies in the second group are for disruptive behavior. They can be thought of as "positive intervention" strategies because they help misbehaving students move away from misbehavior and toward more appropriate ways of conducting themselves.

Undesirable Behavior Will Occur in Your Class

A certain amount of undesirable behavior occurs in almost all classes, even when teachers apply the preventive tactics described in Chapter 7. Because misbehavior has such a deleterious effect of teaching and learning, it is a matter to be taken seriously. You must do what you can: first, keep undesirable behavior to a minimum and, second, deal with it positively and helpfully.

Undesirable behavior varies from benign to serious. With proper effort you can keep most misbehavior benign, nothing more serious than minor violations of class agreements. But you will have to deal with some that is more serious, such as disrupting teaching and learning, behaving cruelly toward peers, and breaching standards of ethics and morality. In this chapter you will encounter a number of tactics for limiting benign misbehavior as well as for managing serious misbehavior in a positive manner.

Supportive Tactics for Benign Misbehavior

Supportive tactics are used when students, who have been behaving properly, begin to show the first signs of incipient misbehavior, such as inattention, fidgeting, yawning, sighing, looking about, or playing with objects or materials. Although such behavior may not bother you or affect most members of the class, you should attend to it. The student involved is not profiting from the lesson, and benign misbehavior can escalate quickly into more serious behavior. Effective tactics to use when you see signs of restlessness include physical proximity, posture, facial expressions, same-side collaboration, added interest, congruent communication, comments to improve student self-control, and helping students feel more capable. The first half of this chapter explains these tactics and how they are used.

Using Physical Proximity

Physical proximity simply means standing close to a student. It is quite effective for those who have wandered away from the task at hand. Suppose you notice, toward the end of the period, that Harrison has stopped working on the seatwork he is to complete during class. He is looking out the window and tapping his pencil. Teachers in years past might have called out Harrison's name and admonished him to get to work, which would have embarrassed him and caused other students to look up from their work. Instead, just move quietly alongside Harrison. Chances are he will get right back to work without your having to say anything at all.

Using Other Body Language Effectively

Fredric Jones (2001) said if it were possible to discipline with the mouth, nagging would have fixed every kid a million years ago. His is a colorful way of saying that "correcting" students verbally does little good. Body language works much better, he says. It includes eye contact, posture, facial expressions, and gestures. You can perform wonders simply by bending over students and giving them an approving nod.

Your posture tells students whether you feel purposeful and in charge, or tired and disillusioned. By standing straight, you say there are things to be done. By watching students you communicate that you are following their efforts and stand ready to help. Your facial expressions such as winks, nods, frowns, smiles, wide eyes, and mouth convey your reactions of humor, enthusiasm, surprise, appreciation, and concern.

Mr. Smathers usually introduces and explains a math concept, questions students to make sure they understand it, and then assigns problems to be completed in class. While students are working, Mr. Smathers sits at his desk and grades papers from the day before. He tells his students that if anyone has difficulty, they may come to him and ask for help. For some reason, several students regularly fail to complete the seatwork assignments, while others make many more errors than they should. Hardly anyone comes to his desk for help. What do you think Mr. Smathers might do to help students profit more from his class?

Developing and Reiterating Same-side Collaboration

Have you had a teacher who stands out in your mind as gruff, unfriendly, and demanding, one you wouldn't have worked with if you had any other option? Conversely, have you ever had a teacher you knew was on your side, doing everything possible to help you succeed? Your feelings toward the two are remarkably different, aren't they?

Teaching, as traditionally done, suggests an adversarial relationship between teacher and students. Students feel teachers are trying to make them engage in activities they don't enjoy and learn material they don't like. They believe teachers will use strong-arm tactics to get their way. Teachers, on the other hand, feel many students will do as little as possible, comply with requests only half-heartedly, if at all, and misbehave when the opportunity arises. The result is an us-against-them attitude that, even when never spoken of, causes mistrust and dampens progress.

Do your best to avoid this harmful antagonistic posture. In its place, install willing cooperation. Barbara Coloroso (1994) urges teachers to treat students with respect, give them power and responsibility, provide support to help them learn to manage their behavior, and help them resolve problems. Alfie Kohn (1996) advises teachers to develop a sense of community in their classrooms, where everyone participates in resolving group concerns and learns to work cooperatively with the teacher and fellow students. Patricia Kyle, Spencer Kagan, and Sally Scott (2001) urge teachers to establish a same-side attitude with students in which everyone works together toward the same goals. They say teachers can do this by showing they genuinely care, are aware of the pressures that affect students, and help students learn to conduct themselves responsibly. C. M. Charles (2002b) urges teachers to look for ways to involve students in examining and making decisions about class matters. He says one of the best ways to support students is to show you are on their side and trust their ability to make sound decisions.

Improving Student Self-control

Student behavior improves as students are taught how to control themselves, cooperate, assume responsibility, and behave in a dignified manner. Jane Nelsen, Lynn Lott, and H. Stephen Glenn (2000) have been promoting that view for many years. Their premise is that behavior problems diminish as students acquire the skills of accepting others, communicating effectively, showing respect, and maintaining a positive attitude. They believe these skills grow in classrooms where students are treated respectfully, suffer no humiliation when they fail, learn how to turn mistakes into successes, are encouraged to cooperate with teachers and fellow students, and are provided a learning environment of excitement and wonder. Nelsen, Lott, and Glenn claim you can achieve 100 percent improvement in relations with your students if you do the following:

- Show you truly care about your students by taking personal interest in them, talking with them, providing many opportunities to learn important life skills, and offering encouragement.
- Listen to your students and take them seriously. Appreciate their uniqueness.
- Help your students perceive themselves as capable, significant, and in control of their own lives. Involve them in making decisions about the class and curriculum. Use class meetings to discuss and resolve class problems.
- Remove barriers to good relationships and replace them with builders of good relationships. Examples of barriers are assuming you know how students are feeling and what they are capable of; telling students what to do and how to do it; and using

"adultisms" when speaking with students, such as "Why can't you ever . . . ? Why do you always . . . ?" Barriers should be replaced with builders such as checking with students to determine their feelings and capabilities; exploring with students what they might do and how they might do it; and communicating with them respectfully: "What do you think this assignment is about?" "Will you allow me to make a couple of suggestions?"

Injecting Interest and Enjoyment

Your three best allies in teaching are treating students respectfully, making class interesting, and providing help. If you do these things, you will have few discipline problems. Students rarely misbehave when they are having an enjoyable time learning (although they may occasionally go to excess because of excitement). You can be sure that most teachers want their classes to be enjoyable and want their students to behave properly while having a happy experience. Nevertheless, many of those same teachers subject students to topics and activities that, in students' minds, are boring and useless. Alfie Kohn says the difference between our intentions and what we ask students to do is particularly unsettling because

> it exposes a yawning chasm between what we want and what we are doing, between how we would like students to turn out and how our classrooms and schools actually work. We want children to continue reading and thinking after school has ended, yet we focus their attention on grades, which have been shown to reduce interest in learning. We want them to be critical thinkers, yet we feed them predigested facts and discrete skills—partly because of pressure from various constituencies to pump up standardized test scores. We act as though our goal is short-term retention of right answers rather than genuine understanding (1996, p. 61).

How do we get around the problem Kohn addresses? We do so by capitalizing on interests and involving students in making decisions about their learning. Interests bring natural motivation, and involvement makes students feel responsible for their learning. It is relatively easy to identify what students like and dislike, and relatively easy to provide the former while avoiding the latter. We have already seen (if experience doesn't convey the message) that students don't like to sit still and keep quiet. They don't like to work by themselves. They don't like to memorize meaningless names, dates, and events. They don't like long drawn-out reading or writing assignments. They don't like to take tests. This is not a knock on students. They are only reflecting their feelings honestly. And certainly there are exceptions in all cases, but ask yourself: do we really need to make students do things they don't like, which is certain to promote resistance, boredom, and frustration for everyone?

Certainly not. There are plenty of things we can provide in lessons that students enjoy. They like working with others, talking, and moving about. They like productive, participative, and creative activities, as opposed to worksheets and tests. They very much appreciate wit, variety, novelty, challenge, and mystery. They enjoy team competition and trying to set new standards of personal and class achievement. They like to use computers and media. They like to hear and learn language that has rhythm, rhyme, and metaphor.

They like to tell and listen to stories. They like to role-play, perform skits, and give performances. They like rhythmic activities with repetition, music, chanting, clapping, and dancing. Any of these things can be incorporated into most lessons.

You don't have to go overboard. Students don't want constant frenzy any more than you do. They need times of quiet and calm, too, that allow them to watch, listen to, think about, or work at things they enjoy.

And how about your needs? We noted earlier that you have needs that require attention just as students do. Your professional needs probably center on good student achievement, student enjoyment and satisfaction, and the conviction you are helping students build better lives. Here are some suggestions you might find helpful:

make frequent use of your favorite teaching activities;

emphasize topics you know well and are enthusiastic about, because students warm up when they see your enthusiasm;

relate personal experiences that have to do with the topic;

tell stories, do artwork, put on skits, use music, hold debates, or even have students wear costume props.

No need to hold back. The more fun you have teaching, the more likely students will appreciate your work and show it.

Mr. Smathers, as we saw earlier, teaches math lessons by explaining a new concept and then having students do a number of pencil-and-paper problems to practice what they have learned. They comply reluctantly and most do not enjoy the activities. Mr. Smathers grades papers while students work at their desks. If Mr. Smathers wanted to add some interest to his lessons, which approach might he use? How do you think students would respond?

Using Congruent Communication

Congruent communication, a concept introduced by Haim Ginott in 1971, involves saying things that are helpful to students and are, at the same time, harmonious with their feelings about situations and themselves. When we respond congruently to student behavior, especially behavior that does not please us, we can address misbehavior and accidents without embarrassing students or putting them on the defensive.

Mr. Smathers says to Samantha, who mistakenly thought she did all the problems correctly, "Well, you didn't get the point I was explaining to you." What effect do you think his statement has on Samantha? Does it encourage her? Does it help her do better? Presently we will see what Mr. Smathers could say that would be more helpful to Samantha.

Ginott said teachers often preach, moralize, impose guilt, and demand promises, unaware of the detrimental effect these things have on students. You don't need to do any of those things. In fact, you should conscientiously avoid them. Instead, confer dignity on your students by treating them as social equals capable of making good decisions. Give up asking "why" questions, too. They carry blame, as in, "Why didn't you finish this work? Why am I having to tell you again?" Instead, ask them, "When do you think you can have the work completed?" or say, "Have another try. Let's see what you can do." These examples of congruent communication encourage students to proceed without making them feel bad.

Here are some reminders about congruent communication:

- Don't deny students' feelings with statements such as, "You are too old to cry" or "You have absolutely nothing to worry about." A congruent statement would be: "I can see this is troubling you quite a bit. Is there anything I might do to help?"
- Do not demand student cooperation with statements such as, "Get back in your seat and get to work." A congruent statement would be: "I could really use your help."
- Do not lose your self-control. Instead of saying, "Once and for all, stop talking back to me!" you can calmly say, "Let's think for a moment about our agreement concerning how we will treat each other in this class."
- Give up you-messages such as, "You are being too noisy again." Instead, use *I-messages,* such as, "I am feeling a bit uncomfortable about the noise level." (By the way, simply including the words *you* and *I* does not automatically make you-messages and I-messages. The difference is that you-messages place blame on students, while with I-messages the teacher expresses personal feelings without assigning blame.)
- When students are not doing well, avoid looking exasperated. Try making a comment such as:

  "Let's make a fresh start on this tomorrow and try it again."
  "This is more difficult than I thought. Let's see if we can make it a bit easier."
  "I can see this isn't holding your attention. Let me try something else."

Helping Students Feel Capable

Some students don't make much effort to participate in class because they don't feel capable of doing as well as others. Linda Albert (1996) has provided some good suggestions for helping students feel more capable. She says student persistence is dependent on the "I-can level," which is students' sense of being capable of doing the work expected of them in school. Albert suggests the following to increase the I-can level, and hence persistence:

1. *Make mistakes okay.* The fear of making mistakes undermines students' sense of capability, and many, when fearful, stop trying. To minimize this fear, talk with your students about what mistakes are. Help them understand that everyone makes mistakes and that mistakes are a natural part of learning. Point out that the more an individual tries to accomplish, the more mistakes he or she will make. And be careful how you correct students' mistakes. Too many corrections are overwhelming and demoralizing. Make corrections in small steps, one or two at a time. Make sure they take effect before moving on to further corrections.

2. *Build confidence.* In order to feel capable, students must be confident that success is possible. Help them see learning as a process of improvement, not an end product. When improvement is evident, acknowledge it. Remember that students can be successful in a number of ways aside from high test scores, such as showing neatness, good handwriting, persistence, creativity, and responsibility. Draw attention to improvements in those areas, too. New tasks seem difficult to practically everyone, so there is little point in calling a task "easy" or saying "Oh, anybody can do this." It is better to tell students, "I know this may seem difficult at first, but keep at it. Let's see how you do."

3. *Draw attention to past success.* When students know they are being successful, they are inclined to continue what they are doing. Albert suggests asking students why they think they were successful in a particular task. If they say it was because the task was easy, you can say "It seemed easy because you had developed the skills to do it." If they say it was because they tried hard, you can say "You surely did. That is one of the main reasons you were successful." These responses help students learn that true success is dependent in part on their capability and in part on the effort they expend.

4. *Show tangible evidence of learning.* Albert advises teachers to provide tangible evidence of student progress. Grades such as "B" and "satisfactory" are ineffective because they tell little about specific accomplishments. More effective evidence, which can be kept in albums and portfolios, includes compositions written, titles and synopses of books read, projects completed, and special skills attained. (Students should not be allowed to compare their accomplishment albums against each other. The contents are used solely to document personal growth, which is made evident by comparing what students can do now that they couldn't do before.)

5. *It is also useful to hold discussions about "yesterday, today, and tomorrow."* These discussions help students visualize improvements they have made. "Remember when you had difficulty writing a five-paragraph essay? Look how easily you do it now, and how well. You are learning fast. By the end of the year you will be able to . . . " Or, "Remember three weeks ago when you couldn't even read these Spanish verbs? Now you can use all of them in the present tense, and, by next month, you'll be able to use them in the past tense as well."

> **FIELD APPLICATION 1:** Observe a classroom teacher at work. Using the list of supportive tactics described in the foregoing paragraphs, identify which of them you see the teacher use to help students maintain desirable behavior.

Positive Intervention Techniques for Misbehavior

We now move ahead to explore ways of dealing with more troublesome misbehavior, such as wantonly breaking class agreements, provoking or mistreating others, refusing to participate, or defying your requests. Here you must intervene to stop the misbehavior and get the student back on track positively. For many teachers, this aspect of behavior management produces more stress, worry, and anxiety than all other teaching factors combined. That need not be the case. As you will see, it is possible to deal effectively with undesirable behavior while preserving positive relationships and personal dignity. The remainder of this chapter identifies effective tactics and explains how to use them.

Development of Behavior Management in the Past Half Century

Here is a brief review of the major developments in discipline strategies and techniques that have occurred over the past half century. These developments show the progressive movement from old-fashioned discipline to present-day behavior management. You will see that virtually all of the qualities we strive for now were developed years ago, but for one reason or another remained isolated from the mainstream of educational practice.

Prior to 1950.   Through the history of education prior to World War II, teachers organized and dispensed discipline as they pleased. While they were not allowed to maim students physically, they doled out varying degrees of demand, humiliation, and physical abuse. They neither asked for, nor wanted, input from others concerning discipline, which they considered their prerogative. They didn't often discuss discipline plans, per se, with anyone. Most teachers didn't use organized discipline plans at all, but merely showed strong disapproval when students misbehaved. That approach was expected by everyone and supported by parents and community. We now know it does little to encourage students to improve their behavior. In many cases it produces a highly undesirable backlash.

> **FIELD APPLICATION 2:**   Reflect on teachers you have had and identify one (if any) who used old-fashioned punitive discipline. Jot down specifically what that teacher did and how it affected you and other students.

1951 Fritz Redl and William Wattenberg (Group Dynamics).   In the 1950s, the behavior management picture began to change. In 1951, Fritz Redl, a psychiatrist, and William Wattenberg, an educational psychologist, published *Mental Hygiene in Teaching,* in which they set forth the first widely recognized plan for managing student behavior. They explained that people in groups behaved differently than when alone, that teachers should use diagnostic procedures to try to determine what was causing students to behave, that behavior could be controlled through systematic application of pleasurable and unpleasurable consequences, that aversive punishment was counterproductive and should not be used, and that students should be given a say in establishing class rules and consequences.

1954 B. F. Skinner (Reinforcement and Behavior Modification).   Burrhus Frederic Skinner has been called the greatest behavioral psychologist of the twentieth century. He is renowned for his scientific work on principles of reinforcement and how reinforcing stimuli can be used to "shape" behavior—that is, to gradually change the behavior of various creatures, including humans. Skinner made most of his discoveries in the 1930s and 1940s, and then wrote several books and articles explaining them and how they could be applied to human behavior. One of his pivotal publications was a journal article called "The Science of Learning and the Art of Teaching" (1954). In that article Skinner spoke of the art of teaching, with emphasis on shaping student behavior through reinforcement. Out of Skinner's work grew a behavior management strategy called "behavior modification," which is still widely used today. Many teachers, especially at the primary level, have used behavior modification extensively in managing the behavior of younger students.

1969 William Glasser (Student Behavior as Choice). In 1969, psychiatrist William Glasser published *Schools without Failure,* called one of the most influential education books of the twentieth century. In that book he made three contributions that significantly influenced educational practice. The first was the conclusion that students choose to behave as they do in school. Neither society, misfortune, nor bad upbringing forces students to misbehave. Rather, they do so intentionally because they like the results it brings. Because behavior is a matter of choice, students should be helped to make choices that bring success, not failure. This approach was based on "reality therapy," a therapeutic approach Glasser developed for working with psychologically troubled individuals.

The second of Glasser's contributions was that failure is very hurtful and damaging to students; hence, schools should do everything possible to help students be successful. The third contribution was a procedure called "classroom meetings," now used widely for students and teachers to discuss and resolve a variety of class problems.

Glasser maintained that every class should have a printed-out, agreed-on set of class rules governing behavior, and, further, that teachers should never accept excuses from students for breaking those rules. He provided a carefully organized protocol for teachers to use with students who broke rules, intended to help those students make better choices in the future.

1971 Jacob Kounin (Class Management). In 1971, educational psychologist Jacob Kounin published *Discipline and Group Management in Classrooms,* which reported research he had been conducting in a large number of classrooms. His major conclusion was that the key to good discipline lies in how teachers conduct lessons and manage students in groups. Kounin found, in particular, that teachers most effective in maintaining positive student behavior keep students attentive and actively involved. They make instructional activities enjoyable and challenging and know what is going on in all parts of the classroom at all times. They conduct lessons smoothly and change activities as necessary to prevent student boredom.

1971 Haim Ginott (Congruent Communication). We have previously noted the contributions of psychologist Haim Ginott, who did more than anyone before him to help teachers relate humanely with students. His suggestions are set forth in *Teacher and Child* (1971), which is still in print. He stressed that teachers who are adept at managing student behavior have good self-discipline, meaning they can control their emotions and actions. He pointed out that students are very sensitive to what happens to them, personally. He urged teachers to use congruent communication when talking with students, meaning communication that is harmonious with students' feelings about situations and themselves and addresses situations rather than the personality of the student. Teachers provoke resistance when they preach and moralize, and they damage students' self-respect when they impose guilt. Teachers are much more successful when they confer dignity on students and invite cooperation by identifying a situation and indicating what needs to be done.

1972 Rudolf Dreikurs (Democratic Teaching and Classrooms).   Rudolf Dreikurs, an Austrian psychiatrist who immigrated to the United States, was an early proponent of democratic teaching and democratic classrooms. By democratic, he meant that students are allowed significant input into decisions about class matters, including teaching and discipline, and that everyone is allowed an opportunity to express concerns and opinions. He said good discipline cannot occur in classes run by highly autocratic or permissive teachers. He also explained that student behavior can be understood in terms of the basic need for belonging. Misbehavior occurs when students experience difficulty meeting that need and turn to "mistaken goals" of attention, power, revenge, and withdrawal. Dreikurs's work has been carried on with better application to school practice by Linda Albert (1996) through a program she calls Cooperative Discipline.

1976 Lee and Marlene Canter (Assertive Discipline).   In 1976 Lee and Marlene Canter published *Assertive Discipline: A Take-Charge Approach for Today's Educator,* in which they proposed a method of classroom discipline that enabled teachers to remain positively in control of student behavior. Their program emphasized teachers' clearly communicating instructional needs and requirements, assertively responding to student misbehavior, keeping themselves under control, remaining positive, and assiduously following through. Teachers were to establish rules for class behavior and communicate those rules thoroughly to students. Consequences, both positive and negative, were associated with the rules, so that students knew clearly in advance what would happen to them as they complied with the rules or violated them. The Canters' suggestions came at a time when teachers were feeling overwhelmed by student misbehavior, and Assertive Discipline immediately became immensely popular. The Canters' program, still quite popular, has been progressively modified to attend more closely to students' needs and give them a greater say in program implementation.

1979 Fredric Jones (Organization, Incentives, and Help).   In the early 1970s, Fredric Jones and his associates studied thousands of hours of videos they recorded in elementary and secondary classrooms. From what he learned, Jones devised Positive Classroom Discipline, a program of behavior management that emphasizes keeping students on track (hence, out of mischief). This is accomplished by means of incentives, working the crowd, and providing help efficiently. Jones urged teachers to use preferred activity times (PAT) as incentives to encourage students to complete work as directed. When they did so, they got to choose, from an approved list, an activity they enjoyed as a group. In addition, Jones advocated "working the crowd," by being very attentive to students, moving among them, and interacting with them continually while presenting instruction. He proposed a style of teaching—called say-see-do teaching—that is helpful in working the crowd. Finally, Jones noted that teachers wasted a great deal of time working with students who requested teacher help by raising their hands (helpless hand-raising, he called it). Jones showed how to give needed help in only a few seconds. Be positive, be brief, and be gone, he said. Jones's contributions continue to be popular. His most recent book is entitled *Fredric Jones's Tools for Teaching* (2001).

1986 William Glasser (Student Needs).   By 1986, William Glasser, who in 1969 had popularized classroom meetings and helping students make better behavior choices, presented a new scheme for managing student behavior. It is based on attending to five predominant needs that motivate student behavior (and misbehavior). Those five needs survival, belonging, power, fun, and freedom. Glasser described this new approach in *Control Theory in the Classroom* (1986). In that book and a series of others that followed, he has described the kind of classroom and teaching that best helps students meet those needs, the result of which is accelerated learning, sense of satisfaction, and proper classroom behavior. Glasser holds that classrooms should be warm, supportive places of learning, where student needs are met and students are asked to do only work that they consider useful. Teachers function as leaders (lead-teachers) who encourage and stimulate, rather than boss. Lead teachers help students to take active roles in learning, in contrast to boss teachers who plan everything, direct, and make demands on students. Teachers should emphasize quality teaching and learning, and realize that power struggles between teacher and students are a major enemy of quality education.

1988 Richard Curwin and Allen Mendler (Discipline with Dignity).   In 1988, Richard Curwin, an educator, and Allen Mendler, a school psychologist, published *Discipline with Dignity,* a book that clarified the importance of personal dignity in behavior management. They pointed out that students do all they can to protect their personal sense of dignity (self-respect) and that classroom misbehavior often occurs as students try to protect themselves. They say teachers should work to remove threats to student dignity while helping students assume responsibility for their actions. Respect, responsibility, and hope are the keys to desirable behavior. Teachers and students should speak with each other in a respectful adult manner. In confrontations between teachers and students, both try to win the argument. This often leads to more serious problems. Teachers should make use of conflict resolution strategies that allow both sides to save face while both get most of what they want.

1989 Thomas Gordon (Discipline as Self-Control).   In 1989, Thomas Gordon, a clinical psychologist, published *Discipline That Works: Promoting Self-discipline in Children.* Gordon, who earlier gained fame with his *Parent Effectiveness Training: A Tested New Way to Raise Responsible Children* (1970) and *T.E.T.: Teacher Effectiveness Training* (1974), says that when teachers use authoritative power to demand things of students, they almost always provoke resistance. Instead of demanding that students behave in certain ways, teachers should do what they can to help students develop self-discipline. This is accomplished, Gordon says, when teachers relinquish power in favor of positive influence. A strong step in this direction is to involve students in solving problems and making decisions about class rules and procedures. Gordon summed up his prescription for behavior management as follows:

> As a society we must urgently adopt the goal of finding and teaching effective alternatives to authority and power in dealing with other persons—children or adults—alternatives that will produce human beings with sufficient courage, autonomy, and self-discipline to resist being controlled by authority when obedience to that authority would contradict their own sense of what is right and what is wrong (1989, p. 98).

Gordon adds that the more teachers use power to control students, the less real influence they have, and that you actually increase your influence with young people when you stop using power to control them. Gordon believes rules of conduct are necessary to make classrooms safe, efficient, and harmonious. He advises teachers, in class discussions, to state what they need in the class and encourage students to do the same. Rules of conduct should grow out of those discussions.

1994 Barbara Coloroso (Inner Discipline).   Barbara Coloroso, in *Kids Are Worth It! Giving Your Child the Gift of Inner Discipline* (1994), describes an approach to behavior management that many authorities now advocate. She believes good management depends on three things: (1) treating students with respect and dignity, (2) giving them a sense of positive power over their own lives, and (3) giving them opportunities to make decisions, take responsibility for their actions, and learn from their successes and mistakes. She says responsibility grows best within an environment of trust, which teachers and administrators must cultivate.

As students grow accustomed to the provisions Coloroso suggests, they come to understand that they have a rightful place in school, but also a responsibility to respect the rights of others and remain actively involved in their own learning. They take ownership of their decisions and deal with them, without rationalizing their mistakes. Should they violate class rules, they are helped to see what they did wrong and why it was wrong. They are expected to accept ownership of the problems they have created and propose ways to resolve them. For more serious problems, students should be helped to fix what they did wrong, determine how to keep it from happening again, and reestablish relationships with people they have offended or harmed. At the same time, they learn that it is all right, even beneficial at times, to make mistakes, provided they plan how to avoid those mistakes in the future.

1996 Alfie Kohn (Communities of Learners).   Alfie Kohn, a former teacher who is now a full-time author and lecturer, has championed the concept of classrooms as communities of learners, rather than groups of students who passively receive information from the teacher. Students and teacher should take joint responsibility for the classroom, instructional activities therein, and relationships among class members. Kohn's suggestions for how this is accomplished are detailed in *Beyond Discipline: From Compliance to Community* (1996). He urges teachers to develop caring, supportive classrooms where students pursue topics that interest them and participate fully in solving class problems. He has roundly criticized teaching and behavior management that do things *to* students rather than *involving* students as partners. He says approaches based on reward and punishment are counterproductive because they cause students to mistrust their own judgment and work for rewards only. He advises teachers to concentrate on establishing an atmosphere in which students feel safe, care about each other, and are continually urged to make judgments, express their opinions, and work cooperatively toward solutions that affect themselves and the class.

2002 C. M. Charles (Synergy in Behavior Management).   C. M. Charles, an educational psychologist and teacher educator, believes that behavior management need not be an onerous task, but an ongoing opportunity for making class life better for students and teachers. One of the benefits that results from helpful behavior management is an increase in class energy. In *The Synergetic Classroom* (2000), *Building Classroom Discipline* (2002a), and *Essential Elements of Effective Discipline* (2002b), Charles explains that behavior management is intertwined with teaching and that it is most useful when thought of as helpful. Helpful efforts, he says, not only assist students in conducting themselves appropriately, but actually energize the class by, first, eliminating causes of misbehavior while attending to students' needs, and second, by promoting "mutually enhancing" relationships between teachers and students. Such relationships, in which teacher and students support and help each other, often produce a sense of joy, excitement, and well-being. These emotions energize class members, promote initiative and productivity, and reduce class disruptions.

When using helpful discipline, teachers do not make demands on students, do not struggle against them, and do not use coercive measures to try to force them to comply. Instead, they bring students into willing partnership where everyone works together to accomplish class goals. Class agreements are developed cooperatively, as are steps to be taken when those agreements are violated. Force is rejected as ineffective. Enticement to cooperate is stressed instead. Class character receives attention, too, because it strongly affects classroom behavior. A nonconfrontational approach is used to deal positively with misbehavior. Charles urges teachers never to argue with students, put them down, or back them into a corner, but instead show continual willingness to help. The way to approach misbehaving students is to ask them, "Is there a problem I can help you with?" or "Can you help me understand why this is happening? I'd like to see if we can fix the problem." Should a conflict arise between you and a student, remain calm and resist the urge to fight back. Drop your defenses. Be positive and helpful. Your challenge is to win the student over, not show that you can dominate. Finally, don't take misbehavior personally. Conduct yourself in a helpful, respectful manner and do what you can to resolve the underlying issues.

Developing Your Approach to Behavior Management

Schoolwide or Individual–Teacher Approach?

By and large, individual teachers are allowed to use systems of behavior management they judge appropriate for their classes. Usually, they have to design those systems for themselves. Should that be the case for you, the following pages will help you organize and implement a system of behavior management that meets your needs. However, many middle-level schools have developed overarching behavior management approaches for the entire school, in the belief that schoolwide plans better coordinate efforts, support teachers, and provide consistent expectations. If a schoolwide plan is in use where you teach, you are expected to adhere to its basic structure, although you may be allowed to make certain modifications you consider necessary. Should you want to make variations in a schoolwide plan, discuss them with your site administrator.

Establishing Your Personal Approach

Traditional discipline, when the teacher makes all the rules and enforces them adamantly, accomplishes little. Because it produces so many undesirable side effects, you should not consider using it. Instead, use a helping approach that is consistent with students' needs and comfortable for you. Consider the advantages of involving students in deciding on appropriate class behavior, as well as helping plan and make decisions about other aspects of the program. It is true that some classes are not capable of cooperating extensively in this partnership role. If you are in that situation, it is up to you to plan the program, organize instruction, establish the code of conduct that helps the class most, and stipulate how students will be dealt with. Even then, however, be sure to explain your system very carefully. Let students ask questions and voice concerns they might have.

As you seek to develop an appropriate approach to teaching and behavior management, take a few minutes to answer the following questions for yourself. Once you have thought these matters through, you will be ready to discuss them with your students.

1. What is this class supposed to do for students?
2. What should the class be like in order to achieve its purposes?
3. What kind of teacher behavior best leads to those outcomes?
4. What kind of student behavior best leads to those outcomes?
5. How can the students and teacher work cooperatively toward the desired outcomes?
6. How do we formalize a behavior management plan and implement it in the classroom?

Let's proceed through those questions. You will see boxed exercises to help you explore the questions. Please do the exercises, perhaps with a small group of colleagues, if possible.

What Is This Class Supposed to Do for Students?   Pretend this is an ideal world. Select a particular class and ask yourself: What can this class do for students that will make a genuine difference in their lives?

> Please think about this question for a moment before reading ahead. Select a class you are qualified to teach and see if you can specify three or four genuinely important outcomes for the class.

Have you identified knowledge that will make a true difference for students? Skills? Attitudes? Development of personal talents? Increased ability to relate productively with others? Stronger ethical character? Increased respect for oneself and others? Increased sense of self-control and responsibility? Higher value placed on education?

Once you have thought through these matters, you will be prepared to discuss these desirable outcomes meaningfully with your students. (If you can't come up with any genuinely important outcomes for your class, prepare yourself as soon as you can to teach a different subject.)

What Should the Class Be Like to Achieve Its Purposes?

> Before proceeding, think for a moment about class environment, activities, and relationship skills that will enable your students to achieve the outcomes you have identified as important. What sort of ambience is needed? How should class members interact and treat each other? How do they work individually and cooperatively?

Perhaps you have identified as desirable class qualities such as challenging, provocative, enjoyable, helpful, responsible, friendly, cooperative, satisfying, pleasant, participatory, and mutually respectful. Perhaps you have identified additional traits as well.

How I Should Conduct Myself in Order to Achieve Those Outcomes?

> See if you can specify at least five specific things you would do, and five ways you would behave in order to promote the outcomes you desire.

You may have identified things such as setting up a good environment for learning, teaching information effectively, being a good model, being a good leader, being charismatic, being always considerate and ethical, emphasizing interest and excitement in learning, taking students seriously, treating students respectfully, meeting their needs, showing them kindness and friendship, enabling them to see evidence of progress, and being as helpful as you can. Perhaps you identified additional behaviors that you feel will serve your students well.

How Should Students Conduct Themselves in Order to Achieve Those Outcomes?

> See if you can specify five kinds of behavior students will regularly exhibit as they work toward the outcomes you have identified.

You may have identified student behaviors such as being open to new learning, being friendly and well-mannered, trying hard, being prompt and punctual, showing self-control, showing consideration for you and other students, and accepting responsibility for learning.

How Can I Get Students to Work Cooperatively with Me?   Suppose you believe that close cooperation between teacher and students is important. How might you encourage such cooperation?

> See if you can think of five specific things you could do to encourage students to cooperate with you (and you with them).

What ideas did you come up with? Perhaps they are included in the following:

> Be friendly toward students.
>
> Be enthusiastic.
>
> Show them personal attention.
>
> Explain teacher–student collaboration and the advantages it brings.

Ask students if they will cooperate with you to make the class enjoyable for everyone.

Use highly interesting activities in your lessons.

Be the best model you can for students to emulate.

Arrange the environment and activities so cooperation occurs naturally.

Propose desirable class qualities such as good personal relations and mutual concern for each other, and ask students how they feel the class can establish those qualities.

Formalizing a Behavior Management Plan for Your Class

The behavior management program you devise should take into account your personality and philosophy while remaining consonant with the nature and social realities of your students. Your approach will be affected by the level of comfort you feel in working with a particular class, which derives from your experience, self-confidence, sense of control, and students' overall behavior. Let's see how your approach might be affected by your level of security.

If Your Sense of Security with the Class Is Relatively Low.   If you are worried your students will disregard your requests, slack off, disrupt, and treat you and each other disrespectfully—and if you are uneasy about your ability to get them to do otherwise—consider writing out a structured behavior management plan comprising the following:

1. A statement concerning what the class is intended to accomplish.
2. A description of desirable and necessary characteristics of the class.
3. A description of what you will do in order to establish the class characteristics you have listed.
4. A description of how students need to conduct themselves in order to make the class function as you envision it.
5. A set of class rules, five or six in number, to govern class behavior.
6. A set of consequences attached to the rules that you will invoke whenever a rule is broken. Organize the consequences to be applied in order from less severe for a single violation to more severe for repeated violations. Reserve the right to jump to more severe consequences for severe misbehavior.
7. A description of how you and other class members can help each other behave advantageously.

When you introduce the plan to students, make sure they understand each part fully and why it is necessary. Ask students for reactions. Ask if they feel the plan will present difficulties for them. Ask them if they can, and will, support the plan wholeheartedly. Tell them you want to send copies of the plan home for their parent or guardian to read, so everyone understands it fully and supports it.

If You Feel Relatively Secure Concerning Student Conduct and Your Ability to Influence It Positively.   If you feel fairly comfortable with your students' behavior and your ability to keep students working productively and happily, you might wish to do one of the following:

1. Think through a behavior management structure such as that just reviewed. Present it to your students tentatively, as preliminary thoughts. Ask them to give you feedback, make suggestions, and tell what they like and dislike. Show your willingness to modify the plan, so long as it does not violate any of your strong feelings or beliefs. Following those discussions, finalize the plan, communicate it to parents or guardians, and put it into effect.

2. Bring your students into full collaboration in developing the behavior management plan. Begin with a series of class meetings, as described in Chapter 3, in which you initiate discussions by asking certain questions. As students respond, take notes and summarize their ideas, then later write them on charts. When the series of discussions is completed, you have in hand a finalized plan, produced by you and your students as equal collaborators. If your students are able to work with you in this way, and if you are comfortable with the process, this approach is likely to yield a highly effective program for your class.

Establishing Behavior Expectations and Teacher Interventions.   Students must understand clearly how they are expected to behave in class and what will happen if they violate those expectations. Some teachers are reluctant to broach this subject directly, feeling they may appear overly dogmatic. When their students misbehave, those teachers usually tell students what they have done wrong and then reprimand them or apply other consequences. Middle school students usually know how to behave properly but sometimes need reminders. Occasionally, you may have to teach them proper behavior.

Examples of Rules.   Teachers who decide by themselves class rules of behavior must explain those rules carefully. It is best to print them out so students can have a copy to take to their parents. Post the rules in the classroom and go over them with students. Be explicit about the rules. Give examples of behavior that complies with them and behavior that violates them. If necessary, have students act out and practice behaviors that comply. Keep the number of rules to no more than six. Otherwise, students cannot remember them. Refer to the posted list as needed to remind students how to conduct themselves. The following are examples of rules excerpted from several different teachers' discipline plans. You can see they overlap.

> Be in your seat on time, ready to work.
>
> Do your best work at all times.
>
> Treat others considerately, as you would like them to treat you.
>
> Do not disrupt teaching or learning.
>
> Bring your textbook, notebook, and pencil every day.
>
> Pay attention when the teacher, or a student who has been called on, is talking.
>
> Bring no candy, gum, hats, or sunglasses to class.
>
> Never use profanity or verbal abuse.
>
> When the period ends, remain seated until you are dismissed.

Examples of Consequences.   If you are using rules to guide behavior, you must also consider a means of enforcing those rules. This is accomplished by linking rules to "reasonable consequences" that are applied when rules are broken. Discuss these consequences with students to clarify their nature, purpose, and application. Everyone—students, teacher, and parents—knows in advance what those consequences are. When a student breaks a rule and you must intervene, you do so by applying the appropriate consequence.

The Canters were the first to suggest a hierarchy of consequences to be applied for rules violations. They suggest a hierarchy similar to the following, although they encourage teachers to select alternative consequences they prefer, provided those consequences are both effective and humane (Canter and Canter, 2001).

First time a student breaks a rule: Indicate that a rule is being broken and remind the student of more appropriate behavior.

Second time a student breaks the same rule: Remind the student of the rule being broken and indicate he or she has chosen to accept the established consequence, such as five minutes time-out from the lesson.

Third time a student breaks the same rule: Remind the student of the rule being broken and indicate that he or she has chosen the established consequence, such as going to the in-school suspension room to work alone.

Fourth time a student breaks the same rule: Remind the student of the rule being broken and indicate that he or she has chosen to accept the consequence of meeting with the vice principal or counselor to discuss the situation.

Severe clause. Sometimes behavior is so severe that it is best to send the student to the vice principal's office on the first offense. You meet with the student later to try to iron out the problem.

Linda Albert (1996) also offers good advice about consequences. She suggests four kinds of consequences she believes are most effective:

- loss or delay of privileges, such as loss or delay of a favorite activity;
- loss of freedom of interaction, such as talking with other students;
- restitution, such as return, repair, or replacement of objects, doing school service, or helping other students whom one has offended;
- meeting between teacher and students to compose a plan for improving that student's behavior.

Albert advises talking with the offending student when applying consequences, using a series of questions such as the following:

- What behavior are you choosing at this moment?
- Is this behavior in keeping with our class agreement about (*name agreement*)?
- Can you help me understand why you are violating our agreement?
- Given our agreements, what should I say to you right now?

By speaking with the student in that way, you can usually avoid applying consequences altogether, but the process does take time.

Richard Curwin (1992) suggests establishing four categories of consequences that students understand easily: reminders, warnings, choosing, and planning. Depending on the misbehavior, its severity, and its frequency, you invoke the consequence you think most suitable—less severe to more severe—from the appropriate category, which might be:

- Reminders: "We need to get this work completed in five minutes."
- Warnings: "If I have to remind you again, you will need to take time-out."
- Choosing: "Janet, you have broken our rule against disrupting the class. You can either sit at the back table by yourself for ten minutes or meet with me briefly after class to discuss this problem. You choose which you prefer."
- Planning (which Curwin calls the most effective of all consequences): "Michael, please sit at the back table and write out a plan for how you can stop breaking our rule about (*name the agreement*). I'd like the plan by the end of this period so we can go over it together."

FIELD APPLICATION 3: Identify and observe a teacher who uses established consequences in conjunction with class rules. Describe the consequences and how they are applied.

Using Class Agreements instead of Rules.   When students work collaboratively with you to establish class expectations, the results are more appropriately called "class agreements." We have noted that the best way to establish class agreements and intervention plans is by using a series of class discussions that lead to a set of clear, workable agreements. That process, described in detail in Chapter 3, involved classroom meetings for the purpose of becoming acquainted with students and then:

- drawing them out on how they'd like the class to function;
- drawing them out on the traits they prefer in teachers;
- drawing them out on how they would like students to behave in the class;
- exploring undesirable student behavior;
- preparing agreements about the class and student behavior; and
- establishing procedures for intervening helpfully when students misbehave.

Agreements imply that students have, through their involvement, made a commitment to abide by their provisions, while rules seem to suggest directives set down by the teacher. If you are sufficiently comfortable about doing so, invite your students to collaborate with you to (1) agree on desirable behaviors, (2) put the agreements into words, (3) explore how to abide by them, and (4) decide clearly what is to happen when anyone (including you) breaks an agreement. When you have to intervene in misbehavior, you only need follow the agreed-on procedure: "Zelia, you have not lived up to our agreement about always doing our best work. We have agreed that I should remind you of it, which should be all that is necessary." If Zelia continues to break the agreement, you will meet with her, per class agreement, to work out a plan to help her become more responsible.

Reminders Concerning Interventions

Your behavior management plan should explain clearly how you will intervene when agreements are violated. Students need to understand the procedures clearly. Regardless of the method of behavior management you use, make it evident that the plan is for students' benefit. Make absolutely sure you never attack students, denigrate them, or back them into a corner. Never use force or intimidation to make them comply. Instead, provide encouragement and help, which will enable you to maintain a positive relationship with them. Here are further reminders to help you intervene appropriately in various kinds of misbehavior.

If You Are Using Rules and Consequences. If you are using a system of class rules linked to specific consequences, you have only to make statements such as:

- Randall, you are breaking our rule about no talking during quiet time. This is a reminder.
- Randall, this is the second time you have broken our rule about no talking during quiet time. The consequence is to meet with me right after class to see what we can do to help you abide by the rule.

If You Are Using Class Agreements. If your behavior management system does not specify consequences, it ought, nevertheless, to explain what will be done when agreements are broken. You will have worked these out with your students. Examples include:

For Benign Behavior:
- Establish eye contact.
- Move alongside the student.
- Ask very quietly, "May I remind you of this agreement?"
- Say, "I am not comfortable with what is happening here. Could I ask for your consideration and help?"
- Say, "I can tell you are not very interested in this (*topic or activity*). What can I do to make the experience better for you?" (Suggestions are considered at this time.)
- "Class, this doesn't seem to be working as we had hoped. What do you think the problem is? Can we resolve it, or should we change to a different activity?" (Suggestions are considered at this time.)
- "Class, I don't feel (*something such as the quality of our work recently*) has been up to the expectations we hold for ourselves. Perhaps we might discuss this matter in a class meeting." (Class meeting is used later, involving problem solving.)

For Frequently Repeated Misbehavior:
- "We are having difficulty keeping this agreement. Can you help me understand why, and how we can resolve the matter?" (Suggestions are considered at this point.)

If Misbehavior Consists of Personal Conflict or Overt Resistance:
- "Could you meet with me later? We need to work together to straighten this out." (Public discussion or private conference follows. Problem solving and conflict resolution are used. Win–win conflict resolution is described briefly in Chapter 14.)

If Misbehavior Is Hurtful or Involves Serious Conflict:

■ "Let's meet together and see if we can find a way to work this out." (Conference ensues. Plans are made for resolution and follow-up.)

■ "When you have cooled down, let's talk together to see if we can settle this problem." (Private conference follows. Conflict resolution is used.)

If Misbehavior Involves Gross Defiance or Possibility of Physical Danger:

■ "You must go immediately to (*separate parts of the room, suspension room, principal's office*). I really hope we can talk about this later and get it settled."

■ Call office for immediate assistance, if necessary.

> **FIELD APPLICATION 4:**   Informally interview three or four teachers concerning the procedures they follow when students seriously misbehave, such as fight, swear at the teacher, or bully other students.

QUESTIONS

1. On which would you place greater emphasis: doing what you can to prevent misbehavior from occurring, or establishing humane, helpful ways of working with students who have misbehaved? Explain your reasons.

2. What do you think is meant by the terms *democratic classrooms, democratic teaching, congruent communication,* and *student needs?*

3. What, if anything, is wrong with teachers' laying down the law concerning student behavior and using the procedures necessary to enforce it?

4. What do you think of involving students closely in determining how the class will function and how behavior will be managed? Explain.

5. Do you see a substantive difference between rules and agreements, or is the distinction superficial? Explain.

6. To what extent do you feel the information presented in this chapter helps you to deal positively and helpfully with students who misbehave in your class? What sorts of student behavior, if any, still give you concern?

ACTIVITY

In no more than three pages, outline an approach to classroom behavior management that you feel would be most effective for you and your students. Make your plan consistent with what you want your class to achieve.

REFERENCES

Albert, L. 1996. *Cooperative discipline.* Circle Pines, MN: American Guidance Service.

Canter, L., and Canter, M. 1976. *Assertive discipline: A take-charge approach for today's educator:* Seal Beach, CA: Canter & Associates. (The 2001 edition is entitled *Assertive discipline: Positive behavior management for today's classroom.*)

Charles, C. 2000. *The synergetic classroom: Joyful teaching and gentle discipline.* New York: Longman.

———. 2002a. *Building classroom discipline* (7th ed.). Boston: Allyn & Bacon.

———. 2002b. *Essential elements of effective discipline.* Boston: Allyn & Bacon.

Coloroso, B. 1994. *Kids are worth it!: Giving your child the gift of inner discipline.* New York: Avon Books.

———. 1999. *Parenting with wit and wisdom in times of chaos and confusion.* Littleton, CO: Kids Are Worth It!

Curwin, R. 1992. *Rediscovering hope: Our greatest teaching strategy.* Bloomington, IN: National Educational Service.

Curwin, R., and Mendler, A. 1988. *Discipline with dignity.* Alexandria, VA: Association for Supervision and Curriculum Development.

Dreikurs R., and Cassel, P. 1972. *Discipline without tears.* New York: Hawthorne.

Ginott, H. 1971. *Teacher and child.* New York: Macmillan.

Glasser, W. 1969. *Schools without failure.* New York: Harper & Row.

———. 1986. *Control theory in the classroom.* New York: Harper & Row.

———. 1998. *The quality school: Managing students without coercion.* New York: HarperCollins.

Gordon, T. 1970. *Parent effectiveness training: A tested new way to raise responsible children.* New York: New American Library.

———. 1974. *T.E.T.: Teacher effectiveness training.* New York: David McKay.

———. 1989. *Discipline that works: Promoting self-discipline in children.* New York: Random House.

Jones, F. 1979. The gentle art of classroom discipline. *National Elementary Principal, 58,* 26–32.

———. 2001. *Fred Jones's tools for teaching.* Santa Cruz, CA: Fredric H. Jones &Associates.

Kohn, A. 1996. *Beyond discipline: From compliance to community.* Alexandria, VA: Association for Supervision and Curriculum Development.

———. 1999. *The schools our children deserve: Moving beyond traditional classrooms and "tougher standards."* Boston: Houghton Mifflin.

Kounin, J. 1971. *Discipline and group management in classrooms.* New York: Holt, Rinehart, and Winston.

Kyle, P., Kagan, S., and Scott, S. 2001. *Win-win discipline: Structures for all discipline problems.* San Clemente, CA: Kagan.

Nelsen, J., Lott, L., and Glenn, H. 2000. *Positive discipline in the classroom.* Rocklin, CA: Prima.

Redl, F., and Wattenberg, W. 1951. *Mental hygiene in teaching.* New York: Harcourt, Brace, and World.

Skinner, B. 1954. The science of learning and the art of teaching. *Harvard Educational Review, 24,* 86–97.

Improving Behavior by Strengthening Class Character

Chapter Preview

This chapter explores class character, its nature, its relationship with behavior management, and how it can be strengthened. Class character is described as a composite of individual students' ethical qualities and personality traits that reflect the nature of the class as a whole. In this chapter such qualities and traits are identified, a guide is provided for appraising them, and suggestions are offered for improving desirable qualities.

Caveat: "Character Education" May Be a Sensitive Topic

Character education, which involves attempting to strengthen students' character traits, is widely lauded as a means of improving individual and group behavior. It emphasizes such things as treating others with respect and consideration, taking personal responsibility, and collaborating effectively. While most people consider character education to be one of the most important focuses of education, not everyone agrees. You should be aware that it is a sensitive matter in some communities, where parents may consider it an invasion of privacy and unwarranted tampering with the moral development of their children. The majority, however, believes character education is eminently worthwhile, attested to by the numbers of national organizations that support it and the numbers of schools that implement it. As you will see, there is growing evidence that teachers and schools who stress character education have fewer discipline problems and a greater sense of student community.

> **FIELD APPLICATION 1:** Check with the school where you are assigned or about which you want to know more. Determine if the school and community favor character education and whether they have a character education program in effect.

Class Character and Why It Is Considered Important

Classes have distinct personalities, just as individuals do. Some classes are happy and outgoing, some serious and hardworking, some boorish, some lethargic, and a few aimlessly chaotic. These outward personalities are indicators of class character. While personality and character are closely related, a connotative distinction differentiates them. Personality usually refers to all observable traits of individuals or classes, while character usually refers to ethical values and qualities such as honesty, correct behavior, determination, responsibility, and steadfastness.

Character has strong bearing on behavior management. In classes where students are purposeful, responsible, and considerate, instruction and learning occur relatively smoothly, with little misbehavior. Students learn rapidly and enjoy themselves. But in classes where students are irresponsible, purposeless, and inconsiderate, misbehavior is the rule. Lessons do not proceed well. Students progress fitfully and find little pleasure in the class.

Fortunately, we know a number of ways to improve the overall character of our classes. Effort you expend in that regard is usually well worthwhile. Not only does it yield improvement in progress and morale, but it also produces positive behavioral changes in individual students that seem to persist for years. Overall, efforts to help students develop better personal character, and, hence, class character, are referred to as *character education.* Whereas some programs of character education give attention to civic education and democratic processes, in most cases character education deals more with individuals' sense of moral conduct and relations with others.

Evelyn Otten (2000), in introducing her review of the literature related to character education, explains that character education helps students connect morality with the social aspects of their lives. The core values emphasized in character education come from community values, which teachers attempt to instill or strengthen in students. Some people are concerned about exactly which values should be taught or, indeed, whether any at all should be explicitly taught. However, we know that virtually all cultures emphasize certain values such as honesty, fairness, and respect for others. If we focus on those overarching values prized by all people, we need not be concerned about indoctrinating students with values contrary to those of their society.

As for the effectiveness of character education, schools that have implemented such programs report fewer disciplinary problems, better attendance, fewer dropouts, and even higher performance on standardized achievement tests (Wynne and Ryan, 1997). Those are commendable results, but so far as teachers and students are concerned, an equally important result is a calm, purposeful, well-mannered classroom and school in which to work and learn.

The Nature and Role of Character Education

Groups working to further character education agree on its purpose and importance, but sometimes have different views concerning the content of programs. Some of the best guidelines for character education are provided in the Character Education Manifesto (1996), a statement put forth by the Center for the Advancement of Ethics and Character located at Boston University's School of Education. The manifesto emphasizes the following:

- The purpose of character education is to help students develop good habits and dispositions that lead to responsible adulthood.
- Young people should be helped to recognize that sound personal character is necessary for living a meaningful and satisfying life.

- Parents, guardians, and other family members are the primary moral educators of their children; hence, schools should address character education in partnership with the home.
- Character education should be an integral, ongoing part of school life.
- The teacher and the school principal are central figures in character education and should be prepared and encouraged to provide it.
- Character education should call on the collective moral wisdom that exists in humanity's great stories, works of art, literature, history, and biography.

The manifesto is signed by representatives of educational institutions, federal government, industry, and educational and youth foundations.

In a similar vein, the Character Education Partnership in Alexandria, Virginia, has listed a group of principles including the following (see Lickona, Schaps, and Lewis, 2001):

- "Character" is made evident in how individuals think, feel, and behave.
- Ethical values are the basis of good character, and character education should promote those values, intentionally and comprehensively.
- Effective character education includes a meaningful and challenging academic curriculum that respects all learners and helps them succeed.
- To make this possible, schools and classrooms must be organized into caring communities of learners where there is strong moral leadership and frequent opportunities for moral action.
- The school staff must participate in this moral community by adhering to the core moral values and sharing responsibility for character development in students.
- The school must bring family members and community members into full partnership in the character-building effort.
- Evaluation of character education should assess the character of the school, the staff's effectiveness in promoting character education, and the extent to which students manifest good character.

For additional suggestions from the Character Education Partnership, see the Web site at *www.character.org*

Successes in Character Education

Evidence from various locations is showing that character education can bring about the results intended. Frequently cited in the literature is a program conducted in Oakland, California, where fifty students received character education from kindergarten through eighth grade (see Walters, 1997). In that program, students participated in lessons built around moral and ethical issues. Teachers modeled desirable behavior and looked for opportunities to ask students to consider what it means to be helpful, caring, honest, and kind. The school held "family reading nights" when students, family members, and teachers got together for stories and discussions at school. Teachers also assigned occasional "family homework" that focused on matters such as chores and family ancestry.

When those students were later compared with "nonprogram" students, they were found to be more spontaneously helpful, friendly, and collaborative in the classroom. Their conflict-resolution skills were more advanced, and they were judged to be less lonely and "socially anxious" in school. The Oakland program is now being used in over fifty schools nationwide, including Louisville, Kentucky, White Plains, New York, and Cupertino, California.

A number of other success stories in character education have emerged in recent years. One of many is the Emerald Way, a character education program at Emerald Middle School, Cajon Valley Schools, California, which in 2001 received a coveted Golden Bell award for excellence (see *www.csba.org/PA/GoldenBell*).

The Emerald Way

The Emerald Way is a schoolwide program for improving student behavior that has been used at Emerald Middle School in El Cajon, California, since 1996. Developed by the principal and teacher leaders, it presents a theme and a common language that help create a sense of community in the school. It emphasizes the development of ten specific character traits believed to enable students to lead more effective lives, increasing class civility while reducing misbehavior. When students do misbehave, teachers intervene with supportive techniques that are in keeping with the schoolwide plan.

The program is undergirded by counseling and parent support. A *Student Success Team* is in place to deal with more serious offenses and to support students who are at risk of failure. A *Homework Club* meets four afternoons a week to help students keep up in classes—the teachers at Emerald Middle School believe a main cause of misbehavior is students' dropping behind academically, leaving them feeling hopeless and disengaged. *Supervised peer mediation* is used to resolve conflicts between students and help them deal with personal problems. Should students fight or talk disrespectfully to teachers or other adults on campus, they face the possibility of detention or in-school suspension.

Goals of The Emerald Way

The Emerald Way sets forth the following goals for students:

to interact more effectively and successfully with others;

to feel connected to the school;

to learn specific behaviors that demonstrate the ten character traits specified in the program;

to develop students' positive feelings toward themselves, their school, and their community.

The Ten Targeted Traits

A separate character trait is featured each month. During that month it is emphasized by all teachers and administrators. A number of activities are built around the trait. The character traits are considered in the following sequence:

1. Courtesy—showing behavior that is gracious, kind, and thoughtful of others
2. Commitment—making and living up to pledges or agreements
3. Respect—showing high regard or strong consideration for something or someone
4. Appreciation—showing sensitive enjoyment, awareness, or grateful recognition
5. Initiative—taking the first step; thinking or acting without being urged
6. Responsibility—showing reliability and accountability in one's own actions
7. Self-discipline—maintaining self-control; taking charge of one's own conduct
8. Honesty—behaving in a fair and straightforward manner, without intending to deceive
9. Cooperation—participating helpfully with others for the benefit of all
10. Success—experiencing a feeling of accomplishment and satisfaction

Schoolwide Procedures

The Emerald Way is put into effect through teacher teams, schoolwide reinforcement procedures, and daily support from school administrators.

Character trait posters are displayed in all classrooms, showing the ten traits for the year. The trait being emphasized in a given month is highlighted.

Teacher teams and a schedule are established. The teams each select one of their members to introduce the trait for the month and plan associated activities. The activities are discussed and approved by the team before being used and are reviewed during weekly team meetings.

Incentives and rewards are approved and applied by members of the team. They are given for demonstration of good character and for academic achievement. For example, all teachers and staff members have access to Emerald Way Knight Cards, which they can present to students who show exemplary behavior. Students use the cards to purchase items in the Student Store or to put in the Knight Card drawing in hopes of winning a school T-shirt.

Time commitment to the program is at least fifty-five minutes of instruction per month, divided into sessions as the team sees fit.

Scheduling of activities is as follows: In week one of each month the designated teachers introduce and explain to students the character trait being emphasized. They identify its objectives and preview instructional activities. Throughout the month teachers teach the trait using activities such as role plays, readings, writing, and discussions. Each week, teachers nominate students who are exemplary or have shown great improvement. Three of those students from each grade level are recognized as Knights of the Week and their names are read during the morning bulletin. Their names go into a pool, from which faculty select the Knights of the Month.

At the end of each month, all faculty members vote for one Knight of the Month from each grade level, 6, 7, and 8. Student recipients are treated to lunch with the principal at a local restaurant. Teams also implement other incentive programs they have put in place, such as bonus points, assembly programs, guest speakers, or field trips.

Suggested teaching activities are in keeping with the program guide, but teachers are allowed latitude in selecting activities they find effective. Examples include journal writing, skits, role plays, cooperative learning tasks, debates, discussions, keeping daily logs, service projects, art projects, guest speakers, and inspirational sayings and readings.

Daily support from administrators is provided as follows: Each day on the closed-circuit TV broadcast, a school administrator, usually the principal, presents special announcements, "Powerful Learners" statements, examples of character traits noted in action, and the principal's Thought for the Day related to the character trait. The TV is also used as an electronic bulletin board to display motivational information about The Emerald Way and showcase photos of Knights of the Month with their teachers and peers.

Examples of Monthly Plans and Lessons

To illustrate more clearly the activities teachers provide, here are the contents of the school plan for improving *Courtesy*.

Target Behaviors

- Use the words *please* and *thank you.*
- Extend friendly greetings (smile, make eye contact, say something considerate).
- Listen and wait (don't interrupt, wait your turn, say "Excuse me").
- Be aware of people and space around you (share space with others, don't crowd halls or doorways, show kindness, don't laugh at others' mistakes or embarrassment, no name-calling).

Thoughts and Quotes (Only three of many suggestions are shown here.):

- Do unto others as you'd have them do unto you.
- All doors open to courtesy.
- Rudeness is the weak person's imitation of strength.

Suggested Classroom Activities (Only a few examples from many are shown here.):

- Describe what school would be like if people were more courteous to each other.
- Describe the differences in norms of courtesy when you are with friends as contrasted with when you are with your parents, grandparents, teachers, or other adults.
- Write or act a brief conversation for each of these types of language: Formal (with adults in school or business), Informal (with friends), and Family (used with family and loved ones).

- In groups, write skits that demonstrate courtesy in various settings and present the skits to the class.
- Have a vocabulary enhancement lesson related to courtesy, including words such as *polite, empathetic, faux pas, diplomacy, gracious, etiquette, chivalry, manners, gaffe.*
- Learn about and practice communication door openers, road blocks, active listening, and I-statements to take the place of you-statements.

Program Effectiveness

Teachers at Emerald Middle School are seldom able, given time restrictions, to do all the activities contained in the program guide. They report, however, that their efforts seem to be effective. There has been a marked decline in referrals to the assistant principal's office, and visitors to the campus invariably comment on how well-behaved, polite, and friendly the students are.

For results of programs in other schools and classes, see the success stories presented at Dr. Tom Lickona's Web site (see *www.cortland.edu/c4n5rs/suxhom.htm*).

Character Education Is Not Easy

Successful efforts such as those described in the Emerald Way and the Oakland Program might make it appear that character education involves little more than describing desirable traits and urging students to conduct themselves accordingly. Several authorities warn against that conclusion. Alfie Kohn (1997) says that too often educators try to instill good character and values in students, as if those virtues were fully formed, floating about, and simply waiting to be stuffed into passive students. He contends that teaching *about* values and *urging* students to behave in certain ways have little effect, because that doesn't help students go through the process of integrating the new values into their value structure. The result is, students develop no lasting commitment to the desired behavior. Kohn says better results are likely when educators, family members, and other adults offer guidance, act as good models, pose challenges that promote moral growth, and help children understand the effects of their actions on others.

In a similar vein, Eric Schaps, Esther Schaeffer, and Sanford McDonnell, all of the Character Education Partnership (www.character.org, 2001), write that, while they are staunch advocates for character education,

> we are concerned about, and critical of, what many are doing in the name of character education. Well-intentioned as these efforts may be, we believe that they will make little difference for students, and thus may soon discredit the entire field. Moreover, they can easily distract us from what really matters in helping students become caring, principled, and responsible adults.

In particular, Schaps, Schaeffer, and McDonnell express concern that educators have an erroneously shallow perspective of character development. Character develops over time and is formed in many ways, such as through exposure to the attitudes and actions of people who are trusted. Schaps, Schaeffer, and McDonnell claim that little, if any, benefit comes from moralizing to students or giving them direct instruction in moral principles. Neither does it do much good, they warn, to use any of the approaches they call "cheerleading," "praise and reward," "define and drill," and "forced formality." Instead of those approaches, Schaps, Schaeffer, and McDonnell advocate the following:

- Meet students' basic needs. Students tend to bond with adults who attend to their needs.
- Enlist students as active, influential participants in creating a caring and just environment in the classroom and school.
- Involve students in honest, thoughtful discussion and reflection about the moral implications of what they see around them, what they are told, and what they personally do and experience.
- Work to see that the class and school reflect the values emphasized in character education.
- Create "caring communities of learners" that feature class meetings, ethics-rich academic work, collaborative learning, "buddies" programs that bring together younger and older students, whole-school events involving students and their families, and service opportunities inside and outside the school.

Are Teachers Prepared for Character Education?

There is some concern about how well classroom teachers can deliver effective programs of character education. Barbara Munson (2000) says research indicates that the overwhelming majority of preservice teacher education programs in the United States do not offer significant instruction in the methodology of teaching character, morals, values, and virtue. Consequently, beginning teachers are ill-equipped to deal with the complex social and behavioral problems they face in the classroom and, hence, are unable to foster strong character in their classes. Munson believes teacher education programs should include a component on character education that emphasizes the nature of and need for character education as well as tactics teachers can use to help their students become "intellectually smart and morally good."

Marvin Berkowitz (1998) also cites the need for specific teacher training, but identifies six obstacles that stand in its way: (1) lack of agreement on what character means; (2) disagreements about what constitutes character education; (3) limited space in the preservice teacher education curriculum that can be devoted to character education; (4) limited data concerning which elements of character education are effective; (5) lack of resources and expertise; and (6) ambivalence about the appropriateness of educating for character. These points merit consideration, but it seems fairly certain that teachers, when prepared for doing so, can promote significant development in students' moral sensitivities and ethical qualities. The question for us now is, how do we prepare ourselves to provide the experiences students need?

FIELD APPLICATION 2:   Inquire about character education in the program where you have done your preparation for teaching. Determine whether character education is given attention, and, if so, through what means.

How to Proceed in Character Education

We have seen a number of suggestions concerning desirable components of character education and how character can be improved. Now let's briefly review desirable character traits to be developed, the teaching strategies used to promote them, and the support strategies needed to make the program workable.

Desirable Character Traits

What specific character traits should we try to help students develop? At least twelve traits, it appears, should receive attention in character education. The stronger we can make the traits in individual students, the better the overall class character becomes. If you observe any class (and have a list of the twelve traits in hand), you can fairly easily see evidence of the traits and their relative strength. The traits are:

1. *Ethics*—a sense of the right and wrong ways of conducting oneself and treating others, especially with regard to kindness, honesty, and fairness.
2. *Trust*—having confidence in others, and earning their confidence in return, that we will conduct ourselves properly, won't harm others, and will help in times of need.
3. *Consideration*—recognizing the individuality of other people and interacting with them in keeping with their needs, traits, and personal circumstances.
4. *Dignity*—assigning respect to ourselves and others, as people of competence and value.
5. *Personal power*—sensing the ability and opportunity to influence others and control various aspects of our lives.
6. *Purposefulness*—having a clear idea of what we want to achieve, why, and how to go about it.
7. *Persistence*—sticking with tasks and following them through to completion, even when they are difficult and frustrating.
8. *Responsibility*—taking on tasks, carrying them out to the best of our ability, showing reliability and self-control, and being willing to accept the results of our actions.
9. *Energy*—experiencing high levels of motivation and activity.
10. *Helpfulness*—willingly assisting others when the need is present.
11. *Collaboration*—working together cooperatively to make progress and resolve difficulties.
12. *Joy*—maintaining a sense of happiness and satisfaction.

You might want to display this list in your classroom so you can refer to it regularly in discussions with your students.

Effective Teaching Strategies

Earlier we saw Schaps, Schaeffer, and McDonnell's (2001) suggestions concerning what teachers should do when presenting their programs of character education, including:

- Meet students' basic needs.
- Enlist students as active, influential participants in creating a caring and just environment in the classroom and school.

- Involve students in honest, thoughtful discussion and reflection about the moral implications of what they see around them, what they are told, and what they personally do and experience. (Here, one strives for conditions mentioned previously—communities of learners that use class meetings and feature ethics-rich academic work, collaborative learning, whole-school events involving students and their families, and service opportunities inside and outside the school.)
- Provide opportunity for students to learn about and practice ethical and personal qualities. Help students find needed resources and show them how to evaluate both their efforts and their overall experience.
- Model desirable character qualities for your students. Modeling means teaching through example. As you conduct yourself in certain ways—for example, showing kindness, consideration, responsibility, and persistence—you notice that your students begin to imitate the behaviors. This is more likely to occur when students like and respect you.
- Conduct discussions about character and its development. In previous chapters, you have read about class meetings and other venues in which you and your students, working in collaboration, confront issues and make joint decisions. Use this process to help students engage in discussions about morality and analyze situations that place one in moral dilemmas where a decision must be made between what is believed to be "right" and what may be more appealing.

Strengthening Ethics.   Ethics has to do with values concerning proper self-conduct and the treatment of others. For the most part, ethics involves honesty, fairness, and kindness.

Honesty.   Honesty means being truthful with oneself and others in all matters of consequence. It requires keeping one's word, refusing to cheat and lie, admitting mistakes and failures, and never resorting to deceit. Teachers want students to tell the truth, and students expect the same of teachers.

Life teaches us that honesty usually *is* the best policy. When we behave honestly, we look better to others and to ourselves, even when we have to admit we made a mistake or failed at something. Making mistakes is always acceptable and can even be useful when we learn from them and, thus, improve. Most people will tell you that mistakes they have made taught them a great deal. Any embarrassment associated with confessing a true mistake will be short-lived. But deceit is another matter. It destroys trust and is never forgotten.

Why, then, do we lie when honesty works best? Usually it is to take advantage of someone, make ourselves look better, get out of a task we find distasteful, avoid the consequences of what we have done, keep people from getting upset with us, avoid appearing inept or ignorant, or just make stories seem grander than they really are. (We seldom fool others, however, and so damage our reputation or get deeper into hot water.) Draw your students into exploring the benefits of behaving honestly, even when doing so produces temporary discomfort. Help them to see the difference between dishonesty and making mistakes and to understand that, while mistakes are a natural and beneficial part of learning, dishonesty can damage personal relations and one's self-respect.

Fairness.   Our students have a keen sense of fairness and want fairness to prevail. Gerry Spence says, "(Children) know when they are being wrongfully repressed. They know right from wrong and they have a nearly perfect sense of justice" (1995, p. 240). Students eagerly call attention to what they perceive as unfairness, especially when they are affected by it. Teachers get tired of that in a hurry, and when students' voices become whiney with, "That's not *fair*," teachers want to retort (and sometimes do), "The world is not a fair place, honey. Get a grip." As if such a comment would immediately set things right in the student's mind.

We miss an opportunity to encourage trust when we dismiss students' concerns about fairness and disregard their complaints. At such times we should explore with them the meaning of fairness, which does not necessarily mean treating everyone the same, but treating individuals in accordance with their individual needs (Curwin and Mendler, 1988). Be up front and honestly tell your students, "I will always try to treat you as fairly as possible and will help you treat each other the same. Sometimes I might treat one of you differently from another. When that happens, it is because of differences I see in the situation or your feelings. But I will always try for fairness. When I fail in that, or anyone in the class fails, it is important that we discuss it." Most students, once the "fair does not mean equal" concept is explained to them, see the justice in it.

Kindness.   The golden rule best expresses what kindness is, treating others as we, ourselves, want to be treated. No one wants to be disrespected, derided, or treated coldly. Students need to learn that kindness overrides the negative impressions one might otherwise make and is, therefore, the key to good relationships. Students give us strong clues about what they consider to be kind treatment. They want us to acknowledge them, call them by name, and chat with them occasionally. They want us to treat them gently, with a smile. They want us to show them respect by being polite and courteous. They want us to understand their fears and difficulties. They definitely do not want us to scold, yell at them, call them names, intimidate or punish them. Remember: while many acts of kindness go into building trust, a single unkind act can destroy it.

Your students may not seem to be overly ethical when you first begin working with them, but they learn from observing your example and from discussing with you the importance of honesty, fairness, and kindness. They will certainly notice any of your lapses in those areas.

> Do you sometimes feel you are being treated inconsiderately, unfairly, or unkindly? Think of such an instance and ask yourself how you would prefer to be treated. Do you think you can treat others pretty much as you would like to be treated? Ask these questions of your students.

Strengthening Trust.   To trust someone is to have strong confidence in him or her. None of us likes to work with people we think might renege on commitments or run us down behind our backs, whereas we feel secure and comfortable with people we believe to be ethical and reliable.

Trust develops naturally when a class operates on ethical principles and teachers show genuine concern for students. To encourage trust, you and your students must commit yourselves to behavior that is honest, fair, and kind. Further, you must always be helpful and show you have faith in each student's potential. Trust grows slowly, if at all, when students remain wary of you and each other. You can establish trust if you persevere, but be warned: it is easily lost, much more quickly that it is gained. Stephen Covey reminds us:

> People will forgive mistakes, because mistakes are usually of the mind, mistakes of judgment. But people will not easily forgive the mistakes of the heart, the ill intention, the bad motives, the prideful justifying cover-up of the first mistake (1989, p. 199).

Here are some things you and your students can work on together to build mutual trust. Discuss them with your students.

- Listen to each other carefully and take each other seriously.
- Recognize and appreciate the uniqueness of each person.
- Speak kindly with others, in a supportive tone of voice.
- Never intentionally deceive others, or harm or slight them.
- Draw attention to others and give credit where it is due.
- Do not expect others to be perfect: make allowance for their imperfections and ask them to make allowance for yours.

In your middle school years, did you ever have a teacher you really trusted, fully and completely? If so, to what specifically do you attribute that trust? Ask this question of your students.

Strengthening Consideration.   Consideration means sensitively recognizing and showing tolerance for other people's beliefs, attitudes, values, and needs. We might condense consideration into one succinct admonition: do not damage the other person's dignity. Dignity refers to self-respect and involves a sense of one's competence, power, control, and self-direction. We show consideration for students when we hesitate to intrude into their inner lives. We accept them as they are, do not threaten them, and keep alive their sense of hope. Students avoid situations and people they fear will make them look stupid. They will lie, cheat, and feign indifference rather than allow themselves to appear incompetent.

Students want to be accepted and treated with kindness. Sometimes they need encouragement, sometimes sympathy, sometimes support. Always they need tolerance. To strengthen consideration in your classes, do two things: first, always make sure you do not threaten students' dignity. Second, in class discussions ask questions that make students reflect on matters.

- Think of a time when your feelings were really hurt. How did you want to be treated at that time?
- Think of a time when you felt quite out of place because you were among people different from you. How did you feel? How did you want to be treated? How do you think you should have acted toward them?
- How can we tell when others are feeling ill at ease or worried or hurt? What do you see that tells you?

- What do you think it means to be considerate of others? How do you act when being considerate?
- Why do you think it is important for all of us to be considerate of each other? What does it do for us personally? For fellow students? For the class as a whole?

At this point we should mention the role that patience plays in consideration. Patience might not seem an ethical principle and may not usually be in life, but in teaching it is. The best teachers are enthusiastic and motivating, but they are patient, too. They know students work and learn at different speeds. They know some grasp concepts quickly, while others take awhile. They know some do their work accurately while others make many mistakes, sometimes over and over. It is very easy to become impatient with students who repeat an error. The considerate teacher sticks with the student, gives help over and over, and tolerates repeated mistakes, but tactfully tries to help the student improve. The considerate teacher knows these students may ultimately master the material as well or better than the faster students. The patient teacher remains pleasant, never showing exasperation and never putting the student down. Students develop an abiding trust in teachers who treat them in that manner.

Strengthening Dignity. Dignity, or self-respect, lies at the center of self-concept and has an enormous effect on how we conduct ourselves and relate to others. Dignity grows stronger as we become more competent and feel valued and respected. One of the most powerful ways to influence students is to help them acquire and maintain dignity. We can do this in several ways: by showing we admire and value them, by drawing positive attention to them, by mentioning things they have accomplished, by treating them courteously, and by asking their opinions and listening to what they say.

In addition, all students want something we don't talk about much, which is for somebody to believe in them, to consider they have worth and the potential to become better. Our students want this from their family members and they want it from us. They want us to show interest in them, stick with them, and tell them we are glad they are in the class. They want us to acknowledge their progress. They want to think we see rosy possibilities for their future. When you give your students those things, they begin to trust you. Without them, they don't.

When we treat students in these ways, they begin to seek us out, ask our advice, and cooperate with us. They give us a great bonus in return: they confer dignity on us, by showing respect, and even affection. Help your students understand that, if they want to build a solid reputation for themselves, the best way to do so is by being ethical, showing respect for others, and mentioning others' positive qualities. Encourage them to practice those things when relating with each other. Be alert for such behavior and, when you see it, mention it favorably in class.

Have you ever had a teacher you felt really believed in you, in your worth and potential? If so, how was that made evident to you? Did it affect you in a lasting way? How? Ask these questions of your students.

Strengthening Personal Power.   Personal power is identified by many psychologists as a fundamental human need. It is strengthened when we are allowed to make choices, make decisions, and assume control of certain aspects of our lives. When you empower your students in these ways, they begin to feel more in control of themselves and better able to deal with what life brings. You can provide this sense of power and strengthen it in a number of ways:

- treat your students as social equals;
- ask for and listen to their opinions;
- allow them to make choices about how they will work, what they will try to accomplish, and how they will show evidence of accomplishment;
- involve them as partners in planning class matters;
- take their views into account and build on them;
- assign them responsibilities in maintaining the well-being of the class;
- allow them to be self-directing in undertaking and completing tasks or projects;
- encourage them to accept responsibility for the outcomes of their efforts, whether those outcomes are good or bad. This helps them understand that their decisions have consequences.
- Allow them to try to correct or make amends for mistakes.

Students will make mistakes when exercising power. Make it possible for them to deal with those mistakes in a positive way. Help them see that power over others can be helpful or hurtful, depending on how it is used.

Strengthening Purposefulness.   Purposefulness means being dedicated to achieving a particular outcome. It entails knowing what we want to accomplish and having a reasonable idea of how to proceed. Many students, by the time they reach the middle school years, are beginning to wonder whether school has much to offer them. Some of those students will already have lost hope in that regard and may have stopped trying.

You can help students grasp a sense of purpose in school, and in their lives, by doing the following:

- Allow them to identify and pursue topics they truly want to learn about.
- Ask them to plan what they hope to accomplish, how they will go about it, what resources they will need and where to get them, and what evidence will tell them they have accomplished their goal.
- Talk with them about obstacles they may encounter, or have encountered, and satisfactions in and from the process of overcoming them.

Have you ever pursued a topic you were keenly interested in? Why did you think it was worthwhile? How much time did you invest in it? Was it something taught at school or something you pursued on your own? What implications for teachers do you see in your experience? Ask these questions of your students, too.

Strengthening Persistence.   Persistence is strengthened as we help students stick with tasks to completion, even when the tasks are difficult and frustrating. Many teachers complain that students show no persistence, that they won't follow work through to completion. Persistence in the face of strong obstacles is a quality much admired, but we get better results in school when we allow persistence to occur naturally in response to an interesting curriculum and engaging teaching. Here are some suggestions you might consider:

- Provide an interesting, worthwhile curriculum and teach it well.
- Provide a warm, supportive, helpful class climate.
- If students are expected to pursue topics they don't enjoy, explain convincingly why the topics are necessary and devise ways of making them interesting.
- Help students see the advantages of doing the best work they can. Teach them the process for doing quality work, which involves evaluating their own work, improving it, and, after that, trying to find ways to improve it still further. Students may resist this process at first, but over time they come to rely on it.

Strengthening Responsibility.   Responsibility—undertaking tasks, seeing them through, and accepting blame or credit—is one of the traits we most admire in others. It is difficult to be responsible when we see no point to what we are doing. Responsibility can be strengthened when we make the following provisions for our students:

- Encourage them to undertake tasks they consider important.
- Allow them to make decisions and behave in accordance with the requirements of the task.
- Help them complete tasks satisfactorily, given existing conditions.
- Help them learn to accept the results of their efforts whether they bring success, failure, excellence, mediocrity, compliments, or criticism.
- Encourage them to acknowledge that they have played the major role in producing the results, whatever they may be.
- Help them learn how to evaluate their efforts with an eye to making future improvements.

Strengthening Energy.   There are a number of ways to increase class energy, or the vitality of the class. An interesting curriculum, enjoyable activities, rewarding relationships, enthusiasm, and teacher charisma all contribute. A sense of class purpose is especially energizing. It might involve working with others to complete a project, put on a performance, or compete against another class. When you can, find ways for students to work cooperatively in groups or teams. This gives everyone a stake in the outcome and often produces high levels of energy. Class synergy, in which students feed energy to each other, also results in high levels of motivation (see Charles, 2000). So do cooperation and competition. Cooperation produces enjoyment and quantity and divergence of ideas, while competition produces motivation, independent thought, responsibility, and efficiency. (However, remember that competition tends to demoralize those who never have a chance of winning. It can also cause them to lie and cheat in attempting to win.)

Margarita Carlos provides an anecdote that illustrates the energy levels of thirteen-year-old students when involved in activities they enjoy.

This year, on the day before Spring Break, I let my students have a talent show and I filmed them on video. You would have thought I was giving them money, they were so excited. Among the "talents" they shared were wrestling in the World Wrestling Federation style, saying words with burps, arching eyebrows, singing *a cappella,* lip-synching and dancing to a current song, performing like rock stars using lacrosse sticks as guitars, doing impersonations of teachers, dancing, juggling, and singing little children's songs in a big group. I'm not sure how I would justify all that educationally, but, let me tell you, my students sure enjoyed it, and it gave me an opportunity to understand them in contexts other than lessons and paper and pencil.

Strengthening Helpfulness.   Helpfulness refers to an attitude of providing assistance to all members of the class. You help students, they help you, and they help each other. Helpfulness becomes a satisfying way of life when you and your students sense they are cared about and learn to care about each other. Helpfulness is also a powerful catalyst for building trust. Students see it in small personal things, such as quietly getting another pencil for Marisa who has broken hers, patiently showing Jason once more how to sequence paragraphs so his essay flows, or suggesting reference materials that help a group complete its project more easily. They especially see it when you help them in troubling situations. "Justin, I know you didn't intentionally break the window. I'll take care of that with the principal," or "Desiree, I can tell the assignment you turned in is not entirely your own work. I suspect you felt you couldn't do it on your own. Let me see if I can make a few suggestions so you can do work you'll be proud of." Or, "Sara, I could tell that what Alicia and Connie did hurt your feelings. Sometimes people do that without thinking. By the way, I was wondering: could you stay for a few minutes and help me get these plants watered?"

In an earlier chapter, we noted Haim Ginott's (1971) contention that teachers have a hidden asset they can always count on, which is looking for ways to be most helpful to students at any given time. He would have you always ask yourself, "What can I do to help my students right now?" When students misbehave or get stuck in their work, you can ask them directly, "What can I do to help you?" Once the class commits itself to helpfulness, much of their misbehavior disappears.

Strengthening Collaboration.   You can strengthen collaboration by drawing students into genuine partnership with you to make all aspects of class life pleasurable and rewarding. Consult with students and involve them however you can in:

- making curriculum and instruction enjoyable and satisfying;
- meeting students' needs as well as your own;
- living by the golden rule;
- removing or reducing the known causes of misbehavior;
- showing consideration and accepting responsibility;
- planning the discipline system;
- enhancing class character;
- establishing quality in all aspects of the school experience.

Strengthening Joy.   Joy is a prevailing sense of happiness and satisfaction, a quality many students claim they don't often experience in school. It grows when students pursue topics they find fascinating, participate in highly interesting activities, and associate with teachers and fellow students who are trustworthy and engaging. Teacher enthusiasm and charisma add greatly.

As you work with students, provide examples and do demonstrations that keep the class lively. Communicate with students on a one-to-one basis. Inject humor as appropriate. Encourage students to look for what is fun, intriguing, or exciting in class activities and new learning. Never speak sarcastically to students, denigrate them, or put them on the defensive. If you are unhappy about what is happening in class, discuss your concerns with the group and see if, together, you can work things out.

> Think back to see if you can identify the most enjoyable class you ever attended. What made it so—teacher personality? activities? topics studied? personal relationships? camaraderie? Can the qualities you identify be applied to other subjects and age levels? Ask your students this question.

Assessing Your Efforts in Character Education

Every so often, consider reviewing your class in terms of the teaching strategies you have been using and the resultant strength of the twelve character traits we have been examining. Involve students in the assessment if you can, because they have a strong stake in the matter. Seek feedback from fellow teachers and students' family members, as well. Here are criteria you can use for judging the character of your class and identifying qualities that require attention:

- *Regarding ethics*—Class members treat each other kindly, honestly, and fairly.
- *Regarding trust*—Class members are comfortable with the teacher and each other, confident of being treated in a kind and helpful manner.
- *Regarding consideration*—Class members show concern for each other's feelings, comfort, and dignity.
- *Regarding dignity*—Class members are laudatory of each other and treat each other with courtesy and respect.
- *Regarding personal power*—Class members have frequent opportunities to make decisions, assume responsibilities, and plan their own activities.
- *Regarding purposefulness*—Class members have clear notions of what they are to accomplish, why it is important, and how they are to proceed.
- *Regarding persistence*—Class members work diligently, do not give up easily, and strive for quality.
- *Regarding responsibility*—Class members pursue tasks, complete them satisfactorily in accordance with existing conditions, accept credit or blame for the results, and make corrections or recompense when necessary.
- *Regarding energy*—Class members show a high level of purposeful activity when it is appropriate to do so.
- *Regarding helpfulness*—Class members routinely offer to help others in need.

- *Regarding collaboration*—Teacher and students work together toward the goals of education in a manner each considers productive and enjoyable.
- *Regarding joy*—A sense of pleasure and satisfaction pervades the class.

When assessing your teaching tactics, judge how well you believe you are accomplishing the following:

- *Needs*—meeting students' basic needs for security, belonging, hope, dignity, power, enjoyment, and competence.
- *Trust*—building trust with students through consideration, helpfulness, and reliability.
- *Community*—enlisting students as colleagues who carry out roles as decision makers within a learning community characterized by mutual respect and consideration.
- *Moral judgments*—involving students in honest, thoughtful discussions and reflections on the moral implications of events in their lives.
- *Modeling*—continually behaving in a manner that offers a good model of the twelve character traits for students to emulate.
- *Opportunity*—ensuring that all class members have access to appropriate materials and abundant opportunity to investigate, participate, and make sense of what they learn.

> **FIELD APPLICATION 3:**   Earlier, it was suggested that if you visited any given class and had in hand the twelve aspects of class character stressed in this chapter, you could fairly easily assess the overall character of that class. Put that assertion to the test by assessing a class. Exchange classes with a colleague or, if you are more comfortable in doing so, assess your own class.

Assessing Support for Your Program

We have noted that character education is much more likely to succeed when supported by administrators, family members, school staff, and the community. If you are undertaking to promote character development, make sure your site administrator understands your program, approves of it, and expresses support for it. Make sure students' family members understand and support your program, too. Determine if there is need for further efforts to gain family members' support and involvement. Make sure you regularly report your efforts and results to them. Review linkages you have established with agencies and organizations that provide community services. Assess the extent and value of your class's involvement with the community and determine whether additional linkages might be valuable.

Other Support and Resources in Character Education

The United States government has committed a great deal of effort and financial support to character education in the nation's schools. Dianne Wilber (2000) reports that, since 1996, the U.S. Department of Education has awarded more than $25 million in seed money to encourage schools to develop programs of character education. Laurel Walters, writing in the *Christian Science Monitor,* reported in 1997 that more than thirty states had received U.S. Department of Education grants to support program development and sixteen states had enacted legislation pertaining to character education. She noted that, in 1995, the Indiana General Assembly passed a mandate for good citizenship education and delineated thirteen desirable character qualities. Soon thereafter, the Indiana Department of Education created a guide entitled "Partners for Good Citizenship: Parents, Schools, Communities," that suggests how various educational entities can work collaboratively toward character development.

In addition, numerous school districts in many states have service-learning projects funded by the Corporation for National Service (*www.cns.gov*), created in 1993 as part of the National Community Service Trust Act. Service learning promotes character education by involving students in addressing real community needs. It is mandatory for students in some schools; optional in others.

A number of other organizations offer resources for character education in middle schools.

Character Counts! (www.charactercounts.org)   A voluntary partnership that supports character education emphasizing respect, responsibility, trustworthiness, caring, fairness, and citizenship. The partnership provides resource materials, training sessions, and awards recognition.

Character Education (www.usoe.k12.ut.us/curr/char)   Information concerning the State of Utah's efforts to implement character education in the schools.

Character Education Clearinghouse (www.cde.ca.gov/character)   Information concerning the California Department of Education's effort to incorporate character education in the regular curriculum.

Character Education Network (www.charactered.net/)   A network that provides on-line interactive lessons, scrapbooks, networking tools, activities, and other resources for integrating character education in schools.

Character Education Partnership, The (www.character.org)   A national nonpartisan coalition for character education. It recognizes schools of high character that can serve as models in character education for other schools.

Character Education Resources and Conferences (www.charactereducationinfo. org)   A listing of information and resources relating to developing and implementing character-education curricula.

Giraffe Project, The (www.giraffe.org)   Offers examples of heroes who "stuck their necks out" for the care and concern of others. The project provides resource materials for helping students work toward a caring community in the classroom.

Goodcharacter (www.goodcharacter.com)   Provides a number of resources on character education including lesson plans, writing assignments, discussion questions, and group activities.

Hurt-Free Schools (www.hurt-free-character.com)   Provides suggestions for using character education and social skills training to create a safe environment for prevention of bullying, harassment, and violence (designed for elementary schools, but suitable for middle schools as well).

Keeter Center for Character Education (www.keetercenter.edu/) Promotes the teaching of values such as honesty, good citizenship, generosity, honor, courage, and the work ethic.

Skc's Character Education Website (www.skce.cjb.net/) Features information on social harmony, self-discipline, responsibility, excellence, and self-reliance.

QUESTIONS

1. How important do you feel character education is? Is it worth the time it requires in a curriculum already overcrowded with other expectations? Should it be given only incidental attention within established areas of the curriculum, or should it be singled out as a major educational objective?

2. How would you explain the relationship among good teaching, discipline, class management, and character education?

3. In the program entitled the Emerald Way, you saw that specific character traits were singled out for concerted attention for about a month, then the class moved ahead to focus on another character trait. Commentators on character education have warned against the "trait of the month" approach. To what extent are you persuaded by their arguments? Do you think the Emerald Way epitomizes what they criticize?

4. How well do you feel you are prepared for helping students develop more desirable character? Do you think character education should be given specific attention in programs of teacher education? If so, how?

5. Authors Schaps, Schaeffer, and McDonnell, in the section on cautions about character education, refer to approaches they call "cheerleading," "praise and reward," "define and drill," and "forced formality." Those terms were not explained in the text. What do you think they mean, and why do you think those approaches might be ineffective?

6. What three things do you feel you could do to bring about a positive, sustainable increase in class energy?

ACTIVITIES

1. Contact four or five of the listed Web sites that provide character education resources for teachers. What do you find there of value?

2. Analyze yourself in terms of the twelve traits presented as important in class character. In which do you feel strongest? In which do you feel weakest? How might you strengthen some of your weaker traits?

3. In the section concerning effective teaching, you were advised to involve students in honest, thoughtful discussion and reflection about the moral implications of what they see around them, what they are told, and what they personally do and experience. Identify one problem or situation from each of those areas that might contain moral dilemmas: what you see

around you, what you are told, and what you personally do and experience. Do this either from your own perspective or from that of a middle school student.

4. Suppose you intend to implement planned attention to character education in your class. Explain how you would try to obtain the support of principal and family members.

REFERENCES

Berkowitz, M. 1998. Obstacles to teacher training in character education. *Action in Teacher Education, 20* (4), 1–10.

Character Education Manifesto. 1996. Center for the Advancement of Ethics and Character, Boston University School of Education.

Charles, C. M. 2000. *The synergetic classroom: Joyful teaching and gentle discipline.* New York: Longman.

Corporation for National Service. 2001. <www.cns.gov>.

Covey, S. 1989. *The seven habits of highly effective people.* New York: Simon & Schuster.

Curwin, R., and Mendler, A. 1988. *Discipline with dignity.* Washington, DC: Association for Supervision and Curriculum Development.

Ginott, H. 1971. *Teacher and child.* New York: Macmillan.

Kohn, A. 1997. How not to teach values: A critical look at character education. *Phi Delta Kappan, 78* (6), 428–439.

Lickona, T. 1991. *Educating for character: How our schools can teach respect and responsibility.* New York: Bantam.

———. 2002. Web site on character education: <www.cortland.edu/c4n5rs/suxhom.htm>.

Lickona, T., Schaps, E., Lewis, C. 2001. Eleven principles of character education. The Character Education Partnership, 1025 Connecticut Avenue, NW, Suite 1011, Washington, DC 20036, <www.character.org>.

Munson, B. 2000. Character education: The missing ingredient of preservice teacher education programs. Paper presented at the Annual Meeting of the American Association of Colleges for Teacher Education (52nd, Chicago, IL, February 26–29).

Otten, E. 2000. Character education (*ERIC Digest*). Bloomington, IN: ERIC Clearinghouse for Social Studies/Social Science Education. ERIC #: ED444932.

Schaps, E., Schaeffer, E., and McDonnell, S. 2001. What's right and wrong with character education today. *Education Week on the Web.* <www.edweek.org/ew/newstory.cfm?slug=02schaps.h21>.

Spence, G. 1995. *How to argue and win every time.* New York: St. Martin's Press.

Walters, L. 1997. How some schools make a success of character education. *Christian Science Monitor, 89* (132), p. 1.

Wilber, D. September 2000. Character education: Finding ways to foster ethical behavior in youth. *Changing Schools.* Quarterly issue.

Wynne, E., and Ryan, K. 1997. *Reclaiming our schools: Teaching character, academics, and discipline.* Upper Saddle River, NJ: Prentice-Hall.

Addressing Issues of Diversity: Cultural, Ethnic, Linguistic, and Economic

Chapter Preview

Gone are the days—if, in fact, they ever existed in the United States—when teachers could walk into a classroom expecting all students to speak English well, share the same customs, and function from a common set of values. From the beginning, America's schools enrolled students from different economic, cultural, ethnic, and linguistic backgrounds. Many of those students spoke languages other than English. Educators did the best for them they could and, in truth, performed remarkably in educating diverse youth, despite the difficulties they encountered. However, for one reason or another, many students did not receive their educational due.

Today, we are better able to provide education for diverse groups of students. This chapter reviews efforts now being made. We begin with some considerations for working with diverse students in general and how teachers can be prepared for this task. Then we move to specific observations and suggestions for five categories of students: one referred to as "economically disadvantaged" and four referred to as "minorities," namely African American, American Indian/Alaskan Native, Asian American, and Hispanic American. Some students from all ethnic, racial, and linguistic groups are included in the economically disadvantaged group.

The Numbers of Students from Diverse Backgrounds

In 2002, almost 40 percent of public school students were considered to come from minority ethnic and racial groups, an increase of 19 percentage points since 1972. This increase was largely due to the growth in the proportion of Hispanic American students. Hispanic Americans and African Americans in 2002 accounted for approximately 17 and 16.5 percent of the public school enrollment, up since 1972 by 11 and 2 percentage points, respectively. The percentage of students from other racial/ethnic groups also increased, from a combined 1 percent in 1972 to approximately 6.5 percent in 2002, with Asian/Pacific Islanders accounting for 4 percent, American Indian/Alaska Native for just over 1 percent, and all others approximately 1 percent. In recent years substantial numbers of students have arrived from Asia, the Middle East, the Caribbean, and Latin America. Other Western countries are also experiencing increased diversity in their school populations as world-wide migration increases.

As for economically disadvantaged students, in 2001 the U.S. Census Bureau considered families to be in poverty if their annual income was less than $21,000 for a family of four, up to $38,000 for a family of nine (U.S. Census Bureau, Poverty 2001). This determination is based on the cost of an "economy food plan," a low-cost but nutritionally adequate diet as established by the U.S. Department of Agriculture. If more than one-third of a family's disposable income is required for the economy food plan, then that family and all of its members are considered to be in poverty. This definition places just over 10 percent of American families "in poverty." As we shall see presently, students from these families, irrespective of their ethnic or racial origins, have certain characteristics that may interfere with their educational progress.

Preparing Teachers to Work with the Culturally Diverse

For decades, educators have been concerned about how best to teach students from diverse cultures. Authoritative opinion now holds that schools and teachers, in general, need to know and attune their programs in accordance with the following factors:

- cultural backgrounds of the students;
- linguistic capabilities and characteristics that affect learning;
- typical behaviors of students as concerns involvement in instructional activities, ability and willingness to speak out, and relations with teachers and fellow students;
- effective methods of interacting with students individually and in groups;
- effective ways of relating with family members and communities and drawing them into partnership with the school.

Suggestions for accomplishing these tasks are now available in books, journal literature, universities, and elsewhere for a wide number of ethnic, racial, linguistic, and cultural groups. Also available are specialized classes and materials that provide information about learning first and second languages, including English. And, finally, we are beginning to learn more about worldviews and lifestyles that affect students from poverty.

In this chapter we do not attempt to delve deeply into these matters, but only to present synopses of cultural and economic differences together with suggestions for teachers. Many of these suggestions may at first seem insignificant, yet may strongly influence teacher effectiveness and student learning. The specific suggestions are mostly concerned with:

- misunderstandings that occur between teachers and students because of assumptions about cultural traits and background;
- students' ways of getting attention, responding to questions, and interacting with others;
- the helpful effects of cooperative activities that are emphasized in certain cultures;
- how students interact with and respond to adults.

In order to teach minority and economically disadvantaged students well, you need to learn as much as you can about the students with whom you work, the views they hold, and the customs by which they live. At the same time, you must understand that any conclusions you draw do not automatically apply to all members of a given group. There are great behavioral and values differences among individuals in ethnic and cultural groups concerning how students should behave, react, and learn. For that reason, you must deal with students as individuals, at the same time recognizing that they are strongly influenced by the customs of their culture. It is also important that you know something about activities that help students acquire English-language capability. You will have access to specialists in your school district to help with this task, but you will still need to coordinate your efforts with bilingual teachers and teachers of English as a second language.

> **FIELD APPLICATION 1:**   Analyze your own preparation for teaching. What were you taught about cultural diversity and how to teach accordingly? How helpful were the information and experiences you received?

Working with Immigrant Students

A 1998 ERIC Digest entitled "Qualities of Effective Programs for Immigrant Adolescents with Limited Schooling" presents a number of suggestions for working with students new to the dominant culture. It points out that immigrant students have needs not only for academic learning, but also (and sometimes more importantly) for socialization and language development. The success of these students is heightened when we are able to involve parents, family, and community, along with health and counseling services.

Some immigrant students arrive well-schooled, but many have had little or no prior schooling. Their literacy skills may be poor even in their native language. By middle-grades level many have fallen behind in academic achievement, despite being taught in their native language. For students to have a reasonable opportunity for success in school, they must quickly learn to understand, speak, read, and write English, which is necessary not only for success in school, but for further education and transition into the labor force. English competency is therefore emphasized, but there are other factors that come strongly into play, as you will see later in the chapter.

What Schools Can Do

The following list specifies what schools can do when designing programs for minority students who are recent immigrants (see Lockwood and Secada, 2000, for elaboration).

■ *Decide where the special programs for immigrant students should be located.* Some authorities advocate special schools or separate wings of the schools, where resources can be concentrated for bilingual teaching, adapted English learning, and social integration. Others say separate locations stigmatize students and reduce exposure to English and socialization. They would have students integrated into regular classes where they receive special attention both within the class and on a pull-out basis. It is not yet clear which procedure is better. Family members and community members should be involved in making this decision.

■ *Emphasize learning English.* Learning the English language is probably the most valuable thing minority students can do in school. This does not mean they should slight their native languages. To the contrary, command of two or more languages gives people distinct advantages in life. But learning a language is a difficult and tedious process, and it is, therefore, not advisable to have students concentrate solely on learning English while putting academic learning aside. In order for academic learning to occur, many students require bilingual instruction for a time.

■ *Decide which option to use for teaching academic content.* Three options are being used for teaching academic content to students who are still acquiring English: (1) instruction in the native language, (2) sheltered English, which is organized to facilitate rapid literacy in English, and (3) standard English. There is no consensus at present concerning which of these options is best. It should be noted that, regardless of the method used, schools grant the same number of course credits to students who satisfactorily complete the class.

■ *Provide for quick entry into the regular program.* Instructional programs for minority students present the normal course content, together with help in learning English as rapidly as possible. Courses can be taught at first in native languages, but students are expected to develop English capability quickly and move into the mainstream.

■ *Make interpreters available.* Interpreters help students and their family members understand the educational program, what it provides, and what is expected. When possible, materials printed in the appropriate native language should be available to everyone who requires them.

■ *Design individual programs for students based on needs.* This process relies on assessing levels of English proficiency, literacy in the native language, overall achievement, and prior school experience.

■ *Plan for expeditious exit from special programs into the regular program.* Students should be able to exit from temporary programs such as sheltered English into standard programs fairly quickly. Requirements and procedures for doing so must be made clear. Language proficiency, achievement, and socialization are given primary attention.

■ *Work for parent, family, and community involvement.* Most students do better in school if parents, extended family, and community pay attention to their progress. To make this possible, schools should help families understand the nature and expectations of formal schooling and the roles family members and community can play. This requires that channels of communication be established and kept open, with interpreters to surmount language difficulties.

■ *Organize student academies.* Students usually do better when organized into small groups or "academies" that remain together and have ongoing contact with caring teachers. This arrangement, used for all students in many middle-level schools, provides security, direction, and support. It also keeps students current with expectations and comfortably connected with other students.

■ *Provide suitable counselors.* Immigrant students do better when assisted by counselors who speak their native languages, have the same or similar cultural backgrounds, and are knowledgeable about further educational opportunities for them.

■ *Provide professional development.* Faculty and staff require special help in learning how to relate and work effectively with immigrant students. They must maintain academic standards, but, at the same time, understand students' cultural backgrounds and show sensitivity toward them.

What Teachers Can Do

Unfortunately, relatively little has been written about what, exactly, teachers can do to provide quality instruction for students recently arrived in the United States. Suggestions set forth in the early 1990s still prevail. They can be summarized as follows (from Lucas, Henze, and Donato, 1990; Walsh, 1991; and the National Coalition of Advocates for Students, 1994):

- Have a repertoire of instructional approaches that upholds high expectations of all students, while affirming the acceptance of differences among them.
- Be knowledgeable about issues of acculturation and second-language acquisition and teach with materials that reflect a diversity of cultures, experiences, and perspectives.
- Have the ability to work together across differences of race and ethnicity, and work well with a variety of individuals and groups.
- Learn as much as possible about students' families. Teachers can serve students better when they know the educational backgrounds of the family. This information is valuable in developing academic support in the home.
- Show appreciation for and enjoyment of ethnic language and culture.
- Hold high expectations of students and frequently recognize their achievement publicly.
- Become familiar with English as a Second Language (ESL) and sheltered English instruction. Also, learn a bit of the language spoken by students in the class.
- Find ways to give much personal attention to each student.
- Use a flexible approach that involves, when appropriate, peer tutoring, language experience, process writing, reciprocal teaching, whole language, mentoring by sympathetic adults, home–school liaisons, and links with community agencies.

The Resiliency Factor

The difficulties immigrant students experience in American schools have been well documented, yet many students succeed in spite of them. Recently, attention has been directed to what causes some minority students to be more successful in school than others. One important factor, called "resiliency," has been identified. It is defined as the ability to cope with adversity. Bonnie Benard (1997) suggests that resilient students display the following four traits: social competence, problem-solving skills, autonomy, and sense of purpose and future. Resiliency theory holds that these traits are present to some degree in all people, but are sometimes not strong enough in given individuals to ensure success, unless certain "protective factors" are provided by families, schools, and communities during childhood or early adolescence (Krovetz, 1999). Those protective factors seem to be the following:

- supportive relationships, particularly encouragement from school personnel and other adults;
- student self-esteem, motivation, and willingness to accept responsibility;
- parental support, concern about education, and involvement with the school;
- community youth programs such as clubs and organized sports activities;
- school emphasis on acquisition of pro-social skills and academic success.

Nancy Chavkin and John Gonzalez (2000) have reviewed a number of approaches to helping educators capitalize on the resiliency factor. They refer to Emmy Werner and Ruth Smith's 1992 study of 700 at-risk residents of Hawaii who lived in adverse circumstances. Two-thirds of the sample experienced significant problems during childhood, but by the time they had reached their midthirties, all but thirty had become constructive, responsible adults. One factor those successful persons shared was a long-term, close relationship with a caring, responsible parent or other adult. Socioeconomic and ethnic backgrounds did not seem to affect the results. Lingxin Hao and Melissa Bonstead-Burns (1998) studied Hispanic students and found that these who speak their family members' language well make higher than average grades in school. Kimberly Gordon (1996) determined that the most important trait of resilient Hispanic students is their faith in their ability to understand what was taught in class and to do well on tests and homework. Other promising leads for helping minority students mentioned by Chavkin and Gonzalez include:

- placing students from low-income, ethnic, and linguistic minority backgrounds in academic programs alongside high-achieving peers, which helps them develop an academic identity and form relationships with academically oriented groups;
- begin preparing students for higher education while they are still in their elementary school years, which seems to result in higher attendance, fewer discipline problems, and better achievement scores;
- making use of existing family structures, where low-income mothers can provide their children with educational stimulation and emotional encouragement (this benefits the mothers as well);
- instilling a sense of pride in self and appreciation for personal culture and language;
- making explicit the personal traits and skills needed for success at school and work, such as confidence, effort, responsibility, perseverance, initiative, and teamwork (see Mattox, 1999);
- beginning early, drawing on community talents and resources, and keeping teachers, staff, family members, students, and community all closely involved with each other.

> **FIELD APPLICATION 2:** Check at a middle-grades school with which you have contact. Inquire about the numbers of recent immigrant students in attendance and the special provisions being made for them.

Working with Specific Ethnic and Racial Groups

At this point we begin a review of the characteristics of ethnic and cultural groups with which you are most likely to work. The groups, considered in alphabetical order, are African American, American Indian/Alaska Native (AI/AN), Asian American, and Hispanic (Latino) American.

African American Students

African American students comprise approximately 16.5 percent of the total school population. Many of those students are bright and talented high achievers, while others have become alienated from the education process (Schwartz, 2001). This is especially so for African American male students, many of whom begin to drop behind academically at around the third or fourth grade (Kunjufu, 1984). As they move into adolescence, they tend to fall farther behind, and many drop out of school. At this stage of life, they become especially prone to adolescent risk-taking behavior that can lead to delinquency, early fathering, drug use, and violence (Ascher, 1991).

The causes of these difficulties are properly assigned to society, not schools, but there seem to be some things schools can do to counter them. Frequently suggested are decreasing the suspension and expulsion rates, increasing students' representation in programs for the gifted and talented, and improving the recruitment and training of teachers and counselors in predominantly black schools (Gibbs, 1988; Reed, 1988).

Programmatic Needs. In 1991, Carol Ascher described a number of programmatic changes in education that she believed would benefit African American male students. They included:

Appropriate Male Models/Male Bonding. Providing positive images of African American male adults, as teachers, mentors, and advocates. African American male students often have few appropriate males with whom to bond in their homes, neighborhoods, or at school. At the same time, they are surrounded by numerous negative images.

Identity/Self-Esteem. The same positive influences can help students develop better self-esteem. It is generally accepted that the self-esteem of African American male students suffers because of negative images prevalent in society. It is believed that this can be countered by drawing attention to the achievements of African American adults and their contributions to society.

Academic Values and Skills.   Many African American students resist learning and being successful at school, which they equate with "acting white." Schools need to find ways to improve students' success, encourage good attendance, provide better assistance with schoolwork, and teach nonviolent conflict resolution, all within the context of African American behavior they find acceptable. This effort can raise the level of achievement across the board, thus limiting the association in students' minds between success and acting white.

Parent and Community Strengthening.   Schools must find ways to strengthen ties between school, families, and communities. One way to do this is through a community service requirement. This might be especially helpful to African American males from fragmented and stressed families.

Linguistic and Cultural Factors.   Cultural and linguistic characteristics are believed to interfere with African American students' progress in schools where students and teachers are predominantly white. It does seem that teachers who understand and respond to linguistic patterns used by African American students tend to be more successful than others (Foster, 1995). Most people agree that it would be good to have greater numbers of African American teachers in schools, but that is not to say that white teachers cannot do the job well, especially if they make a point of doing the following:

- expressing cultural understanding and acceptance;
- showing solidarity with students and eagerness to help;
- emphasizing the knowledge, skills, and values needed for school success and a healthy cultural identity;
- linking curriculum content to students' out-of-school experiences.

Complaints are frequently heard that most teachers misunderstand and mis-assess African American students because they know so little about the culture and ways of speaking (McCollough, 2000). Michele Foster (1999) of Claremont Graduate University is addressing this complaint by helping teachers understand black students' linguistic and cultural traits. One thing she advises teachers to do is use the "5 Rs"—ritual, rhythm, recitation, repetition, and relationships—to promote better learning. She explains that rhythm, recitation, and repetition are often used together, and she points to the effectiveness of one middle school teacher who uses rhythm to teach weekly spelling words.

Foster's efforts seem a strong step in the right direction, but Gloria Ladson-Billings (2000) reminds us of the dearth of research and literature concerning how teachers should be prepared to work with African American students. It serves little purpose to admonish teachers for knowing so little, when practical advice and resources are not available to them. Perhaps teachers might consider doing as Debbie Diller did (1999), a white teacher who improved her relations with African American students by making a concerted effort to emphasize multicultural literature and maintain a dialog with African American friends, fellow teachers, and students.

Janine Bempechat (2001) believes homes can play a major role in improving education for African American students. She maintains that children whose family members organize their homes around learning do better in school. Those family members communicate subtle but powerful messages about the importance of learning, achievement, and personal responsibility. Bempechat contends that having African American adults as educational mentors improves achievement of African American students. She emphasizes that schools should be warm and welcoming, rather than places students and family find threatening.

Wendy Schwartz (2001) suggests making some changes in the perceptions educators have of African American students and the ways they react to them, such as:

- gaining knowledge about African American social styles;
- ceasing to speak disparagingly of African American traditions;
- attempting to mentor students, especially troublesome ones, rather than avoid them;
- taking into account the knowledge, culture, values, and abilities of African American students;
- creating a more hospitable environment by communicating the expectation that all students can succeed, providing the opportunity for them to do so, and evaluating them on the basis of their strengths, not their weaknesses;
- developing classroom codes that are culturally sensitive and that stress responsibility and respect;
- using a discipline system that emphasizes modeling good behavior rather than punishment and gives students a voice in deciding how it will function;
- keeping family members informed about their child's school performance and behavior, good and bad, and asking them to cooperate for the child's benefit.

Web Site Resources.   You may wish to contact the following Web sites, which contain information on the education of African Americans that supplements what is provided in this chapter.

The Black Male in Contemporary Society: Social and Educational Challenges. An excerpt from *Saving The Native Son: Empowerment Strategies for Young Black Males* (ericcass.uncg.edu/virtuallib/diversity/1044.html).

School, Family, Community Partnerships, and the Academic Achievement of African American Urban Students. An investigation into whether certain social institutions can influence school-related attitudes, behaviors, and academic achievement (www.csos.jhu.edu/crespar/Reports/report07entire.html).

Improving Black Student Achievement by Enhancing Student's Self-Image. A booklet that helps teachers understand the factors that lead to a positive self-image for black students and suggests instructional strategies that enhance their academic self-concept (http://www.nwrel.org/cnorse/booklets/achieve).

Selections from *The African-American Mosaic.* A Library of Congress resource guide covering nearly 500 years of the black experience in the Western hemisphere, it includes books, periodicals, prints, photographs, music, film, and recorded sound (lcweb.loc.gov/exhibits/african/intro.html).

Afro-American Black History Museum. A set of interactive exhibits spotlighting major events and people in African American History. It includes: "Black Resistance:

Slavery in the U.S.," "Tuskegee Airmen: The First Black Combat Pilots in America," "Jackie Robinson," "The Black Panther Party," "Black or White: The Environment of the 20s and 30s When Black America Was on a Binge to Undo its Blackness by Concentrating on Making Itself as White as It Could Be," "The Million Man March," "The Scottsboro Boys," and "This is Our War: A Compilation of Articles Written by AFRO Correspondents while Following Black American Troops during World War II."

Library of Congress American Memory Project: The African-American Experience in Ohio, 1850–1920. Text and images drawn from the Ohio Historical Society dealing with the history of black Ohio from 1850 to 1920 that deal with slavery and freedom, segregation and integration, religion and politics, migrations and restrictions, harmony and discord, and struggles and successes.

American Indian/Alaska Native Students

Susan Faircloth and John Tippeconnic reported in 2000 that there were approximately 500,000 American Indian and Alaska Native (AI/AN) students attending K–12 schools in the United States. About 90 percent of these students attended public schools, 10 percent attended schools operated or funded by the Bureau of Indian Affairs (BIA) and tribes, and a small number attended private schools. These students come from more than 500 tribal groups that have unique government and social systems and speak an estimated 200 different languages.

Despite their differences, these students have many things in common, including similar value systems. Overall, they are not being very successful in school, compared to most other groups. Their academic achievement trails that of other groups, and they have the highest dropout rate of all racial/ethnic groups in the United States (U.S. National Center for Education Statistics, 2001).

Possible Reasons for Difficulties.   The precise reasons for AI/AN students' relative lack of success in school are not known, although various explanations have been suggested. Richard St. Germaine (1995) has summarized four main theories.

1. The *deficit theory* suggests that students are hampered by impoverished home and community experiences. The remedy for this condition has students master what they are supposed to learn before moving ahead to the next step in school. Enriched environments are also needed to help overcome deficits in background experiences.

2. The *organizational theory* holds that schools and school systems are to blame because they are inappropriate for educating AI/AN students. The remedy is to restructure schools and reform school practices. The curriculum would address important themes connected to students' lives, instruction would emphasize problem solving, and teachers would function as coaches.

3. The *sociolinguist theory* places blame on endemic miscommunication between students and teachers. The remedy requires teachers to become knowledgeable about students' culture and language and adapt instruction to students' traits and needs.

4. Recently, the theory of *cultural discontinuity* has come to the fore. It holds that there is usually little interaction between Native and majority cultures, especially in rural areas where AI/AN students attend small community or reservation elementary schools and are the majority or the entirety of the school population. When they transition into larger middle schools or high schools, they often suddenly become the minority in a student body that is mostly white. At this point they encounter the trauma of seeing emphasis on a culture different from their own. St. Germaine says this produces a self-defeating paradox that is difficult to remedy: success in school is seen as abandoning traditional cultural values in favor of those of the dominant society. Hence, being successful in school means being a failure as a community member.

Efforts to Redress the Problems.   In 1992, the U.S. Government and Department of Education made a strong push to increase the school success rate of AI/AN students. Their strategy is presented in the final reports of the Indian Nations at Risk Task Force (see Cahape and Howley, 1992) and the White House Conference on Indian Education (see Atencio, and others, 1992). The following paragraphs review their recommendations.

Fostering Intercultural Harmony.   The following approaches to building intercultural harmony in schools seem potentially beneficial (Cotton, 1994).

Esteem-Building.   Practices that emphasize behaviors and activities believed to build self-esteem such as:

- teacher warmth and encouragement
- academic success
- close association with people who have physical or mental handicaps
- participation in activities that give positive portrayals of one's cultural group or gender
- association with teachers and administrators of one's own cultural group

Intergroup Contact and Experience.   Practices that increase contact among diverse cultural groups under conditions in which students:

- have equal status;
- get to know one another as individuals;
- have common interests and similar characteristics;
- cooperate with each other as equals;
- work in culturally heterogeneous study teams;
- experience in-depth, long-term, and high-quality multicultural activities across the curriculum;
- use materials that portray cultural groups in a positive light.

Improving Teacher Preparation.   The recruitment and retention of AI/AN administrators and teachers are recommended, but it is acknowledged that professionals are not available in sufficient numbers to meet the need. Therefore, non-Native teachers are urged to prepare themselves to work more effectively with AI/AN students. In particular, they should familiarize themselves with the lifeways and worldviews of AI/AN people and learn about Native history, language, culture, and spiritual values.

Understanding AI/AN Learning Styles.   Learning style refers to the personal ways students acquire information, concepts, and skills. We know that some students learn better through visual means, some through hands-on activities, some through reading, some through logical explanations, and others through reorganizing informational input.

In Anglo American culture, most students learn well by reading information, organizing it in the mind, and committing it to memory. They also learn well by observing what others do and emulating those behaviors.

There is reason to believe that AI/AN students have learning styles that differ somewhat from those of students in the dominant culture (Cornett, 1983; Swisher, 1991). Many have very strong capabilities for learning visually, perceptively, and spatially, as opposed to the verbal processes emphasized in school. They may tend to use mental images in thought processes rather than word associations. They may learn better by seeing, from the outset, the entire picture of what is to be learned, rather than learning bits of information that slowly build up to the full picture. They show an affinity for manipulatives and hands-on activities and seem to work and learn better in cooperative groups than individually. They seem to show the ability to learn from experience without constant supervision and feedback. They tend to demonstrate their learning in contexts similar to those from which they have learned.

Many Anglo teachers observe that AI/AN students are quiet and not very talkative in the classroom. While these students may be hesitant to participate in large- and small-group recitations, they are said to be more talkative than other students when working in student-led group projects (Philips, 1983). Philips explains that AI/AN students tend to acquire competence through a process of observation, careful listening, supervised participation, and individualized self-correction or testing.

Other studies suggest that AI/AN students become uncomfortable when asked, in school, to behave in ways not valued in the communities where they live. For example, it was established years ago that Cherokee students are more cooperative and less competitive than Anglo students, a trait that probably contributes to lower school achievement (Brown, 1980). Traditional Cherokee norms of behavior stress group achievement rather than individual achievement, which is frowned on. For that reason, very able students often hide their academic competence to avoid appearing superior. This same value is seen in most AI/AN groups. Individuals simply do not try to advance above others or display self-importance.

Suggestions for Teachers of AI/AN Students.   A number of suggestions have been made to help teachers work more effectively with students from AI/AN groups (Cox and Ramirez, 1981; Cornett, 1983; Cajete, 1986; Swisher, 1991; Butterfield, 1994). Keeping in mind that no set of expectations can apply fully to all students among the hundreds of tribal groups, the following suggestions are worth considering:

- Get to know the norms and values of the community from which the students come.
- Know as much as possible about the students' background knowledge and experiences.
- Fit new learning into the immediate contexts of home, community, and school.

- Note students' preferred ways of learning and the ways student behaviors change from situation to situation. Discuss learning styles with students and help them understand why they do what they do in learning situations. Take learning styles into account in instruction.
- Provide activities that are more cooperative and less competitive. However, encourage independent learning, too.
- Provide feedback that is immediate, helpful, and private.
- Allow students to use direct personal experience as much as possible in learning.
- Emphasize art and creative writing about personal experiences in both teaching and evaluation.
- Continue to provide familiar, comfortable, successful experiences, but gradually introduce new ways of learning.
- Evaluate student progress in terms of goal attainment, student behavior, and involvement.
- Employ a flexible time frame for activities rather than always staying on a rigid schedule.
- Remember that most students do not like to be in the spotlight.

Involving AI/AN Family Members. Involving AI/AN family members in their child's education increases their support for education and improves student behavior, achievement, motivation, self-esteem, and behavior (Butterfield and Pepper, 1991). Schools must take the lead in involving family members. They need to set up good communication, provide parent education opportunities for learning about the school program and student needs, and make positive contact with families at home.

Adopting a New Paradigm for Evaluating Student Progress. Standardized tests, used throughout U.S. education, may not give AI/AN students a fair and equal chance. Those students often read or interpret the test items incorrectly, while their cultural values may discourage competitive behavior. For those reasons, it is important to find ways of evaluating student progress that better allow AI/AN students to show what they know and can do. More authentic assessment might include allowing them to demonstrate mastery of essential tasks rather than recalling basic facts and using portfolios of materials to document progress.

Web Site Resources. You might wish to contact the following Web sites for additional information useful in AI/AN education.

> **Native American Authors.** A Web site provides information on Native North American authors with bibliographies of their published works, biographical information, and links to on-line resources including interviews, online texts and tribal Web sites (www.ipl.org/ref/native).
>
> **Native American Sites.** A list assembled and maintained by Lisa Mitten, librarian at the University of Pittsburgh (www.nativeculture.com/lisamitten/indians.html).
>
> **StoneE's WebLodge.** Includes Native American lore and other related links (www.ilhawaii.net:80/~stony).

Native American Links. An extensive list of Web sites (http://sun3.lib.uci.edu/~mlriweb/m2martin.htm).

NativeWeb (http://www.nativeweb.org).

Asian American Students

Jianhua Feng (1994) points out that the term *Asian American* covers a variety of national, cultural, and religious groups, more than twenty-nine of which differ in language, religion, and customs. Among them are four major groups, identified as East Asian, Southeast Asian, South Asian, and Pacific Islanders. Examples of East Asian groups are Chinese, Japanese, and Koreans. Examples of Southeast Asian groups are Thais and Vietnamese. Examples of South Asian groups are Indians and Pakistanis. Examples of Pacific Islanders are Hawaiians and Samoans. While these distinct groups often get lumped together as "Asian," they have different origins, languages, customs, and histories. In addition, some students from these groups have only recently arrived and therefore experience difficulty with language and customs. Others, born in the country where they reside, speak the dominant language fluently and are highly acculturated.

Characteristics of Asian American Students.   Asian Americans are generally stereotyped as successful, law-abiding, conforming, and high-achieving. Indeed, their school behavior is much in keeping with those perceptions, and only occasionally do they present behavior problems for teachers. They tend to be strongly group- and family-oriented, which for newly arrived students may hamper their adaptation to the independence, competition, and individualism emphasized in Western education.

Students from many East and Southeast Asian cultures are imbued with Confucian ideals, which include learning, respect for elders, responsibility for relatives, deferred gratification, and self-discipline. They tend to view failure as a lack of individual will. They tend to be conforming and willing to place family welfare over individual wishes. They are usually self-effacing, willing to wait patiently (Feng, 1994), and seem to learn best in well-structured, quiet environments (Baruth and Manning, 1992). They tend to dislike having attention drawn to them as individuals. Many have been socialized to listen carefully, speak after consideration, speak in soft voices, and show modesty in personal dress and grooming.

Immigrants from Japan, Korea, Taiwan, and Hong Kong frequently come from middle-class backgrounds and have high intellectual proclivities and strong self-direction. They and their family members are usually able to interact easily with teachers. Immigrants from Southeast Asia are more likely to have backgrounds as rural villagers or urban poor. They tend to be more fatalistic in world orientation and rigid in their thinking. Communication between them and Western school personnel is at times difficult.

In conversations and other verbal communication, Asians seldom speak their minds as plainly as do Westerners. They often display verbal hesitancy and ambiguity to avoid giving offense, and they do not make spontaneous or critical remarks (Kim, 1985). Their body language is noticeably different from that of Westerners, too, characterized by head-nodding and lack of eye contact (Matsuda, 1989). The Japanese and Vietnamese are noted for being unwilling to use the word *no* even when they actually disagree with you (Coker, 1988;

Wierzbicka, 1991). Seldom are Asian students, their family members, or their teachers aware of the cultural differences that affect communication. This leads to one side or the other being misunderstood or ignored.

A sense of time unfamiliar to teachers in Western schools can also cause difficulties. Many Asian cultures operate on what is called "polychronic time," which differs from the "monochronic time" familiar to Western people (Storti, 1999). Polychronic time allows different social interactions to happen at the same time, while monochronic time is linear: you do one thing at a time, in a fixed sequence. This difference in time orientation sometimes causes misunderstandings because Asians may not be prompt or ready to get down to business as quickly as Westerners would like.

Li-Rong Cheng (1998) points out that Asian students with school experience elsewhere are accustomed to learning through listening, observing, reading, and imitating; responding to teachers' questions based on lectures and textbooks; and taking tests that require only the recall of factual information. They may be left feeling ambivalent and confused by classroom activities that involve group work, discussions, and creative activities, at which times the following behaviors may be observed:

- *Delay or hesitation.* Students may be unsure of an answer, unfamiliar with the discourse style, or simply disengaged and lost.
- *Failure to stick with the topic.* This may be due to insufficient knowledge, unfamiliarity with how to gain the floor, or fear and avoidance of interactions.
- *Inappropriate nonverbal expressions.* Students will often avoid eye contact with adults (a sign of respect), frown (in concentration, as opposed to displeasure), or giggle (from embarrassment or lack of understanding, not in response to something perceived as humorous).
- *Giving short responses.* Students may not be proficient enough to reply in long, cohesive utterances, or too shy to respond.
- *Overly soft voice.* This is typical for children in some Asian cultures.
- *Unwillingness to take risks.* Students may fear being embarrassed or ridiculed.
- *Lack of participation.* In some Asian classrooms, volunteering information is considered overly bold.
- *Embarrassment over receiving praise.* Students' native culture may regard humility and self-criticism highly.
- *Atypical greetings.* Students may appear impolite or unfriendly because they look down (out of respect or fear) when the teacher approaches instead of offering a greeting.

It is natural that Asian students and family members expect teachers to understand their ways, concerns, confusion, and hesitance. It is also understandable that teachers misinterpret Asian's head-nodding, frowning, smiling, giggling, and averted eyes. The approach taken in Western education places the onus for resolving possible misunderstandings on teachers. Suggestions for doing so are presented in the section on how to work with Asian students.

Despite these difficulties, students from Asian origins tend quickly to become notably successful in school. They learn English well and tend to be high achievers. Of course, not all are superior students. Some have learning problems. Some lack motivation. Some gravitate to gang behavior. Some struggle with English or other Western languages, at least at first. But all in all, Asian students are cooperative, hardworking, successful, and eager to please.

How Can Teachers Work Most Effectively with Asian American Students?   Matsuda (1989), Baruth and Manning (1992), Trueba and Cheng (1993), Huang (1993), Feng (1994), and Cheng (1996, 1998) make a number of suggestions to help teachers work more effectively with Asian students, including:

- Learn about the values, traditions, and customs of the cultures from which your students come.
- Carefully observe and understand students' sense of communication and time, and adjust your interactions accordingly.
- Do not assume all groups have the same traits. You will encounter large differences concerning basic cultural patterns, language skills, and familiarity with Western society.
- Learn at least a few words of the students' native languages. Ask students to teach them to you.
- Understand students' general nature, but base your academic expectations on individual ability rather than group stereotypes.
- Help students understand that, while at school, they may offer their opinions and challenge the views of others.
- Consider peer teaching for students who are not proficient in English.
- Use to advantage the student's natural support system of family, friends, and community. Encourage family members to assist one another in serving as facilitators and sources of information. Those established in the community can assist new arrivals.
- Explain to family members that parental involvement in their child's education is a tradition in the Western world.
- Examine your own communication patterns as a step to better appreciating those of Asian students and family members. Realize that their ways, just like yours, are learned and considered appropriate and reasonable for the culture.
- In meetings, assume the role of authority. Provide clear and full information, such as what will be provided by, and is expected from, each participant in the discussion. Address immediate needs and give concrete advice.
- When joint decisions must be made, reach consensus through compromising.
- Be patient during verbal exchanges. Consider periods of silence opportunities for reflection on what has been said. Be attentive to nonverbal cues.
- When you can do so, use individual rather than group meetings and oral communication rather than written memos.
- Consider the individual first. While it is important to incorporate the student's culture in an effective manner, focusing on the individual rather than a group is key to improving the quality of service in school settings.
- Encourage students to join student clubs to increase their exposure to language, socialization, and different types of discourse.
- Facilitate students' transition into mainstream culture through activities and discussions of culturally unique experiences and celebrations, such as birthday parties and Thanksgiving.

- Role-play, practice colloquialisms, and act out skits that involve typical verbal exchanges.
- Read to students to increase their vocabulary, and expose them to various narrative styles used in letters, stories, articles, biographies, and poetry.
- Families can play an important role in students' success in school. Try to involve them.

Web Site Resource

Asian/Pacific Pathway. To inform teachers, administrators, family members, and community leaders about the Asian/Pacific American student population and its educational and cultural characteristics (http://eric-web.tc.columbia.edu/pathways/asian_pacific).

Hispanic American Students

Hispanic American students, often called Latinos, come from ethnic groups whose native or ancestral language is Spanish. As reported in *Latinos in School: Some Facts and Findings* (2001), the number of Hispanic American children and youth in public schools in the United States has, for a number of years, been steadily and rapidly increasing. The Hispanic American population is quite young, with approximately one-third under age eighteen. Hispanic American students comprise approximately 17 percent of the public school population in the United States. That figure is projected to reach 25 percent by the year 2025. Students in this group are the second most likely to drop out before completing high school, trailing only American Indians/Native Alaskans. Their high school completion rate in 1999 was 63 percent, as compared with 81 percent for African Americans and 90 percent for Anglo Americans. The dropout rate among Hispanic immigrants is double that of U.S.-born Hispanic students—44 percent compared to 21 percent. The reason for this high dropout rate is not clear, but it is usually attributed to attendance at overcrowded, inadequately staffed, and under-resourced schools that fail to meet students' educational needs while serving as breeding grounds for antisocial activities. Many of these students live in economically distressed areas and do not believe that remaining in school will materially improve their future lives.

Characteristics of Hispanic American Students.   Nearly 50 percent of Hispanic American students attend urban schools. In 1999, fewer than 18 percent had access to a home computer, compared with 52 percent for white students. Yet, in secondary schools, Hispanic American students earn more credits than white students in computer science, foreign languages, and English, while other ethnic groups earn proportionately more credits in history, science, and mathematics. Only 35 percent of Hispanic American students enroll in college preparatory or academic programs, compared with 43 percent of African Americans and 50 percent of whites. They tend to be tracked into programs that only satisfy the basic requirements for high school graduation.

How Can Teachers Work Most Effectively with Hispanic American Students?
Wendy Schwartz (2000) and Anne Lockwood and Walter Secada (2000) have made several

suggestions for improving the quality of classroom experiences for Hispanic American youth, including:

- Make the classroom a safe and inviting place to learn.
- Personalize instruction and give students the opportunity to assume positions of leadership and responsibility. Target these students for pro-social roles and protect them from intimidation.
- Provide help in reducing student anger and building trust as a means of countering attitudes that result from negative experiences with schools and adults.
- Treat Hispanic students' language and culture as desirable resources.
- Convey high expectations, present options, and provide resources needed for an effective education.
- Emphasize the prevention of problems and respond effectively to early-warning signs that a student is beginning to disengage from school.
- Teach content so that it interests and challenges Hispanic students.
- Respect and show interest in students' language, culture, and ethnicity.

The school as a whole can contribute to this effort by doing the following:

1. Identify for each Hispanic student an adult in the school who is committed to nurturing a sense of self-worth and supporting the student's efforts to succeed in school. Such mentors can help students withstand the peer, economic, and societal pressures that lead to dropping out.
2. Find ways to provide smaller classes or lower student–teacher ratio to increase the personal attention given each student.
3. Seek out and replicate programs being used effectively in other schools. Continually try to improve them.
4. Engage family members and the community in the education of their children.
5. Look for ways to improve communication with Hispanic families.
6. Recruit Hispanic family members into a partnership to envision a future for their children and a reasonable plan for realizing it.

Web Sites of Interest.   You might wish to access the following Web sites for additional information on Hispanic American education.

Transforming Education for Hispanic Youth: Exemplary Practices, Programs, and Schools by Anne Turnbaugh Lockwood and Walter G. Secada. Full text on-line in HTML and PDF formats (http://www.ncbe.gwu.edu/ncbepubs/resource/hispanic youth/hdp.htm).

Latino Web—Education. Categories at this Web site include Bilingual Education, Financial Aid, Learning Tools, Research, Scholarships, School Groups, Supplies, and Teaching Tools (http://www.latinoweb.com/education.html).

Latino Education Directory. A directory that helps individuals and organizations make contact with each other, share resources, and form networks of support for Latino students (http://www.ael.org/eric/maed).

Migrant Education Technology and Curriculum Resources (http://lone-eagles. com/migrant.htm).

Center for the Study of Books in Spanish for Children and Adolescents. This Web site can be viewed in English or Spanish (http://public.csusm.edu/campus_ centers/csb).

> **FIELD APPLICATION 3:** Select one of the four minority groups discussed in previous paragraphs. Inquire at a middle-grades school about the number of students from that group in attendance. Ask about special provisions being made to increase their success levels.

Working with Economically Disadvantaged Students

Early in the chapter, economic disadvantage was described in terms of poverty. A family and its members are said to be in poverty if they have to spend more than one-third of their disposable income to purchase food adequate to meet the family's nutritional needs. Further, it was said that groups living in poverty tend to have life views that are different from those of the dominant society and that those differences can hinder students' education.

For some time, Ruby Payne (2001) has been investigating the effects that economic disadvantage exerts on people in poverty. Her findings are interesting and helpful. Most teachers assume that children from poverty think and behave much as do children from more affluent families, but Payne concludes differently. She says poverty produces, or is associated with, a number of views and behaviors that are distinct from those in the dominant society. She provides information that is helpful to teachers.

Hidden Rules

Each economic class has its own set of hidden rules for survival. Individuals internalize those rules and apply them in new situations. Schools and teachers use the hidden rules of the middle-class dominant society, which include future time orientation, planning for the future, a strong work ethic, competition, an emphasis on individuality, verbal learning, and willingness to take risks. However, increasing numbers of school students do not come from the middle class and do not share all those values. Hence, barriers to understanding arise between educators and students from poverty.

Areas of Conflict

Misunderstanding and conflict often occur when hidden rules clash. Payne (2001, pp. 68–70, 76–78) also advises teachers to learn some of the hidden rules of poverty in order to understand students and communicate better with them.

- Speech—Students from economically disadvantaged families tend to use a casual, informal style of speech. School emphasizes a more formal style of speech. (Teachers should point out the difference, help students use the appropriate language for various situations, and help them understand that a formal style is helpful in school and the workplace.)
- Money—Money is to be used, to be spent. The school teaches it is to be managed, saved, and made to grow.
- Personality—Having "personality" is highly valued and appreciated for entertainment. The school places a higher value on achievement.
- Major thought about food—People who are poor wonder if there is enough. Middle-class people want to know whether you liked it.
- Clothing—Clothing is seen as an expression of personality.
- Time—The present is most important. School emphasizes looking to the future.
- Language—Use of English is casual, and focused on survival. School language is more formal, about negotiation.
- Family structure—The family tends to be matriarchal, whereas the family is usually patriarchal in the dominant society.
- Perspective—Individuals' perspective tends to be local for students of poverty, while national for the dominant society.
- Driving forces in life—Among the poor, survival, relationships, and entertainment are the driving forces, whereas schools promote work and achievement as driving forces.
- Background noise—In the homes of the poor, volume levels are high, the television is almost always on, and conversation is participatory, with more than one person talking at a time. Schools value quiet, with speakers taking turns.

Cultural differences are also evident in the following views and behaviors of economically disadvantaged students:

- Individual personality is prized, especially in entertaining and telling stories. Students love humor and entertaining others.
- Overall orientation to life tends to be somewhat negative.
- School discipline is not about improvement. It is about punishment. Students may laugh when disciplined, as a way of saving face.
- Present time is most important, so there is little effort to plan ahead or to consider future implications of present actions.
- Lack of order or organization in one's personal life is normal. Students may lose papers, neglect to get required signatures on forms, not do homework, and have a difficult time getting started on assignments.
- Likable teachers are attractive and should be pleased. Others are not worth the trouble.
- Conflicts are settled verbally and physically, rather than with calm reason.
- Survival language is emphasized, and students say what is on their minds.
- Emotional warmth is needed from the teacher, in order to feel comfortable.
- A high level of integrity is needed from those in power, as organizations and authority are seldom trusted.
- Students don't know or use middle-class courtesies and may talk back.

Payne gives this advice to teachers of students in poverty (she uses the term *generational poverty* to refer to the continuing cycle from parent to offspring): The key to helping these students achieve in school is to create caring relationships with them. Relationships are what motivate them most.

> **FIELD APPLICATION 4:**   Arrange to interview a middle-level teacher who works with economically disadvantaged students. Use the list of traits presented in previous paragraphs. Ask the teacher about the extent to which he or she observes those traits in students from poverty, and how much those traits interfere with student learning, if at all.

QUESTIONS

1. If you were asked to draw one major conclusion from all the suggestions presented in this chapter about teaching minority students and students from poverty, what would it be?

2. Which of the five groups considered in this chapter would present the greatest challenge for you? Which would be easiest for you? Why?

3. Many teachers say, "Kids are kids. If you can teach one, you can teach any of them." In what ways do you feel that comment is correct, and in what ways do you think it is misleading?

4. Assume all groups of people have approximately the same overall level of intelligence. That being the case, why do some do better in school than others?

5. The suggestions presented in this chapter seem to assign teachers the entire burden for student success. If you could get students to do one thing that would make education go better for them *and* you, what would it be?

6. Critics of education are wont to say that schools fail students, while students never fail schools. To what extent do you agree and/or disagree with that assertion? Explain.

ACTIVITIES

1. Suppose your community has in influx of immigrant students from Sri Lanka. The students assigned to you all speak English well enough to communicate. What steps would you take to help them achieve maximum benefit from being in your class?

2. Select one of the five groups described in this chapter. For a grade-level or subject-matter class of your choice, list all the things you can think of that you would do to help them learn and enjoy school.

3. Suppose you have a class made up of 50 percent minority students and 50 percent non-minority. Describe how you could have the two groups work together for the mutual benefit of both.

4. You have probably experienced a fairly typical program of teacher education, and you probably have middle-class values. What modifications would you suggest in your teacher-education program that would prepare you better for working with economically disadvantaged students?

REFERENCES

Ascher, C. 1991. *School programs for African American males.* New York: ERIC Clearinghouse on Urban Education.

Atencio, B., and others. 1992. White House Conference on Indian Education (Washington, DC, January 22–24, 1992). Final Report, volumes 1 and 2.

Baruth, L., and Manning, M. 1992. *Multicultural education of children and adolescents.* Boston: Allyn & Bacon.

Bempechat, J. 2001. *Fostering high achievement in African American children: Home, school, and public policy influences.* <http://eric-web.tc. columbia.edu/monographs/ti16_index.html>.

Benard, B. 1997. Drawing forth resilience in all our youth. *Reclaiming Children and Youth, 6* (1), 29–32.

Brown, A. 1980. Cherokee culture and school achievement. *American Indian Culture and Research Journal, 4,* 55–74.

Butterfield, R. 1994. *Blueprints for Indian education: Improving mainstream schooling.* Charleston, WV: ERIC Clearinghouse on Rural Education and Small Schools.

Butterfield, R., and Pepper, F. 1991. Improving parental participation in elementary and secondary education for American Indian and Alaska Native students. ERIC: Identifier RC018622.

Cahape, P., and Howley, C. 1992. Indian nations at risk: Listening to the people. Summaries of Papers Commissioned by the Indian Nations At Risk Task Force of the U.S. Department of Education.

Cajete, G. 1986. *Science: A Native American perspective* (A Culturally Based Science Education Curriculum). Unpublished Ph.D. dissertation, International College/William Lyon University, San Diego, CA.

Chavkin, N., and Gonzalez, J. 2000. *Mexican immigrant youth and resiliency: Research and promising programs.* Charleston, WV: ERIC Clearinghouse on Rural Education. ED447990.

Cheng, L. 1996. Enhancing communication: Toward optimal language learning for limited English proficient students. *Language, Speech and Hearing Services in Schools, 28* (2), 347–354.

———. 1998. Enhancing the communication skills of newly arrived Asian American students. ERIC/ CUE Digest No. 136. New York: ERIC Clearinghouse on Urban Education.

Coker, D. 1988. The Asian students in the classroom. *Education and Society, 1* (3), 19–20.

Cornett, C. 1983. What you should know about teaching and learning styles (Fastback No. 191). Bloomington, IN: Phi Delta Kappa Foundation.

Cotton, K. 1994. Fostering intercultural harmony in schools: Research findings (Topical Synthesis No. 7). Portland, OR: Northwest Regional Educational Laboratory.

Cox, B., and Ramirez, M. 1981. Cognitive styles: Implications for multiethnic education. In J. Banks (Ed.), *Education in the 80s: Multiethnic Education* (pp. 61–71). Washington, DC: National Education Association.

Diller, D. 1999. Opening the dialogue: Using culture as a tool in teaching young African American children. *Reading Teacher, 52* (8), 820–858.

Faircloth, S., and Tippeconnic, J. 2000. Issues in the education of American Indian and Alaska Native students with disabilities. Charleston, WV: ERIC Clearinghouse on Rural Education and Small Schools.

Feng, J. 1994. Asian-American children: What teachers should know. Urbana, IL: ERIC.

Foster, M. 1995. Talking that talk: The language of control, curriculum, and conflict. *Linguistics and Education, 7,* 129–150.

———. 1999. Teaching and learning in the contexts of African American English and culture. *Education and Urban Society. 31* (2), 177ff.

Gibbs, J. (Ed.). 1988. *Young, black, and male in America: An endangered species.* Dover: Auburn.

Gordon, K. 1996. Resilience and motivation in two ethnic minority populations. ERIC Identifier ED404401.

Hao, L., and Bonstead-Bruns, M. 1998. Parent–child differences in educational expectations and the academic achievement of immigrant and Native students. *Sociology of Education, 71* (3), 175–198.

Huang, G. 1993. Beyond culture: Communicating with Asian American children and families. *ERIC/CUE Digest Number 94.* New York: ERIC.

Kim, B. (Ed.). 1985. *Literacy and languages. The Second Yearbook of Literacy and Languages in Asia, International Reading Association Special Interest Group.* Selection of Speeches and Papers from the International Conference on Literacy and Languages (Seoul, South Korea, August 12–14).

Krovetz, M. 1999. *Fostering resiliency: Expecting all students to use their minds and hearts well.* Thousand Oaks, CA: Corwin.

Kunjufu, J. 1984. *Developing positive self-images and discipline in black children.* Chicago: African American Images.

Ladson-Billings, G. 2000. Fighting for our lives: Preparing teachers to teach African American students. *Journal of Teacher Education 51* (3), 206–214.

Latinos in School: Some facts and findings. 2001. *ERIC Digest Number 162.*

Lockwood, A., and Secada, W. 2000. Transforming education for Hispanic youth: Exemplary practices, programs, and schools. *ERIC Digest.* <www.ncbe. gwu.edu/ncbepubs/resource/hispanicyouth/hdp. htm>.

Lucas, T., Henze, R., and Donato, R. 1990. Promoting the success of Latino language minority students: An exploratory study of six high schools. *Harvard Educational Review, 60,* 315–340.

Matsuda, M. 1989. Working with Asian Family members: Some communication strategies. *Topics in Language Disorders, 9* (3), 45–53.

Mattox, B. 1999. Impact of the MegaSkills Program for students, teachers, family members schoolwide. <http://www.megaskillshsi.org/training%20 programs/schoolprogram.htm>.

McCollough, Shawn. 2000. Teaching African American students. *Clearing House 74* (1), 5–6.

National Coalition of Advocates for Students. 1994. *Delivering on the promise:Positive practices for immigrant students.* Boston: Author.

Payne, R. 2001. *A framework for understanding poverty.* Highlands, TX: aha! Process.

Philips, S. 1983. *The invisible culture.* New York: Longman.

Qualities of effective programs for immigrant adolescents with limited schooling. 1998. Washington, DC: ERIC.

Reed, R. 1988. Education and achievement of young black males. In J. W. Gibbs (Ed.), *Young, black, and male in America: An endangered species.* Dover: Auburn.

Schwartz, W. 2000. New trends in language education for Hispanic students. *ERIC/CUE Digest Number 155.* New York: ERIC.

———. 2001. School practices for equitable discipline of African American students. New York: ERIC Clearinghouse on Urban Education.

St. Germaine, R. 1995. Drop-out rates among American Indian and Alaska Natives Students: Beyond cultural discontinuity. Charleston, WV: ERIC Clearinghouse on Rural Education and Small Schools.

Storti, C. 1999. *Figuring foreigners out: A practical guide.* Yarmouth, ME: Intercultural Press.

Swisher, K. 1991. American Indian/Alaskan Native learning styles: Research and practice. Charleston, WV: ERIC Clearinghouse on Rural Education and Small Schools. ED335175.

Trueba, H., and Cheng, L. 1993. *Myth or reality: Adaptive strategies of Asian Americans in California.* Bristol, PA: Falmer.

U.S. Census Bureau. *Poverty 2001.* <www.census.gov/ hhes>.

U.S. National Center for Education Statistics. 2001. <http://nces.ed.gov/>.

Walqui, A. 2000. Strategies for success: Engaging immigrant students in secondary schools. Washington, DC: ERIC.

Walsh, C. 1991. Literacy and school success: Considerations for programming and instruction. In C. Walsh and H. Prashker (Eds.), *Literacy development for bilingual students.* Boston: New England Multifunctional Resource Center for Language and Culture Education.

Wierzbicka, A. 1991. Japanese key words and core cultural values. *Language in Society, 20* (3), 333–385.

11 Working with Students Who Require Special Accommodations or Management

Chapter Preview

Our obligation (and privilege) is to teach all students the best we know how, regardless of their intellectual or physical traits that might affect learning. Some of our students have higher than normal levels of intelligence that call for special programs. Some, often for reasons we do not understand, have difficulty learning, and a few behave in ways that violate normal standards of decorum. You must make special accommodations for students who are at the edges of the mainstream of learning and behavior. Some of those accommodations will be in the program you offer, some in your methods of teaching, and some in how you relate to students who are withdrawn, disruptive, overly energetic, or confrontational.

This chapter explores some of your duties in helping those students, together with suggestions for doing so. You will encounter discussions about:

1. students who are gifted or talented
2. students who have disabilities
3. students who are behaviorally at risk of failure
4. students diagnosed with ADHD
5. students who abuse drugs and alcohol
6. students who are prone to violence, vandalism, and bullying

Students Who Are Gifted or Talented

Giftedness refers to untrained and spontaneously expressed intellectual, artistic, or sensori-motor capabilities, sufficiently high to place the student in the top 5 percent of his or her age peers. Talented refers to capability made evident through learning, sufficient to place a student in the upper 15 percent of his or her peers.

It has long been recognized that the normal school curriculum, designed for approximately the middle 70 percent of students, does not adequately help gifted or talented students, given their advanced capabilities. Therefore, special programs are made available to them in most school systems. In small schools that cannot provide special programs, classroom teachers often enrich the curricula by providing selected experiences, activities, and self-directed work in greater depth than normal.

Programs and Practices

The Council for Exceptional Children (2002) points out that we have no reliable list of best practices for teachers to use with gifted and talented students. Research in this matter has produced inconclusive results. When new approaches are evaluated, such as a resource room, ability grouping, or a particular method of instruction, varied results are found, leaving the conclusion that many different approaches sometimes work well with gifted and talented students, but not always. The evaluation of these approaches may be invalid because program changes are usually made on a limited scale. Changing the learning environment without changing the content of lessons, for example, seems ineffective, as does modifying the curriculum without giving attention to how it is organized through successive grade levels.

At present, the favored plan for helping gifted and talented students involves bringing gifted students together, presenting them intellectually stimulating and important ideas, encouraging them to identify and solve problems, and making sure their learning progresses through grade levels in a sequential manner. One project of this type that is producing recognized results is the National Curriculum Project for High Ability Learners, located at the College of William and Mary (http://ericec.org/facs/html). It is a focused, integrated program designed to produce significant learning gains in core curriculum areas. The effectiveness of the program may be due to its broader view of intelligence and giftedness than is ordinarily seen. Another notable program is the Schoolwide Enrichment Model, summarized in the following section.

Schoolwide Enrichment Model

The Schoolwide Enrichment Model evolved from Joseph Renzulli's Enrichment Triad Model, first developed in the mid-1970s and implemented in school districts in New England (Renzulli, 1996). Now, with the growing success of the model, it has been adopted across the country. The basic premise of the Schoolwide Enrichment Model is that school's primary purpose is to develop talent. Therefore, instruction usually reserved for gifted students is used with all students in the school. The result is a curriculum that is more challenging, enjoyable, and productive than normal. A broad range of enrichment experiences is provided, and student responses are used to improve the program further. Flexibility of implementation is encouraged, and each school develops a program that meets its students' needs and matches its faculty's strengths.

Instruction is based on the following beliefs: (1) each learner is unique, (2) learning is more effective when students enjoy what they are doing, and (3) learning is more effective when content and process involve real problems. In the program, students contribute their best work samples that reflect their strengths and interests as learners. Activities that follow focus on those strengths rather than shortcomings the students might have. For further information on the Schoolwide Enrichment Model, contact the following Web site: <www.gifted.uconn.edu>.

Other Widely Accepted Programs

Several other new programs for gifted students are receiving wide attention. Three such programs are Multiple Intelligences, Talents Unlimited, and the Triarchic Method.

Multiple Intelligences. This approach uses the multiple-intelligences theory set forth by Howard Gardner in 1983 (see Gardner, 2000; also see Reid and Romanoff, 1997). The Charlotte–Mecklenburg (North Carolina) Public Schools are using this approach, with large numbers of gifted students involved in programs that fuse multiple-intelligences theory, problem-centered learning, and critical and creative thinking. For further information, check various Web sites on multiple intelligences.

Talents Unlimited. Rena Subotnik and Laurence Coleman (1996) describe a program designed to meet the atypical learning styles and needs of gifted students. It attempts to remove factors from the conventional curriculum that are antithetical to talent development and replace them with scholarly inquiry and apprenticeships. Carol Schlichter et al. (1997) describe the Multiple Abilities Program at the University of Alabama, in which preservice teachers team with general and special elementary education classroom mentors to teach students with average and above average abilities and students with mild learning or behavior problems. The program helps preservice teachers develop enrichment minicourses based on the Talents Unlimited Model.

Triarchic Method. The triarchic model builds education around three intellectual abilities: memory–analytic, creative–synthetic, and practical–contextual. Robert Sternberg and Pamela Clinkenbeard (1995) describe the triarchic model and explain how it is used for identifying, teaching, and assessing gifted students.

> **FIELD APPLICATION 1:** At a middle-level school with which you have contact, inquire as to whether there are special provisions made for educating gifted and talented students. Make a list of what is available to those students.

Students Who Have Disabilities

According to the U.S. Department of Education, about 13 percent of the school population is enrolled in special education programs. The largest numbers among those students are categorized as follows:

- Specific learning disabilities—2.7 million students
- Speech impairments—1.06 million
- Mental retardation—592,000
- Serious emotional disturbance—457,000, with two-thirds of this category accounted for by hyperkinetic syndrome (ADHD)
- Health impairments—166,900
- Mobility or orthopedic impairments—69,000

- Hearing impairments—69,000
- Autism and traumatic brain injury—65,000
- Visual impairments—28,000

National Law: Individuals with Disabilities Education Act, 1997

Federal law contains a number of provisions concerning how students with disabilities are to be educated. The Individuals with Disabilities Education Act (IDEA), Amendments of 1997, mandates a free appropriate public education for eligible children and youth with disabilities, age three through twenty-one. Other regulations indicate how special education teachers and regular classroom teachers must contribute to the education of students with disabilities:

- Each child with a disability must be educated with nondisabled children to the maximum extent appropriate.
- Each child with a disability must be removed from the regular educational environment only when the nature or severity of the child's disability is such that education in regular classes with the use of supplementary aids and services cannot be achieved satisfactorily.
- To the maximum extent appropriate to the child's needs, each child with a disability must participate with nondisabled children in nonacademic and extracurricular services and activities.
- An individualized education program (IEP) must be developed for each child and include a statement of the child's present levels of educational performance, including how the child's disability affects the child's involvement and progress in the general curriculum. A copy of the resultant IEP must be furnished to family members at no cost.
- The IEP team for a child with a disability must include at least one regular education teacher of the child. The regular education teacher must, to the extent appropriate, participate in the development, review, and revision of the child's IEP, including assisting in
  1. the determination of appropriate positive behavioral interventions and strategies for the child; and
  2. the determination of supplementary aids and services, program modifications, and supports for school personnel provided for the child.
- Parents or guardians may participate in meetings devoted to the identification, evaluation, and educational placement of the child. They are to be allowed membership in the group that determines what additional data are needed as part of an evaluation of their child, the group that determines their child's eligibility, and the group that makes decisions on the educational placement of their child.

Parents' or Guardians' Rights

It is important that you know parents' and guardians' legal rights associated with the education of special students. This knowledge will help you understand and anticipate what family members may say, do, and request. Here are the rights under IDEA, 1997 (wording revised):

1. *Entitlement:* Your child is entitled to a free, appropriate public education, at no cost to you. The program must meet the unique educational needs of your child, and your child will be provided the services and supports he or she needs.
2. *Notification:* You will be notified whenever the school wishes to evaluate your child for potential special education needs, wants to change your child's educational placement, or refuses your request for an evaluation or a change in placement.
3. *Request:* You may request an evaluation if you think your child needs special education or related services.
4. *Informed, voluntary consent:* You will be asked by your school to provide "informed consent" (meaning you understand and agree in writing to the evaluation and educational program decisions for your child). Your consent is voluntary and may be withdrawn at any time.
5. *Independent evaluation:* You may obtain an independent evaluation if you disagree with the school's evaluation.
6. *Reevaluation:* You may request a reevaluation if you think your child's current educational placement is no longer appropriate.
7. *Regular evaluation:* The school must reevaluate your child at least every three years. Your child's educational program must be reviewed at least once during each calendar year.
8. *Language:* You may have your child tested for special education needs in the language he or she knows best. Also, students who are hearing impaired have the right to an interpreter during the testing.
9. *Records review:* You may review all of your child's records and obtain copies of these records, but the school may charge you a reasonable fee for making copies.
10. *Records access:* Only you, as parent or guardian, and those directly involved in the education of your child, will be given access to personal records. If you feel that any of the information in your child's records is inaccurate, misleading, or violates the privacy or other rights of your child, you may request that the information be changed.
11. *Full information:* You must be fully informed by the school about all of the rights provided to you and your child under the law.
12. *Participation in IEP:* You may participate in the development of your child's Individualized Education Program (IEP).
13. *IEP decisions:* You may participate in all IEP team decisions, including placement.
14. *IEP meeting requests:* You may request an IEP meeting at any time during the school year.
15. *Least restrictive environment.* You may have your child educated in the least restrictive school setting possible, meaning in settings with children who do not have disabilities.
16. *Due process:* You may request a due process hearing or voluntary mediation to resolve differences with the school that can't be resolved informally.
17. *Progress information:* You should be kept informed about your child's progress at least as often as family members of children who do not have disabilities.

Parents' and Guardians' Responsibilities

In addition to knowing parents' and guardians' rights regarding students with disabilities, you should also know their responsibilities. When parents or guardians have been fully informed by your school district, you can expect them to understand their role as follows:

1. *Partnership:* Develop a partnership with the school and share relevant information about your child's education and development. Regard your child's education as a cooperative effort.
2. *Preparation:* Before attending an IEP meeting, make a list of things you want your child to learn.
3. *Furnish information:* Bring to the IEP meeting any information that the school or agency may not already have. This could include copies of medical records, past school records, and test and medical information. You can also discuss real-life examples to demonstrate your child's abilities in certain areas.
4. *Discuss:* Discuss any related services your child may need. Ask each professional to describe the kind of service he or she will be providing and what improvement you might expect to see in your child as a result of these services.
5. *Discipline:* Discuss methods for handling discipline problems that you know are effective with your child.
6. *Support at home:* Ask what you can do at home to support the program.
7. *Request clarification:* Ask for clarification of any aspect of the program that is unclear to you.
8. *Understand before signing:* Make sure you understand the program specified in the IEP before agreeing to it or signing the form.
9. *Discuss with teacher:* Consider and discuss with your child's teacher how your child might be included in the regular school activities program, including lunch, nutrition breaks, art, music, physical education, and extracurricular activities.
10. *Monitor progress:* Monitor your child's progress and periodically ask for a report. If your child is not progressing, discuss this with the teacher and determine whether the program should be modified.
11. *Discuss with school:* Discuss with the school any problems that occur with your child's assessment, placement, or educational program.
12. *Keep records:* There may be many questions and comments about your child that you will want to discuss, as well as meetings and phone conversations you will want to remember. Keep these as notes. Document their resolution.
13. *Failure to reach agreement:* If you and the school cannot reach an agreement about your child's educational and developmental needs, ask to have another meeting with the school. If, after a second meeting, there is still a conflict over your child's program, you may ask for a state mediator or a due process hearing.

Programs and Practices

IDEA directs that disabled students, to the extent feasible, must be accommodated in regular classrooms. Hence, you will have some of them in your classes and will be partly, or sometimes entirely, responsible for the education they receive while with you. You need to know what you are required to do, adopt a positive attitude toward working with students with disabilities, and learn to provide needed services as best you can.

Listed here are attitudes, activities, and support systems common to successful inclusion programs (adapted from *Including Students with Disabilities in General Education Classrooms,* 1993). If you have students with disabilities in your classes, you should make sure the following are in place:

Desirable Attitudes and Beliefs

- The regular teacher believes the student can succeed.
- School personnel are committed to accepting responsibility for the learning outcomes of students with disabilities.
- School personnel and other students in the class have been prepared to receive a student with disabilities.
- Family members are informed and duties of the support program are clear.
- Special education staff are committed to collaborative practice in regular classrooms.

Services and Physical Accommodations

- Services needed by the student are available (e.g., health, physical, occupational, or speech therapy).
- Accommodations to the physical plant and equipment are adequate to meet the student's needs (e.g., toys, building and playground facilities, learning materials, assistive devices).

School Support

- The principal understands the needs of students with disabilities.
- Adequate numbers of personnel, including aides and support personnel, are available.
- Adequate staff development and technical assistance, based on the needs of the school personnel, are being provided (e.g., information on disabilities, instructional methods, awareness and acceptance activities for students, and team-building skills).
- Appropriate policies and procedures are in place for monitoring individual student progress, including grading and testing.

Collaboration

- Special educators are part of the instructional or planning team.
- Teaming approaches are used for problem solving and program implementation.
- Regular teachers, special education teachers, and other specialists collaborate (e.g., co-teaching, team teaching, teacher-assistance teams).

Instructional Methods

- Teachers have the knowledge and skills needed to select and adapt curricula and instructional methods according to individual student needs.
- A variety of instructional arrangements is available (e.g., team teaching, cross-grade grouping, peer tutoring, teacher-assistance teams).
- Teachers foster a cooperative learning environment and promote socialization.

A Case of Making It Work

The composite case report presented here has been modified from one that appears in *Including Students with Disabilities in General Education Classrooms* (1993). It describes briefly how Jane Smith (or you) can work collaboratively with special education teachers to provide the services required by students with disabilities.

Jane Smith teaches Language Arts at Lincoln Middle School. Three days a week, she co-teaches the class with Lynn Vogel, a special education teacher. Their twenty-five students include four who have special needs due to disabilities and two who need special help in certain curriculum areas. Each of the students with a disability uses an IEP developed by a team that included both teachers. The teachers and other school personnel have attended training sessions to develop collaborative skills for teaming, problem solving, and building an inclusive classroom environment.

The school principal, Ben Parks, has received training on the impact of new special education developments and instructional arrangements. Periodically he confers with the staff to identify areas where new training is needed. For specific questions that may arise, technical assistance is available through a regional special education cooperative.

Mrs. Smith and Miss Vogel share responsibility for teaching and for supervising their two paraprofessionals. In addition to their time together in the classroom, they spend one to four hours per week resolving problems, planning instruction, and deciding how best to help students who need special assistance. They also spend time planning with other teachers and support personnel who work with their students.

Monitoring and adapting instruction is an ongoing activity. Curriculum-based measurement is used to assess their students' learning progress. Curricula and lessons are adapted to students' levels of knowledge and skills, allowing new material to be added at the students' pace and in keeping with their learning styles. For some students, advance organizers or previews are used to direct attention to the most important points of the material to be learned; for other students, new vocabulary words are highlighted or levels of reading are made easier. Some students use special activity worksheets, while others learn by using media or computer-assisted instruction.

The teachers group students differently for different activities. Sometimes teachers and paraprofessionals divide the class, each teaching a small group or tutoring individuals. They use cooperative learning projects to help the students learn to work together and develop social relationships. Peer tutors provide extra help to students who need it.

Students Who Are Behaviorally At-Risk of Failure

Behaviorally at-risk refers to students whose behavior severely inhibits learning and puts them in danger of failing in school. Richard Curwin and Allen Mendler (1992) have taken a special interest in these students, whom teachers usually consider lazy, turned off, angry, hostile, irresponsible, disruptive, withdrawn, having attitude problems, or out of control. Curwin and Mendler describe them in less pejorative terms:

They are failing.

They have received, and do not respond to, most of the punishments and/or consequences offered by the school.

They have low self-concepts in relation to school.

They have little or no hope they will be successful in school.

They associate with and are reinforced by students similar to themselves.

The number of behaviorally at-risk students is increasing steadily. Many of those students can see no role for themselves in the educational mainstream. They have lost hope that school will ever be worthwhile for them. Consequently, many do not care how they behave in the classroom. It does not worry them if they fail, bother the teacher, or disrupt the class.

Why At-Risk Students Are Difficult to Work With

Behaviorally at-risk students are difficult to work with for several reasons. They usually, though not always, have a history of academic failure. This failure has lowered their sense of personal dignity, causing them to protect themselves from further insult by withdrawing or acting as if they don't care. They have learned that it feels better to misbehave than to follow rules that provide no payoff. Curwin (1992) illustrates this point.

> Ask yourself, if you got a 56 on an important test, what would make you feel better about failing? Telling your friends, "I studied hard and was just too stupid to pass," or "It was a stupid test anyway, and besides I hate that dumb class and that boring teacher" (p. 49).

When students' dignity has been damaged repeatedly, it makes them feel good to lash out at others. As they continue to misbehave, they find themselves systematically removed from opportunities to act responsibly. When they break rules, they are made to sit by themselves in isolation. When they fight, they are made to apologize and shake hands when they don't want to do so. In such cases they are taken out of the very situations in which they might learn to behave responsibly. Curwin (1992) makes the point as follows:

> No one would tell a batter who was struggling at the plate that he could not participate in batting practice until he improved. No one would tell a poor reader that he could not look at any books until his reading improved. In the same way, no student can learn how to play in a playground by being removed from the playground, or how to learn time-management skills by being told when to schedule everything. Learning responsibility requires participation (p. 50).

Students who are behaviorally at-risk know and accept that they are labeled "discipline problems." They know that they can't do academic work very well and are considered bothersome and irritating. Wherever they turn, they receive negative messages about themselves. They have become, in their own eyes, bad persons. How can teachers help students who see themselves as bad persons and whose only gratification in school comes from causing trouble?

Helping Students Regain Hope

Many of these students are not beyond redemption. Many can be successful, provided they regain a sense of hope. Curwin and Mendler (1992) say we can help students regain hope simply by treating them with respect and making instruction more interesting and worthwhile. Students will involve themselves in learning they find interesting, although interest is not enough by itself. Learning must also bring success and lead to competence. At-risk students will not persevere unless they experience pleasure and success often and regularly.

Discipline for Students Who Are Difficult to Control

Traditional methods of discipline have little effect on students who are behaviorally at-risk. These students have grown immune to scolding, lecturing, sarcasm, detention, extra writing assignments, isolation, their names on the board, and trips to the principal's office. It does no good to tell them what they did wrong, or to grill them about their failure to do class work or follow rules. Teachers who speak sarcastically to these students almost always make matters worse.

Dealing with the chronic rule breaker is never easy, and we need to understand that the success rate is far from perfect. Nevertheless, there is good reason to believe that by making certain changes in the ways we deal with at-risk students, we can significantly help 25 to 50 percent of them, especially if we do the following:

■ *Always treat students with dignity.* Dignity is a basic need that is essential for healthy life. To treat students with dignity is to respect them as individuals, to be concerned about their needs and understand their viewpoints. Effective discipline does not attack student dignity but instead offers hope.

> Curwin and Mendler advise teachers to ask themselves this question when reacting to student misbehavior: "How would this strategy affect my dignity if a teacher did it to me?"

■ *Don't allow discipline to interfere with student motivation.* Any discipline technique that reduces motivation to learn is self-defeating. Students who are enjoying their lessons cause few discipline problems. The question, therefore, is: How do I organize instruction to make it fun and worthwhile?

■ *Emphasize responsibility rather than obedience.* Obedience means "do as you are told." Responsibility means "make the best decision possible." Obedience is desirable in matters of health and safety, but when applied to most misbehavior it is a short-term solution against which students rebel. Responsibility grows, albeit slowly, as students have the opportunity to sort out facts and make decisions.

Example of a Master Plan for Services for Students at Risk

Schools everywhere have begun seeking ways to help students who are at risk of failure. One example, from the State of Utah, is provided in the following case adapted from a publication of the "At-Risk Task Force," Utah State Office of Education <www.usoe.k12.1998>.

The Utah *Master Plan for Services for Students at Risk,* revised in 1998, provides for appropriate and effective education for students who are at risk of failing in school. The plan is based on the following beliefs:

- Equity in education is sought through valuing individual differences, holding high expectations for all, providing instruction in inclusive environments, recognizing and appreciating diversity, and doing away with discrimination, stereotyping, and bias.
- A student's decision to drop out of school evolves over time and is the product of negative experiences in school and sometimes other external factors.
- School failure places a student at an extreme disadvantage in the workplace and in pursuing opportunities for further education.
- Rigorous standards and high expectations, when combined with integrated and continuous systems of support, have the capacity to reduce school failures.
- Prevention, intervention, and recovery are critical elements in helping students who are at risk.

The plan is designed to:

- develop, promote, and deliver child-focused, family-centered, community-based, and culturally appropriate services that improve the health, safety, education, and economic well-being of children and families in Utah;
- address the range of needs, factors, circumstances, and situations that contribute to students' inability to succeed in school;
- establish a continuum of strategies and practices to support student learning, beginning with the earliest learning years through elementary, middle, and high school years, that includes key points of transition;
- engage families and communities by inviting and facilitating their ongoing participation in the education process;
- support schools in meeting the needs of minority students and increase graduation rates among minority students and other students at risk of not graduating.

Curricular and instructional provisions include:

- a continuum of formal reading instruction across grade levels that overcomes the problem of illiteracy;
- books and other information resources made available to students at-risk and their families;
- ways for students with diverse needs to meet the requirements of the state core curriculum and high school graduation requirements;
- preservice and in-service training to improve classroom delivery of curriculum that accommodates differences among students;
- instruction made more integrative, challenging, and exploratory;
- comprehensive guidance for middle-grades students and reduction in class size;
- educational alternatives for students who have been expelled;
- efforts to combat truancy;
- assistance to help students make the transition from one educational setting to another.

Using Accelerated Programs to Help Students at Risk

We don't often think of using programs of accelerated learning to help students who are at risk. However, they may prove valuable, as indicated in the following description of the Accelerated School Program (Levin, 2002). For other examples see Freeberg (1989) and Brunner (1997).

Accelerated School Program

Purpose: Established to bring "at-risk" students into the educational mainstream by the end of elementary school.

Goals
- Enhance academic growth through challenging and stimulating activities instead of slowing down student learning with remediation.
- Treat "at-risk" students as gifted and talented students by identifying and building on their strengths instead of lowering expectations for these children.
- Create a schoolwide unity of purpose that would encompass all children, staff, and family members.
- Incorporate the entire staff into governance and decision making for creating powerful learning experiences for *all* children, instead of using state and district mandated "canned" curriculum packages as solutions to learning challenges for the children.

Principles of the Accelerated School
- unity of purpose
- empowerment coupled with responsibility
- building on the strength of students, staff, and family members

Students Diagnosed with Attention Deficit and Hyperactivity Disorder (ADHD)

Attention deficit and hyperactivity disorder (ADHD) is a behavior syndrome that that involves three persistent difficulties that inhibit student learning and lead to misbehavior:

- poor attention span
- weak impulse control
- hyperactivity

ADHD can begin in infancy and extend into adulthood, with negative effects on the individual's life at home, school, and in the community. It is now estimated that ADHD afflicts 3 to 5 percent of the school-age population. The exact cause of ADHD is unknown, but is believed to be neurological in nature. Accurate diagnosis is difficult, and can be done accurately only by well-trained developmental pediatricians, child psychologists, child psychiatrists, and pediatric neurologists.

ADHD symptoms affect people in various ways, ranging from inability to get organized to inability to remain employed after leaving school. It occurs in varying degrees of severity, and some people do not exhibit all the symptoms. ADHD is recognized in several variations (Amen, 2001). Males are more likely to be diagnosed with the condition than are females. Males typically have ADD with hyperactivity, while females typically have it without hyperactivity.

Programs and Practices

Dawn Hogan (1997) provides a number of suggestions, described in the following list, to help teachers work more effectively with ADHD students.

Relationships with Students.   Engage in personal, friendly conversation with the students, and show that you value their opinions and include them in the decision-making process when possible. Validate their strengths and offer activities in which they can excel. Respond favorably as they improve.

Environment for Learning.   Provide a calm, structured, positive environment. Establish clear standards of behavior. In the room, post realistic, predictable consequences for infractions. Immediate and consistent feedback is important, as is modeling positive behavior instead of focusing on the negative. Students with ADHD often act without thinking, so help them develop an awareness of their behavior. Use "I-messages" to explain your feelings to students after they are disruptive. Discuss the incident and brainstorm possible solutions together.

Assigned Work.   Make sure that assigned work is within or just beyond the student's capabilities. The material may need to be broken into tasks that can be accomplished in short amounts of time. Divide long assignments into shorter parts to make them more manageable.

Dealing with Upsets.   When ADHD students become upset, a time-out may be helpful to allow them time to think quietly about the conflict and resolve it on their own. They can rejoin the group when they feel calm and in control.

Fatigue.   Fatigue, stress, and pressure can easily overwhelm students' self-control and lead to inappropriate behavior. Provide opportunities for rest and relaxation such as stretching and times of quiet. Overactive individuals who need movement can run errands, sharpen pencils, water plants, and stand up when called on in class.

Interactive Learning.   Engage students in interactive learning. Assign peer partners to model organization skills and offer assistance. ADHD students do not always know how to initiate and complete tasks on their own, so provide checklists students can use when working on assignments.

Consistency.   Develop daily routines and prepare students for any change in the procedure to avoid disorientation.

Homework.   Make sure homework can be completed easily and gets done.

Relationships with Family Members.   Communicate closely with parents, and invite family members to become involved in the student's homework. Write out the assignment in clear terms. Include a homework schedule with due dates and places for family members to sign after work is done. Suggest that parents provide a set time for homework and a quiet study space away from the distractions of television, video games, and busy family activities.

Reinforcement. Provide frequent reinforcement in the form of nods, smiles, pats on the back, and words of praise. If stronger reinforcement is needed, consider point systems or tangible items. Encourage self-talk, allowing students to talk about how good behavior is self-gratifying. When you compliment students, use their name and a description of what they did right.

Dianna McFarland, Rosemarie Kolstad, and L. D. Biggs (1995) offer these succinct tips to teachers who work with ADHD students:

- Seat students near you, away from distractions.
- Keep the classroom uncluttered and well organized. Put unneeded materials away to minimize distractions.
- Surround ADHD students with well-behaved students who serve as positive models.
- Make instructions clear and concise.
- Give only one direction at a time.
- Make eye contact before giving instructions.
- Use realistic, achievable goals and objectives.
- Use lots of visual aids.
- Establish specific rules such as "Stay in your seat" and "Do not talk."
- When misbehavior occurs, respond immediately.
- Provide a structured routine with small segments of work followed by breaks.
- Keep a chart that tracks individual students' progress. This helps them remain focused.
- Frequently ask the student to repeat instructions you have given.
- Adjust your expectations and the student's workload. ADHD students can seldom do as much work as can other students.
- Coach students on how to make friends and relate to others.
- Interact with students through smiling, recognition, pleasant words, or giving notes of approval.

Finally, here are seven tips adapted from an article by Connie Weaver (1994).

Become Informed. Learn all you can about ADHD, its characteristics and how it affects learning and behavior.

Move Toward a Project-Based Classroom. Allow students to choose a project from two or three options. Also allow them to select from alternatives how they want to work and complete a task. Keep the number of choices limited.

Help Students Use Tools to Compensate for Difficulties They Experience. Make checklists of steps for completing specific tasks. Let students use the word processor and spell checker.

Make Directions as Easy to Follow as Possible. Always get students' attention before introducing something new. Give them time to begin homework in class so you can answer questions they might have.

Monitor Student Progress. Examine students' assignment notebooks and/or folders on a regular basis to make sure they are doing what they are supposed to. Ask them to tell you about the goals they have for some of their assignments and feelings they have about the class.

Use Alternative Assessments to Evaluate Students' Learning. Don't rely solely on written or standardized tests, which are very unpleasant for most ADHD students. Give oral exams, allow students to act out what they've learned, evaluate results of projects, and let students show you rather than tell you.

Ask for Help When You Need It. Your ADHD student might qualify for a classroom aide or some other type of services under section 504 of the Rehabilitation Act. Check with your principal to see if additional help can be obtained.

Behavior Management for ADHD Students

Frankly speaking, ADHD students are usually disruptive and hard to handle. Keeping them productively engaged is difficult even for experienced teachers, and the discipline suggestions presented in Chapters 7 and 8 may not work well with them. The following behavior management ideas are adapted from suggestions supplied by the Attention Deficit Disorders Association, Southern Region (2002). The association credits Dan Steinfink, M. D., and Harvey Oshman, Ph.D., for supplying the suggestions, which were originally intended for family members.

- Establish clear rules for behavior.
- Enforce the rules in a firm, consistent, and kind manner. Be positive, not punitive. Never degrade these students or put them down in any way. Do all you can to help them maintain their self-esteem.
- Listen actively to the students.
- Don't haggle or negotiate over small things. Make a reasonable and clear decision and stick with it.
- Assign class responsibilities. This helps students build self-discipline and a sense of responsibility.
- Help the students remember. ADHD students are distractible and forgetful. Help them keep a short list of tasks, which they tick off as each is completed. Also use picture cues and a prominently placed calendar.
- Accept ADHD students' absent-mindedness. These students do not usually process multiple requests quickly or accurately. Before making a request, be sure you have the student's attention.
- Avoid power struggles. Give directions one to three times as needed. Speak clearly and slowly, use a gentle touch, and make eye contact using an encouraging expression. As soon as the student does what is asked, simply say, "Thank you, Marcus. I appreciate your putting the toy away." One of the most potent motivations is a verbal response indicating that you are pleased with the student's efforts.

- Be tolerant of interruptions. Because these students are impulsive, they will speak and act out of turn. Make sure they get their turn.
- Prevent problems to the extent you can. Minimize exposure to highly stimulating situations until the students acquire a measure of self-control.
- Do not let students become fatigued. When they are tired, their self-control breaks down. Provide rest and times of quiet relaxation.
- Be accepting of these students' limitations. You cannot change them through repeated criticism, which often does more harm than good. Much of their misbehavior is not intentional. You cannot completely eliminate it. You get better results through showing tolerance and respect.
- Keep track of what works with individual students and use it repeatedly.

> **FIELD APPLICATION 2:**   Observe a class in which one or more students are identified as ADHD. Make notations about their behavior, relations with other students, and work habits. Ask the teacher if he or she makes special provisions for those students.

Students Who Abuse Drugs and Alcohol

Teachers, schools, and communities are very concerned about students' use of drugs and alcohol. As yet, however, we don't have reliably effective programs for dealing with the problem. Just over 50 percent of high school students report they use alcohol at least once a month (Bosworth, 1997). The use of illicit drugs is almost as prevalent. About 40 percent of high school seniors admit they have used an illicit drug at least once, and 24 percent say they use drugs at least once a month. Students are generally becoming less convinced that drugs and alcohol are bad for them.

Approaches That Have Failed

For three decades, significant public and private resources have been expended in attempting to stop youth from using alcohol, tobacco, and other drugs (abbreviated ATOD). The use of ATOD begins before the age of twenty, so schools are a convenient institution in which to access potential offenders. Most of the tactics we have used heretofore against use of ATOD have been ineffective, to put it mildly. These efforts include scare tactics, providing information on ATOD and their effects, self-esteem building, values clarification, large assembly presentations, and didactic presentation of material (Tobler and Stratton, cited in Bosworth, 1997).

Approaches That Show Promise

Certain approaches have shown some positive results, although the general consensus is that no one kind of intervention prevents abuse of ATOD for everyone. At present, the following seem most likely to help (Bosworth, 1997):

Normative Education. Help students realize that use of ATOD is not the norm for teenagers. Students generally overestimate the proportion of their peers actively involved in ATOD, making it easier to be pressured by the myth that "everybody is doing it." Surveys and opinion polls can be used to help students understand actual use rates.

Social Skills. Help students increase their ease in handling social situations. Decision making, communication skills, and assertiveness skills are particularly important during early adolescence, when puberty prompts changes in the social dynamics among young people as well as with the adults in their lives.

Social Influences. Use advertising, role models, and peer attitudes to help students realize the external pressure for using ATOD. Help them learn how to resist such pressures.

Perceived Harm. Help students understand the risks and short- and long-term consequences of using ATOD. The message must come from credible sources and be reinforced in multiple settings.

Protective Factors. Emphasize close association with peers who provide positive support. Encourage students to focus on positive aspects of life such as helping, caring, setting goals, and meeting challenges successfully.

Refusal Skills. Stress ways of refusing ATOD effectively, while maintaining friendships. Recent research indicates it is most useful in supporting teens who do not want to use drugs. It is most effective when used in conjunction with other activities such as social influences and normative education.

Interactive Learning. Lecture presentations do not seem to produce results. More promising are role plays, simulations, Socratic questioning, brainstorming, small group activities, cooperative learning, class discussions, and engaging students in self-examination and learning. Refusal skills need to be practiced in the classroom through role plays in the context of realistic settings where ATOD might be offered. Videos and multimedia software that are set in real-world environments can be used to provide models of appropriate behavior and stimulate discussion.

Adult Modeling. Teachers and other adults at school should set high expectations, open up supportive communication with students, and show they care and want to help. They can also use prevention messages from literature, movies, songs, or current events that portray substance use/abuse.

FIELD APPLICATION 3: Make an appointment with a counselor at a middle-grades school. Ask the counselor about the levels of alcohol, tobacco, and drug use among students at the school. Inquire about any ATOD prevention programs in effect at the school.

Students Prone to Violence, Vandalism, and Bullying

A few years ago, the United States government formulated a set of educational goals the country was to reach by the year 2000. The seventh of those goals was: "All schools in America will be free of drugs and violence and the unauthorized presence of firearms and alcohol, and offer a disciplined environment that is conducive to learning." To help reach that goal, Congress passed the Safe and Drug-Free Schools and Communities Act of 1994, which supported programs of drug and violence prevention.

Sorry to say, we didn't reach the goal. We didn't even come close to it. In 1998, a survey by the National Center for Education Statistics (NCES) showed that, out of a sample of 1,234 schools, 43 percent reported no incidents of crime, while 37 percent reported from one to five crimes and about 20 percent reported six crimes or more. Ten percent reported at lease one serious violent crime: murder, rape, sexual battery, assault with a weapon, or robbery. Sixty-five percent of school-associated violent deaths were students, 11 percent were teachers or other staff members, and 23 percent were community members who were killed on school property. The breakdown on school crimes reported in 1998 is as follows:

- 190,000 physical attacks or fights without a weapon
- 116,000 incidents of theft or larceny
- 98,000 incidents of vandalism
- 11,000 physical attacks or fights in which weapons were used
- 7,000 robberies
- 4,000 incidents of rape or sexual battery

Programs and Practices

Among the efforts schools have been making to deal with violence, four approaches stand out, with varying rates of effectiveness: (1) zero tolerance policies, (2) increased school security, (3) formal violence prevention programs, and (4) programs in character development, problem resolution, and anger control.

The proportion of schools with zero tolerance programs is high where violent aggression, alcohol, drugs, firearms, and other weapons have been in evidence. Only about 2 percent of schools use stringent security measures, such as full-time guards and daily metal detection checks. Others use part-time guards, protective fencing, and alarms, while 3 percent do not use security measures at all.

Seventy-eight percent of schools surveyed have some type of formal violence-prevention or violence-reduction program or effort, and 50 percent of public schools with violence-prevention programs indicate that all or almost all of their students participate in those programs.

Programs that attempt to develop stronger individual character and better personal relationships are used in many schools, but they vary considerably. The Centers for Disease Control and Prevention (1999) have suggested using (1) curricula that emphasize the development of problem-solving skills, anger management, and other social skills, (2) adult mentoring for young people, and (3) full involvement of the community in developing a sense of ownership of the problem of violence and its solutions.

Efforts in Dealing with Bullying and Hate Crimes

Bullying is a type of violence that teachers encounter regularly. Only seldom do they have to contend with hate crimes. Both bullying and hate crimes have devastating effects on student morale. Both perpetrators and victims need special help, and dealing with their behavior requires special tactics.

Bullying.   Bullying is defined as committing intentional, repeated hurtful acts against others. It is a daily occurrence in most schools. It may consist of physical aggression, sexual aggression, name-calling, threatening, taunting, intimidating, or shunning. Not only does it harm its intended victims, but it also has a negative effect on school climate and opportunity for all students to learn. Four kinds of bullying are common:

1. *Physical bullying:* punching, poking, strangling, hair pulling, beating, biting, kicking, and excessive tickling.
2. *Verbal bullying:* hurtful name-calling, teasing, and gossip.
3. *Emotional bullying:* rejecting, terrorizing, extorting, defaming, humiliating, blackmailing, rating/ranking of personal characteristics such as race, disability, ethnicity, or perceived sexual orientation, manipulating friendships, isolating, ostracizing, and peer pressure.
4. *Sexual bullying:* includes many of the actions listed above as well as exhibitionism, voyeurism, sexual propositioning, sexual harassment, abuse involving physical contact, and sexual assault.

Large numbers of students report that they have been victims of bullying at school. About one in seven says he or she experienced severe reactions to the abuse. Among middle school students, one in four is bullied on a regular basis, while one in five admits to bullying others.

Acts of bullying usually occur away from the eyes of teachers or other responsible adults. As perpetrators go undetected, a climate of fear develops that affects victims adversely. Grades may suffer because attention is deflected away from learning. Fear may lead to absenteeism, truancy, or dropping out. If the problem persists, victims occasionally feel compelled to take drastic measures, such as fighting back, carrying weapons, and, occasionally, committing suicide.

Bystanders and peers of victims can suffer harmful effects as well. They may be afraid to associate with the victim for fear of lowering their own status or of retribution from the bully. They may not report bullying incidents because they do not want to be called a "snitch," a "tattler" or an "informer." Some experience feelings of guilt or helplessness for not standing up to the bully on behalf of their classmate. They may feel unsafe, with loss of control and inability to take action.

Bullies themselves face an uncertain future. They skip school more often and are more likely to drop out early. Further, bullying is considered to be an early warning of violent tendencies, delinquency, and criminality.

Hate Crimes.   Bullying and hate crimes are quite similar, except the latter are related to a dislike for other races, ethnic groups, or religions. A hate crime is an act that causes emotional suffering, physical injury, or property damage. It typically involves intimidation, harassment, bigoted slurs or epithets, force or threat of force, or vandalism.

Preventing Bullying and Hate Crimes.   The incidence and effects of bullying and hate crimes are usually grossly underestimated. Educators, family members, and children concerned with violence prevention must be concerned with these phenomena and their linkage to other violent behaviors. For excellent suggestions on limiting bullying and hate crimes, see *Preventing Bullying: A Manual for Schools and Communities* (U.S. Department of Education, 1998). The suggestions resemble rather closely schoolwide discipline systems, as described in Chapter 8. Here are a few of the many suggestions:

- Regularly schedule classroom meetings during which students and teachers engage in discussion, role-playing, and other activities for preventing bullying, hate crimes, and other forms of school violence.
- Immediately intervene in all bullying incidents.
- Involve parents or guardians of bullies and victims of bullying and hate crimes. Receive and listen receptively to family members who report bullying. Establish procedures whereby such reports are investigated and resolved expeditiously.
- Form "friendship groups" or other supports for students who are victims of bullying or hate crimes.
- Popularize antibullying efforts within the community.
- Closely supervise students on the grounds and in classrooms, hallways, rest rooms, cafeterias, and other areas where bullying occurs.
- Conduct assemblies and teacher/staff in-service training to raise awareness of bullying and hate crimes, communicating zero tolerance for such behavior.
- Post and publicize clear behavior standards, including rules against bullying, for all students. Consistently and fairly enforce such standards.
- Establish a confidential reporting system that allows children to report victimization. Keep records of the incidents.
- Ensure that your school has in force all legally required policies and grievance procedures for sexual discrimination. Make these known to family members and students.
- Provide students with opportunities to talk about bullying and hate crimes and enlist their support in defining bullying as unacceptable behavior.
- Involve students in establishing classroom rules against bullying. Such rules may include a commitment from the teacher not to ignore incidents of bullying.
- Develop an action plan to ensure that students know what to do when they observe a bully/victim episode.
- Confront bullies in private rather than in front of their peers, which might enhance their status and lead to further aggression.
- Don't try to mediate a bullying situation. The difference in power between victims and bullies may cause victims to feel further victimized by the process or to believe that they are somehow at fault.

> **FIELD APPLICATION 4:**   Station yourself inconspicuously at various places in the school, such as corridors, cafeteria, school grounds, and routes to and from school. See if you detect incidences of bullying. If you do, what, if anything, do you feel should be done about it?

QUESTIONS

1. The chapter addressed six areas in which special accommodations or management are needed. Which one of the six presents the greatest challenge for you? With which do you feel the most comfortable?

2. One of the areas addressed was that of students at-risk. What does *at-risk* mean to you? Are not all students at risk?

3. Why do you think it was suggested that you familiarize yourself with the legal rights of parents and guardians of students with disabilities, and, in turn, of those family members' responsibilities?

4. Accelerated programs developed for gifted students are proving useful for nongifted students as well. What does this suggest to you about the normal, standard curriculum?

5. There is plenty of information around us all the time about the harmful effects of tobacco, alcohol, and drugs. Why do you think students are so persistent in using them?

6. Do you see a difference between bullying and hate crimes? If so, what is the difference?

ACTIVITIES

1. Suppose you have a middle-grades child of your own. Outline what you would do to help the child avoid the dangers of alcohol and drugs.

2. Suppose you are informed that you will have in your class two students diagnosed with ADHD. Outline what you would do to prepare for working with them effectively.

3. Suppose you have a student in your class who is clearly on the road to failure, but doesn't appear to be at all concerned about it. Describe what you would try to do to help that student.

4. Suppose you see bullying going on among members of your class. Describe what you would do about it.

REFERENCES

Amen, D. 2001. *Healing ADD: The breakthrough program that allows you to see and heal the six types of attention deficit disorder.* New York: G. P. Putnam's Sons.

At-Risk Task Force, Utah State Office of Education. 1998. <www.usoe.k12.ut>.

Attention Deficit Disorders Association, Southern Region, ADD/ADHD. 2002. <http://www.adda-sr.org/BehaviorManagementIndex.htm>.

Bosworth, K. 1997. Drug abuse prevention: School-based strategies that work. Washington, DC: ERIC Clearinghouse on Teaching and Teacher Education. ED409316.

Brunner, I., and others. 1997. *Accelerated schools as learning organizations: Cases from the University of New Orleans Accelerated School Network.* Paper presented at the Annual Meeting of the American Educational Research Association (Chicago, IL, March 24–28).

Centers for Disease Control and Prevention. 1999. *Facts about violence among youth and violence in schools.* Washington, DC: U.S. Government, Media Relations Division.

Curwin, R. 1992. *Rediscovering hope: Our greatest teaching strategy.* Bloomington, IN: National Educational Service.

Curwin, R., and Mendler, A. 1992. *Discipline with dignity.* Alexandria, VA: Association for Supervision and Curriculum Development.

Freeberg, L. 1989. Don't remediate, accelerate: Can disadvantaged students benefit from fast-forwarded instruction? *Equity and Choice, 5* (2), 40–43.

Gardner, H. 2000. *Intelligence reframed: Multiple intelligences.* New York: Basic Books.

Hogan, D. 1997. ADHD: A travel guide to success. *Childhood Education, 73* (3), 158–160.

Including Students with Disabilities in General Education Classrooms. 1993. ERIC Digest #E521. Arlington, VA: ERIC Clearinghouse on Disabilities and Gifted Education (ERIC EC) <http://ericed.org>.

Levin, H. 2002. *The Accelerated Schools Program,* <www.acceleratedschools.org>.

McFarland, D., Kolstad, R., and Briggs, L. 1995. Educating attention deficit hyperactivity disorder children. *Education, 115* (4), 597–603.

National Center for Education Statistics. 1998. *Violence and discipline problems in U.S. public schools:*

1996–97. Washington, DC: U.S. Government, NCES publication 98–030.

Reid, C., and Romanoff, B. 1997. Using multiple intelligence theory to identify gifted children. *Educational Leadership, 55* (1), 71–74.

Renzulli, J. 1996. Schools for talent development: A practical plan for total school improvement. *School Administrator, 53* (1), 20–22.

Schlichter, C. 1988. Thinking skills instruction for all classrooms. *Gifted Child Today, 11* (2), 24–28.

Schlichter, C., Larkin, M., Casareno, A., Ellis, E., Gregg, M., Mayfield, P., & Roundtree, B. 1997. *Partners in enrichment: Preparing teachers for multiple ability classrooms.* Council for Exceptional Children. <www.cec.sped.org/bk/martec.html>.

Sternberg, R., and Clinkenbeard, P. 1995. The Triarchic Model applied to identifying, teaching, and assessing gifted children. *Roeper Review, 17* (4), 255–260.

Subotnik, R., and Coleman, L. 1996. Establishing the foundations for a talent development school: Applying principles to creating an ideal. *Journal for the Education of the Gifted, 20* (2), 175–189.

The Council for Exceptional Children. 2002. The ERIC Clearinghouse on Disabilities and Gifted Education (ERIC EC) <http://ericec.org>.

U.S. Department of Education. 1995. Disability statistics report #6. National Institute on Disability and Rehabilitation, <http://pstc.brown.edu/disability.html>.

Preventing bullying: A manual for schools and communities. 1998. U.S. Department of Education. <www.cde.ca.gov spbranch/ssp/bullymanual.htm>.

Weaver, C. 1994. Reaching kids with attention deficit disorders: Why whole language helps. *Instructor, 103* (9), 39–43.

Using Computer Technology to Enhance Your Program

Chapter Preview

In this chapter we discuss how to use computer technology to enliven and otherwise enhance the instructional program. You will find a number of suggestions for using computers in student research, communication with families, collaboration with classes in other schools, and expanding instructional activities through WebQuests and virtual field trips. Information is presented to help you set up your own class Web site, if you wish, on which you can post information about your class, students, activities, homework, and other requirements. An extensive list of Web sites that are especially useful to teachers concludes the chapter.

Education and Information Technology

The first nationwide educational technology plan for schools in the United States was set forth in 1996. Called *Getting America's Students Ready for the 21st Century: Meeting the Technology Literacy Challenge,* the plan presented a vision for the effective use of technology in a changing economy. Since its appearance, both government and the private sector have invested substantially in helping schools meet the goals stated in the plan. Because so much progress was made so quickly after the plan was issued, the Department of Education reviewed and revised it in 1999, in collaboration with educators, researchers, students, family members, industry leaders, policymakers, and institutions of higher education. This effort resulted in five new national goals for educational technology in the public schools.

Goal 1: Access. All students and teachers will have access to information-technology in their classrooms, schools, communities, and homes.

Goal 2: Achievement. All teachers will use technology effectively to help students achieve high academic standards.

Goal 3: Literacy skills. All students will acquire technology and information literacy skills.

Goal 4: Improved technology. Research and evaluation will improve the next generation of technology applications for teaching and learning.

Goal 5: Improved teaching and learning. Digital content and networked applications will transform teaching and learning.

The report emphasizes that the use of educational technology must be at the core of students' schooling and that meeting the five goals must be made a national priority. President Bush's administration inserted into this report a segment from his No Child Left Behind education initiative. Called *Enhancing Education through Technology* (2001), the report calls for the following:

- allocation of monies to states and school districts, with special targeting for high-need schools;
- reduction of paperwork, by using formulas for allocation instead of grant applications;
- increased flexibility, allowing the money to be used for software, wiring, and training for teachers;
- allowance for purchase of Internet filters to limit student access to certain sites;
- encouragement for individual states to set performance goals for technology use and student achievement;
- provision of matching grants for the establishment of Community Technology Centers in high poverty areas.

Cautions about Computer Technology

Not everyone is enthralled with computers in education. Many educators make the point that increased expenditure of money, even if it comes, will not in and of itself bring about higher student achievement. They emphasize that the quality of teachers remains the most important factor in the classroom. Other voices are asking us to clarify the goals we hope to attain through computer technology and are raising questions about availability of computers, knowledge of how to use them effectively, availability of quality software, and reliable technical support (Kirkpatrick and Cuban, 1998; Kleiman, 2000; Soloway, et al., 2001).

Nevertheless, the prevailing view is that computers have the potential to improve teaching and learning greatly (Kurland, 1997). While most teachers are not yet well prepared to use computers in teaching and management, they know how appealing computers are to students and remain largely convinced that newer programs can help students think, solve problems, and deal with real-world situations and problems. They know that computers give greatly expanded access to resources, communication, and connections around the world.

FIELD APPLICATION 1:   Assess your school, or one you know about, to determine the extent to which computers are available to students, whether they are used in the instructional program, and whether teachers make use of them for planning, record keeping, or other management duties.

Two Different Approaches to Teaching

In earlier chapters it was emphasized that early adolescent students enjoy hands-on learning activities, learning teams, and subject matter presented through appealing themes.

Computers provide these benefits, but they are educationally beneficial only if we use them properly. We must remember that technology is a tool for learning, not an end in itself. To amplify this point, let's examine two different approaches to instruction by well-intentioned, energetic teachers, one using a more typical approach while the other is relying more heavily on computers.

Mr. Middleton's Approach

Peter Middleton is a conscientious teacher who cares about his students and truly wants them to learn. He does his best to engage them and make the class interesting and relevant. For example, in his unit on Egypt, he brings slides he personally took while traveling there and shares an abundance of information and anecdotes as he narrates his slide show. He allows the students to work in cooperative groups to investigate topics about Egypt, and later asks the groups to share their findings with other students in jigsaw groups. Everyone takes notes on presentations made by oth-ers. Mr. Middleton believes this helps students learn a great deal in a short amount of time. All students are responsible for remembering the information, and they are tested on it at the end of the unit. In addition, each student selects a topic to research from a list provided by Mr. Middleton. This research leads to a final project, which can be a written paper, an art project, a speech, or a dramatized scene. Students share their projects with others as a culminating activity. Mr. Middleton is satisfied these activities help his students learn while enjoying the process.

Ms. Blair's Approach

Sonia Blair is also a conscientious teacher who cares about her students and their learning. She designed a unit that involved students searching the Web for information on Egypt. The unit calls on students to collaborate in collecting information, analyzing it, compiling the results, and recording what has been learned. The compiled information is then presented in various ways, including class presentations and entries on a class Web site.

Most teachers find Ms. Blair's approach interesting. They especially like learners being active, seeking out knowledge, cooperating in teams, and learning how to find, organize, and present information. Nevertheless, most would at first be hesitant to use this approach. They would be wondering how to organize it: what kind of instructions to give, what sort of preparation students need, and what happens when students make no progress. They know you won't get far if you just tell students to get busy and do some research on Egypt. They need to know how Ms. Blair helps students pose questions, seek answers, document findings, and report them. They need to know how she keeps students actively involved, how she phrases questions and makes suggestions, and how she is able to organize the work without giving numerous explicit directions. Clearly, Ms. Blair values exploration and divergence, but all teachers know that students are not likely to do very well unless given a workable structure and adequate support.

Using Computer Technology with Middle-Grades Students

Teachers have two questions when they think of computers in their classrooms. The first is, What are they good for? The second is, How do I use them? The following sections of this chapter provide information related to those questions. Specific attention is given to teaching via computers, using computers for communication, establishing electronic portfolios for students, and using computers for distance education.

FIELD APPLICATION 2: Speak with fellow teachers or student teachers. Ask how comfortable they feel with using computers in the classroom and whether they have a reasonable understanding of how to use them advantageously.

Teaching and Computers

Turning Points 2000 (Jackson and Davis, 2000) offers a number of recommendations concerning how teaching should be done, with or without computers. These recommendations can be summarized as follows:

- Create a student-centered classroom in which students' prior knowledge is accessed and connected to the new, with the focus on students rather than the teacher.
- Provide for diversity of teaching strategies, opinions, and options.
- Organize content so students can connect parts to the whole.
- Help students see the real-world relevance of what they are learning.
- Stress hands-on learning.
- Allow for collaborative learning.
- Encourage reflection on what is being learned.
- Provide ongoing assessment, so you can adjust instruction as necessary.

If you wish to follow these recommendations when integrating computer technology, what do you do? You must go through a learning process yourself. A good first step is to consult your district or school's technology director for suggestions. That person can probably provide a wealth of information. You can also access on-line information that focuses on teaching and learning with technology, such as:

- Instructional uses of the Internet for elementary age students: <www.lburkhart.com/elem/internet.htm>.
- Computers and classrooms: <www.davidpearcesnyder.com/computers_and_classrooms.htm>.

Begin slowly. Do some experimenting to familiarize yourself with available software. Add technology to one of your own tried-and-true lessons. Create a list of sites with URLs and add it to your binder of lesson activities. Remember that, while middle-grades students can learn to use computers easily, they need you as their coach and advisor.

Beginning Points.   Here are suggestions for ways to use computers in your class (Burkhart and Kelly, 2000):

- *Send E-mail.* E-mail exchanges with other classes and schools can be very informative and rewarding. You might wish merely to exchange information about each other, or share samples of class work. Have groups of students write to other groups, so the problem of exact matching on numbers is eliminated. Consider using Gaggle.net, a search engine that provides free E-mail service with good filters and controls (http://gaggle.net).

- *Gather information.* This works well for small-group activities and collaborative learning projects. Each group can be assigned an element of the project to research and present.
- *Follow an on-line trip.* Classroom Connect and Online Expeditions, which you can access through your Internet browser, offer many such trips.
- *Check current events.* Current events are presented on numerous on-line television, newspaper, and radio sites. Useful sites are provided at the end of the chapter. Check the site out beforehand to make sure the content is appropriate.
- *Take virtual field trips.* Many museums offer field trips via computer (see appendix at end of chapter). You will need to prepare your students by helping them understand what to look for and what to do.
- *Create your own on-line project.* Base this on your class's curricular interests. There are Web sites such as PBS TeacherSource—Teaching with Technology (www.pbs.org/teachersource/teachtech.htm) that show you how to write your own project.

Informing Students' Families.   If you are using technology, inform students' parents about what students are doing and learning. Ask your principal if there are parent technology classes, or if the school could provide them, as a way of letting family members see firsthand what their children are doing. Consider asking students to show parents, using the home computer, some of the activities that are being used. This also provides a valuable service in educating family members. The more you learn about technology, the better you become at using it. Don't expect to be perfect at first (or ever). Using computer technology is learned over time. No need to rush. A slower pace is actually beneficial.

Conserving Time.   If you have ever conducted a search on the Web, you know how time gets away as you go from one interesting link to another. The information is beguiling and seems endless. In the classroom, time available for using the Internet is limited. To work most efficiently, prepare your students in advance for what they can do once on the computer. Don't conduct a Web-based lesson without first creating a Hot List of pertinent sites or a folder of bookmarked sites, so that students can get right to the sources of information. With practice, you will know how much time students need to complete a given assignment, and you will be able to allocate time precisely. At first, take note of where students get to in a lesson and then modify time allocations in the future. You may also wish to inform students in advance about any support structures (scaffolding) you have done for them such as templates, graphic organizers, and folders of searchable sites.

Don't forget another thing—your own time. Before you begin building Web lessons, check to see if there are similar lessons that other educators have made available on the Web. See selected lesson-plan sites listed in the Resources at the end of this chapter. There you will find many superb techniques, tips, and ideas you can adapt to your particular needs.

Teaching Rules for Using Computers.   Establish specific rules for students to follow when using computers in class or in the lab. Here are suggestions from experienced teachers (Starr, 2000a):

- Listen for instructions before touching your computer.
- Use only "safe" search engines and access only teacher-bookmarked files.

- Consult with the teacher before printing from the Internet.
- When using information from a site, copy and paste it along with the URLs into a text document so you can later create a bibliography.

Students should also be educated about their ethical responsibilities as users of technology. Give attention to issues such as copyright law and its violation, plagiarism, and cybercheating. Discuss these matters in terms students can understand. Add impact by using role-playing situations about fairness, a concern for most students. Should students commit infractions, treat them as mistakes, but ask students to discuss or practice the correct procedures. They will need occasional reminders, but will usually abide by established expectations.

Using the Internet for Research.   When students use the Internet, some won't resist the urge to seek out areas they should not. To limit this possibility, most schools use filtering or blocking software to screen out sites considered inappropriate for students, but there is still a need for helping them learn to make responsible choices concerning on-line contacts. Therefore:

- Be very clear to yourself and your students about what you want them to do and accomplish.
- Be equally clear about what you do *not* want them to do.
- Carefully preview all of the sites you bookmark. Consider appropriateness, reading level, source of information, date of information, author's intent, and nature of and amount of advertisements.
- Save all bookmarked selections in a special folder for students to access.
- Present a preview of the Web sites and their activities before students begin work at the computers.
- Remind students not to search Web sites other than those you have bookmarked.
- Provide graphic organizers or outlines to assist students in organizing content.
- Design methods of assessment as you plan the lesson. Inform students and show them the assessment rubric. This will help them know what you expect and stay on track.
- Think through what you will do when the inevitable hardware and/or software glitches occur. Have a backup plan.

Middle school students need guidance as they develop their research skills. They may have success in drawing information from approved sources, but they probably won't know what constitutes a good source of information. Don't encourage students to use a general search engine that will bring forth far too much material for them to handle. This produces confusion, wastes time, and calls up sites that contain baseless opinion. If you use computers extensively, you may want to give students a checklist to help evaluate sites. Check out a Web site that can help you get started with lesson plans and activities for integrating technology into your program: <http://www.mcrel.org/resources/links/techlessons.asp>.

Using the Internet to Find Lessons in Content Areas.   There is an abundance of excellent teaching ideas and good lesson plans on the Internet. Take a moment when you can to check the following:

- (www.bluewebn.com/wired/bluewebn) Library of Blue Ribbon learning sites on the Web are organized by grade level and subject area. Included are tutorials, activities, projects, unit and lesson plans, hot lists, other resources, references, and tools. It is an excellent place to start.
- (www.teachnet.com) This site provides lesson plans, power tools, teacher-to-teacher conference boards, and education news.
- (www.thesolutionsite.comk12) This site has interactive lesson plans.
- (http://askeric.org/Virtual/Lessons) You'll find lesson plans organized by subject at this site.
- (http://lessonplanz.com) Free searchable on-line lesson plans, organized by grade level and subject, can be found at this site.

Using the Internet for WebQuests.   Among the excellent resources available on the Internet is WebQuest, an inquiry-oriented activity in which learners access most of their information on the Web. Developed by Bernie Dodge (2001), WebQuests are teacher-made structures that engage learners and cause them to use higher-level thinking skills. The following are examples of sites that help you make good use of WebQuests:

- (http://edweb.sdsu.edu/webquest/webquest.html) The official site contains information on WebQuests, training materials, examples, and a community for discussion.
- (http://edweb.sdsu.edu/webquest/matrix.html) This is a selective list of WebQuests, listed by grade level and subject area.
- (http://www.ozline.com/webquests/intro.html) This site provides WebQuests for learning produced by Tom March, who collaborated with WebQuest creator Bernie Dodge.

Using the Internet for Virtual Field Trips.   Virtual field trips are similar to WebQuests. They allow students to explore, via computer, sites and locales all over the world. Students find them quite interesting. Here are some links to popular sites that provide virtual trips:

- (http://www.field-trips.org/) This site features virtual field trips for grades K-12 and includes objectives and resources for a variety of trips.
- (http://www.surfaquarium.com/virtual.htm) This site has links to dozens of cyber trips.
- (http://www.education-world.com/awards/past/topics/internet.shtml) This site has an extensive list of sites reviewed (reviews dated 1996–2001) with links to these sites.

Using the Internet for Telecollaboration.   Telecollaboration allows your students to collaborate with other classes around the world. A good place to explore this option is *NickNacks Telecollaborate!* (http://telecollaborate.net/education/edjoin.html), which provides a participant's guide, on-line resources, and innovative project demonstrations. At its simplest, telecollaboration exchanges information about hobbies and activities, locale, descriptions of school, and the like. More involved activities can include data collection (questionnaires, measuring), creation (original writing or art), research (finding and reporting), and live conferencing (real-time meetings via the Internet).

Using Computers for Communication

Computers can be of great assistance in managing communications for you and your class. Students enjoy and learn by exchanging E-mail with other students and classes. You can develop a class Web site where you post your class activities, requirements, standards, and examples of student work. Students and parents are very interested in such sites. You can also use them for communicating with students' family members and building electronic portfolios, as explained in the following paragraphs.

Communicating with Pen Pal Classes

Many teachers find their students greatly enjoy and benefit from communication exchanges with pen pal classes. They like to exchange information about class members, what the class is learning, and activities in which the class and school might be involved. These exchanges provide reason and motivation for students to do quality work, reflect on what they are learning, and express themselves clearly.

Many school systems have their own Internet service providers. If yours does not, you can find several Internet sites that offer free E-mail for teachers and students. They are very easy to use. One site popular with teachers is Gaggle.net (www.gaggle.net). Gaggle.net has built-in monitoring software that screens for certain words or phrases, curse words, pornography, and SPAM. Any questionable E-mails are diverted to the teacher's "Blocked" folder to be read and either deleted or sent on. This gives the positive benefits of E-mail without many of the risks otherwise encountered. Schools set up this service so individual students can establish accounts only through the school. Students can access their mail from classroom computers, the computer lab, home, the school library, the public library, and elsewhere.

To find pals for your classes, use one of the sites that connects classroom to classroom or student to student. Here are some good sites for you to consider:

- EPALS (http://www.epals.com) offers correspondence capabilities with over 8,000 K-12 students, schools, teachers.
- Mighty Media Keypals Club (http://www.mightymedia.com/keypals/) is a worldwide pen pal service with over 25,000 users in seventy-six countries.
- Intercultural E-Mail Classroom Connections (IECC) (http://www.iecc.org) allows teachers to join a mailing list or explore the IECC Web pages to look for partner classrooms or projects. Besides offering connections with other students throughout the world, IECC has information for teachers seeking intergenerational connections (volunteers of age fifty and over) for their students.

Posting Student Work on the Web

Web publishing allows family members, community members, pen pals, collaborative classes, and others to learn about the class and what individual students are doing. This exposure helps students learn to express themselves better and builds confidence and self-esteem. Here are some suggestions:

- Use your school's Web site. Speak with your school or district's Webmaster. Depending on the sophistication of the system, you may easily be able to post student work.

- Use an existing educational Web site. These are free and designed specifically for teachers. They will probably contain advertising, so check on your school policy first.
- Ask your media technologist to help you design and post a Web site for your class.
- Make your Web site yourself. There are several free sites on the Web that tell you how to create pages and upload your content. Here are three good sources to contact:
  1. (http://ccwf.cc.utexas.edu/~jbharris/Virtual-Architecture) This site provides user-friendly information on the whys and hows of creating Web-based projects and includes "foundational ideas," telecollaboration, teleresearch, designing and directing projects, and assessment. There are many examples of projects and many links to annotated Web sites. It is an excellent place to start.
  2. (http://www.thinkquest.com) This site provides links to educational Web sites created by youth.
  3. (http://www.educationindex.com/7–12) This site provides free service arranged by subject or grade level, and the sites are annotated.

How to Post Student Work.   Students create their work in the computer and then upload the files directly to the site. It may be best to have students save the material as a text file or .jpeg or .gif. For work not created on the computer, scan the file into the computer, save as .jpeg or .gif file and upload to the site. For photographs, scan and upload normal photos. Digital photos of schoolwork, products, and the like can be uploaded from computer to the site. In these ways, you make your students' work and other items of interest available for any interested people to see.

Cautions about Web Sites.   You are well advised to take certain precautions when posting information on a Web site. For example:

- Do not post pictures in which individual students are identifiable unless you first get a signed release from the family members. See your building principal for copies of this form.
- Do not publish students' surnames, addresses, or other personal information.
- Copyright law requires that you get signed permission from family members before posting any student work on-line. Most people do not know that all original work is automatically protected by copyright.

Posting Information about Classes.   For information you wish to post about your classes, follow the uploading procedures, cautions, and guidelines as presented previously. You can give out any information about yourself you think advisable and post any of your original work that you don't mind others copying.

Communicating with Family Members.   For making information available to parents and family members, you can either establish a class Web site or use a free Internet site that provides a place to post class assignments, publish student work, and communicate with family members via E-mail. Sites recommended for this purpose include:

- SchoolNotes (http://www.edgate.com/edgate/about.html) provides a simple and effective way to communicate with family members and students. This is a free service that allows individual teachers to post information about classes for access by students and family members. You might include information on weekly study topics, special projects, calendars of activities, homework assignments, reading lists, and so on. No special software is needed, and SchoolNotes can be accessed from any computer with a browser. No programming knowledge is necessary.

- TeacherWeb (http://www.teacherweb.com) offers individual teachers free personal Web sites for posting homework assignments, special announcements, and other matters. TeacherWeb offers templates for customizing the sites, which allows easy updating of information. No programming knowledge is required.
- HomepageScholastic (http://homepage.scholastic.com/classpages/start_hp.cfm) shows you how to create a Web page for your class and its activities. The pages allow students and family members to read class announcements, find homework assignments, download permission slips for field trips and special activities, and peruse reading lists and student projects.

It is not difficult to post information on these sites, but keep in mind that you must update the site frequently and regularly. All the benefits of communication are lost if the information is not kept current. Make sure you are willing to follow through on this commitment before you involve students and family members.

Establishing Electronic Portfolios for Students

Students' portfolios, in which they place selected samples of their work, personal reflections on that work, and other material, provide a good way to keep track of their progress over time. Electronic portfolios offer distinct advantages over traditional portfolios that are kept in binders or large folders. They conserve space, allow students to access Web site material, and publish Web pages. All this work can then be saved on diskette. Scanners are needed for electronic portfolios, and digital cameras are helpful. One teacher reports using HyperStudio multimedia software to help her students showcase their portfolios (South, 2001).

> **FIELD APPLICATION 3:** Try to identify and contact a teacher who uses the computer for communicating with parents or students in other schools. Ask specifically what sort of communication is involved, how it is done, and what it accomplishes.

Using Computers for Distance Education

Many classrooms, schools, and districts have outfitted migrant students with laptop computers so they can continue their education wherever they are. You may find yourself involved in such programs. In 2002, five large projects were operational for migratory students in the United States, supported by funding from the U.S. Department of Education (see *Migrant Education Technology Grant Summaries,* 2000).

MECHA (Migrant Education Consortium for Higher Achievement) is based in Florida, with students traveling to Georgia, South Carolina, North Carolina, and Pennsylvania. It uses Web-TV to keep students and teachers connected. Each student is provided an Individual Learning Plan, which includes information on placement, skill levels, health concerns, and teacher recommendations. These ILPs are available on-line (with restricted access for privacy) to the teachers in the receiving states. Lessons and lesson plans can be accessed on the Web site. All MECHA teachers receive extensive training and professional development. A significant component of this program is the use of on-line mentors, who help participating students remain enthusiastic and connected.

ESTRELLA (Encourage Students through Technology to Reach High Expectations in Learning, Lifeskills, and Achievement) is based in Texas. Students it serves travel to Illinois, Minnesota, Montana, and New York. It provides the opportunity for students to earn credits and meet requirements for graduation from high school while traveling with their families. Each student receives a laptop computer with software to complete his or her courses. Families commit to providing time and space for learning and pledge to learn to use the computer as well. Summer programs in the receiving states provide direct support. Extensive professional development for teachers is a key element, and the use of Cyber-mentors is crucial. The Cybermentors are college students who communicate with their mentees on-line (www.estrella.org).

InTIME (Integrating Technology into Migrant Education) is based in Oregon. It uses technology to improve learning for more than 23,000 migrant students who travel mainly within Oregon, helping with crops, fishing, and forestry.

KMTP (Kentucky Migrant Technology Project) works with the migrant population that moves mostly within the state. The program has developed a set of excellent courses that use Internet-based technologies to help students meet national education standards. These courses can be accessed by students as well as teachers. You might like to look at them (http://www.migrant.org).

Anchor School, based in Florida, offers migrant students a helpline/voice-mail system, Intranet, portable local area network, individualized learning plans, electronic portfolios, and human support in the form of an Instructional Support Team that travels with the migrant students. These team members include teachers, AmeriCorps volunteers, and college students. They serve as liaisons between schools, provide training for teachers and family members, moderate on-line chats, and offer support for students when they arrive at a new school. Anchor School has created a database for correlating teaching standards and materials for Florida, North Carolina, South Carolina, and Tennessee. If you would like to see Anchor School's extensive lists of resources for families, students, and teachers, contact their Web site (http://www.anchorschool.org).

Future Prospects for Computers in the Classroom

In October 2001, leaders in education, government, and technology were asked how they thought learning would evolve over the next twenty-five years (MSNBC/*Newsweek,* 2001). Most foresaw a time when all students would have PC tablets, networked and connected to the Internet wirelessly. They spoke of fluidity and creativity, with students able to manipulate text and multimedia. They anticipated interactive educational technology, personal connections that technology can provide with others, the opportunity to interact with others worldwide, and the ability to connect with others in real time. In short, the entrepreneurs, educators, inventors, and politicians saw our students learning about the world, creating in multimedia, and developing strong interpersonal relationships. They believed teachers would be catalysts at the center of this development.

Futurist David Pearce Snyder (2000) describes a strategy for maximizing the benefits of computers in education. He says four propositions about human learning should guide our efforts. First, we are programmed to learn from birth. Second, the task of the teacher is to engage students' minds. Third, different students learn and respond differently; thus, a variety of teaching tactics is indicated. Fourth, effective ways of engaging students change over time. Snyder believes that technology will transform public education and will do so continually for the foreseeable future as technology advances and we find ways to make it work better. He believes that schools should be reorganized as learning cooperatives where students, helped by teachers, are charged with mastering the curriculum. Meanwhile, teachers must keep themselves up-to-date with the developing technologies.

Snyder thinks the important breakthrough of this decade will be "conversational computing." He and others suggest that in twenty years our computers will have artificial personalities (called personologies) that will be so appealing that we will develop relationships with them. It is only a small leap from there to Snyder's dream of giving every student a "cyber-tutor" to ensure success in learning. These tutors would be personable, engaging, patient, conversant, able to teach, and able to learn.

Internet Resources to Add Verve to Your Program

Here you will see a number of Internet sources judged especially useful for middle level teachers. The sites were all functional in 2002, but sites appear and disappear frequently, so it is possible that a few of those included here may no longer be available when you try to access them.

For Users New to the Web

Consider visiting the Web Teacher for tutorials to help you get started (http://www. webteacher.org/winnet/indextc.html).

Search Engines

Search engines find information for you on the Internet. Here are three teacher favorites:

1. Dogpile (http://www.dogpile.com) simultaneously employs several search engines and returns results quickly.
2. Google (http://www.google.com), a teacher favorite, gets results fast and has filters that block inappropriate language. It returns sites and pages in order of popularity.
3. WebFerret (www.ferretsoft.com/) searches for specific pages across all Web sites, providing quick access to topics of interest.

Sites for New Teachers

A great site for middle-grades educators, MiddleWeb (http://www.middleweb.com) provides news articles, on-line diaries of middle school teachers, a chatlist, help for new teachers, ideas for discipline and classroom management, books for new and restless teachers, and general resources for new teachers.

Teachers Resources (www.bottco.com/Schoolsite/TEACHERS.html) provides access to sites dealing with art, music, computers, language arts, reading, English, spelling, history, math, science, special education and health, and general resources.

The Best on the Web for Teachers (http://teachers.teachnology.com/index.html) is an especially useful service because it features Web sites ranked by users who evaluate them according to helpfulness.

Tips on Teaching and Related Matters

An Online Guide for Dealing with Difficult People (http://mimas.csuchico.edu/~brinkman) helps teachers deal with the inevitable challenging encounters with students, parents, colleagues, and administrators.

Cutting-Edge Teaching Strategies (http://www.middleweb.com/CurrStrategies.html) lists ten Great Web Sites for Teachers, which offer interesting ideas and articles about effective teaching.

Harry Wong's Tips for Teachers (www.glavac.com/harrywong.htm) provides a collection of Wong's ever-popular hints on teaching and management.

New Teacher's Home Page (http://www.inspiringteachers.com/home.newteachers.html) features the "Beginning Teacher's Tool Box," provides links to subject-area content, lesson-plan sites, education resources, and recommended reading, as well as articles and practical tips.

Works4Me (http://www.nea.org/helpfrom/growing/works4me/library.html) is a Tips Library from the National Education Association that provides teaching techniques, content, getting organized, managing the classroom, maintaining good relationships, using technology, and the like submitted by teachers.

Lessons, Units, and Projects

Lessons in General

Apple Learning   http://henson.austin.apple.com/edres/mslessons/ms-menu.shtml
Interchange/
Learning Resources
     Many good middle-grades lessons here. Cross-curricular, electronic yearbook, interactive sports guides, news writing, oral traditions, storytelling.

Ask ERIC   http://www.askeric.org/Virtual/Lessons
     A good collection of lesson plans and other sources of educational information.

EdUniverse Lesson Plans   http://www.eduniverse.com/lessonp.asp
  Over 2,000 teacher-submitted lesson plans integrating technology into curricular areas. A synopsis of each lesson is provided.

Teachers.Net Lesson Bank   http://teachers.net/lessons
  An extensive collection of lesson plans, organized by grade level and subject area.

Teachers Helping Teachers Lesson Plans   http://www.pacificnet.net/~mandel/index.html
  Teacher-submitted lesson plans, teaching tips, educational links, and resources for various subject areas.

The Global Schoolhouse/Global Schoolnet   http://www.gsn.org
  Features collaborative projects organized by topic, grade, and project date; Newsday, for students to write and post articles on the Web; and Online Expeditions, which allows students to participate in exotic adventures such as climbing Mt. Everest and following the Silk Road of China. Features Classroom Conferencing via the Internet with other classrooms or with experts in fields of study.

The JASON Project   http://www.jasonproject.org
  A multidisciplinary program focusing on science, math, and technology that uses exploration and collaboration with leading scientists in biology and geology. Expeditions include the Galapagos Islands, the Peruvian rainforest, the Great Lakes, Hawaii, and coral reefs.

Lessons for Specific Areas

Art, Drama, and Music

Art Lesson Plans and Curriculum from ArtsEdNet   http://www.getty.edu/artsednet/resources
  Art lessons arranged by grade level. Provides access to the Getty Scope and Sequence: A Guide for Learning and Teaching Art.

ArtsEdge (Kennedy Center)   http://artsedge.kennedy-center.org
  Helps educators to teach in, through, and about the arts. Many resources are presented here, plus an idea exchange.

Drama Unit Lesson Plans   http://www.byu.edu/tma/arts-ed
  Creative ideas for teaching drama. Lesson plans and resources on creating characters, fundamentals of acting, improvisation, movement, and theater games.

Drama Teacher's Resource Room   www3.sk.simpatico.ca/erachi
  Links to lesson plans and articles on costume, props, sets, lighting.

Musicians and Middle Schools   www.uctv.tv/mams/intro.shtml
  A series of television presentations designed for use in middle schools. Musicians are professors of music at University of California at San Diego. Provides live music, discussions by artists, and using music to inspire creativity.

English, Literature, and Language Arts

Grammar Resources   www.teachers.net/library/grammar.html
  Resources linked to Web sites dealing with a variety of topics in using the English language properly and writing research papers.

The Teacher's Desk Lesson Plans   www.knownet.net/users/Ackley/lessons.html
  Features language arts lessons.

The Teacher's Desk   http://www.geocities.com/teachersdesk/topics/par_week_program.html
Paragraph a Week
  A year-long writing plan complete with topics and an evaluation form.

Foreign Language

American Council on the Teaching of Foreign Languages   www.actfl.org
  Fosters and supports the teaching and learning of and about foreign languages and cultures in
  the United States.

Anacleta's Spanish and World Language/Culture Links   http://anacleta.homestead.com
  Of interest to parents, students, and teachers. Provides activities and links to sites related to
  art, celebrations, culture, music, and more.

Casa de Joanna: Language Learning Resources   members.aol.com/jporvin/cs_art.htm
  Numerous sites related to French, Spanish, English learning and art. Links to Museo del
  Prado and Diego Rivera MuseoVirtual, among others. Links by theme such as friends, activi-
  ties, sports, clothes, school, food, and family.

FLTeachers' Web Pages   www.geocities.com/Paris/LeftBank/9806/flteacherspgs.html
  Web pages created by teachers of ESL, German, Italian, Russian, Japanese, Spanish, and
  French. Multiple language sites.

Mathematics

AAA Math   www.aaamath.com/lessonplans.html
  Explanation, interactive exercises and problems, and challenge games for a variety of topics,
  ranging from addition to exponents to statistics. Also mathematics lesson plans.

BasketMath Interactive   www.scienceacademy.com/BI/index.html
  An interactive math practice site for students. Extensive problems, including word problems
  and map reading.

Money Math: Lessons for Life   www.savingsbonds.gov/sav/savlearn.htm
  A four-lesson curriculum supplement that can be used to teach practical finances, math skills,
  and use of electronic tools.

Online Math Collection   www.fi.edu/school/math/index.html
  Interactive online lessons, designed for middle school math classes. Recent inclusions are
  Melting Pot Math, Mnemonics, Neighborhood Math, and Puzzling and Perplexing Seasonal
  Math Problems.

The Math Forum   http://mathforum.org/teachers/
  The section for middle school teachers contains links to collections of lessons, problems of
  the week, fun activities for students, and teacher resources. "Ask Dr. Math" provides answers
  to students' math questions on a variety of topics.

Physical Education

P. E. Central   http://pe.central.vt.edu
  Offers lesson ideas, best practices and programs, special techniques, and latest research.

Science

Ask a Volcanologist   http://volcano.und.nodak.edu/vwdocs/ask_a.html
  Provides students an opportunity to get answers to their questions about volcanoes.

Ask-a-Geologist   http://walrus.wr.usgs.gov/ask-a-geologist
Provides students an opportunity to get answers to their questions about volcanoes, earthquakes, mountains, rocks, maps, groundwater, lakes, and rivers.

Ask-An-Earth-Scientist   www.soest.hawaii.edu/GG/ASK/askanerd.html/
A service of the Department of Geology and Geophysics at the University of Hawaii. Questions can be asked about volcanoes, earthquakes, igneous rocks, and hydrology.

Astronomy Online—CERES Project   http://btc.montana.edu/ceres/html.EdActivities.html
Classroom-ready activities created by a team of teachers, university faculty, and NASA researchers.

Center for Improved Engineering and Science Education   http://www.k12science.org
Sponsors and develops interactive projects that science teachers throughout the world can use to enhance their curriculum. Projects feature experts, real-time data, and collaboration. Related to National Science Standards and National Mathematics Standards.

Exploring the Environment   www.cotf.edu/ete
Part of NASA's "Classroom of the Future" project. Modules are organized by grade level and divided into Basic, Comprehensive, and Advanced classifications. Examples of topics: Mars Landing, Mountain Gorillas, Florida Everglades.

How Things Work   http://howthingswork.virginia.edu/home_current.html
Encourages everyone to learn about physics and other sciences in the world around them.

Iron Science Teacher   www.exploratorium.edu/iron_science.index.html
Archived Webcasts of science teachers vying for "Iron Science Teacher" by demonstrating experiments that can be done in the classroom or at home.

Kids in the Creek   www.bpa.gov/corporate/kr/ed/kidsinthecreek/homepage.htm
Provides details on a project in teaching students how to evaluate in detail the health of a stream. There are links to teaching resources, materials, curriculum, and other topics.

National Geographic Online   www.nationalgeographic.com
Offers maps, photography, links to magazine articles and television programs, on-line adventures, lesson plans, and teacher community.

Sea World/Busch Gardens Animal Resources   www.seaworld.org/infobook.html
Information on animal rescue and rehabilitation, animal training, aquariums as a hobby, facts on whales and dolphins.

The Franklin Institute's Education Hotlists   www.fi.edu/tfi/hotlists/hotlists.html
Screened, organized lists of science and other resources available on-line.

The Science Spot   sciencespot.net/Pages/classroom.html
A teacher-created site for middle school science activities and lessons for general science, biology, chemistry, physics, earth science, and astronomy. Presents suggestions for organizing and running a science club.

The Why Files   http://whyfiles.org
Offers scientific explanations for items in the news.

Virtual Frog Dissection Kit   george.lbl.gov/ITG.hm.pg.docs/dissect/info.html
Allows students to dissect a digital representation of a frog interactively.

WhaleNet: Ask a Scientist   http://whatle.wheelock.edu/whalenet-stuff/ASK_SCI.html
Allows students to E-mail questions about whales to participating scientists.

Social Studies

A Teacher's Guide to the Holocaust http://fcit.coedu.usf.edu/holocaust/default.htm
Provides an overview of the events and people of the Holocaust through art, literature, movies, documents, and photographs. There are links for teachers and students.

American Memory: Historical http://lcweb2.loc.gov/ammem/ammemhome.html
Collections for the
National Digital Library
Gateway to primary source materials that relate to U.S. history and culture. Through this site you can access more than 7 million items. This site links to Learning Page, which helps teachers use the site to best advantage. There is also a link to International Horizons, which are digital collections from around the world.

American Originals: www.nara.gov/exhall/american_originals_iv/introduction.html
Treasures from the
National Archives
An on-line version of a changing exhibit that presents the nation's greatest documentary treasures.

Arthuriana Pedagogy: http://dc.smu.edu/arthuriana/teachingmidschool.html
Resources for Teaching
Middle School
Presents interesting lesson plans and classroom exercises and activities for teaching about the Middle Ages.

Lesson Plans and Resources for Social Studies Teachers www.csun.edu/~hcedu013
A useful collection of resources and lesson plans, with links to additional lesson plans, teaching strategies, social studies resources, social studies catalogs, on-line activities, National Council for the Social Studies, Educational Standards and Curriculum Frameworks, teaching current events, newsgroups, and mailing lists.

Mr. Donn's Ancient History Page http://members.aol.com/donnandlee/index.html
Includes resources, lesson plans, maps, time lines, and many links to other sites concerned with ancient civilizations and history.

ESL, Bilingual Education, and Multicultural Studies

Asia Society www.askasia.org
For both students and teachers. References on many Asia topics, access to Asia experts, and extensive Asia links.

AskERIC: Multicultural Education http://ericir.syr.edu/cgibin/print.cgi/Resources/Subjects/
Social_Studies/Multicultural_Education.html
Contains many lessons, activities, ideas, and inspirational thoughts.

China the Beautiful www.chinapage.com/china.html
Good information on Chinese calligraphy and history. Additional information at http://china site.com.

Dave's ESL Idea Page www.pacificnet.net/~sperling/ideas.html
Practical, creative ways to teach English language. Many of the ideas can be adapted for use by foreign language teachers. Group activities, grammar, games, and speaking.

IECC—Intercultural E-mail Classroom Connections www.iecc.org/
A free service to help teachers and their students link with counterparts from different cultures and in different countries for E-mail exchanges and other projects.

Lessons, Lesson Plans and Handouts for the ESL Classroom　　　　　http://iteslj.org/
　　The Internet TESL Journal provides lessons, plans, and articles of interest for teachers as well as access to archived lessons.

Library of Congress Reading Rooms and Information Centers　　　　　www.loc.gov/rr/
　　Offers well-organized information. Collections on Africa, Middle East, American Folklife, Asia, Europe, and Spanish-speaking countries.

MCC: Multicultural Calendar　　　　　www.kidlink.org/KIDPROJ/MCC/
　　Provides a multicultural calendar for dates and celebration days in various cultures.

Smithsonian　　　　　www.si.edu/
　　Information on many different racial, ethnic, and cultural groups, including African American, Asian American, Hispanic, and Native American, with exhibits, references, resources.

Students with Special Needs

American Sign Language Browser　　　　　http://commtechlab.msu.edu/sites/aslweb/browser.htm
　　Video demonstrations of a great number of ASL signs, together with interesting information about those signs.

Council for Exceptional Children　　　　　www.cec.sped.org/home.htm
　　One of the largest and most prestigious organizations working on behalf of exceptional students. Provides directories to excellent resources.

Gifted Child Society　　　　　www.gifted.org
　　Provides information and resources on gifted child education for parents and teachers.

Internet Resources for Special Children (IRSC)　　　　　www.isrc.org/
　　A site maintained by a nonprofit organization whose mission is to communicate information relating to the needs of children with disabilities. Extensive links to information on various disabilities.

LD Online　　　　　www.ldonline.org/
　　A user-friendly site for parents and teachers of students with learning disabilities. Offers free articles, bulletin boards, and links to many resources.

SERI: Special Education Resources on the Internet　　　　　http://seriweb.com/
　　An excellent place to start when looking for Special Education resources. You will find many useful links on a wide variety of topics, including Gifted and Talented.

Character Education

Center for the 4th and 5th R's　　　　　www.cortland.edu.c4n5rs/home.html
　　Information on the history of character education. Publishes and provides access to a newsletter on issues related to character education. Disseminates articles and information about character education. Has an extensive list of links.

Character Counts　　　　　www.charactercounts.org/
　　Information on what research shows us about character education. How to get a program started. Free teaching tools.

Character Education Partnership　　　　　www.character.org/
　　A national nonprofit organization working to promote character education in schools. Extensive links to resources, reports on status of character education, and recognition of "Schools of Character."

Current Events

ABC News   http://abcnews.go.com/
   Offers headlines, audio, video, and other features.

CNN Interactive   www.cnn.com
   Breaking news, video, and European and Asian editions on-line. Offers headlines and full
   stories from the world and the United States.

MSNBC   www.msnbc.com/news/
   Quick and easy access to top stories in news, business, sports, health, technology, and more.
   Live video and audio.

USA Today Online   www.usatoday.com/educate
   Provides daily lesson plans with multidisciplinary activities related to the day's news.

Homework Help

Information, Please   www.infoplease.com
   Access to almanacs on sports, entertainment, and general knowledge, Random House *Web-
   ster's College Dictionary,* and the *Columbia Encyclopedia.*

B. J. Pinchbeck's Homework Helper   http://school.discovery.com/homeworkhelp/bjpinchbeck
   B. J. Pinchbeck created this site when he was eleven. He is currently fourteen, and his site has
   links to over 700 other sites that can help students with their homework.

Research References

Research-It!   www.itools.com/research-it/
   Quick and easy-to-use one-stop researching. Dictionaries, thesaurus, translators, rhyming
   dictionaries, and so on.

Virtual Reference Desk   http://thorplus.lib.purdue.edu/reference/index.htm
   Accesses dictionaries, almanacs, encyclopedias, maps, phone books, science data, zip codes.

FIELD APPLICATION 4:   Contact the Virtual Reference Desk, listed above. Note what
it contains. Determine how it compares with printed reference materials you have available
in your classroom. Might you use it in your daily life as well as teaching?

Bartleby.com: Great Books Online   www.bartleby.com
   Outstanding access to books and information on the Web, free of charge. Reference works,
   verse, fiction, and nonfiction.

Great Libraries on the Web   www.ipl.org/svcs/greatlibs/
   A collection of Web pages of outstanding libraries.

Internet Public Library   www.ipl.org/
   On-line texts, collections for teens and youth, reference materials, magazines, and newspapers.

Lives, the Biography Resource   http://amillionlives.com/
   Links to biographies, autobiographies, memoirs, diaries, letters, and oral histories. Organized
   by subject matter and grade level.

Museums and Exhibitions

Metropolitan Museum of Art www.metmuseum.org
One of the world's foremost art museums. Enormous and rich resources.

Smithsonian Institution www.si.edu/portal/t1-infocenter.htm)
Interactive Web site with many interesting exhibits, teacher materials, plans, and activities.

The American Museum of Photography www.photographymuseum.com/
Everything you could imagine about the art, technology, and techniques of photography.

The Louvre www.paris.org/Musees/Louvre
Possibly the world's most famous art museum.

On-line Journals and Magazines

Creative Classroom Online www.creativeclassroom.org/
For K-8 teachers. Has ready-to-use lessons, advice, teaching tips, and practical information.

Education Week on the Web www.edweek.org/
Will keep you up-to-date on trends and issues in education.

Instructor http://teacher.scholastic.com/products/instructor.htm
Ideas and articles of interest to K-8 teachers. Also has a New Teacher section.

New Teacher Connection www.pdkintl.org/journal.htm
Provides help and support for new teachers. Offers a "Journal of a First-Year Teacher," showing how someone else has reacted to new situations.

Phi Delta Kappan www.pdkintl.org/
The Kappan is one of the very best journals for interesting articles and research findings.

Teacher Magazine www.edweek.org/tm/
A monthly publication of Editorial Projects in Education, Inc., the same nonprofit organization that publishes *Education Week* and *Education Week Online.* Features local, state, and national news for grades preK-12.

Teacher Talk http://education.indiana.edu/cas/tt/tthmpg.html
Addresses topics such as building rapport with students, conflict mediation, your classroom management style, and cultural diversity in the classroom.

Professional Organizations

American Association of School Administrators (AASA) www.aasa.org/
American Educational Research Association (AERA) http://aera.net
American Federation of Teachers (AFT) www.aft.org/
American Library Association (ALA) www.ala.org/
Association for Supervision and Curriculum Development (ASCD) www.ascd.org
Council for Exceptional Children (CEC) www.cec.sped.org/home.htm
International Reading Association (IRA) www.reading.org
International Society for Technology in Education www.iste.org
Music Teachers' National Association www.mtna.org

National Association for Beginning Teachers (NABT)	www.inspiringteachers.com/nabt
National Association of Elementary School Principals	www.naesp.org/
National Association for Gifted Children	www.natgc.org/
National Association for Sport and Physical Education	www.aahperd.org/naspe/naspe.html
National Association of Secondary School Principals	www.nassp.org
National Council for Social Studies	www.ncss.org/
National Council of Teachers of English (NCTE)	www.ncte.org/
National Council of Teachers of Mathematics	www.nctm.org/
National Education Association (NEA)	www.nea.org/
National Science Teachers Association	www.nsta.org
National Parent Teacher Association (NPTA)	www.pta.org

Federal and State Departments of Education

"No Child Left Behind"   www.ed.gov/nclb/
   Information on the Elementary and Secondary Education Act (ESEA) and what this means
   for each particular state.

U.S. Department of Education   www.ed.gov/
   A plethora of information on all aspects of education.

State Departments of Education

Alabama	www.alsde.edu/	Kentucky	www.kde.state.ky.us
Alaska	www.educ.state.ak.us/	Louisiana	www.doe.state.la.us
Arizona	http://azde.state.az.us/	Maine	www.state.me.us/education/homepage.htm
Arkansas	http://arkedu.state.ar.us/		
California	http://cde.ca.gov/	Maryland	www.msde/state/md.us
Colorado	www.cde.state.co.us/	Massachusetts	www.doe.mass.edu/
Connecticut	www.state.ct.us/sde	Michigan	www.mde.state.mi.us
Delaware	www.doe.state.de.us/	Minnesota	www.educ.state.mn.us
Florida	www.firn.edu/doe/index.html	Mississippi	mdek12.state.ms.us
Georgia	www.doe.k12.ga.us	Missouri	www.dese.state.mo.us/
Hawaii	www.k12.hi.us	Montana	www.metnet.state.mt.us/MAIN.html
Idaho	www.sde.state.id.us/Dept/		
Illinois	www.isbe.state.il.us/	Nebraska	http://nde4.nde.state.ne.us/
Indiana	http://doe.state.in.us	Nevada	www.nsn.k12.nv.us/nvdoe
Iowa	www.state.ia.us/educate	New Hampshire	www.state.nh.us/doe
Kansas	www.ksbe.state.ks.us	New Jersey	www.state.nj.us/education/
		New Mexico	http://sde.state.nm.us/

New York	www.nysed.gov	Tennessee	www.state.tn.us/education
North Carolina	www.dpi.state.nc.us/	Texas	www.tea.state.tx.us/
North Dakota	www.dpi.state.nd.us/	Utah	www.usoe.k12.ut.us/
Ohio	www.ode.ohio.gov/	Vermont	www.cit.state.vt.us/educ/
Oklahoma	www.sde.state.ok.us/	Virginia	www.pen.k12.va.us
Oregon	www.ode.state.or.us/	Washington	www.wednet.edu/
Pennsylvania	www.cas.psu.edu/pde.htm/	Washington, D.C.	www.k12.dc.us/
Rhode Island	http://instruct.ride.ri.net/ ride_home_page.html	West Virginia	http://access.k12.wv.us/
South Carolina	www.state.sc.us/sde	Wisconsin	http://badger.state.wi.us/ agencies/dpi
South Dakota	www.state.sd.us/state/ executive.deca/deca.htm	Wyoming	www.k12.wy.us/wdehome.html

QUESTIONS

1. Of the Internet sources provided in this chapter, which five have the greatest initial appeal to you?

2. Generally speaking, how useful do you find teaching tips and ready-made lesson plans, in comparison with what you glean from experience and construct for yourself?

3. To what extent do you feel you are able, or want, to make use of computer technology and the Internet in your teaching? Explain.

4. What do you think of the idea of establishing a Web site for your class? What advantages do you think it might offer for communication, building interest, and encouraging family support? What limitations and cautions can you identify?

ACTIVITIES

1. Access what you consider the five most appealing or useful Internet sites provided in the chapter. Judge the extent to which they meet, exceed, or fall short of your expectations.

2. Suppose you decide to establish a Web site for your class or classes. Describe how you would go about it and what you would post on it. How might you provide for feedback from family members and students regarding the site contents and presentation?

3. Access four of the resource sites listed at various places in the chapter. In terms of your program (or prospective program), how relevant, helpful, and interesting are they?

REFERENCES

Alliance for Childhood. 2001.
<www.allianceforchildhood.net/projects/computers/ computers_reports_fools_gold_contents.htm>.

Bauer, J. 2000. *A technology gender divide: Perceived skill and frustration levels among female preservice teachers.* November. Paper presented at annual meeting of the Mid-South Educational Research Association. <http://askeric.org/plwebcgi/fastweb? getdoc+ericdb+1050500+9+wAAA+%28gen>.

Berenson, S., Drujkova, M., Cavey, L., Smith, N., and Barnes, T. 2000. Girls on track with information technology. *Meridian,* Winter, <www.ncsu.edu/ meridian/archive_of_meridian/2000wint/math/ index.html>.

Bishop, A. 2001. An expert's guide to products for the multilingual classroom. *Technology & Learning,* August, <www.techlearning.com/db_area/archives/ TL/200104/classroom.html>.

Burkhart, L., and Kelly, K. 2000. Instructional uses of the Internet for elementary age students. March, <www. lburkhart.com/elem/internet.htm>.

Catagni, A., and Westat, E. 2001. Internet access in U.S. public schools and classrooms: 1994–2000. National Center for Education Statistics, <http:// nces.ed.gov/pubs200½001071.pdf>.

District 230 students make use of handheld computers. 2001. Consolidated high school district 230, <www.d230.org/handheld/default.htm>.

Dodge, B. 2001. FOCUS: Five rules for writing a great WebQuest. *International Society for Technology in Education,* May. <www.iste.org/L&L/archive/vol28/ no8/featuredarticle/dodge/index.html>.

Education Commission. 2000. The power of the Internet for learning: Moving from promise to practice. Washington, DC: Office of Postsecondary Education, Office of Policy, Planning, and Innovation.

Enhancing Education through Technology. 2001. *No Child Left Behind,* August 21, <www.ed.gov/inits/ nclb/partx.html>.

Getting America's students ready for the 21st Century: Meeting the technology literacy challenge. 1996. Washington, DC: U.S. Department of Education, Office of Educational Technology.

Jackson, A., and Davis, G. 2000. *Turning points 2000: Educating adolescents in the 21st Century.* New York: Teachers College Press.

Kirkpatrick, H., and Cuban, L. 1998. Computers make kids smarter—right? *TECHNOS Quarterly,* Summer, <www.technos.net/journal/volume 7/2cuban. htm>.

Kleiman, G. 2000. Myths and realities about technology in K-12 schools. *LNT Perspectives,* April-June, <www.edc.org/LNT/news/Issue14?feature1.htm>.

Knupfer, N. 1997. New technologies and gender equity: New bottles with old wine. AskERIC/ED409843. February, <http://askeric.org>.

Kurland, D. 1997. Interview with D. Midian Kurlan. *Journal of Design Science,* October, <www.ignition design.com/journal/kurland/index.html>.

Migrant Education Technology Grant Summaries. 2000. August, <www.ed.gov/offices/OESE/MEP/2000tec sum.html>.

MSNBC/*Newsweek.* 2001. The classroom of the future. October 29, <www.msnbc.com/news/645566.asp? pne=msntv&cpl=1>.

Roth-Vinson, C. 2000. Connecting girls to the future in science, math, and technology: Cyber Sisters mentor program empowers girls to succeed. *techLEARNING,* May, <www.techlearning.com/db_area/ archives/WCE/archives/rothvins.htm>.

Smith, L. 2000. The socialization of females with regard to a technology-related career: Recommendations for change. *Meridian,* Summer, <www.ncsu.edu/ meridian/archive_of_meridian/sum2000/career/ index.html>.

Snyder, D. 2000. Computers and classrooms. <www. davidpearcesnyder.com/computers_and_classrooms. htm>.

Soloway, E., Norris, C., Blumenfeld, P., Fishman, B., Krajcik, J., and Marx, R. 2001.Devices are ready-at-hand. *HICE Palm Pages,* June, <www.handheld. hicedev.org/readyAtHand.htm>.

Sorrell, S. 2000. Eminence pocket pc project. November, <www.paperlessclassroom.org/story.htm>.

South, C. 2001. Electronic portfolios: assessment for an advanced society. *Technology & Learning,* March, <www.techlearning.com/db_area/archives/WCE/ archives/csouth.htm>.

Starr, L. 2000a. Computer rules prevent problems! *Education World,* August, <www.education-world.com/a_ tech/tech044.shtml>.

_____. 2000b. Educating girls in the tech age: A report on equity. *Education World,* May, <www.education-world.com/a_tech/tech028.shtml>.

Tech-Savvy: Educating girls in the new computer age. 2000. American Association of University Women Executive Summary, <http://www.aauw.org/2000/ techsavvy.html>.

The power of the Internet for learning: Moving from promise to practice. 2000. Education Commission, <http://interact.hpcnet.org/webcommission/index. htm>.

13 Legal, Ethical, Professional, and Personal Considerations for Teachers

Chapter Preview

You have now seen many suggestions concerning what you should and should not do when working with students. However, until now we have not directly considered the matters of legality, ethics, and professionalism nor have we explored personal considerations that help you function better in teaching. In this chapter we attend to those matters. We begin with legal requirements: what the law says you must and must not do when teaching students. Following that, we move to ethical and professional codes of conduct you are obliged to follow in teaching. Finally, we suggest ways of keeping yourself enthusiastic and satisfied in your work.

Legal Requirements and Responsibilities in Teaching

Each state has the legal authority and responsibility for establishing a school system that provides high-quality free education for its young. Various states take somewhat different approaches to meeting this federal mandate, but their efforts are, overall, quite similar. What each state attempts to do is spelled out in their individual Education Code, which stipulates the rules and regulations that govern education, including licensing requirements and conditions for employment. In addition to state education codes, federal statutes govern issues that are under federal mandate, such as special education and multicultural education. All schools and teachers are subject to certain legal requirements having to do with student safety and well-being, sex equity, family privacy, disabilities, grounds for negligence, and record keeping. In addition to those requirements, we also review the legalities of copyright and fair use.

> *Authors' Note:* We are not qualified to provide legal advice. We believe the legal aspects of this chapter are correct, but our interpretation cannot be considered the final word. Please, therefore, obtain from your school district a description of legal responsibilities of its teachers and consider those provisions authoritative.

Student Safety and Well-Being

Educational law professor Nathan L. Essex (1999) explains that school officials have a moral and legal duty to preserve the safety and well-being of all students while not trampling on the constitutional rights of students involved in disruptive behavior. Essex refers to four principles of which you should be aware: defensible policies, parent understanding, due process, and reasonable actions. There is a fifth principle that applies to you even more directly. It is the principle of diligence.

Defensible Policies. Obtain a copy of the policies in place in your district. Policies are agreed-on ways of doing things in the school district, and they are set by the school board. Administrators act on the basis of these policies, which deal with a large number of concerns such as attendance, discipline, dress codes, and guidelines for class use of the Internet. All these policies must pass the test of "defensibility," meaning they must be reasonable, legal, and ethical.

> **FIELD APPLICATION 1:** At a middle-level school, at the district's central offices, or on a district's Web site, see if you can obtain a copy of at least some of the policies in effect for that school district. Examine them and discuss them with class or colleagues.

Parent Understanding. School policies are to be made public, and parents should be informed of them. Your school district will make provisions for informing parents. In addition, you will have policies you follow in the classes you teach concerning expectations, grading, code of conduct, homework, makeup work, and other matters. Inform parents of your policies. Write them out and send a copy home for review. Attach a signature page to be returned to you verifying that the parent has read and understands the policies. Post the policies on your class Web site.

Due Process. Students accused of violating rules that may result in disciplinary action have the right to know the charges being brought against them, have an opportunity to respond to the charges, and receive a fair and impartial hearing. Students have constitutional rights under the Fourth Amendment as concerns unreasonable search and seizure. However, schools have traditionally operated under the doctrine of *in loco parentis,* which means "in place of parents." This doctrine allows school officials authority over students in school matters involving academics and discipline and permits them to take actions that a reasonable parent would take under similar circumstances.

Reasonable Actions. School officials have the right to establish rules that are necessary to maintain an orderly, peaceful campus conducive to teaching and learning. In doing so, they must act within legal and ethical constraints and their actions must be reasonable and proper, which is usually taken to mean they are what a prudent professional would consider proper under the circumstances. Reasonable actions should also be fair, but fairness does not imply that all students are necessarily treated the same. Prudent teachers make sure they understand the facts in a matter, listen to students' views, and make decisions that take into account the seriousness of the infractions and students' past behavior.

Diligence.   In general, *diligence* means taking reasonable care or giving reasonable attention to a matter, sufficient to avoid a claim of negligence. In school settings this principle is applied in relation to established policies, together with what a reasonable and prudent professional would do in a similar circumstance. For example, when supervising students you must, in accordance with this principle, observe them properly, warn them about dangers, advise them reasonably, and pay attention to their behavior. This includes informing administrators when you hear students make threats against each other. If a student is injured physically or mentally while under your supervision, you, your principal, and the school district may be sued. You can be found liable if you have failed to be duly diligent.

Jamie Goldman

Jamie Goldman was running late. It always seemed the mornings before school moved at warp speed. Jamie was a very conscientious teacher. She had gotten to school even earlier than usual that morning so she would have a chance to get the computer lab properly set up for her social studies classes. They were going to participate in a WebQuest and she wanted to bookmark the desirable sites so students would spend less time searching and more time learning.

That had taken longer than expected, and she still had to run off the papers that explained instructions and activities. She glanced at her watch and groaned. It was time for her morning duty. Of all weeks to be assigned duty in the mornings! Of course, there was never a good time. She sighed. Stand out there in the cold, watching students arrive by foot and by bicycle, supervising students exiting the buses, making sure no one left for the nearby convenience store once they arrived. By this time in the school year, all students knew the rules. There had never been any incident there that she was aware of. After school was a different matter, with disputes and occasional fights. But in the morning, the kids were still pretty much asleep. She told herself no one would notice whether she was there or not. She had to get the papers run. She wished she had thought ahead and arranged to trade duties with a colleague, but it was too late now. She walked as quickly as she could to the copy room. Her mind eased a bit to the rhythmic lull of the copy machine churning out her lessons. She thought with anticipation of the day ahead and how she had planned everything so the students would be successful and enthusiastic. Copies completed, she collected them and headed for her classroom. Maybe she would have time to stand a few minutes of her duty.

A flurry outside caught her attention and she followed the group of students moving swiftly to the front of the school. Her stomach clenched. There was a bus out of place in the bus circle, with a crowd around the front of it. "Leslie! What happened?" she shouted, as one of her students ran by. Leslie yelled back, "I think the bus hit someone on a bike!"

Is Jamie in trouble legally?

She may well be.

Sex Equity and Physical Contact with Students

Title IX of the Education Amendments of 1972 prohibits sex-based discrimination in any educational program or activity receiving federal funding, which includes almost of the nation's schools. One of the obvious effects of this statute has been the increase in number and quality of sports programs for girls. More recently, the protections offered by Title IX have been the basis for lawsuits involving sexual harassment of a student by a teacher (Goorian and Brown, 2002).

One such case was heard by the Supreme Court in 1992. In *Franklin v. Gwinnett County Public Schools,* a female student alleged sexual harassment by a male teacher and sued the school district. The Court ruled that sexual harassment of students by district employees met the standard for discrimination and that monetary damages could be recovered by the plaintiff.

It would take another case, *Gebser v. Lago Vista Independent School District,* to establish the standard for liability. The justices ruled that a plaintiff must prove he or she informed a proper school official of the harassment and that the official was "deliberately indifferent" to the complaint. A "proper school official" was determined to be one with the authority to take action on behalf of the school district, most likely a principal, probably not a teacher.

Student-to-student sexual harassment was the issue in *Davis v. Monroe County Board of Education,* a case heard by the Supreme Court in 1999. The plaintiff was a fifth-grade girl who was repeatedly sexually harassed by a male classmate. After incidences of teasing, groping, and other harassing actions, the girl and her mother repeatedly notified teaching staff and the principal, who did not act sufficiently to stop the harassment. They held that the hostile environment caused by this continual harassment made it impossible for the girl to learn, thereby discriminating against her. The Supreme Court, in a 5–4 decision, ruled for the plaintiffs.

What do these rulings mean for educators? Report to your principal any harassment you witness or hear about, whether it be by teacher or student. Ask your principal to investigate. Document what you have observed or been told by witnesses.

Mary Lou Moore

Mary Lou Moore was sitting at her desk, sipping coffee and jotting down ideas for lessons. The before-school quiet was pleasant and peaceful. Humming to herself, she thought of the day to come. Hearing the door open, she glanced up and gave a surprised smile to Tyler Stone, an active seventh-grader in her first period class. He never came in early to speak with her. Her smile quickly changed to a look of concern and she got to her feet and went over to him. "Why, Tyler, what's wrong? Please tell me." Huge tears were sliding down Tyler's cheeks, and he could barely speak. "I think my dog is dying! She fell down this morning and had a seizure. She was right outside my window and I didn't even hear her!" He was very distressed. Mary Lou put her arm around his shoulder and squeezed. She could feel his grief. She patted his back and gave him a hug and asked if he wanted to use her phone to call his mom, who had taken the dog to the vet. She also asked if he wanted to go rest in the counseling office. He told her that his dog always made him better when he was feeling bad. She said she understood. Tyler buried his face in her shoulder.

A parent happened to see Mary Lou embracing Tyler. Will Mary Lou be accused of unethical contact with a student?

Mary Lou is safe. She is a teacher in her mid-fifties, old enough to be Tyler's grandmother. She frequently shows affection with hugs and pats on the back, more so than most teachers. Please keep in mind that, if you are closer in age to your students, and particularly if you are a male, it is important that you be very careful. Use good judgment and follow district policy regarding touching students. Students and their families can misinterpret your friendliness or sometimes students can be malicious in their accusations, as you will see in the following true story (Donhoff, 1997).

Allen Mann

Four girls in Mr. Mann's class claimed that he "snapped their bra straps," an accusation that under the State Penal Code would be termed "annoying" a child. The girls said he put his hand on their shoulders, which made them feel "uncomfortable." They claimed he was a "pervert" who walked around with mirrors on his shoes, peeked down girls' blouses, and tried to look up girls' skirts. Mr. Mann vehemently denied these allegations, while admitting he did pat both boys and girls on the shoulder as a gesture of encouragement. In this personal and professional nightmare, Mr. Mann temporarily was relieved of his teaching duties, losing his salary and medical benefits in the process. He had to endure an investigation and a trial. The jury deliberated for only twenty minutes before finding him not guilty on all counts. Even though he was vindicated, the whole experience was horrifying. In thirty years of teaching, he had never had a blemish on his record, but suddenly was wrongfully accused and had to defend himself. After the trial, Mr. Mann returned to his school and resumed teaching. The taint of the accusations remained, however.

This cautionary tale is to make plain that you must exercise good judgment and common sense in personal interactions with students. Remember that, should students frustrate or anger you, you must never grab any part of their body, as it is difficult to justify or defend physical contact motivated by anger. Also make sure you never throw pencils, pens, erasers, books, desks, or chairs, no matter how strongly you are provoked.

At times you may be the authority figure present when a fight breaks out on campus or in your classroom. Don't get between the combatants. Teachers can, and do, get injured. Stay where you are and send for administrative support. Call the students by name and attempt to discourage the fighting: "Joey, break it up!" or "Mike, come with me!" Stay calm, and persist with verbal messages. Focus on the task at hand, and make sure later to document your observations of the occurrence. The school administration will deal with the students involved.

Family Privacy

The Family Education Rights and Privacy Act (FERPA) requires that students' educational records be protected under privacy rights and kept confidential. Educational records are defined as "those records, files, documents, and other materials which—(1) contain information directly related to a student; and (2) are maintained by an educational agency or institution or by a person acting for such agency or institution" (Goorian and Brown, 2002). Share a student's confidential information only with those who have a right and a need to know such as other teachers who will be working with the child.

In *Falvo v. Owasso Independent School District,* a parent sued over the practice of peer-grading of assignments. The parent indicated that the practice of having another student grade her child's papers caused him humiliation. The Tenth Circuit Court of Appeals ruled that the practice of having students grade one another's work violated the privacy rights of students by revealing "education records" unlawfully.

The school district appealed, and in 2001 the justices heard *Owasso Independent School District v. Falvo.* In February 2002, the Supreme Court reversed the appellate court, ruling that:

- Students who grade other students' papers are not acting on behalf of the educational institution.
- Peer grading is a way to reinforce lessons, as well as to teach students to assist and respect one another.

If you post grades in your classroom, consider using identification numbers rather than students' names.

Students with Disabilities

As noted in Chapter 11, the Individuals with Disabilities Act (IDEA) guarantees the right to an education for all students with disabilities, ages three through twenty-one. This law affects in one way or another almost every person who works in public education. First enacted in 1975, the law mandates that children with disabilities receive a free appropriate public education in the least restrictive environment possible. The law admitted into schools over a million children who had previously been excluded. It provides for education tailored to individual students' needs, formalized in "individualized education plans," referred to as IEPs. As described in Chapter 11, the IEP is created by a team of teachers, parents, and specialists who meet annually to design or revise educational plans for the student.

In 1997, Congress amended IDEA to clarify discipline practices for disabled students. Essentially, the amendment requires that a determination be made as to whether a disabled student's misconduct is related to his or her disability. A set of procedures is provided for making this determination. A disabled student cannot be suspended or expelled if the misbehavior is related to the disability.

Record Keeping

Your attendance logs and grade book are considered official educational records and will be kept at the school for some time. Take pains to maintain them accurately. In addition, keep good documentation should you observe seriously inappropriate student behavior, together with your interventions to correct behavior or academic problems. Note frequent infractions by given students and steps you have taken in response. Keep a log of phone calls, E-mail, and meetings in which you discuss concerns with parents or guardians. Name the people involved and the results of the actions. Keeping such documentation puts you in a strong position to defend grades and disciplinary actions.

Cautions about Copyright

Copyright means the creator of a particular work has sole right to copy, distribute, perform, and publish the work. A copyright does not have to be applied for, paid for, or even announced. It is bestowed as soon as an original work is created and extends for seventy-five years beyond the creator's death. A work qualifies for copyright if it is original, creative, and tangible ("fixed" on paper, video, CD, Web site, etc.).

Oral works are not copyrighted until they are recorded. An idea cannot be copyrighted, although the creative expression of the idea is covered by copyright. Facts are not copyrighted, but an original expression of those facts is.

Here are some things hypothetical teachers did that may or may not have violated copyright laws. See what you think, then check your conclusions against the legalities described later.

1. History teacher James Meade was so impressed with a television documentary on the Civil War that he recorded it and made three copies—one for himself and two colleagues—to use during the Civil War unit they taught every year.
2. Natasha Clemons found an article that explained the ecology of the pine forest so well that she made a copy for every student in her class.
3. Phillip Baldwin was trying to spice up his class Web site. He found some graphics on another site that he thought would be perfect, so he copied them to his class site.
4. Lisette Brown's department never had enough funds to purchase workbooks for each student, so each year Lisette copied certain workbook pages for her students to use.
5. Jack Welch was always on the lookout for new ideas for teaching math. He read some "best ideas" on the Internet and then used them in class with good success.
6. The student activities club played music for students during lunch on Fridays. The student body had varied musical tastes, funds were tight and the CDs were expensive. Tom O'Dell, advisor, encouraged students to create CDs by compiling music from various sources.
7. Mr. O'Meara liked to play background music while his students worked on their essays. He brought some of his own CDs and played them in class.

Most teachers do not know the technicalities of copyright, so may unintentionally violate the law regularly. Not only should we be cautious about that, but we should also teach students about copyright and the protection it affords. Students often do not know they cannot copy the works of other authors, nor do they know their own original works are automatically copyrighted as soon as they are created, leaving them the sole rights to copy, distribute, and perform their work. We need to teach them that creative work is an entity, and that using somebody else's work without permission is the same as stealing.

However, it is permissible to reproduce portions of copyrighted material if the copyright holder grants permission. We should know, and teach our students, how to ask for permission to use copyrighted material. For a sample template for securing permission, see Willard (2002).

That said, some leeway does exist for educators to use copyrighted material without permission. That tacit permission falls within the parameters of "fair use." Your district will probably have a policy in place regarding copyright and fair use. Make a point to find out about it. Generally speaking, fair use entitles teachers to use the following without permission of the copyright holder:

From printed materials, you may copy for your own use:

- one chapter from a book
- a newspaper or magazine article
- a poem of less than 250 words (or an excerpt of up to 250 words from a longer poem)
- excerpts from music or literature that represent no more than 10 percent of the entire work
- prose of less than 2500 words
- a chart, picture, or illustration from a book or magazine

You are *not* allowed to copy:

- consumable works, such as workbook pages
- a special work in its entirety
- articles from the same newspaper from week to week
- the same works for multiple semesters or years
- material to use for commercial purposes (e.g., to sell)

From television, you may copy and show a recorded program if:

- It was broadcast to the general public.
- It is shown within ten school days after recording.
- The videotape is destroyed within forty-five days after recording.

From sheet music, you may create and use:

- copies of sheet music for a performance to replace purchased copies
- a single recording of a student performance to use for evaluation or rehearsal
- a single copy of a sound recording of copyrighted music to use in exercises

For software: You may make one backup copy but may not load the software on more than one computer unless the license permits multiple copying.

Concerning school Web sites: Content should be limited to original text or graphics (teacher- or student-created), text or pictures clearly designated as being in the public domain or available for free use, and any material for which a license has been acquired (National Association of Secondary School Principals, 2002).

For more information, see the *Education World* on-line series on copyright and fair use for educators (Starr, 2000).

What Constitutes Negligence

Our society is becoming ever more litigious, and public servants, including teachers and other educators, increasingly have lawsuits filed against them. It is very important that you know how to protect yourself against the possibility of a lawsuit.

Most teachers are conscientious, caring individuals who would not intentionally do anything illegal where students are concerned. Good intentions are sometimes not enough, however. If you are sued by a parent, most likely the basis for that suit will be alleged negligence in performing your assigned duties; that is, you did not properly follow the principle of diligence as described earlier. Education laws vary from state to state. Your school district should be able to provide you with legal interpretations of proper performance of duty. Check to see if that material is available.

The concept of negligence in an educational setting typically involves three elements (Drye, 2000):

- A mental or physical injury has occurred.
- The teacher had a duty to oversee the area and activity in which the injury took place.
- The teacher has failed to exercise reasonable care.

Physical or Mental Injury. It is not uncommon to see teachers chatting with other staff members or students while on supervisory duty, or even using the time to grade papers or catch up on some reading. These teachers are probably unaware of their requirement to keep a diligent eye on all students under their supervision. They may feel that their mere presence satisfies their duty. If so, they are certainly mistaken. Unless a student is injured while under a teacher's supervision, no legal complaint will be brought against the teacher. But if a student is injured mentally or physically, and the teacher did not exercise reasonable care, there is a good chance the teacher and school will be sued for negligence.

Duty to Oversee. Teachers and other school personnel have a duty to exercise reasonable care to protect students from harm. As previously noted, they are to function *in loco parentis,* meaning in the place of parents. Their responsibilities include maintaining a safe and orderly campus, foreseeing potential problems, warning students about dangers, teaching students how to use equipment safely, and keeping close watch. Earlier in this chapter, you read Jamie Goldman's case, and a student was injured when she arrived at her duty station too late to supervise the bus area. Jamie may well have a lawsuit filed against her, and, if so, she will have difficulty showing she was diligently performing her assigned duty to oversee.

> **FIELD APPLICATION 2:** Observe as buses arrive before school begins. Watch the procedure as buses move through the area, unload students, and move away. Determine who is on supervisory duty and watch what that person does. Is he or she being thoroughly diligent, or are distractions evident?

Breach of Duty. Breach of duty means failing adequately to perform an assigned duty. Performance is judged in terms of how a reasonable and attentive teacher would have behaved in similar circumstances. Various factors are taken into account when complaints are made against teachers for breach of duty. Those factors include the teacher's training and experience, age of the student, environment where the problem occurred, type of activity, presence (or absence) of a teacher in charge, and any disability of the student if applicable. Jamie Goldman will have difficulty because she was an experienced teacher who knew what her duties were. The school administrator may get in trouble, too, for not making sure Jamie was on duty at a very dangerous part of the school day.

Guarding against Negligence

The following guidelines will help you make sure you are in a defensible position should questions arise about breach of duty:

- Perform your assigned duties as directed, even those that seem boring and unnecessary. Follow your school's policy for supervising students before school, during passing periods, after school, and during any free periods. It is advisable that you be highly visible in the hallway to monitor students during passing periods. Standing at your open door to greet your students will allow you to keep an eye on activities in the hallway and in your classroom at the same time.

- Oversee your students. Be vigilant in monitoring their behavior. Do not leave students unattended in your classroom, shop, or instructional area. If class is in session and you must step out for a moment, contact someone in the office to cover for you or ask the next-door teacher to look in on your class. Deal quickly with misbehaving students who present a hazard to other students. If there is an accident, make sure you write an accurate report and keep a copy.
- Provide thorough instructions and teach safety procedures before undertaking activities that involve risk to students (such as using equipment or going on field trips). Make sure the educational value of a particular activity far outweighs any foreseeable risks. See that all equipment is well maintained. Frequently review safety procedures.
- Supervision must be provided for school-sponsored activities at school, such as dances, assemblies, presentations, intramural games, and club meetings. If you agree to chaperone, make sure you are where you say you will be and are focused on maintaining student safety.
- The standard of care you should use for guidance is the degree of skill, knowledge, and diligence that can reasonably be expected of a normal, prudent practitioner of the same experience and standing (Shoop, 2002).
- Your school will sponsor school activities away from the campus. If you are in charge of these, plan them carefully from start to finish. Always make sure you have a signed permission slip from a parent or guardian for each student. Recruit plenty of parent chaperones or other teachers so there is a workable ratio of adults to students. Assign specific students to specific chaperones. Have plenty of activities designed for students so they will see a purpose to the field trip and understand that you are holding them accountable. Make sure students and their parents understand that all school rules apply on field trips.
- You are required to be vigilant for signs that students might harm themselves. Pay attention to what they do, say, and write. Observe them for changes in behavior. Follow up if you note anything that makes you concerned. Speak with the student privately or contact the counselor and ask that person to speak with the student.
- You are required by law to report it if you suspect one of your students is being abused. Familiarize yourself with some of the common signs of abuse. If you are suspicious, do not confront the child or parent directly. Report your concerns to the school counselor or administrator, who will follow up.
- Respect the confidentiality of students and colleagues; don't discuss performance or personality with others. If you possess information about a student that other school personnel have a right and a need to know, you may share it with the appropriate persons.
- Document incidents involving students and others that might be cause for concern.

Maggie Lindholm

There were two minutes left in the period and the class was in the middle of cleanup when Maggie Lindholm felt a tug at her sleeve. It was Jeremy, a quiet boy who hated calling attention to himself. "Someone stole my thirty dollars," he whispered. "Are you sure, Jeremy? When did you see it last?" "I put it in the front pocket of my backpack and zipped it in and now it is gone." His face looked stricken. "It was for my yearbook."

Maggie raised her voice so she could be heard over the shuffling of papers and books. "Ladies and gentlemen! Has anyone seen Jeremy's money? It was in his backpack and now it is missing. Did someone pick it up by mistake?" A chorus of no's followed. "Well, it has to be here someplace. You will have to stay in while we do a search." The students groaned. Maggie called for administrative support. While she was waiting for the assistant principal to arrive, an anonymous note ended up in her hand. It read, "It's under Richie's shirt." Maggie's next class was waiting impatiently in the hallway, and she was feeling frustrated. "Richie, please take off your shirt."

Is Maggie in trouble for having Richie remove his shirt? See the following commentary.

You have seen that teachers are considered to be acting in place of students' parents while students are at school. The U.S. Supreme Court ruled in 1985 (*New Jersey v. T.L.O.*) that students under supervision at school have reduced protections under the Fourth Amendment. A school employee need only have "reasonable cause" that a search will produce evidence of wrongdoing, rather than the standard of "probable cause" required in law enforcement (Dowling-Sendor, 2000). In 1995, the Supreme Court upheld a school district's right to adopt a policy that required drug testing for all students participating in school athletic programs (*Vernonia School District 47J v. Acton*), and in 2002 decided 5–4 in favor of a school district (*Board of Education of Independent School Dist. No. 92 of Pottawatomie County v. Earls*) that had established a drug testing policy for middle school and high school students who participate in competitive extracurricular activities such as band, chess, choir, and academic bowls (Missouri Department of Elementary and Secondary Education, 2002). While school personnel have the right to search students if there exists "reasonable cause" that rules are being broken or illegal behavior is occurring, the scope of the search must be reasonable and based on the facts of the situation. When possible, teachers should allow administrators to conduct the searches. If you conduct a search in class, document the incident fully.

> *Note of Caution:* Bear in mind that strip searches of students, even when probable cause exists, are overly invasive. When you are in doubt, put the matter in the hands of the administration.

Ethical Considerations for Teachers

Ethics (a noun used in both singular and plural senses) refers to standards of proper behavior. Ethical principles guide us in our personal and professional lives, especially when we face difficult decisions. Ethics involves distinguishing between right and wrong and making a commitment to do what is right, good, and proper (Josephson Institute of Ethics, 2001). Professional ethics refers to standards governing the conduct of the members of a given profession. The National Education Association (NEA) has developed and made available to all educators a Code of Ethics of the Education Profession. This code reflects both commitment to the student and commitment to the profession. The following paragraphs present some of the main points in the NEA Code of Ethics:

In General:
- Educators accept the responsibility to adhere to the highest ethical standards.
- Educators vigorously pursue the provision of equal educational opportunity for all.

In Particular:

In striving to help students realize their potential, educators emphasize inquiry and the acquisition of knowledge and understanding. In so doing, educators will not unreasonably:

- restrain the student from independent action in the pursuit of learning;
- deny the student's access to varying points of view;
- suppress or distort subject matter relevant to the student's progress;
- fail to make reasonable effort to protect the student from conditions harmful to learning or to health and safety;
- intentionally expose the student to embarrassment or disparagement;
- exclude any student from benefits or participation on the basis of race, color, creed, sex, national origin, marital status, political or religious beliefs, family, social or cultural background, or sexual orientation;
- use professional relationships with students for private advantage;
- disclose information about students obtained in the course of professional service unless disclosure serves a compelling professional purpose or is required by law.

Jessica Kaminsky

Jessica Kaminsky is struggling to resolve a matter in her mind. Her local collective bargaining unit, the Pioneer Valley Teachers Association, is involved in tough contract negotiations with the school district over salary and working conditions. Ordinarily, this would not affect her or the students in her classroom, because the negotiations are not normally made public until an agreement is reached, but this year is different. The state funding for school districts has been increased, and teachers across the state are being awarded sizable pay increases. This is welcome news for educators, who have not received pay raises for two years. However, Pioneer Valley's school board and district management team hold the position that local education is best served by giving teachers a modest pay increase and using the remaining funds for strengthening instructional programs in the district.

To put pressure on the school board, the PVTA has issued a strong recommendation that all teachers immediately begin "working to the contract." This means not arriving at school before the time stipulated in the contract and leaving school at the stipulated departure time. If this is done, school clubs will have to be cancelled along with tutoring sessions and special events, plays, and field trips outside the normal school day. This means no speech team or tournament for the kids, no after-school dances (because no teachers would be available to chaperone), no foreign language fair, and no after-school intramural sports. In the interest of union solidarity, all members of the bargaining unit are expected to comply. Union leaders acknowledge the difficulties this presents for teachers, who are accustomed to giving freely of their time, but feel it necessary. Jessica sees the logic and wants to support her fellow teachers. Yet, she can't help feeling that her students are the victims in this power play.

If you were Jessica, would you give your support to your colleagues or to your students? Could there be a middle ground?

Lila Jones

Lila Jones is in her fourth year of teaching music. She just transferred to Ridgecrest Middle School from a nearby district because of a serious personal conflict with another teacher. She is eager to get to know the new staff and students and be part of a collegial working environment. She is friendly and caring and spends extra time with her students preparing for performances, which doesn't always give her the opportunity to visit informally with other staff members. One student in particular, Alyssa, has been staying after school every day, waiting until all the other students leave and wanting to talk. She has opened up about her family, how her father left when she was a baby, and how her mom's current boyfriend has just moved in. She has told Lila about her older sister running away and leaving her there alone. One day Alyssa comes to see Mrs. Jones during her lunch period, tears flowing down her cheeks. She whispers to Mrs. Jones that Mr. Gibson, her math teacher, kept her in for detention because she didn't have her homework. She was the only student there, so Mr. Gibson sat next to her, and as they talked, he had casually touched her leg. Lila's mind raced. She didn't know Mr. Gibson well, but knew he was young and well-liked by the students. Some of the girls were said to have crushes on him, but she had never heard anything like that from Alyssa.

What should Lila do now, if anything?

Todd Franklin

Todd Franklin is a veteran teacher, part of a well-established interdisciplinary team at Diamond Heights Middle School. He and his colleagues have worked at integrating their curriculum, developing a strong team identity for the students, and at making the adjustments and compromises necessary in creating a strong team. Their meetings are characterized by candor and open discussion, and the team prides itself on putting all their cards on the table. This always worked well for Todd, until recently.

Nereyda Valenzuela is one of the superstar students assigned to their team. All four teachers are impressed with the way Nereyda applies herself, shows a positive attitude, relates well with peers, works to the best of her ability, and is eager to learn and to do more than required. She accepts each challenge with determination to succeed. The team is considering naming her their Student of the Year.

One day in their team meeting, Winona Hatch, the mathematics teacher, brought up her personal belief that their Student of the Year should be a U.S. citizen. There seemed to be general consensus, although Todd brought up the question of how they would know about citizenship. After all, they weren't supposed to ask the children or do any investigative work to determine nation of citizenship. Students living here were entitled to an education, regardless of their citizenship. The others weren't sure.

Nereyda is in Todd's first-period class and always comes in before school to receive extra help with reading. She arrived later than usual one morning, her eyes and nose red and her lip quivering. "What's wrong, Nereyda?" "Nothing, Mr. Franklin. I am fine. I am sorry I wasn't here to read this morning." Todd said it was not a problem and to let him know if he could do anything to help. He watched her struggle to regain her composure. Her best friend, Carla, came over to her desk to chat. Mr. Franklin overheard, "La Migra," which he knew meant Immigration and Naturalization. As he eavesdropped he pieced together that her father had returned to Mexico to visit his ill mother. She was afraid he couldn't come back because he had no green card; no one in her family did. She was worried her whole family would be sent back to Mexico. In that way, Todd learned she was in the United States illegally. He decided not to tell his team, or anyone, what he had overheard.

Has Todd done the right thing?

Professionalism and Professional Conduct

Every profession has a code of ethical conduct that preserves public confidence in that profession. In virtually all cases, confidence is maintained when professionals demonstrate competence, integrity, honesty, and fairness (Schmeiser, 1995).

The public tends to expect even more from teachers than from other professionals, with respect to honesty, consideration, responsibility, equality, integrity, and trustworthiness. These expectations are not limited to the classroom and school, but extend far into community and society. Here are some of the provisions set forth in the National Education Association's professional code.

In fulfillment of the obligation to the profession, the educator:

- Shall exert every effort to raise professional standards, to promote a climate that encourages the exercise of professional judgment, to achieve conditions that attract persons worthy of the trust to careers in education, and assist in preventing the practice of the profession by unqualified persons.
- Shall not in an application for a professional position deliberately make a false statement or fail to disclose a material fact related to competency and qualifications.
- Shall not misrepresent his or her professional qualifications.
- Shall not assist any entry into the profession of a person known to be unqualified in respect to character, education, or other relevant attribute.
- Shall not knowingly make a false statement concerning the qualifications of a candidate for a professional position.
- Shall not assist a noneducator in the unauthorized practice of teaching.
- Shall not disclose information about colleagues obtained in the course of professional service unless disclosure serves a compelling professional purpose or is required by law.
- Shall not knowingly make false or malicious statements about a colleague.
- Shall not accept any gratuity, gift, or favor that might impair or appear to influence professional decisions or action.

In addition to the provisions set forth by the National Education Association, the following suggestions can help you maintain high levels of professionalism.

Dress professionally. Dress like an adult in a professional situation. What you wear helps establish your role as the adult in charge—your students' teacher and model. Of course your clothing should be in accordance with the climate and the standards of the school and community. Just remember: you are representing your profession.

Use appropriate language. Use language appropriate for the educational setting. Model correct speech patterns and do not use obscene language. Keep in mind that you demonstrate respect for yourself and your students by the way you speak.

Provide interesting activities. Help students find enjoyable ways to learn. Take their feelings into account and make sure to provide interesting assignments and activities.

Be persistent. Don't give up on students. Keep trying. Find alternative ways to teach concepts if students experience difficulty. Show them you are on their side and want to help them learn.

Use your power wisely. You know you are human and fallible, but your students don't see you that way. You are a role model to them and have much power in influencing their behavior, especially through your enthusiasm for ideas, your creativity and originality, hard work, persistence, fairness, courtesy, kindness, and integrity. Treat students fairly, with respect, and show by example how you deal with difficult situations.

Show appreciation for students. Do your best to know and appreciate students as individuals, with differing personalities, needs, capabilities, and self-concepts. Enjoy them. Do what you can to help. Take pleasure in their successes.

Beware the self-fulfilling prophecy. Guard against forming first impressions of students because you may set in motion a chain of unwarranted expectations. For example, if a boy looks sloppy and lazy, you may inadvertently treat him as such and, in so doing, slow his educational progress. Suspend judgments. Relate positively with every student. Show respect and consideration. That is the way to give all students a good chance at success in your classroom.

Fred LeBlanc

Fred LeBlanc greeted his students at the classroom door on the first day of school. Fred considered himself a good judge of character and believed that he could tell a lot about how each student would achieve and behave throughout the year simply by observing and listening to them for just a short while. He noted which individuals smiled and returned his greeting, which ones looked down at the ground and grunted, which said a perfunctory, "hi," and which ones ignored him completely. Among those entering his room that morning were:

- a tall boy with a pierced eyebrow and pink spiky hair, dressed in black;
- a very small, thin, pale boy, wearing glasses;
- a beautiful girl with long hair and shining eyes, dressed neatly;
- the brother of a boy he had taught the year before, who had been a pain in the neck;
- the principal's daughter, an only child;
- two girls, entering arm-in-arm, laughing boisterously and drawing attention to themselves;
- a boy accompanied by his father, whom Fred knew to be a respected research biologist at the university.

Honestly, what behavioral traits popped into your mind, however fleetingly, as you read about each person on the list?

Continue to grow professionally. Participate in staff development workshops and seminars offered by your school site or district. Attend conferences that pertain to your subject matter and professional needs. Subscribe to professional journals or visit the journals on-line. Keep up with current trends and strive to improve your teaching. Take advantage of opportunities to learn from other teachers.

Reflect on your experiences and on your teaching behaviors. To gain a clear picture of what is working well in your classroom, take a few minutes daily to reflect on how you interacted with students and they with you (see Bailey, 1999). For example, ask yourself:

- Was I consistent in my behavior toward students?
- Was I pleasant or moody?
- Was I considerate, caring, and respectful toward students?
- Did I make my classes interesting and challenging?
- Did my discipline plan work today? Were there disruptions?

Be a good colleague. Be willing to do your fair share with extra duties. Be respectful of other teachers and never publicly (or in the faculty lounge) disparage another staff member. Do not indulge in gossip about others or break their confidentiality. Cooperate with fellow teachers and be flexible when the situation warrants it. Help other teachers when they ask for it by sharing materials, covering a class, or helping with lesson planning when there is an emergency.

> **FIELD APPLICATION 3:**   Arrange to talk with two or three teachers. Tell them you want to know more about professionalism and ask what they think it means and entails. Ask for specific examples to illustrate their points.

Teacher Rights and Protections

When you are hired by a school district, you will sign a contract that stipulates the services you are to provide and what you will receive in compensation. In most states, you are required to work under probationary status for the first two to five years, after which you may be granted tenure, or permanent status. Once you receive tenure, your contract renews automatically as long as your job performance is satisfactory.

Probationary Period

During your probationary period, your contract will be renewed on a yearly basis. Districts stipulate a deadline, usually early in spring, by which time they will notify you if you will be rehired for the following school year. Depending on the state, probationary teachers who are not rehired may have the right to know the reasons why this action was taken and meet with the board and superintendent to discuss the matter. Nineteen states grant this right (Simpson, 2001). Twenty states provide that new teachers deemed to have teaching deficiencies must receive a plan of improvement. Other states grant collective bargaining units (teacher associations) the authority to negotiate for due process rights for beginning teachers.

As of May 2001, the following states offer substantial job protections for new teachers: Alaska, Arkansas, Delaware, Indiana, Kentucky, Nebraska, New Jersey, Ohio, Oklahoma, Oregon, Pennsylvania, Vermont, and West Virginia.

States offering little or no nonrenewal protections for beginning teachers are: Alabama, California, Colorado, Florida, Illinois, Maine, Maryland, Massachusetts, Missouri, North Carolina, South Carolina, Utah, and Wyoming.

Georgia, Mississippi, and Texas have no state tenure law (Simpson, 2001).

Tenure

Tenure is a form of job security whose main purpose is to protect teachers from arbitrary termination for reasons unrelated to teaching, such as conflicts with administrators or school board members (see Scott, 1986). The protection provided by tenure varies from state to state and even district to district. Usually, if procedures are brought against them, tenured teachers are afforded due process, including a hearing in which the administration must prove its case against the teacher. School districts retain the right to discharge a teacher for "just cause," usually meaning immorality, incompetence, or insubordination. Standards of morality may differ from community to community, but it is safe to assume that immorality would encompass sexual conduct with a student, possession of a controlled substance, other criminal activity, and unprofessional conduct. Incompetence could mean mental incapacity, inadequate instruction, or inability to control the class. Insubordination means a persistent failure to comply with reasonable rules or orders clearly stated by someone in authority. Examples might be unauthorized absences, refusal to perform nonteaching duties, and encouraging students to disobey authority.

First Amendment Rights

The Supreme Court ruled in 1969 (*Tinker v. Des Moines Independent School District*) that constitutional rights extend to teachers and students on public school property. Justice Abe Fortas, in writing the Court's opinion, said: "It can hardly be argued that either students or teachers shed their constitutional rights to freedom of speech or expression at the schoolhouse gate." However, keep in mind that one cannot say whatever one wishes. For example, libel, slander, and obscenity are examples of unprotected speech.

When teachers are functioning as employees, critical things they say about the school must be about "matters of public concern," such as safety of students, and not about personal concerns such as perceived administrator incompetence or other grievances. The latter is not protected under the First Amendment (Collins, 2001).

Academic Freedom

University professors place high premium on academic freedom, which allows them to present instruction in the way they deem best. However, the Supreme Court has not directly ruled on whether public school teachers in grades K–12 should be accorded academic freedom. It declined to hear the appeal of a high school biology teacher who was reassigned because he was not following the district's curriculum in science. The teacher refused to teach the theory of evolution without also presenting scientific criticisms of the theory. Administrators reassigned the teacher to another grade level in which evolution was not taught. The teacher sued in state court on the basis of his federal constitutional rights to free speech and freedom of religion. He lost the trial and the appeal. The appeals court affirmed that teachers deserve some academic freedom but must not refuse to comply with the district's curriculum requirements (Walsh, 2002).

The Fourth Circuit Court of Appeals held in 1998 that a public school teacher has no First Amendment right to participate in the makeup of the school curriculum. In the same year the Eighth Circuit Court of Appeals upheld the firing of a teacher for allowing her creative writing students to write and perform skits containing "street language." The message is clear that teachers who use controversial material or teaching methods may be putting their careers at risk (Simpson, 1998).

Personal Considerations for Teachers

You have seen how important it is to adhere to the highest ethical and professional standards and have reviewed legal requirements that affect the performance of your duties. There is a fourth area of concern that also deserves your attention. It has to do with personal considerations that affect your enthusiasm and ability to teach in a professional manner.

Teaching is a very stressful job and often a thankless one. Teachers do their best to meet the learning and behavioral needs of a wide range of students. That effort requires high enthusiasm, abundant energy, and a steady sense of purpose. If you are to remain an excellent teacher, you must keep enthusiasm, energy, and purpose intact. Challenges that may prevent your doing so include stress, frustration, fatigue, and disillusionment. Let us see how we can limit or rise above those conditions.

Stress

Stress refers to a condition of heightened nervous tension that affects us emotionally and physically. In some cases, it helps us perform better and can even be thrilling. That kind of stress, called "eustress," is experienced by people who accept new challenges or engage in performances or competition. It is enlivening and invigorating, but only up to a point, after which it becomes detrimental.

Nervous tension that makes us feel bad and interferes with our work is called "distress." It dampens our spirits and can preoccupy our minds so we do not think well. This kind of stress is often associated with high levels of fear, ongoing responsibilities that are very burdensome, and inability to perform up to expectations.

There is no escaping stress, eustress, and distress. They are part of normal life. But because distress (and excess eustress) can badly affect your work, it is important that you learn how to manage it (Brownell, 1997). Your goal is not just to survive, but to thrive in teaching. Some teachers leave teaching because they simply cannot handle the stress that is part of the profession, while others burn out emotionally but remain in teaching anyway, marking time from weekend to weekend and vacation to vacation. While burnout has become more prevalent in recent years, most teachers can avoid it and continue to grow as educators (Carter, 1994).

Burnout

Teacher burnout is an emotional state (with physical manifestations) in which teachers no longer want to go to work, receive no pleasure from teaching, and make less than adequate efforts to help students learn and succeed. Burnout is not an event that occurs precipitously in a teacher's career, but a process that builds up over time (Brock and Grady, 2001). It is caused by a combination of factors such as persistent stress, unappreciative and unmotivated students, antagonistic parents, demanding administrators, and the feeling that one has become incapable of teaching effectively, given existing conditions. Recent developments in mandated standardized testing ("high-stakes testing") have increased the pressure on teachers (Associated Press, 2002).

Symptoms of burnout usually include most of the following, although all may not be present in early stages (Brock and Grady, 2001):

- *Physical*—fatigue, exhaustion, sometimes frequent accidents and illness, possible abuse of alcohol or drugs
- *Intellectual*—poor concentration, lack of focus, failure to meet deadlines, absence of creativity
- *Emotional*—feeling overwhelmed, alienated, anxious, despairing, irritable, cynical
- *Social*—lack of consideration, withdrawal, avoidance of interactions with others

Amy Carlisle

The incessant buzz of the alarm clock had worked itself into Amy Carlisle's dream. It had morphed into a school fire alarm, and she was trying to get her students out the door, but they wouldn't move. No matter what she did or said, they continued to mill around, pretending not to hear her. She panicked, knowing the flames would consume them. As she became aware that it was her alarm clock she felt relieved and gravely disappointed at the same time—relieved that there was no fire, disappointed that it was morning so soon.

She turned off the alarm and sat wearily on the edge of the bed, exhausted even after ten hours of sleep. Was there any possible way she could take today off? She did a quick accounting of her lesson plans and tried to remember in what state she had left the classroom the day before. A day off would really help. She would use it well, maybe grading that stack of essays that had sat untouched on her desk for over a week. The students were already asking when she expected to turn them back. "Never" is what she wanted to say. She wondered if they would forget about them in time. Or, better yet, she could take a walk in the woods on her glorious free day. Or maybe do some real cooking. Or get some rest. That was what she really needed, rest.

She sat there so long she only had time to shower, dress, and head out the door. She grabbed a cup of coffee for the drive, hoping someone would bring in doughnuts. It was going to be a long day. Her plan period was going to be used for a parent–team meeting regarding Priscilla Jenkins, who had been rude and insolent, the worst of a generally unsatisfactory group of students, most of them lazy, uncooperative, and downright mean. She was certain Mrs. Jenkins would blame her and other teachers for Priscilla's conduct. That's what the parents were like these days—not admitting their offspring had faults, only blaming others. Then after school, there was to be a staff meeting to go over the school scores. Amy dreaded that. She knew the scores were down, and what would that mean? An insinuation that the teachers were not working hard enough, or were not good enough, to teach the students. Ultimately, it would mean more work for her, she was sure of it.

Amy slammed on the brakes to avoid rear-ending the car ahead of her, stopped at a traffic light. She barely noticed it in time. Her coffee sloshed over her shirt and down to her lap. Amy began to cry.

Alex Leonard

Alex Leonard was a colleague of Amy's, although a member of a different teaching team. He was a first-year teacher hired on an emergency credential, and the terms of his employment stipulated that he finish his university coursework as quickly as possible. So, in addition to learning the ropes of teaching and all it entails, Alex attended university classes two nights a week. His coursework required the usual reading, papers, projects, and tests. Alex also had a family, and he and his wife and three children were currently living with his wife's parents, which was not an ideal situation. Alex lived in a pressure cooker, but you would never know it from his demeanor.

Alex liked his students and didn't hesitate to tell them so. Some of the students interpreted his fondness for them as a sign of weakness and attempted to test him with inappropriate behavior. Alex regretted this, but it didn't influence the way he responded to all the students; he was invariably kind, considerate, and respectful. He didn't take their misbehavior personally, but did try to modify the activities to make them more enjoyable. He asked for student input on ways to make the class function better, and he listened to their suggestions. He made many mistakes, but admitted them and tried to learn from them. Although he felt frustrated at times, he did his best not to take it out on the students.

Students would say of him, "He is so nice." "He likes everyone, not just the ones who get A's." "He will always take time to explain it again." "He's funny, but he doesn't make fun of anyone." "He doesn't make me feel stupid if I ask a question or don't get what he is teaching." "The kids who give him a hard time don't know how to treat a nice teacher." "I can learn more because I am not afraid he is going to yell at me."

Lisa Russell

Lisa Russell served as team leader for Amy Carlisle's team, and was concerned about her friend and colleague. Amy had seemed increasingly exhausted, negative, and withdrawn. Once the creative spark of their team, Amy now was often indifferent and apathetic. Students who had enjoyed her class were beginning to grumble: "What's up with Mrs. Carlisle? She looks at us like she hates us." "She takes a really long time to return papers to us." "She lost my makeup test!" "She's always in a bad mood." Lisa was sure Amy was struggling from overload, just as she herself had at one time. She thought she might be able to help.

Lisa had found her way back to feeling happy and confident in teaching by taking a few simple steps. She determined to look at the big picture, rather than focusing on the daily battles. She made a point of looking for positive things in work, students, and col-leagues, rather than negative. That alone helped her a great deal. She also determined to balance her life with exercise, relaxation, and recreation. In doing so, her mood improved and she regained her sense of balance.

Lisa remembered how she had taken a major step to put herself on students' side so they could work together without the former antagonisms. Experience had taught her that, when a teacher views students as adversaries, the classroom can become a hostile place. She reestablished effective learning routines and made reasonable homework assignments, which helped to reduce the feeling of overload.

When Lisa saw Amy that morning in the staff lounge, hair disheveled, shirt stained, tears brimming in her eyes, she knew her suspicions were correct. It was then she determined to take steps to help Amy.

Countering Stress and Avoiding Burnout

It can be disheartening to feel your energy, joy, and enthusiasm for teaching ebbing away. But you are not powerless. You can take control of yourself and your teaching life, as Lisa Russell did. If you find yourself in Amy Carlisle's position, take steps immediately to find a remedy that will bring happiness back to teaching. Consider the following suggestions. (By the way, if you conscientiously follow them from the beginning, you will probably never experience the threat of burnout.)

- Know that you are doing important work. Difficult, but important.
- Do the best you can to enjoy your students. Get to know them. Appreciate their qualities. Talk with them. Work alongside them. Develop the feeling of togetherness. It is invigorating.
- Find ways for students to show parents and others what they are learning. Emphasize creative projects and group activities. Put students in the limelight.
- Be realistic in your expectations of yourself. You cannot do everything and you cannot do anything perfectly. Do the best you can. Focus on the possible and take notice of your achievements.
- Plan lessons thoroughly and make them fun. You will feel confident and in control if you have well-organized lessons that students enjoy.
- Cut down on paperwork as much as possible, then keep up with what you have to do. Don't let it pile up.
- Set aside some time for yourself each day. Teachers are givers by nature, and it is easy to devote all your time to others.
- Find humor and things to laugh about every day. Associate with colleagues who are fun.

- Exercise. It gives you new energy, refreshes your perspective, helps you sleep better, and contributes to a sense of well-being.
- Establish priorities. Decide what is most important for you to accomplish. Make a list, realizing you may not finish everything on a given day.
- Ask for help when you need it, from colleagues, friends, family, and especially students.
- Keep your mind active. Continue learning new things. Share with students some of what you are learning.
- Leave your stress behind when you close the door to your classroom at the end of the day. Think about something else for a while. Do something different.

> **FIELD APPLICATION 4:**   Talk with a middle-grades teacher or counselor. Ask about the incidence of stress and burnout at the school or in the district. Ask what provisions, if any, are available to help teachers contend with stress and guard against burnout.

QUESTIONS

1. How secure do you feel with regard to legal concerns in teaching? What caution do you feel you should keep in mind?

2. What do you see as differences, if any, between ethics and professionalism? Be specific.

3. Do you feel you have a legal and professional right to teach as you see fit? In what ways are you constrained, if at all?

4. Few teachers get in trouble for violating copyright, even though some of their actions are clearly illegal. Why do you think that is so? Do you feel it is all right for teachers to violate copyright laws slightly?

5. Once a teacher has tenure, it is very difficult for a district to dismiss that teacher. Do you think that is a good provision or one that should be changed?

6. Have you known teachers who seemed to be suffering from burnout? If so, what were the specific symptoms you observed?

ACTIVITIES

1. With a group of colleagues, make a list of situations in normal teaching that might have potential legal ramifications, sufficient to worry you. Decide how you would conduct yourself in those situations.

2. Describe what you consider to be a proper professional attitude. To what extent does professionalism merge with ethics?

3. Write out a plan for yourself that you believe will prevent your experiencing burnout and allow you to enjoy teaching throughout your career.

4. Formulate a strategy for yourself (or another teacher) who is in the probationary period of teaching. Indicate how that teacher can make a strong impression and earn tenure.

REFERENCES

Alexander, K., and Alexander, M. 1992. *American public school law.* St. Paul, MN: West.

Associated Press. 7 May 2002. Teachers feel stress of high-stakes testing: Results can make or break some educators' careers, <CNN.com/Education>.

Bailey, G. 1999. A qualitative study of middle grade students' perceptions of their schools, teachers, and classes. <www.education.nsula.edu/lmsa/Qual.htm>.

Brock, B., and Grady, L. 2001. *Rekindling the flame: Principals combating teacher burnout.* Thousand Oaks, CA: Corwin.

Brownell, M. 1997. Coping with stress in the special education classroom: Can individual teachers more effectively manage stress? Reston, VA: ERIC Clearinghouse on Disabilities and Gifted Education. ERIC Digests 545. ED414659 97.

Carter, S. 1994. Organizing systems to support competent social behavior in children and youth: Volume III, *Teacher stress and burnout.* Western Regional Resource Center, U.S. Department of Special Education Programs, University of Oregon, <http://interact.uoregon.edu/wrrc/Burnout.html>.

Collins, K. 2001. Watch your mouth! SAI report. School Administrators of Iowa, <http://www.sai-iowa.org/401Report.html>.

Donhoff, K. 1997. Jury sees through charges. *California Educator, 1* (6), <www.cta.org/cal_educator/v1i6/case_jury.html>.

Dowling-Sendor, B. 2000. Discipline on the road: A case of search and seizure on a school field trip. *American School Board Journal,* <http://asbj.com/2000/02/0200schoollaw.html>.

Drye, J. 2000. Tort liability 101: When are teachers liable? Atlanta, GA: Educator Resources. <http://www.Educator-Resources.com>.

Education Week on the Web. 1 August 2002. Special education. <www.edweek.org/context/topics/issuespage.cfm?id=63>.

Essex, N. 1999. Safeguarding rights, minimizing exposure. *The School Administrator Web Edition.* Arlington, VA: American Association of School Administrators. <http://www.aasa.org/publications/sa/1999_06/essex.htm>.

Golden Mean Online. Spring 2000. Laboratory safety: Keeping our children and teachers safe. Mathematics and Science Network, University of North Carolina. <http://www.unc.edu/depts/msen/goldmean/spring00/labsafe.html>.

Good, T. 1987. Two decades of research on teacher expectations: Findings and future directions. *Journal of Teacher Education, 8* (4), 32–47.

Goorian, B., and Brown, K. 2002. Trends and Issues: School Law. ERIC Clearinghouse on Educational Management. <http://eric.uoregon.edu/trends_issues/law/index.html>.

Josephson Institute of Ethics. 2001. What is ethics anyway? <www.josephsoninstitute.org/MED/MED-whatis ethics.htm>.

Missouri Department of Elementary and Secondary Education. 19 July 2002. School laws and legislation: Search and seizure issues. <www.dese.state.mo.us/schoollaw/freqaskques/searchissues.htm>.

Moyers, B. 15 February 2002. Freedom to teach: History of academic freedom. NOW: In Depth: Politics and economy. PBS Web site, <www.pbs.org/now/politics/acfreehistory.html>.

National Association of Secondary School Principals. 2002. Putting the "right" back in "copyright": Educating principals in copyright law. Chart. <www.principals.org/srvices/legal_chart.htm>.

National Education Association. 1975. Code of Ethics of the Education Profession. <www.nea.org/aboutnea/code.html>

National Education Association. 2002. NEA report on the Individuals with Disabilities Education Act (IDEA). Washington, DC: Author. <http://www.nea.org/publiced/idea/>.

Schmeiser, C. 1995. Ethics in assessment. ERIC Digests. ED 391111. <www.library.unt.edu/ericscs/vl/ethics/digests/assess.htm>.

Scott, J. 1986. Teacher tenure. ERIC Digest, 19. Eugene, OR: ERIC Clearinghouse on Educational Management. <www.ed.gov/databases/ERIC_Digests/ed282352.html>.

Shoop, R. 2002. Identifying a standard of care. *Principal Leadership* (on-line), *2* (7) . National Association of Secondary School Principals. <http://www.principals.org/news/pl_idstandardcare_0302.html>.

Simpson, M. 1998. Academic freedom takes a hit. *NEA Today Online.* <http://www.nea.org/neatoday/9811/rights.html>.

———. 2001. NEA examines the rights of nontenured teachers. *NEA Today Online.* <http://www.nea.org/neatoday/0105/rights.html>.

Starr, L. 2000. The educator's guide to copyright and fair use. *Education World.* <http://www.education-world.com/a_curr/curr280a.shtml>.

Tauber, R. 1998. Good or bad, what teachers expect from students they generally get! Washington, DC: ERIC Clearinghouse on Teaching and Teacher Education. ERIC identifier: ED426985.

Walsh, M. 16 January 2002. High court declines to hear case on teaching of evolution. *Education Week 21* (8), 22. <http://edweek.org/ew/newstory.cfm?slug=18scotus.h21>.

Willard, N. 2002. Schools, the Internet, and copyright law. *Education World.* <http://www.education-world.com/a_tech/tech121.shtml>.

BIBLIOGRAPHY

Albert, L. 1996. *Cooperative discipline.* Circle Pines, MN: American Guidance Service.

Alexander, K., and Alexander, M. 1992. *American public school law.* St. Paul, MN: West.

Alexander, W., Williams, E., Compton, M., Hines, V., and Prescott, D. 1968. *The emergent middle school.* New York: Holt, Rinehart, Winston.

Alliance for Childhood. 2001. <www.allianceforchildhood.net/projects/computers/computers_reports_fools_gold_contents.htm>.

Amen, D. 2001. *Healing ADD: The breakthrough program that allows you to see and heal the six types of attention deficit disorder.* New York: G. P. Putnam's Sons.

Anderman, E., and Kimweli, D. 1977. Victimization and safety in schools serving early adolescents. *Journal of Early Adolescence, 17*(4), 408–438.

Anfara, V. (Ed). 2001. *The handbook of research in middle level education.* Greenwich, CT: Information Age.

Ascher, C. 1988. Improving the school-home connection for low-income urban family members. *ERIC Digests.* <www.ed.gov/databases/ERIC_Digests/ed293973.html>.

———. 1991. School programs for African American males. New York: ERIC Clearinghouse on Urban Education.

———. 1993. Changing schools for urban students: The school development program, Accelerated Schools, and Success for All. Trends and Issues No. 18. New York: ERIC Clearinghouse on Urban Education.

Associated Press. 7 May 2002. Teachers feel stress of high-stakes testing: Results can make or break some educators' careers. <CNN.com/Education>.

Atencio, B., and others. 1992. White House Conference on Indian Education (Washington, DC, January 22–24, 1992). Final Report, volumes 1 and 2.

At-Risk Task Force, Utah State Office of Education. 1998. <www.usoe.k12.ut>.

Attention Deficit Disorders Association, Southern Region, <ADD/ADHD. 2002. http://www.adda-sr.org/BehaviorManagementIndex.htm>.

AVID, an educational reform program that works. 26 August, 2001. *San Diego Union Tribune.* <http://www.middleweb.com/MGNEWS1/MGN0907.html>.

Bailey, G. 1999. A qualitative study of middle grade students' perceptions of their schools, teachers, and classes. <http://www.education.nsula.edu/lmsa/Qual.htm>.

Baruth. L., and Manning. L. 1992. *Multicultural education of children and adolescents.* Boston: Allyn & Bacon.

Bauer, J. 2000. *A technology gender divide: perceived skill and frustration levels among female preservice teachers.* November. Paper presented at annual meeting of the Mid-South Educational Research Association. <http://askeric.org/plwebcgi/fastweb?getdoc+ericdb+1050500+9+wAAA+%28gen>.

Belenardo, S. 2001. Practices and conditions that lead to a sense of community in middle schools. *NASSP Bulletin 85*(627), 29–30. <www.nassp.org/news/bltn_prac_cond1001.html>.

Bempechat, J. 2001. *Fostering high achievement in African American children: Home, school , and public policy influences.* <http://ericweb.tc.columbia.edu/monographs/ti16_index.html>.

Benard, B. 1997. Drawing forth resilience in all our youth. *Reclaiming Children and Youth, 6*(1), 29–32.

Berenson, S., Drujkova, M., Cavey, L., Smith, N., and Barnes, T. 2000. Girls on track with information technology. *Meridian.* Winter. <www.ncsu.edu/meridian/archive_of_meridian/2000wint/math/index.html>.

Berkowitz, M. 1998. Obstacles to teacher training in character education. *Action in Teacher Education, 20*(4): 1–10.

Berliner, D. 28 January, 2001. Our schools vs. theirs: Averages that hide the true extremes. *Washington Post.* Outlook Section OP-ED.

Biddulph, S. 1997. *Raising boys.* Sydney, Australia: Finch.

Bishop, A. August, 2001. An expert's guide to products for the multilingual classroom. *Technology & Learning.* <//www.techlearning.com/db_area/archives/TL/200104/classroom.html>.

Bosworth, K. 1997. Drug abuse prevention: School-based strategies that work. Washington, DC: ERIC Clearinghouse on Teaching and Teacher Education. ED409316.

Bosworth, K., and Sailes, J. 1993. Content and teaching strategies in 10 selected drug abuse prevention curricula. *Journal of School Health, 63*(6), 247–253.

Bradley, A., and Manzo, K. 2000. The weak link. *Education Week.* <http://www.edweek.org/ew/ew_print story.cfm?slug=05msmain.h20>.

Brazee, E. 2000. Exploratory curriculum in the middle school. ERIC Digests. <http://www.ed.gov/databases/ERIC_Digests/ed447970.html>.

Briggs, T. 1920. *The junior high school.* Boston: Houghton Mifflin.

Brock, B. and Grady, L. 2001. *Rekindling the flame: Principals combating teacher burnout.* Thousand Oaks, CA: Corwin.

Brown, A. 1980. Cherokee culture and school achievement. *American Indian Culture and Research Journal, 4,* 55–74.

Brownell, M. 1997. Coping with stress in the special education classroom: Can individual teachers more effectively manage stress? Reston, VA: ERIC Clearinghouse on Disabilities and Gifted Education. ERIC Digests 545. ED414659 97.

Bruner, J. 1960. *The process of education.* New York: Vintage.

Brunner, I., and others. 1997. *Accelerated schools as learning organizations: Cases from the University of New Orleans Accelerated School Network.* Paper presented at the Annual Meeting of the American Educational Research Association (Chicago, IL, March 24–28).

Brylinsky, J., and Moore, J. 1984. The identification of body build stereotypes in young children. *Journal of Research in Personality, 28,* 170–181.

Burkhart, L., and Kelly, K. 2001. Instructional uses of the Internet for elementary age students. March. <www.lburkhart.com/elem/internet.htm>.

Burnett, G. 1993. The assessment and placement of language minority students. ERIC/CUE Digest, Number 89.

Burns, J. 1996. The five attributes of satisfying advisories. *Integrative Design.*<http://www.vla.com/idesign/attributes2.html>.

———. 2001. Frequent inquiries regarding advisory: Ten questions, with answers from Jim Burns. *Integrative Design.* <http://www.vla.com/idesign/advisory2.html>.

Butterfield, R. 1994. *Blueprints for Indian education: Improving mainstream schooling.* Charleston, WV: ERIC Clearinghouse on Rural Education and Small Schools.

Butterfield, R., and Pepper, F. 1991. Improving parental participation in elementary and secondary education for American Indian and Alaska Native students. ERIC RC018622.

Cahape, P., and Howley, C. 1992. Indian nations at risk: Listening to the people. Summaries of Papers Commissioned by the Indian Nations At Risk Task Force of the U.S. Department of Education.

Cajete, G. 1986. *Science: A Native American perspective* (A Culturally Based Science Education Curriculum). Ph.D. dissertation, International College/William Lyon University, San Diego, CA.

Calderón, M. 1996. How a new form of peer coaching helps teachers and students in two-way bilingual programs. Paper presented at the Annual Meeting of the National Association for Bilingual Education (Orlando, FL, March 1996).

Canter, L., and Canter, M. 1976. *Assertive discipline: A take-charge approach for today's educator.* Seal Beach, CA: Canter & Associates.

———. 1991. *Family members on your side.* Santa Monica, CA: Canter & Associates.

———. 2001. *Assertive discipline: Positive behavior management for today's classroom.* Los Angeles, CA: Canter & Associates.

Carnegie Council on Adolescent Development. 1989. *Turning points: Preparing American youth for the 21st Century.* New York: Carnegie Corporation of New York.

Carter, S. 1994. Organizing systems to support competent social behavior in children and youth: Volume III, *Teacher stress and burnout.* Western Regional Resource Center, US Department of Special Education Programs, University of Oregon.

Catagni, A., and Westat, E. 2001. Internet access in US public schools and classrooms: 1994–2000. National Center for Education Statistics. <http://nces.ed.gov/pubs200½001071.pdf>.

CDC. 1999. *Facts about violence among youth and violence in schools.* Washington, DC: U.S. Government. Media Relations. Division. <http://www.cdc.gov/navimages/spacer.gif>.

Chaddock, G. 6 December, 2000. US eighth graders beat global average in math. *Christian Science Monitor.* <http://www.csmonitor.com/durable/2000/12/06/p1s2.htm>.

Character Education Manifesto. 1996. Center for the Advancement of Ethics and Character, Boston University School of Education.

Charles, C. M. 2000. *The synergetic classroom: Joyful teaching and gentle discipline.* New York: Longman.

———. 2002a. *Building classroom discipline* (7th ed.). Boston: Allyn & Bacon.

———. 2002b. *Essential elements of effective discipline.* Boston: Allyn & Bacon.

Chavkin, N., and Gonzalez, J. 2000. *Mexican immigrant youth and resiliency: Research and promising programs.* Charleston, WV: ERIC Clearinghouse on Rural Education ED447990.

Cheng, L. 1996. Enhancing communication: Toward optimal language learning for limited English proficient students. *Language, Speech and Hearing Services in Schools, 28*(2), 347–354.

———. 1998. Enhancing the communication skills of newly arrived Asian American students. ERIC/CUE Digest No. 136. New York: ERIC Clearinghouse on Urban Education.

Clements, B., Lara, J., and Cheung, O. (1992). Limited English proficiency: Recommendations for improving the assessment and monitoring of students. Washington, DC: Council of Chief State School Officers. (ED 347 265).

Coker, D. 1988. The Asian students in the classroom. *Education and Society, 1*(3), 19–20.

Collins, J., and Plahn, M. 1988. Recognition, accuracy, stereotypic preference, aversion, and subjective judgment of body appearance in adolescents and young adults. *Journal of Youth and Adolescence, 17*(4), 317–334.

Collins, K. April, 2001.Watch your mouth! SAI report. School Administrators of Iowa. <http://www.sai-iowa.org/401Report.html>.

Coloroso, B. 1994. *Kids are worth it!: Giving your child the gift of inner discipline.* New York: Avon Books.

———. 1999. *Parenting with wit and wisdom in times of chaos and confusion.* Littleton, CO: Kids Are Worth It!

Cornett, C. 1983. What you should know about teaching and learning styles (Fastback No. 191). Bloomington, IN: Phi Delta Kappa Foundation.

Corporation for National Service. 2001. <www.cns.gov>.

Cotton, K. 1994. Fostering intercultural harmony in schools: Research findings (Topical Synthesis No. 7). Portland, OR: Northwest Regional Educational Laboratory.

Covey, S. 1989. *The seven habits of highly effective people.* New York: Simon & Schuster.

Cox, B., and Ramirez, M. 1981. Cognitive styles: Implications for multiethnic education. In J. Banks (Ed.), *Education in the 80s: Multiethnic Education* (pp. 61–71). Washington, DC: National Education Association.

Crawford, J. 1998. Ten common fallacies about bilingual education. ERIC Digest. Washington, DC: http://www.cal.org/ericcll

Cromwell, S. 26 April 1999. Student-led conferences: A growing trend. *Education World.* <http://www.education-world.com/a_admin/admin112.shtml>.

Cruickshank, D., Bainer, D., and Metcalf, K. 1999. *The act of teaching* (2nd ed.). Boston: McGraw-Hill College.

Curwin, R. 1992. *Rediscovering hope: Our greatest teaching strategy.* Bloomington, IN: National Educational Service.

Curwin, R., and Mendler, A. 1988. *Discipline with dignity.* Alexandria, VA: Association for Supervision and Curriculum Development.

———. 2001. *Discipline with dignity.* Upper Saddle River, NJ: Merrill.

Davis, B. 1993. Grading practices. *Tools for teaching.* <http://uga.berkeley.edu/sled/bgd/grading.html>.

de la Pena, F. (1991). Democracy or babel? The case for official English in the United States. Washington, DC: U.S. English.

Department of Education, Office of the Secretary. (1991). The condition of bilingual education in the nation: A report to the Congress and the President. Washington, DC: Author.

Diamond, M., and Hopson, J. 1998. Magic trees of the mind: *How to nurture your child's intelligence, creativity and healthy emotions from birth through adolescence.* New York: Dutton.

Dianda, M., and McLaren, A. July, 1996. A pocket guide to building partnerships for student learning. NEA. <www.nea.org/partners/pocket.html>.

Diller, D. 1999. Opening the dialogue: Using culture as a tool in teaching young African American children. *Reading Teacher, 52*(8), 820–858.

District 230 students make use of handheld computers. 2001. Consolidated high school district 230. <www.d230.org/handheld/default.htm>.

Dodge, B. 1997. Some thoughts about WebQuests. http://edweb.sdsu.edu/courses/edtec 596/about_webquests.html>.

———. May, 2001. FOCUS: Five rules for writing a great WebQuest. *International Society for Technology in Education.* <www.iste.org/L&L/archive/vol28/no8/featuredarticle/dodge/index.html>.

Donhoff, K. March 1997. Jury sees through charges. *California Educator,* 1 (6). <www.cta.org/cal_educator/v1i6/case_jury.html>.

Dowling-Sendor, B. 2000. Discipline on the road: A case of search and seizure on a school field trip. *American School Board Journal.* <http://asbj.com/2000/02/0200schoollaw.html>.

Dreikurs, R., and Cassel, P. 1972. *Discipline without tears.* New York: Hawthorne. Reissued 1995, Penguin-NAL.

Drye, J. 2000. Tort liability 101: When are teachers liable? Atlanta, GA: Educator Resources. <http://www.Educator-Resources.com>.

Education Week on the Web, 1 August 2002. Special education. <www.edweek.org/context/topics/issuespage.cfm?id=63>.

Education World. 2001. Selection of first-day ice breakers. <http://www.education world.com/a_lesson/lesson196.shtml>.

Enhancing education through technology. 21 August, 2001. *No Child Left Behind.* <www.ed.gov/inits/nclb/partx.html>.

Epstein, J., Salinas, C., and Jackson, V. 1995. *Manual for teachers and prototype activities: Teachers involve family members in schoolwork (TIPS) language arts, science/health, and math interactive homework in the middle grades.* (Rev. ed.) Baltimore: Center on School, Family, and Community Partnerships, Johns Hopkins University.

Essex, N.. June 1999. Safeguarding rights, minimizing exposure. *The School Administrator Web Edition.* Arlington, VA: American Association of School Administrators. <http://www.aasa.org/publications/sa/1999_06/essex.htm>.

Faircloth, S., and Tippeconnic, J. 2000. Issues in the education of American Indian and Alaska Native students with disabilities. Charleston, WV: ERIC Clearinghouse on Rural Education and Small Schools.

Felner, R., Jackson, A., Kasak, D., Mullhall, P., Brand, S., and Flowers, N. 1997. The impact of school reform for the middle years: Longitudinal study of a network engaged in Turning Points-based comprehensive school transformation. *Phi Delta Kappan, 78* (7), 528.

Feng, J. 1994. Asian-American children: What teachers should know. Urbana, IL: ERIC.

Fillmore, L., and Snow, C. 2000. What teachers need to know about language. Washington DC: Center for Applied Linguistics. ERIC Issue: RIEFEB2001.

Folsom, K. 1994. Developing and implementing a plan involving family members to improve the reading interests of middle school students. Nova Southeastern University: Ed.D.practicum.

Foster, M. 1995. Talking that talk: The language of control, curriculum, and conflict. *Linguistics and Education, 7,* 129–150.

Freeberg, L. 1989. Don't remediate, accelerate: Can disadvantaged students benefit from fast-forwarded instruction? *Equity and Choice, 5*(2), 40–43.

———. 1999. Teaching and learning in the contexts of African American English and culture. *Education and Urban Society. 31*(2), 177ff.

Gardner, H. 2000. *Intelligence reframed: Multiple intelligences.* New York: Basic Books.

Gatewood, T. 1975. The middle school we need: A report from the ASCD working group on the emerging adolescent learner. Washington, DC: Association for Supervision and Curriculum Development.

George, P., and Alexander, W. 1993. *The exemplary middle school.* (2nd ed.). New York: Harcourt Brace.

Getting America's students ready for the 21st Century: Meeting the technology literacy challenge. 1996. Washington, DC: U.S. Department of Education, Office of Educational Technology.

Gibbs, J. W. (Ed.).1988. *Young, black, and male in America: An endangered species.* Dover: Auburn.

Ginott, H. 1971. *Teacher and child.* New York: Macmillan.

Glasser, W. 1969. *Schools without failure.* New York: Harper & Row.

———. 1986. *Control theory in the classroom.* New York: Harper and Row.

———. 1993. *The quality school teacher.* New York: Harper Perennial.

———. 1998a. *The quality school: Managing students without coercion.* New York: HarperCollins.

———. 1998b. *The quality school teacher.* New York: HarperCollins.

Glasser, W., and Dotson, K. 1998. *Choice theory in the classroom.* New York: HarperCollins.

Goldenberg, C. (1992/1993). Instructional conversations: Promoting comprehension through discussion. *The Reading Teacher, 46,* 316–326.

Golden Mean Online. 2000. Laboratory safety: Keeping our children and teachers safe. Mathematics and Science Network, University of North Carolina.

Gonzalez, J., and Darling-Hammond, L. 2000. Programs that prepare teachers to work effectively with students learning English. ERIC Digests. Washington DC: ERIC Clearinghouse on Languages and Linguistics. <http://www.unc.edu/depts/msen/goldmean/spring00/labsafe.html>.

Good, T., 1987. Two decades of research on teacher expectations: Findings and future directions. *Journal of Teacher Education, 8*(4), 32–47.

Goorian, B., and Brown, K. 2002. Trends and Issues: School Law. ERIC Clearinghouse on Educational Management. <http://eric.uoregon.edu/trends_issues/law/index.html>.

Gordon, K. 1996. Resilience and motivation in two ethnic minority populations. ERIC Identifier ED404401.

Gordon, T. 1970. *Parent effectiveness training: A tested new way to raise responsible children.* New York: New American Library.

———. 1974. T. .E. T.: Teacher effectiveness training. New York: David McKay.

———. 1989. *Discipline that works: Promoting self-discipline in children.* New York: Random House.

Green, C. 2001. *Total memory workouts: 8 easy steps to maximum memory fitness.* New York. Bantam.

Green, M. 2000, September. Getting help from home. *NEA Today Online.* <www.nea.org/neatoday/0009/cover.html>.

Gutloff, K. 1997, October. Make it happen: How to involve hard-to-reach families. *NEA Today.* <www.nea.org/neatoday/9710/cover.html>.

Hao, L., and Bonstead-Bruns, M. 1998. Parent-child differences in educational expectations and the academic achievement of immigrant and Native students. *Sociology of Education, 71*(3), 175–198.

Harrington-Lueker, D. 2001. Middle schools fail to make the grade. *MiddleWeb.* <http://www.middleweb.com/MGNEWS1/MGN0319.html>.

Harnett, A. 1991. Preparation of middle school teachers. *ERIC Digest 90–1.* Washington, DC: ERIC Clearinghouse on Teacher Education. ERIC Identifier: ED335 356.

Hebert, E. 1998. Lessons learned about student portfolios. *Kappan Online Article.* <www.pdkintl.org/kappan/kheb9804.htm>.

Henderson, A. 1996. *Parents are powerful.* Washington, DC: Center for Law and Education. <www.cleweb.org/>.

Henderson, A., and Berla, N. (Eds.). 1994. *A new generation of evidence: The family is critical to student achievement.* Washington, DC: Center for Law and Education.

Henderson, A., and Raimondo, B. 2001, September. Unlocking parent potential. *Principal Leadership 2*(1). <www.principals.org/news/pl_prnt_ptntl.html>.

Hogan, D. 1997. ADHD: A travel guide to success. *Childhood Education, 73*(3), 158–160.

Hopstock, P., Bucaro, B., Fleischman, H., Zehler, A., and Eu, H. 1993. *Descriptive study of services to limited English proficient students.* Arlington, VA: Development Associates.

Hopkins, G. 1999. Advice about middle school advisories. *Education World.* <http://www.education-world.com/a_curr/curr127.shtml>.

Huang, G. 1993. Beyond culture: Communicating with Asian American children and families. *ERIC/CUE Digest Number 94.* New York: ERIC.

Hughes, M., Schumm, J, and Vaughn, S. 1999. Home literacy activities: perceptions and practices of Hispanic family members of children with learning disabilities. *Learning Disabilities Quarterly 22* (3), 224–35.

Hunsberger, B., and Cavanagh, B. 1988. Physical attractiveness and children's expectations of potential teachers. *Psychology in the Schools, 25*(1), 70–74.

Hunter, M. 1967. *Teach more—faster!* Originally published: El Segundo, CA: TIP. Re-issued in 1995, Thousand Oaks, CA: Corwin.

Hyslop, N. 2000. Hispanic parental involvement in home literacy. ERIC Digest 158.

Including students with disabilities in general education classrooms. 1993. ERIC Digest #E521. Arlington, VA: ERIC Clearinghouse on Disabilities and Gifted Education (ERIC EC) <http://ericed.org>.

Jackson, A. 1997. Middle Grade School State Policy Initiative. *Phi Delta Kappan International.* <http://pdkintl.org/kappan/hfels973.htm>.

Jackson, A. and Davis, G. 2000. *Turning points 2000: Educating adolescents in the 21st Century.* New York: Teachers College Press.

Johnson, W. 2001, September. CTA President's message to members. Mailing to CTA Members. Sacramento: California Teachers Association.

Jones, F. 1979. The gentle art of classroom discipline. *National Elementary Principal, 58,* 26–32.

———. 2001. *Fred Jones's tools for teaching.* Santa Cruz, CA: Fredric H. Jones & Associates.

Jones, J. 2001. How to make a practice of reflection. *TeachNet.* <www.teachersnetwork.org/docs/ntol/howto/develop/c13310,.htm>.

———. 2001. How to prepare a professional portfolio. *TeachNet.* <www.teachersnetwork.org/docs/ntol/howto/develop/c13309,.htm>.

Josephson Institute of Ethics. 2001. What is ethics anyway? <www.josephsoninstitute.org/MED/MED-whatisethics.htm>.

Joyce, B., Weil, M., and Calhoun, E. 2000. *Models of teaching* (6th ed.). Boston: Allyn and Bacon.

Kelty, J. 1997. An examination of Hispanic parent involvement in early childhood programs. ERIC. Document no: ED420406.

Krashen, S. 1996. *Under attack: The case against bilingual education.* Culver City, CA: Language Education Associates.

Kenealy, P., Frude, N., and Shaw, W. 1988. Influence of children's physical attractiveness on teacher expectations. *Journal of Social Psychology, 128*(3), 373–383.

Kim, B. (Ed.). 1985. *Literacy and languages. The second yearbook of literacy and languages in Asia, International Reading Association Special Interest Group.* Selection of Speeches and Papers from the International Conference on Literacy and Languages (Seoul, South Korea, August 12–14, 1985).

Kirkpatrick, H., and Cuban, L. Summer, 1998. Computers make kids smarter—right? *TECHNOS Quarterly.* <www.technos.net/journal/volume 7/2cuban.htm>.

Kleiman, G. April–June, 2000. Myths and realities about technology in K–12 schools. *LNT Perspectives.* <www.edc.org/LNT/news/Issue14?feature1.htm>.

Knupfer, N. 1997. New technologies and gender equity: New bottles with old wine. AskERIC/ED409843. February. <http://askeric.org/>.

Kohn, A. 1993. *Punished by rewards: The trouble with gold stars, incentive plans, A's, praise, and other bribes.* Boston: Houghton Mifflin.

———. 1996. *Beyond discipline: From compliance to community.* Alexandria, VA: Association for Supervision and Curriculum Development.

———. 1997. How not to teach values: A critical look at character education. *Phi Delta Kappan 78*(6), 428–39.

———. 1999. *The schools our children deserve: Moving beyond traditional classrooms and "tougher standards."* Boston: Houghton Mifflin.

Kounin, J. 1971. *Discipline and group management in classrooms.* New York: Holt, Rinehart, and Winston.

Krashen, S. 1997. Why bilingual education? ERIC Digests.

Krovetz, M. 1999. *Fostering resiliency: Expecting all students to use their minds and hearts well.* Thousand Oaks, CA: Corwin.

Kunjufu, J.1984. *Developing positive self-images and discipline in black children.* Chicago: African American Images.

Kurlan, D. 1997. Interview with D. Midian Kurlan. *Journal of Design Science.* October. <www.ignitiondesign.com/journal/kurland/index.html>.

Kyle, P., Kagan, S., and Scott, S. 2001. *Win-win discipline: Structures for all discipline problems.* San Clemente, CA: Kagan.

Ladson-Billings, G. 2000. Fighting for our lives: Preparing teachers to teach African American students. *Journal of Teacher Education 51*(3), 206–214.

Lambourne, K., and Zinn, M. 1993. *Education, race, and family: Issues for the 1990s.* East Lansing, MI: Julian Samora Research Institute, Michigan State University.

Latinos in school: Some facts and findings. 2001. *ERIC Digests Number 162.*

Levin, H. 2002. *The Accelerated Schools Program,* <www.acceleratedschools.org>.

Lickona, T. 1991. *Educating for character: How our schools can teach respect and responsibility.* New York: Bantam.

———. 2002. Web site on character education. <www.cortland.edu/c4n5rs/suxhom.htm>.

Lickona, T., Schaps, E., and Lewis, C. 2001. Eleven principles of character education. The Character Education Partnership. <www.character.org>.

Lipsitz, J. 1997. Program description (Middle Grades Improvement Program). *Phi Delta Kappan, 78* (7), 554.

———. 21 March, 1997. What works in middle-grades reform. *Phi Delta Kappa International.* <http://www.pdkintl.org/klip973.htm>.

Lipsitz, J., Jackson, A, and Austin, L. 21 March 1997. Speaking with one voice: A manifesto for middle-grades reform. *Phi Delta Kappa International.* <http://www.pdkintl.org/kappan/kman973.htm>.

Listserv, MiddleWeb. 16 November 2000. A Listserv conversation with John Lounsbury. *MiddleWeb.* <http://www.middleweb.com/MWLISTCONT/lounsburychat.html>.

Lockwood, A., and Secada, W. 2000. Transforming education for Hispanic youth: Exemplary practices, programs, and schools. *ERIC Digest.* <www.ncbe.gwu.edu/ncbepubs/resource/hispanicyouth/hdp.htm>.

Lorayne, H., and Lucas, J. 1996. *The memory book.* New York: Ballantine.

Lounsbury, J. 1996. Key characteristics of middle level schools. ERIC Digests. <http://www.ed.gov/databases/ERIC_Digests/ed401050.html>.

———. 2000. Understanding and appreciating the wonder years. Month of the Young Adolescent. <www.nmsa.org/moya/moyajhl.htm>.

Lucas, T., Henze, R., and Donato, R. 1990. Promoting the success of Latino language minority students. An exploratory study of six high schools. *Harvard Educational Review, 60,* 315–40.

Mac Iver, D. 1990. Meeting the needs of young adolescents: Advisory groups, interdisciplinary teaching teams, and school transition programs. *Phi Delta Kappan. 71:*458–464.

Marzano, R. 2000. Transforming classroom grading. <www.ascd.org/readingroom/books/marzano00book.html>.

Maslow, A. 1954. *Motivation and personality.* New York: Harper.

Matsuda, M. 1989. Working with Asian family members: Some communication strategies. *Topics in Language Disorders, 9*(3), 45–53.

Mattox, B.1999. Impact of the MegaSkills Program for students, teachers, family members school wide. <http://www.megaskillshsi.org/Default.htm>.

McCollough, Shawn. 2000. Teaching African American students. *Clearing House 74*(1), 5–6.

McFarland, D., Kolstad, R., and Briggs, L. 1995. Educating attention deficit hyperactivity disorder children. *Education, 115* (4), 597–603.

McTighe, J. 1996/1997. What happens between assessments? *Educational Leadership 54*(4). <http://www.ascd.org/readingroom/edlead/9612/mctighe.html>.

Mee, C. 1997. *2,000 voices: Young adolescents' perceptions and curriculum implications.* Columbus, OH: National Middle School Association.

Migrant Education Technology Grant Summaries. August, 2000. <www.ed.gov/offices/OESE/MEP/2000tecsum.html>.

Miles, M. 1971. *Annie and the old one.* Boston: Little, Brown.

Millican, A. 29 October, 2001. Cafe gives at-risk kids a real lift in life. *San Diego Union Tribune,* Local news B1, B3.

Mills, J. 1916. The six-three-three plan. *Journal of Education: New England and National 84* (4) p. 92.

Mills, R. 1998. Grouping students for instruction in middle schools. *ERIC Digests.* <http://www.ed.gov/databases/ERIC_Digests/ed419631.html>.

Missouri Department of Elementary and Secondary Education. 19 July 2002. School laws and legislation: Search and seizure issues. <www.dese.state.mo.us/schoollaw/freqaskques/searchissues.htm>.

Mizell, H. 2001. Professional development: The state it's in. *MiddleWeb.* <http://www.middleweb.com/HMstate.html>.

Mizelle, N. 1999. Helping middle school students make the transition into high school. ERIC Digests. <http://www.ed/gov/databases/ERIC_Digests/ed432411.html>.

Mizelle, N., and Mullins, E. 1997. Transition into and out of middle school. In Judith L. Irvin (Ed.) *What research says to the middle level practitioner.* Columbus, OH: National Middle School Association.

Moles, O. 1993. Collaboration between schools and disadvantaged family members. In F. Chavkin (Ed.) *Families and schools in a pluralistic society.* Pp. 21–53. Albany, NY: State University of New York Press.

Moreno, R., and Lopez, J. 1999. Latina mothers' involvement in their children's schooling: The role of maternal education and acculturation. Julian Samora Research Institute. Working Paper Series.

Morris, N., and Kaplan, I. 1994. Middle school family members are good partners for reading. *Journal of Reading 38*(2), 130–31.

Moyers, B. 15 February, 2002. Freedom to teach: History of academic freedom. NOW: In Depth: Politics and economy. <PBS Web site. www.pbs.org/now/politics/acfreehistory.html>.

MSNBC/*Newsweek.* 29 October, 2001. *The classroom of the future.* <www.msnbc.com/news/645566.asp?pne=msntv&cpl=1>.

Munson, B. 2000. Character education: The missing ingredient of preservice teacher education programs. Paper presented at the Annual Meeting of the American Association of Colleges for Teacher Education (52nd, Chicago, IL, February 26–29).

National Association of Secondary School Principals. 2002. Putting the "right" back in "copyright": Educating principals in copyright law. Chart. http://www.principals.org/srvices/legal_chart.htm>.

National Center for Education Statistics. 1998. Violence and discipline problems in U.S. public schools: 1996–97. U.S. Government. NCES publication 98–030.

National Coalition of Advocates for Students. 1994. *Delivering on the promise: Positive practices for immigrant students.* Boston: Author.

National Education Association. 1975. Code of Ethics of the Education Profession. <www.nea.org/aboutnea/code.html>.

———. 2002. NEA report on the Individuals with Disabilities Education Act (IDEA). Washington, DC: Author. <http://www.nea.org/publiced/idea/>.

National Forum to Accelerate Middle Grades Reform. 2002. <http://www.mgforum.org _www.mgforum.org>.

National Middle School Association. 1982. This we believe. Columbus, OH: Author.

———. 1995. This we believe: Developmentally responsive middle level schools. Columbus, OH: Author.

———. 2001. Research Summary #3. 2001. <http://www.nmsa.org/research/ressum3.htm>.

NCES. 1983. *A nation at risk: The imperative for educational reform.* Washington, DC: U.S. Government Printing Office.

———. 1998. *Violence and discipline problems in U.S. public schools: 1996–97.* Washington, DC: U.S. Government. NCES publication 98–030.

Nelsen, J., Lott, L.. and Glenn, H. 2000. *Positive discipline in the classroom.* Rocklin, CA.: Prima.

Niedowski, E. 15 September, 2001. Middle school reform is off to a bumpy start. *Baltimore Sun.* <http://www.sunspot.net/templates/misc/printstory.jsp?slug=bal%2Dte%2Emd% Emiddle11 . . . >.

Nistler, R., and Maiers, A. 1999. Exploring home-school connections: A family literacy perspective on improving urban schools. *Education and Urban Society, 32* (1), 2–17.

Norton, J., and Lewis, A. 2000. Middle grades reform. <http://www.pdkintl.org/kappan/klew0006.htm>.

O'Malley, J., and Chamot, A. 1989. *Learning strategies in second language acquisition.* Cambridge, England: Cambridge University Press.

Otten, E. 2000. Character education. *ERIC Digest.* Bloomington, IN: ERIC Clearinghouse for Social Studies/Social Science Education. ERIC no: ED444932.

Oxford, R. 1989. The role of styles and strategies in second language learning. ERIC Digests.

———.1994. Language learning strategies: An update. ERIC Digests. Washington, DC: ERIC/CLL.

Paratore, J., Melzi, G., and Krol-Sinclair, B. 1999. What should we expect of family literacy? Experiences of Latino children whose family members participated in an Intergenerational Literacy Project. <http://www.ncbe.gwu.edu/pathways/newimmigrant/family members.htm>.

Payne, R. 2001. *A framework for understanding poverty.* Highlands, TX: aha! Process.

Philips, S. 1983. *The invisible culture.* New York: Longman.

Piaget, J. 1950. *The psychology of intelligence.* London: Routledge & Kegan Paul. Pocket Books.

Powell, R., and Van Zandt Allen, L., 2001. In Anfara, V. (Ed). Middle school curriculum. *The handbook of research in middle level education.* Greenwich, CT: Information Age.

Promoting successful transition to the mainstream: Effective instructional strategies for bilingual students. 1999. ERIC Digest. Washington, DC: ERIC/CLL.

Pucci, S. 1994. Supporting Spanish language literacy: Latino children and free reading resources in schools. *Bilingual Research Journal, 18*(1–2), 67–82.

Purkey, W. 2002. Invitational education. <www.invitationaleducation.net>.

Purkey, W., and Stanley, P. 1991. *Invitational teaching, learning, and living.* Washington, DC: NEA Professional Library.

Purkey, W., and Strahan, D. 2002. *Inviting positive classroom discipline.* Westerville, OH: National Middle School Association.

Qualities of effective programs for immigrant adolescents with limited schooling. 1998. Washington, DC: ERIC.

Quinn, D., and, Valentine, J. 2001. What impact does the use of technology have on middle level education, specifically student achievement? National Middle School Association research summary #19: *National Middle School Association.* <http://www.nmsa.org/services/ressum19.html>.

Ravitch, D. 2000. *Left back: A century of failed school reforms.* New York: Simon & Schuster.

Redl, F., and Wattenberg, W. 1951. *Mental hygiene in teaching.* New York: Harcourt, Brace, and World.

Reed, R.1988. Education and achievement of young black males. In J. W. Gibbs (Ed.), *Young, black, and male in America: An endangered species.* Dover: Auburn.

Reid, C., and Romanoff, B. 1997. Using multiple intelligence theory to identify gifted children. *Educational Leadership, 55* (1), 71–74.

Renzulli, J. 1996. Schools for talent development: A practical plan for total school improvement. *School Administrator, 53*(1), 20–22.

Rodríguez, R. 1982. *Hunger of memory: The education of Richard Rodríguez. An autobiography.* Boston: D. R. Godine.

Rodríguez-Brown, F., Li, R., and Albom, J.1999. Hispanic family members' awareness and use of literacy-rich environments at home and in the community. *Education and Urban Society, 32* (1), 41–58.

Roth-Vinson, C. May, 2000. Connecting girls to the future in science, math, and technology: CyberSisters mentor program empowers girls to succeed. *techLEARNING.* <www.techlearning.com/db_area/archives/WCE/archives/rothvins.htm>.

Rutherford, B., and Billig, S. 1995. Parent, family, and community involvement in the middle grades. *ERIC Digests.* <www.ed.gov/databases/ERIC_Digests/ed387273.html>.

Schaps, E., Schaeffer, E., and McDonnell, S. 2001. What's right and wrong with character education today. *Education Week on the Web.* <www.edweek.org/ew/newstory.cfm?slug=02schaps.h21>.

Schemo, D. 6 December 2000. Worldwide survey finds U.S. students are not keeping up. *New York Times.* <http://www.nytimes.com/2000/12/06/national/06EXAM.html>.

Schlichter, C. 1988. Thinking skills instruction for all classrooms. *Gifted Child Today (GCT), 11*(2), 24–28.

Schlichter, C., Larkin, M., Casareno, A., Ellis, E., Gregg, M., Mayfield, P., & Rountree, B. 1997. Partners in enrichment: Preparing teachers for multiple ability classrooms. Council for exceptional children. <www.cec.sped.org/bk/martec.html>.

Schmeiser, C. 1995. Ethics in assessment. *ERIC Digests.* ED 391111. <www.library.unt.edu/ericscs/vl/ethics/digests/assess.htm>.

Schumacher, D. 1998. The transition to middle school. *ERIC Digests.* ERIC Identifier:422 119.

Schwartz, F. 1981. Supporting or subverting learning: Peer group patterns in four tracked schools. *Anthropology and Education Quarterly, 12*(2), 99–120.

Schwartz, W. 2000. New trends in language education for Hispanic students. *ERIC/CUE Digest Number 155.* New York: ERIC.

———. 2001. School practices for equitable discipline of African American students. New York: ERIC Clearinghouse on Urban Education.

Scott, J. 1986. Teacher tenure. *ERIC Digest,* 19. Eugene, OR: ERIC Clearinghouse on Educational Management. ED282352. <www.ed.gov/databases/ERIC_Digests/ed282352.html>.

Shoop, R. March 2002. Identifying a standard of care. *Principal Leadership* (online), 2 (7) . National Association of Secondary School Principals. <http://www.principals.org/news/pl_idstandardcare_0302.html>.

Short, D. 1998. Secondary newcomer program: helping recent immigrants prepare for school success. *ERIC Digest.* ERIC/CLL

Simpson, M. 1998. Academic freedom takes a hit. *NEA Today Online.* <http://www.nea.org/neatoday/9811/rights.html>.

———. 2001. NEA examines the rights of nontenured teachers. *NEA Today Online.* <http://www.nea.org/neatoday/0105/rights.html>.

Skinner, B. 1953. *Science and human behavior.* New York: Macmillan.

———. 1954. The science of learning and the art of teaching. *Harvard Educational Review, 24,* 86–97.

Slavin, R. 1991. Synthesis of research on cooperative learning. *Educational Leadership. 48,* 71–82.

Slavin, R., and Calderón, M. (Eds.) 2001. *Effective programs for Latino students.* Mahwah, N.J.: L. Erlbaum Associates.

Smith, L. Summer, 2000. The socialization of females with regard to a technology-related career: Recommendations for change. *Meridian.* <www.ncsu.edu/meridian/archive_of_meridian/sum2000/career/index.html>.

Snyder, D. 2000. Computers and classrooms. <www.davidpearcesnyder.com/computers_and_classrooms.htm>.

Soloway, E., Norris, C., Blumenfeld, P., Fishman, B., Krajcik, J., and Marx, R. June, 2001. Devices are ready-at-hand. *HICE Palm Pages.* <www.handheld.hice dev.org/readyAtHand.htm>.

Sorrell, S. November, 2000. Eminence pocket pc project. <www.paperlessclassroom.org/story.htm>.

Sosa, A. 1996. Involving Hispanic family members in improving educational opportunities for their children. Chapter 20 in: *Children of La Frontera: Binational efforts to serve Mexican migrant and immigrant students.* ERIC no: ED393649

South, C. March, 2001. Electronic portfolios: assessment for an advanced society. *Technology & Learning.* <www.techlearning.com/db_area/archives/WCE/archives/csouth.htm>.

Spence, G. 1995. *How to argue and win every time.* New York: St. Martin's Press.

St. Germaine, R. 1995. Drop-out rates among American Indian and Alaska Natives Students: Beyond cultural discontinuity. Charleston, WV: ERIC Clearinghouse on Rural Education and Small Schools.

Starr, L. August, 2000a. Computer rules prevent problems! *Education World.* <www.education-world.com/a_tech/tech044.shtml>.

———. May, 2000b. Educating girls in the tech age: a report on equity. *Education World.* <www.education-world.com/a_tech/tech028.shtml>.

———. 2000c. The educator's guide to copyright and fair use. *Education World.* <http://www.education-world.com/a_curr/curr280a.shtml>.

Sternberg, R., and Clinkenbeard, P. 1995. The Triarchic Model applied to identifying, teaching, and assessing gifted children. *Roeper Review, 17*(4), 255–60.

Sternberg, R., and others. 1996. Identification, instruction, and assessment of gifted children: A construct validation of a Triarchic Model. *Gifted Child Quarterly, 40*(3), 129–37.

Stevenson, C. 1998. *Teaching ten to fourteen year olds.* (2nd ed.). New York: Addison Wesley Longman.

Storti, C. 1999. *Figuring foreigners out: A practical guide.* Yarmouth, ME: Intercultural Press.

Subotnik, R., and Coleman, L. 1996. Establishing the foundations for a talent development school: Applying principles to creating an ideal. *Journal for the Education of the Gifted, 20*(2), 175–189.

Swisher, K. 1991. American Indian/Alaskan Native learning styles: Research and practice. Charleston, WV: ERIC Clearinghouse on Rural Education and Small Schools. ED335175.

Tauber, R. 1997. *Self-fulfilling prophecy: A practical guide to its use in education.* Westport, CT: Praeger.

———. 1998. Good or bad, what teachers expect from students they generally get! Washington, DC: ERIC Clearinghouse on Teaching and Teacher Education. ERIC identifier: ED426985.

Tech-Savvy: Educating Girls in the New Computer Age. 2000. American Association of University Women Executive Summary. <www.aauw.org/2000/techsavvy.html>.

Terry, S. 6 August 2001. Rookie teachers aren't on their own. *The Dallas Morning News.* <http://www.dallasnews.com/education/433256_mentors-02irv.html>.

Tharp, R., and Gallimore, R. 1988. *Rousing minds to life: Teaching, learning and schooling in social context.* Cambridge: Cambridge University Press.

The Council for Exceptional Children. 2002. The ERIC Clearinghouse on Disabilities and Gifted Education (ERIC EC) <http://ericec.org>.

The power of the Internet for learning: Moving from promise to practice. 2000. Education Commission, <http:// interact.hpcnet.org/webcommission/index.htm>.

Tomlinson, C. 1995. Gifted learners and the middle school: Problem or promise? *ERIC Digest.* <http://www.ed. gov/databases/ERIC_Digests/ed386832.html>.

Trueba, H., and Cheng, L. 1993. *Myth or reality: Adaptive strategies of Asian Americans in California.* Bristol, PA: Falmer.

Tucker, G. 1999. A global perspective on bilingualism. *ERIC Digest.* Washington, DC: ERIC Clearinghouse on Languages and Linguistics.

U.S. Census Bureau. *Poverty 2001.* <www. census.gov/ hhes>.

U.S. Department of Education. 1995. Disability statistics report #6. National Institute on Disability and Rehabilitation. <http://pstc.brown.edu/disability.html>.

———. *Preventing bullying: A manual for schools and communities.* 1998. U.S. Department of Education. <www.cde.ca.gov spbranch/ssp/bullymanual.htm>.

U.S. Department of Education, Office of Educational Technology. 2001. E-learning: Putting a world-class education at the fingertips of all children. <www.ed.gov/ technology/elearning>.

U.S. National Center for Education Statistics. 2001. <http:// nces.ed.gov/>.

Van Voorhis, F. 2001. Interactive science homework: an experiment in home and school connections. *NASSP Bulletin.* <www.nassp.org/news/bltn_sci_hmwrk1001.html>.

Walqui, A. 2000. Strategies for success: Engaging immigrant students in secondary schools. Washington, DC: ERIC.

Walsh, C. 1991. Literacy and school success: Considerations for programming and instruction. In C. Walsh and H. Prashker (Eds.), *Literacy development for bilingual students.* Boston: New England Multifunctional Resource Center for Language and Culture Education.

Walsh, M. 2002. High court declines to hear case on teaching of evolution. 16 January. *Education Week 21* (8), 22. <http://edweek.org/ew/newstory.cfm?slug= 18scotus.h21>.

Walters, L. 1997. How some schools make a success of character education. *Christian Science Monitor, 89* (132) p. 1.

Weaver, C. 1994. Reaching kids with attention deficit disorders: Why whole language helps. *Instructor, 103*(9), 39–43.

Weldy, G. (Ed.) 1991. Stronger school transitions improve student achievement: A final report on a three-year demonstration project "Strengthening Total Transitions for Students K–13." Reston, VA: National Association of Secondary School Principals.

———. 1995. Critical transitions. *Schools in the Middle, 4*(3), 4–7.

Wierzbicka, A. 1991. Japanese key words and core cultural values. *Language in Society, 20*(3): 333–85.

Wilber, D. September, 2000. Character education: Finding ways to foster ethical behavior in youth. *Changing Schools.* Quarterly issue.

Willard, N. 2002. Schools, the Internet, and copyright law. *Education World.* <http://www.education-world.com/ a_tech/tech121.shtml>.

W. K. Kellogg Foundation. 2002. Middle start overview. <www.wkkf.org/Programming/Overview.asp?CID=40>.

Wong. H. 2001. (selection of tips for teachers). <www. glavac.com/harrywong.htm>.

Wong, H., and Wong, R. 1998. *The first days of school.* Singapore: Harry K. Wong Publications.

Wynne, E., and Ryan, K. 1997. *Reclaiming our schools: Teaching character, academics, and discipline.* Upper Saddle River, NJ: Prentice-Hall.

INDEX